Blood for Thought

Blood for Thought

The Reinvention of Sacrifice in
Early Rabbinic Literature

———

Mira Balberg

UNIVERSITY OF CALIFORNIA PRESS

University of California Press, one of the most distinguished university presses in the United States, enriches lives around the world by advancing scholarship in the humanities, social sciences, and natural sciences. Its activities are supported by the UC Press Foundation and by philanthropic contributions from individuals and institutions. For more information, visit www.ucpress.edu.

University of California Press
Oakland, California

Library of Congress Cataloging-in-Publication Data

Names: Balberg, Mira, author.
Title: Blood for thought : the reinvention of sacrifice in early rabbinic
    literature / Mira Balberg.
Description: Oakland, California : University of California Press, [2017] |
    Includes bibliographical references and index. |
Identifiers: LCCN 2017013391 (print) | LCCN 2017015219 (ebook) |
    ISBN 9780520968660 () | ISBN 9780520295926 (cloth : alk. paper)
Subjects: LCSH: Sacrifice—Judaism. | Blood--Religious aspects—Judaism. |
    Rabbinical literature—History and criticism. | Rabbis—Jerusalem. |
    Judaism—Liturgy.
Classification: LCC BM715 (ebook) | LCC BM715 .B35 2017 (print) |
    DDC 296.4/92—dc23
LC record available at https://lccn.loc.gov/2017013391

Manufactured in the United States of America

24 23 22 21 20 19 18 17
10 9 8 7 6 5 4 3 2 1

For Tim

Nulla venit sine te nox mihi, nulla dies.

CONTENTS

ACKNOWLEDGMENTS

Much of this book was written during 2014–15, a year that I blissfully spent as a fellow at the Frankel Institute for Advanced Judaic Studies at the University of Michigan. I thank Mikhail Krutikov and Deborah Dash Moore for extending to me the invitation to the institute, and to the institute's fellows and staff for creating a wonderfully nurturing and stimulating intellectual environment. I completed the book at my academic home at Northwestern University, where my colleagues in the Department of Religious Studies continue to offer support, advice, wisdom, camaraderie, and laughs on a daily basis. A generous grant from the Alice Kaplan Institute for the Humanities at Northwestern helped this book see the light of day.

The seed from which this book sprouted was sown almost two decades ago, in the classes that I took as an undergraduate student at the Hebrew University in Jerusalem with Baruch Schwartz, and particularly in his memorable class on the book of Leviticus. My ongoing interest in the intersection of cult and literature was born in Professor Schwartz's classes, as was my emerging understanding of the complexity—and the rewards—of careful and close work with ancient texts. His outstanding classes have profoundly shaped me as a scholar and a teacher for years to come.

Moulie Vidas was the guardian of this book from its very inception: from his initial "this needs to be a book" response when I first shared with him some very incoherent thoughts on the topic of sacrifice in rabbinic Judaism, through avid inquiries about how the project was coming along and constant encouragement that it was a worthwhile project, to his accurate and insightful comments that made many arguments suddenly come together. Thanks to my friendship with Moulie, writing is often transformed from a lonely and frustrating process to a stimulating and exciting opportunity for dialogue.

Four colleagues, whom I consider both mentors and friends, read the manuscript in its entirety and offered perceptive comments and highly useful observations. Azzan Yadin-Israel's attention to details while keeping track of the bigger picture was unparalleled. Richard Kieckhefer was a wonderful conversation partner, who gave solid advice on all fronts—intellectual, stylistic, and pragmatic. Haim Weiss's literary sensibility, and the depth of his cultural insights, helped me greatly in fine-tuning my presentation. Finally, Ellen Muehlberger read the manuscript in the same way that she has read every single thing I have written in the past few years: with a keen eye for elegance and coherence, and with unfailing support and encouragement.

I am truly grateful to the two readers for the press, who gave this book the closest, most engaged, and most charitable reading I could hope for. In their comments they astutely identified arguments that needed to be strengthened, connections that needed to be tightened, overstatements that needed to be refined, and vague points that needed to be clarified, and the book is much improved thanks to their suggestions. One of the readers, Yair Furstenberg, was kind enough not only to reveal his identity but also to share with me extensive and highly detailed comments on the manuscript, well beyond the call of duty: I was therefore fortunate to benefit from his vast knowledge and insurmountable textual skills while working on this book, as I have been in the past. I also wish to thank Ra'anan Boustan, for his enthusiastic support of this book from beginning to end.

The ideas and analyses in this book were shared, in multiple configurations and forms, with several brilliant friends who offered valuable thoughts during multiple stages of the project. I wish to thank Ishay Rosen-Zvi for steering me away from the trite and the obvious, and especially for stressing the importance of looking at ritual narratives; Alexei Sivertsev, for enriching my readings both with theoretical sophistication and with broader cross-cultural knowledge; Simeon Chavel, for helping me to engage with biblical texts in a multilayered and nuanced way; and Gil Klein, for wonderfully innovative approaches to rabbinic texts and delightfully fun conversations. Special heartfelt thanks to Rachel Neis, an inspiring and incisive thinker and dialogue partner, and to Yair Lipshitz, my intellectual and emotional kindred spirit, not only for making my academic work more interesting and exciting, but also for true friendship in a time of need, which will never be forgotten.

In the course of my work on this book I have had the opportunity to present parts of it at Princeton University, Yale University, the University of Michigan, the Hebrew University in Jerusalem, Northwestern University, DePaul University, and the University of California, Los Angeles. I am grateful to all those institutions for their kind invitations, and to their faculty and students for their thoughtful feedback.

It has been, once again, a true pleasure to work with Eric Schmidt of the University of California Press, a wonderfully engaged and supportive editor who is genuinely committed to furthering good scholarship. I am grateful to Eric, to Maeve Cornell-Taylor, and to Cindy Fulton for bringing this book to life. I am also indebted to Marian Rogers for meticulously copyediting the manuscript, and to Al Peters for the skillful preparation of the indices.

My parents are a steady source of love and support, unfailingly enthusiastic about all that I do, and unfailingly generous in all matters, great and small. To them, as well as to my brother and sister, my mother-in-law and father-in-law, and my extended family, I am profoundly indebted and eternally grateful.

My gratitude to Tim DeBold goes well beyond the fact that he read every page of this book and patiently endured many hours of conversations about its most minute details. I thank him for knowing how to make the mundane exciting and the frustrating amusing, for giving me a home and for showing me the world outside of it. *Te vox mea nominat unam.*

Introduction

In his novel *The Time of Trimming* ('*et ha-zamir*), Israeli author Haim Be'er describes the emergence of messianic zeal among religious Zionist circles in Israel right before the 1967 war. In one unforgettable scene, the military undertaker Süsser listens with great dismay to Benny Brimmer, an enthusiastic young man talking about the Jewish people's obligation to rebuild the Jerusalem temple and to renew the sacrificial cult. Unable to contain his rage, Süsser interrupts the young man's sermon:

> "I don't need a temple," Süsser cut Brimmer's tripartite plan off, "so that Zvi Yehuda Kook and 'the Nazarite' David Cohen[1] would be able to sprinkle the blood of lambs on the wall of the altar and offer the fat of rams. . . . If the minister of education[2] had appointed me as a judge for the Israel Prize, I would give the prize for the Wisdom of Israel to Titus Vespasian who with the aid of Heaven liberated us once and for all from this nightmare of a slaughterhouse and a station for the distribution of breasts and thighs on the Temple Mount."[3]

Many readers, I suspect, will find Süsser's appalled and disgusted outlook on sacrifices highly relatable. In the course of the last two millennia animal sacrifice turned

---

1. Zvi Yehuda Kook (1891–1982) was the most influential spiritual leader of Merkaz ha-rav yeshivah in Jerusalem, which pioneered the settlement movement after 1967 and called for active efforts to bring about a messianic redemption. Along with Rabbi David Cohen (1887–1972), also known as "the Nazarite" because of his ascetic practices, Zvi Yehuda Kook is considered the most prominent disciple of his father, Rabbi Avraham Yitzhak haKohen Kook. Zvi Yehudah Kook and David Cohen were the first rabbis to ascend to the Temple Mount on June 7, 1967, the day that the Israeli army took over East Jerusalem.

2. In the original Hebrew, Be'er specifically mentions the name of Zalman Aran, Israeli minister of education between 1963 and 1969.

3. Haim Be'er, *The Time of Trimming* [Heb.] (Tel-Aviv: Am Oved, 1987), 438 (my translation).

from a quintessential, indeed almost universal, channel of religious expression into a reviled trait of otherness—either the otherness of the past or the otherness of the "uncivilized"—such that the idea itself seems to most of us abhorrent.[4] What I find particularly instructive about this passage from Be'er's novel is not so much Süsser's critique of sacrifices (which echoes many similar critiques, ancient and modern alike), but his comment that he finds Titus Vespasian worthy of a prize for "the Wisdom of Israel." Süsser does not designate for Titus, the Roman emperor-to-be who sacked Jerusalem during the Great Revolt against Rome and eventually commanded the burning of the Jerusalem temple in 70 C.E., a prize for military accomplishments or political leadership. He wants to give him the prize for "the Wisdom of Israel," which is regularly given by the State of Israel to scholars who specialize in various facets of the Jewish canon—rabbinic literature, liturgy, mysticism, philosophy, and so on.[5] Titus, for Süsser, is a quintessential contributor to Jewish culture: in fact, he is perhaps the *founder* of Jewish culture.

Süsser's statement is radical, to be sure, but it powerfully echoes one of the most prevalent notions in the scholarly study of early Judaism, namely, that the destruction of the Jerusalem temple in 70 C.E. and the subsequent cessation of the Judean sacrificial cult[6] effectively set in motion the Jewish culture of learning and of literary production, whose pioneers were the rabbis of late antiquity.[7] According to this view, the rabbis, who had to adjust to a world with no center, with no cult, with no

---

4. On contemporary approaches to sacrifice, see Annette Yoshiko Reed, "From Sacrifice to the Slaughterhouse: Ancient and Modern Perspectives on Meat, Ritual, and Civilization," *Method and Theory in the Study of Religion* 26, no. 2 (2014): 111–58.

5. For the sake of accuracy, it should be noted that the prize given annually for "the Wisdom of Israel" is actually called "the Bialik Prize" rather than "the Israel Prize."

6. There is some debate among scholars on whether certain sacrificial practices persisted after 70 C.E. despite the absence of the temple; for a helpful survey of the relevant evidence, see James R. Brown, *Temple and Sacrifice in Rabbinic Judaism* (Evanston, IL: Seabury Theological Seminary, 1963), 20–24. I am in agreement with Alexander Guttmann's assessment that while private sacrifices may have continued in different configurations, public sacrifices did come to an end after 70 C.E.; see Alexander Guttmann, "The End of the Jewish Sacrificial Cult," *Hebrew Union College Annual* 38 (1967): 137–48. This question, however, is largely inconsequential for this book, since it is clear that what the rabbis envision as sacrifice in their literature—an institutionalized, centralized, and highly structured and supervised cultic practice—did not exist in their own time.

7. The view that identifies the rabbis as the founders of Jewish textual culture often ignores the rich priestly library of the Second Temple period, as it ignores the Greek textual creation of Hellenistic Jews. To a great extent, this view stems from the fact that nonrabbinic works were not traditionally preserved by Jews and have thus been eradicated from Jewish cultural memory: on this, see Rachel Elior, *Memory and Oblivion: The Secret of the Dead Sea Scrolls* [Heb.] (Jerusalem: Van Leer Institute and ha-kibbutz ha-me'uhad, 2009). In other ways, those who endorse this view identify a substantial difference between priestly literature, which is based on an ethos of esoteric revelation, and rabbinic literature, which is based on an ethos of learning and inquiry. For elaborate discussion on this difference, see Azzan Yadin-Israel, *Scripture and Tradition: Rabbi Akiva and the Triumph of Midrash* (Philadelphia: University of Pennsylvania Press, 2014), 161–82.

established ways of approaching the deity, allowed their tradition to survive against all odds by turning it into texts and generating a whole intellectual culture around those texts.[8] In the words of Jonathan Z. Smith, in the works of the rabbis "the locus of sacrifice was shifted from temple to domicile, and the act of sacrifice was wholly replaced by narrative and discourse."[9] In this regard, the destruction of the temple and the beginnings of "the Wisdom of Israel" are perceived as deeply intertwined.[10] While scholars continue to disagree on whether the rabbis were devastated by the inability to perform sacrifices or secretly thought to themselves, "Good riddance,"[11] there does seem to be one shared premise among most scholars who approach the topic of sacrifices in rabbinic literature, which is that the most important thing about sacrifices in the world of the rabbis is their absence. That is to say, the most common answer to the question, "What did the rabbis think about animal sacrifices?" is "They thought that they can do without them."

Various scholars described the rabbinic project, at least in part, as a project of creating a postsacrificial version of Judaism.[12] Whether as legislators acting "on the ground," as theologians dealing with crisis and despair, or as a cultural elite creating new modes of religious expression and performance, the rabbis are often perceived as offering both discursive and practical "substitutes" for sacrifice.[13] This

8. See, for example, David Goodblatt, "The Jews of the Land of Israel in the Years 70–135" [Heb.], in *Judea and Rome: The Rebellions of the Jews*, ed. Uriel Rappaport (Jerusalem: Am Oved, 1983), 178–80; Guy Stroumsa, *The End of Sacrifice: Religious Transformations in Late Antiquity*, trans. Susan Emanuel (Chicago: University of Chicago Press, 2009), 66–69; Stanley Stowers, "The Religion of Plant and Animal Offerings versus the Religion of Meanings, Essences, and Textual Mysteries," in *Ancient Mediterranean Sacrifice*, ed. Jennifer Wright Knust and Zsuzsanna Várhelyi (New York: Oxford University Press, 2011), 47–48.

9. Jonathan Z. Smith, "Trading Places," in *Relating Religion: Essays in the Study of Religion* (Chicago: University of Chicago Press, 2004), 223.

10. Indeed, Stroumsa (*The End of Sacrifice*, 63) uncannily echoes Süsser when he writes: "The Jews should no doubt pay thanks to Titus, whose memory they hold in contempt, for having destroyed their temple for the second time, for imposing on them the need to free themselves from sacrifice and its ritual violence, before any other society."

11. On this contention, see Jonathan Klawans, *Purity, Sacrifice, and the Temple: Symbolism and Supersessionism in the Study of Ancient Judaism* (New York: Oxford University Press, 2006), 203–11.

12. For notable examples of this view, see Robert Goldenberg, "The Broken Axis: Rabbinic Judaism and the Fall of Jerusalem," *Journal of the American Academy of Religion* 45 (1977): 869–82; Shmuel Safrai, "The Recovery of the Jewish Population in the Yavneh Generation" [Heb.], in *Eretz Israel from the Destruction of the Second Temple to the Muslim Conquest*, ed. Zvi Baras, Shmuel Safrai, Menahem Stern, and Yoram Tsafrir (Jerusalem: Yad Ben Zvi, 1982), 18–37; Baruch Bokser, "Rabbinic Responses to Catastrophe," *Proceedings of the American Academy for Jewish Research* 50 (1983): 37–61; Shaye J. D. Cohen, "The Temple and the Synagogue," in *The Temple in Antiquity: Ancient Records and Modern Perspectives*, ed. Truman G. Madsen (Provo, UT: Religious Studies Center, Brigham Young University, 1984), 151–74.

13. See, for example, Ben-Zion Rosenfeld, "Sage and Temple in Rabbinic Thought after the Destruction of the Second Temple," *Journal for the Study of Judaism in the Persian, Hellenistic and Roman Period* 28, no. 4 (1997): 437–64; Michael Fishbane, *The Exegetical Imagination: On Jewish Thought and Theology* (Cambridge, MA: Harvard University Press, 1998), 123–35; Paul Heger, *The Three Biblical Altar*

view of the rabbis as replacing sacrifices relies primarily on about two dozen state-ments found in the later strata of rabbinic literature, particularly in the Babylonian Talmud, in which certain practices—prayer, fast, Torah study, charity, and the death of the righteous—are compared to sacrifices in their efficacy or value.[14] Not-withstanding the question of whether those statements should necessarily be understood in terms of substitution or supersession,[15] the immense emphasis given to those statements in assessing how the rabbis responded and adjusted to the destruction of the Jerusalem temple created a picture in which sacrifices play a part in rabbinic literature only as that-which-is-lost, as the past against which the rabbis carve their own present and future.

And yet, this picture is far from reflecting the contents of the rabbinic texts themselves. Roughly speaking, about a quarter of early rabbinic (Tannaitic) litera-ture consists of elaborate instructions, discussions, and descriptions concerning the temple and the sacrificial cult,[16] and much of this Tannaitic material continues to be debated and elaborated in later rabbinic (Amoraic) compilations, primarily in the Babylonian Talmud.[17] The rabbinic sacrificial corpus, as I will refer to it throughout this book, does not treat sacrifices as metaphors or as placeholders of the forlorn past: rather, sacrifices are construed in this corpus as integral parts of the greater picture rabbinic texts aim to construct, a picture of life in accordance with the rabbis' interpretation of the Torah's law. This book's point of departure is the implicit claim that the early rabbinic sacrificial corpus makes through its very existence, namely, that sacrificial worship is an inherent component of the rabbis' legal, social, and religious vision. It thus sets out to explore how the early rabbis thought about the function, purpose, workings, and value of sacrifices by turning to the abundant rabbinic material that speaks at length about sacrifices, rather than to the relatively small collection of passages that speak about the lack thereof.

To be clear, this book is not an inquiry into sacrificial practices in early Judaism, whether before or after the destruction of the Jerusalem temple. Rather, it is an

---

Laws: Developments in the Sacrificial Cult in Practice and Theology (Berlin: Walter de Gruyter, 1999), 377–82; most recently, Moshe Halbertal, *On Sacrifice* (Princeton: Princeton University Press, 2012), 37–53. The paradigm of "substitution" will be discussed at length in the conclusion.

14. For some of the most oft-quoted examples, see BT Berakhot 17a, 26b; BT Sukkah 49b; BT Mo'ed Qatan 28a; BT Sotah 5b; BT Menahot 110a.

15. For an insightful discussion of this question, see Klawans, *Purity, Sacrifice, and the Temple,* 198–202.

16. This includes twenty of the sixty tractates of the Mishnah (and seventeen of the fifty-seven tractates of the parallel Tosefta), and about two-thirds of Midrash Sifra on Leviticus, in addition to substantial discussions in Sifre on Numbers and Sifre on Deuteronomy.

17. The Palestinian Talmud as it stands before us does not include the tractates of Order Qodashim ("Holy Things") of the Mishnah, in which the majority of sacrificial material is contained. On the ques-tion of whether such tractates existed and in what form, see Yehoshafat Harel, "Palestinian Sugyot for Seder Qodashim" (PhD diss., Hebrew University, 2004).

inquiry into intellectual history: it ventures to understand how sacrifice as a religious concept and as a biblical trope was interpreted, reworked, and approached by a group of Jewish intellectuals in Roman Palestine in the first three centuries of the Common Era. Put differently, my purpose is to use Tannaitic sources to reconstruct a rabbinic *theory of sacrifice* and a rabbinic *ethos of sacrifice*. I am guided by the premise that rabbinic legal-ritual discourse (often referred to as *halakhah*) is a quintessential mode of intellectual and ideational expression, and by the conviction that the rabbis do not use their normative compilations simply to "tell people what to do" but also and perhaps especially to articulate religious views and ideals.[18] My argument, as it will unfold throughout the book, is that the early rabbis present remarkably innovative perspectives on sacrifices, and radical interpretations of biblical cultic institutions, and that their reinvention of sacrifice gives it new meanings within the greater context of the rabbis' social and religious ideology. Whether the rabbis' transformations of the biblical sacrificial system took place despite the impracticality of sacrifice at their time or because of the impracticality of sacrifice at their time we cannot know: but what I will show in detail is that the impracticality of sacrifice did not in any way make this area of biblical law a fossilized, stagnant, or inconsequential one in the rabbis' creation.

Throughout the book I will frequently refer to the panoply of rabbinic ideas and ideals on sacrifices as "the rabbis' sacrificial vision" (without suggesting, as I will explain below, that the rabbis all speak in the same voice). I use this phrase as a way of suggesting that the rabbis create in their works an elaborate and vivid picture of sacrificial processes, actions, structures, substances, and even accidents, which rests on their notions of what sacrifice should be. In other words, the rabbis generate a *descriptive* account of sacrifices that is guided by a *prescriptive* view of cult, worship, individual, and community. In this regard the rabbinic sacrificial corpus is not entirely unlike two earlier textual compilations that offer an idealized description/prescription of sacrifice and cult, on which the rabbis heavily rely: chapters 40–48 of the book of Ezekiel and the Priestly and Holiness Codes of the Pentateuch. Neither of these texts describes a sacrificial setting that actually existed and functioned in its authors' own time. Ezekiel walks the reader through a temple that was revealed to him "in the visions of God" fourteen years after the destruction of Jerusalem by the armies of Nebuchadnezzar,[19] whereas the Priestly and Holiness Codes, which were presumably composed during or after the Babylonian

---

18. In this conviction I follow Jon Levenson, who put it in the following succinct words: "In the Hebrew Bible, as elsewhere in the cultural world in which it was composed, law often articulates a theological and moral ideal: it does not always stipulate a practice that all can reasonably be expected to undertake." Jon D. Levenson, *The Death and Resurrection of the Beloved Son: The Transformation of Child Sacrifice in Judaism and Christianity* (New Haven: Yale University Press, 1993), 15.

19. Ezekiel 40:1–2.

exile of the sixth century B.C.E., present their ritual legislation as pertaining to the tabernacle or "the Tent of Meeting" that the Israelites carried through the wilderness.[20] Both Ezekiel and the Priestly and Holiness Codes (which agree on many details of the sacrificial cult, but not on all of them) conjoin sacrificial practices with which they were actually familiar, literary themes and ideas found in earlier traditions, neo-Babylonian concepts of worship and of civil religion, and fantasies on the ideal relations of space, society, and authority.[21] It is virtually impossible to tell whether any of those authors were concretely interested in reforming an existing set of cultic practices, or in instituting a new set of cultic practices, in their own time and place or in a foreseeable or distant future. What matters for our purposes is that both Ezekiel and the Priestly and Holiness Codes are literary creations that put forth textual accounts of an idealized sacrificial cult as part of a more comprehensive religious and social agenda. I maintain that this is exactly how we should approach the rabbinic sacrificial corpus.

While the rabbinic sacrificial corpus is not a "vision" in the same way that Ezekiel 40–48 is a vision (that is, the rabbis do not claim to have "seen" the workings of the temple through divine revelation), this corpus does present a vision insofar as it builds a complex and vivid picture not of what is, but of what the authors think can be and should be. This picture is woven of threads of imagination and interpretation, memory and hope, necessity and fantasy. The fact that the rabbis have such a robust vision of the sacrificial cult does not tell us anything about whether, how, and when they thought this vision would ever be materialized. The only thing it tells us is that when the rabbis approached the topic of sacrifice as part of the greater edifice of Torah-based practice, they had distinct ideas about what sacrifice is, how it ought to be performed, and what its place is in the overarching scheme of Jewish life.

This book, then, seeks to understand the rabbinic sacrificial vision by tracing the junctures at which the rabbis, in reworking the biblical material that forms the basis of their legislation regarding sacrifices and temple cult, significantly depart from the biblical texts and present revolutionary perspectives. By piecing together those different departures and the innovations that the rabbis introduce to the sacrificial system we are able, I argue, to identify some of the conceptual and ideological underpinnings of the rabbis' interpretive and legislative enterprise as they approach the topic of sacrifice. This book proposes that through careful scrutiniz-

20. On the historical context of the Priestly and Holiness Codes' cultic legislation, see Ronald E. Clements, *God and Temple* (Philadelphia: Fortress Press, 1965), 100–122.

21. On the Priestly and Holiness Codes and their construction of the cult, see David P. Wright, "Ritual Theory, Ritual Texts, and the Priestly-Holiness Writings of the Pentateuch," in *Social Theory and the Study of Israelite Religion: Essays in Retrospect and Prospect,* ed. Saul Olyan (Atlanta: Society of Biblical Literature, 2012), 195–216; on Ezekiel's Temple vision, see Kalinda Rose Stevenson, *The Vision of Transformation: The Territorial Rhetoric of Ezekiel 40–48* (Atlanta: Scholars Press, 1996).

ing and analysis, out of the minute and often very technical details of the rabbinic texts on sacrifices emerges a rich and intriguing theory of sacrifice as a religious, social, and political practice.

THE SACRIFICIAL CORPUS

This book focuses in particular on the portions of early rabbinic literature, commonly known as Tannaitic literature,[22] that deal extensively with the topic of sacrifice and temple cult. The Tannaitic compilations (all, to the best of our knowledge, composed in Roman Palestine) include the Mishnah, a normative codex that was finalized in the first quarter of the third century C.E.; the Tosefta, a codex structured as parallel and complementary to the Mishnah, which is presumably contemporaneous with it or somewhat later;[23] and the Tannaitic or "halakhic" midrashim, exegetical works on the books of Exodus, Leviticus, Numbers, and Deuteronomy, all roughly dated to the third century as well.[24] These works are all collective, composite, and multilayered: they have no single author, but contain an array of traditions, both anonymous and attributed to named rabbis, collected and compiled over a lengthy period of time. These works consist of a wide variety of genres—narratives, apodictic rulings, hermeneutic discussions, homilies, lists, and inquiries into case studies—and they also contain a wide variety of opinions: sometimes named rabbis are explicitly presented as disagreeing with each other on

22. The term "Tannaitic" comes from the noun *tanna*, literally "reciter." The word *tanna* is used in the later strata of rabbinic literature to refer both to the early rabbis whose traditions are collected in the Mishnah and other contemporaneous compilations, and to individuals who memorized and recited those traditions in later periods upon demand.

23. For several decades, scholars have been debating whether the Tosefta is later than the Mishnah and should be seen as an early commentary on it, earlier than the Mishnah and should be seen as its main source, or the two are free renditions of the same essential text. See Abraham Goldberg, "The Tosefta—Companion to the Mishna," in *The Literature of the Sages,* vol.1, ed. Shmuel Safrai (Assen: Van Gorcum, 1987), 283–302; Shamma Friedman, "Mishna-Tosefta Parallels" [Heb.], *Proceedings of the 11th World Congress of Jewish Studies* C.1 (1994): 15–22; Friedman, "The Primacy of Tosefta to Mishnah in Synoptic Parallels," in *Introducing Tosefta: Textual, Intratextual, and Intertextual Studies,* ed. Harry Fox, Tirzah Meacham, and Diane Kriger (Hoboken, NJ: Ktav, 1999), 99–121; Martin Jaffee, *Torah in the Mouth: Writing and Oral Tradition in Palestinian Judaism, 200 BCE–400 CE* (New York: Oxford University Press, 2001), 39–61; Judith Hauptman, *Rereading the Mishnah: A New Approach to Ancient Jewish Texts* (Tübingen: Mohr Siebeck, 2005); Elizabeth Shanks Alexander, *Transmitting Mishnah: The Shaping Influence of Oral Tradition* (New York: Cambridge University Press, 2006), 35–55. I tend to adopt Shamma Friedman's view of the Tosefta as a compilation of various materials *relevant* to the Mishnah: some of these materials are the sources of the Mishnah, some of them are later interpretations, etc., but the compilation as a whole is later.

24. See the helpful survey in Menahem Kahana, "The Halakhic Midrashim," in *The Literature of the Sages,* vol. 2, ed. Shmuel Safrai, Peter Tomson, and Zeev Safrai (Assen: Uitgeverij Van Gorcum, 2006), 3–106.

a given matter, and other times a close study of the texts reveals incongruities and differences in approach either within the same compilation or across different compilations. All of this is to say that the term "the rabbis," which I use repeatedly in the book to refer to the agents behind the ideas, interpretations, and innovations that will be examined in the following chapters, is very much an artificial construct. "The (early) rabbis" are essentially the aggregate of many voices that were preserved through the compilations mentioned above, voices that speak of different things, from different perspectives, with different concerns. Moreover, these voices themselves arrive at us mediated by centuries of additions, emendations, interpolations, and scribal errors, such that our ability to construct any real flesh-and-blood rabbis through these texts is very limited.

Nevertheless, despite the great variety and multivocality that characterize rabbinic literature, a close examination of the Tannaitic sacrificial corpus in its entirety reveals that there are fundamental ideas, convictions, and legal and ritual principles that prevail throughout the corpus and constitute a shared and uncontested foundation. In other words, there is a certain horizon of possibilities and expectations that determines how and with which conceptual categories the rabbis approach the topic of sacrifice, and this horizon is traceable in the Tannaitic corpus notwithstanding the many variations of opinion, rhetoric, and focal points found in specific texts. For example, as will be discussed in chapter 2, a fundamental principle that governs rabbinic sacrificial legislation across the board is that the application of the victim's blood to the altar is the most important and decisive component of the sacrificial ritual. Different passages then present a variety of opinions on the extent to which blood is more critical than other components and on the dispensability of sacrificial substances that are not blood, but they all nonetheless work within the same framework that identifies the primacy of blood in the process. To take another example, there is an overwhelming consensus across different rabbinic compilations that congregational offerings can only be made using public funds, as will be discussed in chapter 3, although there is some nuance between different compilations as to what makes funds "public." The book aims to reconstruct the horizon of possibilities and expectations that orients the rabbinic discourse on sacrifice in its broadest terms, while also giving account of the controversies, divergences, and shifting emphases that emerge in different textual junctures.

By referring to the ideational principles and frameworks that we see in Tannaitic compilations as "rabbinic" I am not presuming to make a claim on the exact point in time in which these frameworks and principles emerged. It is certainly possible that some of the rulings and concepts that appear in the Tannaitic literature were developed during the time of the temple, and perhaps were shared or even taken for granted among different Judean circles around the turn of the Common Era.[25] There are various areas of legislation in which we can identify strong resonance between Tannatic texts and earlier texts from the Second Temple period (537 B.C.E.–70 C.E.),[26] and it is not inconceivable that if we had elaborate treatises on sacrifice from this period we would find in them echoes of the sacrificial discourse of the rabbis. However, extant texts from the Second Temple period offer nothing even remotely similar to the Tannaitic sacrificial corpus insofar as none of them is concerned with the actual *workings* of sacrifice. Texts from the Second Temple period dedicate much attention to the appearance of the temple and the priests,[27] to the types of offerings made on different festivals,[28] to the substances that can be used for sacrificial purposes,[29] and to the behavior of the priests and of the worshippers during the rituals.[30] But no text that precedes the Tannaitic corpus—at least none that is available to us—engages with questions such as what makes a sacrifice valid, how to correct sacrificial mishaps, what the relation between public and private offerings is, what constitutes a fulfillment of a sacrificial duty, and similar questions that stand at the heart of the rabbinic corpus. As Joshua Schwartz has shown in detail, Second Temple sources tell us almost nothing about the actual mechanisms of sacrifice, perhaps because while the temple cult was still active and vibrant these issues were too trivial to be of concern.[31] Thus, when I describe certain rabbinic ideas as innovative or revolutionary, I do not propose that the innovation is necessarily a product of the second or third

25. Thus, for example, Meir Bar-Ilan argues that tractates Tamid and Middot of the Mishnah should both be understood as polemical documents, created specifically in contestation of sectarian positions found in various compilations from the Second Temple period and thus reflecting more general debates about the temple and its cult in Judea of the turn of the Common Era. See Meir Bar-Ilan, "Are Tamid and Middot Polemical Tractates?" [Heb.], *Sidra* 5 (1989): 27–40.

26. See, for example, Hanoch Albeck, "The Book of Jubilees and the Halakhah," *Jewish Studies* 45 (2008): 3–48; Ya'akov Sussman, "The Study of the History of Halakhah and the Dead Sea Scrolls: First Talmudic Contemplations in Light of the *Miqsat Ma'ase ha-Torah* Scroll" [Heb.], *Tarbitz* 59 (1990): 12–76; Ahron Shemesh, *Halakhah in the Making: The Development of Jewish Law from Qumran to the Rabbis* (Berkeley and Los Angeles: University of California Press, 2009); Vered Noam, *From Qumran to the Rabbinic Revolution: Conceptions of Impurity* [Heb.] (Jerusalem: Yad Ben Zvi Press, 2010).

27. See Steven Weitzman, *Surviving Sacrilege: Cultural Persistence in Jewish Antiquity* (Cambridge, MA: Harvard University Press, 2005), 79–95.

28. See especially Lawrence Schiffman, *The Courtyards of the House of the Lord: Studies on the Temple Scroll* (Leiden: Brill, 2008), 297–380; Schiffman, "Sacrifice in the Dead Sea Scrolls," in *The Actuality of Sacrifice: Past and Present,* ed. Alberdina Houtman, Marcel Poorthuis, Joshua Schwartz, and Joseph Turner (Leiden: Brill, 2014), 89–106.

29. See Martha Himmelfarb, *Between Temple and Torah: Essays on Priests, Scribes, and Visionaries in the Second Temple Period and Beyond* (Tübingen: Mohr Siebeck, 2013), 61–78.

30. See Jutta Leonhardt, *Jewish Worship in Philo of Alexandria* (Tübingen: Mohr Siebeck,), 2001.

31. Joshua Schwartz, "Sacrifice without the Rabbis: Ritual and Sacrifice in the Second Temple Period according to Contemporary Sources," in Houtman et al., *The Actuality of Sacrifice,* 146.

century C.E., but only that there is no textual precedent for this idea that predates the Tannaitic corpus.

The systematic and innovative treatment of sacrifice in rabbinic literature is not limited to the Tannaitic corpus, but can be found also in the Amoraic literature that was composed in Palestine and Babylonia approximately between the third and sixth centuries C.E. Several tractates of the Palestinian and Babylonian Talmuds are dedicated in part or in their entirety to aspects of the sacrificial cult,[32] and random discussions about sacrifices regularly appear as part of larger scholastic endeavors in hundreds of places throughout the two Talmuds. The Talmudic material on sacrifices, however, is not included in this book's inquiry and is not mentioned except on occasion, when it provides important alternative versions or pertinent explanations for the Tannaitic material. Although many traditions that appear in the Talmuds are presented as Tannaitic in provenance through their attributions to early rabbis or through the terminology with which they are introduced, I am generally reluctant to include those traditions in the Tannaitic corpus, as I find it virtually impossible to assess the "authenticity" of such passages. My choice to restrict the book to the material that appears in the Tannaitic compilations derives from my aim to present a relatively synchronic picture of rabbinic approaches to sacrifices, rather than to outline a trajectory of development or change throughout the rabbinic period as a whole. Since the Talmudic discussions on sacrifice almost exclusively rely on and set out from the Tannaitic corpus, I consider Talmudic materials to be important aids in approaching the earlier material, but see them as a "second story" on top of the Tannaitic foundations rather than as sources through which the foundations themselves can be reconstructed.

To the extent that aspects or components of the Tannaitic sacrificial corpus received attention in modern scholarship, this attention was most often guided—explicitly or implicitly—by one predominant question, namely, why this material exists in the first place. This question pertained less to the Tannaitic midrashim, whose engagement with sacrificial issues can easily be understood as dictated by the content of the Pentateuchal books around which the midrashim are structured, but was forcefully presented in regard to the Mishnah (and the parallel Tosefta), which are self-standing normative codices. Taking it for granted that the Mishnah is a legislative code that seeks to enforce certain modes of behavior on the Jewish populace of the authors' time, scholars pondered the question of why such significant portions of the Mishnah are dedicated to practices and institu-

---

32. The Talmudic tractates that discuss sacrifices and temple cult extensively are Pesaḥim, Yoma, and Ḥagigah (both in the Palestinian Talmud and in the Babylonian Talmud); Sheqalim (Palestinian Talmud only); Zevaḥim, Menaḥot, Ḥullin, Bekhorot, ʿArkahin, Temurah, Karetot, Meʿila (Babylonian Talmud only).

tions that are no longer applicable. Four central models for answering this question can be traced in different scholarly works:

1. *Preservation.* Tannaitic texts that describe or discuss sacrifices either date back
   to the time of the Second Temple or conserve traditions and rulings that
   already prevailed at the time of the temple, with or without adding layers of
   explanation or complication. The purpose of this preservation is either
   past-facing (remembering what was lost) or future-facing (preparing for when
   the temple will be rebuilt).[33]

2. *Recitation.* Rabbinic texts on sacrifices were created as substitutes for sacrificial practices. Their aim is not prescriptive but rather performative: those texts
   can be read, recited, or learned in the synagogue or study house, thereby
   allowing individuals or groups to continue engaging in sacrifices verbally even
   when it is impossible to engage in them physically. As such, rabbinic sacrificial
   texts correspond to other liturgical components that invoke or describe
   sacrificial practices.[34]

3. *Appropriation.* It was important for the rabbis to create a discourse on
   sacrifices and on the temple cult because of their power struggle with the
   priests. Since after the destruction of the temple the rabbis set out to emerge as
   the new intellectual and religious elite and to marginalize the priests who
   claimed this role in the past, it was imperative for them to claim that even in
   the area of knowledge most closely associated with the priests the rabbis were
   the ultimate figures of authority.[35]

---

33. This was the dominant approach among the founders of the academic study of rabbinic literature. See, for example, David Zwi Hoffmann, *Die erste Mischna und die Controversen der Tannaim*
(Berlin, 1882); Ya'akov N. Epstein, *Prolegomena to Tannaitic Literature: Mishnah, Tosefta, and Halakhic
Midrashim* [Heb.] (Jerusalem: Magnes Press, 1959), 25–58. While contemporary scholars tend to see the
texts themselves as products of a later period, the paradigm of preservation is still the most common
one in scholarship of rabbinic literature. This paradigm is lucidly expressed in David Henshke's summary of his study of pilgrimage traditions in Tannaitic literature: "Throughout the Tannaitic period the
concepts pertaining to pilgrimage all remained in their original framework: the memory of the temple
and its cult was still vibrant enough, and the mindset of 'soon the temple shall be rebuilt' preserved
it in a restorative orientation." David Henshke, *Festival Joy in Tannaitic Discourse* [Heb.] (Jerusalem:
Magnes Press, 2007), 324 (my translation). See also Francis Schmidt, *How the Temple Thinks: Identity
and Social Cohesion in Ancient Judaism*, trans. J. Edward Crowley (Sheffield: Sheffield Academic Press,
2001), 263–66.

34. See, for example, Smith, "Trading Places," 223; Stroumsa, *The End of Sacrifice*, 67–68; Michael
D. Swartz, "Liturgy, Poetry, and the Persistence of Sacrifice," in *Was 70 CE a Watershed in Jewish His-
tory? On Jews and Judaism before and after the Destruction of the Second Temple*, ed. Daniel R. Schwartz,
Zeev Weiss, and Ruth A. Clements (Leiden: Brill, 2012), 393–412.

35. This idea is most forcefully proposed by Peter Schäfer, "Rabbis and Priests, or: How to Do Away
with the Glorious Past of the Sons of Aaron," in *Antiquity in Antiquity: Jewish and Christian Pasts in the
Greco-Roman World*, ed. Gregg Gardner and Kevin Osterloh (Tübingen: Mohr Siebeck, 2008), 155–72.

4. *Defiance of reality.* The rabbis' engagement with sacrifices in a world in which the temple and its cult were absent was their way of shutting out this reality and declaring that "nothing has changed." The rabbis did not operate out of genuine interest in sacrifices as such, but rather out of a desire to maintain in their works the only model of reality that they saw as complete and coherent—namely, the scriptural model—which by definition includes a temple and sacrificial practices.[36]

There is certainly truth, to some extent, to each of these models (which are not necessarily mutually exclusive). It stands to reason that the rabbis indeed built on earlier foundations, conceptual or practical, that date back to the Second Temple period—although is it very difficult to identify particular texts or ideas as quintessentially "early" with any degree of certainty.[37] Mishnaic texts that describe sacrificial procedures have indeed become part of the liturgy, and later on their study was hailed as equivalent to actual sacrifice,[38] but we will never know whether the rabbis who authored these texts intended them as such. These texts certainly helped the rabbis build their authority as interpreters and legislators who were empowered to adjudicate every area of Jewish life, although there is room to question how salient the rabbis' competition with the priests actually was.[39] Finally, it is true that if one reads the rabbinic sacrificial corpus against the backdrop of the absence of the temple and the cult this corpus conspicuously seems to be proclaiming "nothing has changed," as Tannaitic texts almost never mention that the temple is no longer functional and that its laws are not applicable.

It is also the guiding principle in Naftali S. Cohn, *The Memory of the Temple and the Making of the Rabbis* (Philadelphia: University of Pennsylvania Press, 2012); see also Kathryn McClymond, "Don't Cry over Spilled Blood," in Knust and Várhelyi, *Ancient Mediterranean Sacrifice,* 235–50.

36. This approach was influentially put forth by Jacob Neusner, "Map without Territory: Mishnah's System of Sacrifice and Sanctuary," *History of Religions* 19, no. 2 (1979): 103–27.

37. Scholars of rabbinic literature traditionally regarded statements attributed to or associated with early sages as early in provenance: this method, however, is problematic insofar as we have no way of knowing whether and to what extent attributions are reliable, and whether early statements continued to be worked and modified by later transmitters. On the unreliability of rabbinic attributions, see Amram Tropper, *Rewriting Ancient Jewish History: The History of the Jews in Roman Times and the New Historical Method* (New York: Routledge, 2016), 120–25. Likewise, the method of relying on "antiquated language" in dating rabbinic passages is highly questionable, as such language can be incorporated purposefully as a stylistic feature.

38. See especially BT Menaḥot 110a.

39. On the presumed competition and enmity between priests and rabbis, see Stuart A. Cohen, *The Three Crowns: Structures of Communal Politics in Early Rabbinic Jewry* (Cambridge: Cambridge University Press, 1990), 147–78; for a more refined argument, see Martha Himmelfarb, *A Kingdom of Priests: Ancestry and Merit in Ancient Judaism* (Philadelphia: University of Pennsylvania Press, 2006), 165–70.

However, I would like to contest the very premise behind these four models, that is, that the very existence of the sacrificial corpus ought to be explained specifically vis-à-vis the absence of the temple. In truth, every one of these four explanatory models could be applied to other areas of rabbinic legislation as well. Many rabbinic traditions presumably date back, in one configuration or another, to the time of the Second Temple and were transmitted by later generations; various rabbinic passages were integrated into the liturgy, or developed as "textual rituals," which are effectively performed only when they are studied;[40] rabbinic legislation is a means of constructing authority and asserting expertise regardless of the area of legislation, as this is the essence of creating a normative codex;[41] and perhaps most importantly, the Mishnah covers many areas of biblical law that were not applicable at the time of the rabbis or may never have been applicable at all (such as the laws of the king, the laws of the Jubilee year, laws of cities of refuge, etc.). As Ishay Rosen-Zvi has observed, "What makes [the mishnaic discussions pertaining to the temple] unique is not the fact that they are detached from the reality, but rather that they are not dependent on it. . . . Practiced and unpracticed laws appear side by side without any hint of this essential difference between them."[42] In the greater scheme of Tannaitic literature, there is really nothing unique or exceptional about the sacrificial corpus. It is only necessary to account for the existence of this corpus if one assumes, as I mentioned in the beginning, that the most important thing about the temple cult in the world of the rabbis is its absence.

It is not my intention here to argue that the destruction of the temple was not a significant event for many Jews who lived at the time, and for the rabbis among them. Rather, I am merely pointing out that the destruction of the temple plays little to no role in the rabbis' sacrificial corpus. We can explain the texts' silence on this matter as a sign that the core of the texts precedes the destruction or as an indication of denial inherent in trauma[43] or as a mode of political resistance or in any other way, but all these explanations are projections that rest on certain assumptions about how the destruction of the temple *must have* affected the early rabbis and their Jewish contemporaries. Assumptions and projections are, of

40. On "textual rituals" in rabbinic literature, see Beth Berkowitz, *Execution and Invention: Death Penalty Discourse in Early Rabbinic and Christian Cultures* (New York: Oxford University Press, 2006), 68–71; Ishay Rosen-Zvi, *The Mishnaic Sotah Ritual: Temple, Gender, and Midrash,* trans. Orr Scharf (Leiden: Brill, 2013), 234–38; Michael D. Swartz, "Judaism and the Idea of Ancient Ritual Theory," in *Jewish Studies at the Crossroads of Anthropology and History: Authority, Diaspora, Tradition,* ed. Ra'anan S. Boustan, Oren Kosansky, and Marina Rustow (Philadelphia: University of Pennsylvania Press, 2011), 294–317.

41. See Michael Berger, *Rabbinic Authority* (New York: Oxford University Press, 1998).

42. Rosen-Zvi, *The Mishnaic Sotah Ritual,* 246.

43. As argued by Bokser, "Rabbinic Responses to Catastrophe."

course, an inevitable part of textual analysis, and there is no fault in them as long as they are recognized as such. However, the danger in reducing the vast Tannaitic sacrificial corpus to a "response" to the destruction of the temple is that it all too easily leads to seeing the rabbis' investment in the topic of sacrifice as formalistic at best, or disingenuous at worst.[44] Simply put, if the rabbis care about sacrifices only as scriptural tropes or as vestiges of the past or as possibilities for the distant future or as the domain of the priests that should be taken over, then the rabbis probably do not have anything interesting to say about sacrifices per se. This position was put forth most bluntly by Jacob Neusner, who asserted that the Mishnah "says little more than it learns from an already available scripture" about sacrifices, and that the sacrificial corpus is essentially an "elaborate construction with no new and actual content: a design of an imaginary system which, if it were realized, would be all formalism and no fresh meaning."[45]

The study presented in this book is guided by the premise that sacrifices are a topic of utmost importance for the early rabbis, and it works to show that their investment in this topic generated radically new ideas on the workings and meanings of sacrificial practices.[46] This investment should be understood, first and foremost, as deriving from the prominence of sacrifices and temple cult in the legal codes of the Pentateuch, which function both overtly and covertly as the rabbis' pivotal point of reference. The rabbis' commitment to presenting themselves as the ultimate authorities in interpreting scripture, and in translating scripture into a way of life, suffices in and of itself to explain their extensive engagement with a set of practices that is so definitive of biblical religion. As several recent studies showed, the fact that certain scriptural themes are not grounded in the rabbis' own lived experience does not mean that the rabbis do not put incredible amounts of

---

44. The view of the rabbis' engagement with the temple as disingenuous is especially manifest in Peter Schäfer's summary of the rabbis' state of mind: "We (i.e., the rabbis) are now the ones who dictate to the priests what it is all about, what they are and are not supposed to do—whenever, God forbid, their time will come again." (Schäfer, "Rabbis and Priests," 172).

45. Neusner, "Map without Territory," 113, 117. See also Maria-Zoe Petropoulou's sweeping statement that when the Mishnah is compared to earlier sources on sacrifice, "a factor of development over time is only rarely visible." Maria-Zoe Petropoulou, *Animal Sacrifice in Ancient Greek Religion, Judaism, and Christianity, 100 BC to AD 200* (Oxford: Oxford University Press, 2008), 129.

46. This book thus joins a few works that explored various innovative facets of the rabbinic sacrificial corpus, primarily Noam Zohar, "Purification Offering in Tannaitic Literature" (master's thesis, Hebrew University, 1988); Ishay Rosen-Zvi, "The Body and the Temple: The List of Priestly Blemishes in the Mishnah and the Place of the Temple in the Tannaitic Study House" [Heb.], *Jewish Studies* 43 (2006): 49–87; Rosen-Zvi, "The Mishnaic Mental Revolution: A Reassessment," *Journal of Jewish Studies* 66, no. 1 (2015): 36–58; Michael D. Swartz, "Ritual Is with People: Sacrifice and Society in Palestinian Yoma Traditions," in Houtman et al., *The Actuality of Sacrifice*, 206–27.

creative energy and interpretive audacity into their own construction of those themes.[47]

In the case of sacrifices, however, I believe that the rabbis' investment in the topic stemmed not only from its centrality in the Bible but also from its centrality in the world around them. The ancient Mediterranean world was a world suffused with sacrifices: in many ways, sacrificial practices were almost synonymous with what the Romans called *cultus deorum,* "care of the gods," which perhaps comes closest to what we would define as "religion."[48] Moreover, as I will discuss in the conclusion, sacrifice in antiquity was a constitutive social and political practice, which was instrumental in forming and maintaining relations of kinship, class, citizenship, and community. To a denizen of Roman Palestine of the second century C.E., sacrifice was a pervasive reality whether or not he or she actually participated in sacrificial practices. Indeed, I will argue, certain aspects of the rabbinic sacrificial vision are best understood against sacrificial institutions, ideas, and practices that were at play among Greeks, Romans, and early Christians of the first centuries C.E. Thus, in addition to illuminating the ways in which the rabbis thought of and developed ideas pertaining to sacrifice as part of their greater legal and interpretive creation, this book also seeks to integrate the rabbinic creation into the broader cultural context in which it came to be.

WHAT WE TALK ABOUT WHEN WE TALK ABOUT SACRIFICE

Since the subject of this book is textual constructions of sacrifice, it is imperative, first, to provide a working definition of "sacrifice" for the purposes of this book, and second, to explain my methodology in approaching textual representations of sacrifice as opposed to live performances of sacrificial rituals. My approach can be succinctly summarized in a paraphrase of the famous saying of Yiddish author Sholem Aleichem, "Dumplings in a dream are a dream and not dumplings": ritual in a text is text and not ritual. Following the astute observations of historian Philippe Buc, I maintain that rabbinic texts about sacrifices teach us primarily about rabbinic texts. Only secondarily, and only with great caution, do they allow us to reconstruct actual sacrificial practices with which the rabbis were familiar,

47. Most notably, see Berkowitz, *Execution and Invention;* and Rosen-Zvi, *The Mishnaic Sotah Ritual.* See also Yair Lorberbaum, *Disempowered King: Monarchy in Classical Jewish Literature* (New York: Continuum Books, 2011); Mira Balberg, "Rabbinic Authority, Medical Rhetoric, and Body Hermeneutics in Mishnah Negaʿim," *AJS Review* 35, no. 2 (2011): 323–46.

48. See Hans Schilderman, "Religion as Concept and Measure," *Journal of Empirical Theology* 27, no. 1 (2014): 7.

"with full and *constant* sensitivity to their [the practices'] status as texts."[49] The types of questions with which this book engages, and the kinds of texts that stand at its center, reflect my interest in the Tannaitic sacrificial corpus as a textual creation and not as a historical or ethnographic document.

The term "sacrifice" is a remarkably open-ended and pliable one, and it and its cognates have been used for centuries to denote a whole range of actions or events that generally fall under the category of giving (or giving up on) something for the sake of someone or something else[50]—from Jesus's crucifixion to parents losing sleep to care for their infants, from soldiers dying on the battlefield to passing on dessert during Lent. When discussing sacrifice in the biblical and early rabbinic context, however, I am emphatically using this term in a very limited way, to refer distinctly to a ritual process in which an individual or a group physically transfers an animal or another edible substance to the possession of the "High"—whether this "High" is perceived as the deity himself or as the institution and personnel associated with him.[51] Throughout this book, I use the term "sacrifice" to refer to the *process* (that is, the series of actions) in which a substance is transferred in this way, and I use the term "offering" to refer to the transferred substance.

The word *process* is key here, since sacrifice in this restricted sense by definition consists of multiple activities. Broadly speaking, the sacrificial process can be divided into three key stages: (1) delivery, in which the offerer enters the sacred precinct and presents the sacrificial substance (animal or grain offering) to the officiating priests; (2) transformation of the substance, to prepare it for consumption, performed partially or exclusively by priests; (3) distribution and consumption, either by humans (owners, priests, or both) or by fire. Each one of these three stages in turn consists of multiple actions: the delivery stage requires a journey to the temple, selection of the sacrificial substance, and a gesture marking ownership of the animal (laying hands on an animal's head, ceremoniously lifting up a grain offering); the transformation stage requires slaughter, dissection, disposal of blood, mixing of oil and other substances (for grain offerings), libations, and arrangement on the altar; and the consumption stage involves cooking or roasting, burning on an altar, and/or eating. Which activities exactly are performed, how they are performed, and by whom vary depending on the exact type of offering.

Various scholars who engaged with the topic of sacrifice tended to isolate within this multiphase process a single action that they identified as the essence of

49. Philippe Buc, *The Dangers of Ritual: Between Early Medieval Texts and Social Scientific Theory* (Princeton: Princeton University Press, 2001), 4 (emphasis in the original).

50. See, for example, Halbertal, *On Sacrifice*, 1; Olli Pyyhtinen, *The Gift and Its Paradoxes: Beyond Mauss* (Surrey: Ashgate Publishing, 2014), 24–33.

51. In general, the Hebrew word *qorban* (offering) and its cognates are never used in rabbinic literature in metaphorical or figurative senses. While various acts of piety can be said to function *like* sacrificial offerings, the term is reserved for offerings brought to the altar.

"sacrifice" as such, or as bespeaking its original meaning, and bracketed other actions as merely complementary or rudimentary. Thus, for example, both Walter Burkert[52] and René Girard[53] identified the act of killing the animal as the essence of the sacrificial process, the former because he associated sacrifice with hunting, and the latter because he saw animal sacrifice primarily as an act of premeditated violence. In contrast, William Robertson Smith[54] and, to a different end, Jean-Pierre Vernant and Marcel Detienne[55] identified the consumption of the offering as the driving purpose of the sacrificial process, the former because he saw sacrifice as communion between humans and deity, and the latter because they saw it as a form of commensality among humans.[56] For Henri Hubert and Marcel Mauss, sacrifice is defined by the entry and exit of the offerer into and out of the sacred realm;[57] for Georges Bataille, it is defined by the destruction or demolition of the sacrificial substance;[58] and for Jonathan Z. Smith, the key to the sacrificial process is the careful selection of the animal.[59] In a helpful endeavor to recalibrate the prominent scholarly approaches to sacrifice and reassess some deep-seated dogmas, Kathryn McClymond recently argued that sacrifice must be viewed as a series of actions rather than as a single action, and be explored through a holistic and inclusive lens rather than in an attempt to capture an "original" purpose.[60]

While I am in full agreement with McClymond that there is no universal and transhistorical essence to sacrifice except in the eye of the beholder, and that no one action of which a sacrificial process is comprised is necessarily more fundamental than another, I want to draw attention to the fact that scholars of religion, more often than not, engage with *representations* of sacrifice and not with sacrifice as such. These representations, whether visual or textual, oftentimes do emphasize

---

52. Walter Burkert, *Homo Necans: The Anthropology of Ancient Greek Sacrificial Ritual and Myth,* trans. Peter Bing (Berkeley and Los Angeles: University of California Press, 1983).

53. René Girard, *Violence and the Sacred,* trans. Patrick Gregory (Baltimore: Johns Hopkins University Press, 1979).

54. William Robertson Smith, *Lectures on the Religion of the Semites* (New York: Macmillan, 1927), 211–384.

55. Marcel Detienne and Jean-Pierre Vernant, *The Cuisine of Sacrifice among the Greek*s, trans. Paula Wissing (Chicago: University of Chicago Press, 1989).

56. On "violence" vs. "food" as prominent trends in theories of sacrifice, see James W. Watts, "The Rhetoric of Sacrifice," in *Ritual and Metaphor: Sacrifice in the Hebrew Bible* (Atlanta: Society of Biblical Literature, 2011), 3–16.

57. Henri Hubert and Marcel Mauss, *Sacrifice: Its Nature and Functions,* trans. Wilfred D. Halls (Chicago: University of Chicago Press, 1981).

58. Georges Bataille, *Theory of Religion,* trans. Robert Hurley (New York: Zone Books, 1992).

59. Jonathan Z. Smith, "The Domestication of Sacrifice," in *Relating Religion: Essays in the Study of Religion* (Chicago: University of Chicago Press, 2004), 145–59.

60. Kathryn McClymond, *Beyond Sacred Violence: A Comparative Study of Sacrifice* (Baltimore: Johns Hopkins University Press, 2008).

one component of the sacrificial process over others, and do place significant rhetorical and dramatic weight on one dimension of sacrifice over others.[61] Indeed,
the different theories of sacrifice developed by the different scholars mentioned
above are in no small measure attributable to the texts on which these scholars
heavily relied: it is rather unsurprising that Girard, whose main point of reference
was Greek tragedy, saw sacrifice as a form of murder, whereas Vernant and
Detienne, who focused on Homer and Hesiod, saw it as a meal.[62] McClymond is
certainly correct that if we were to observe the performance of a sacrificial ritual
from beginning to end, we would probably not be able to point to one particular
action as the raison d'être of the process as a whole. But when we encounter
accounts of sacrificial rituals that were produced with a certain set of convictions
and educational purposes in mind, it is extremely important to examine which
sacrificial actions are highlighted in a given depiction of sacrifice and which are
marginalized or ignored. If we approach depictions of sacrifice as carefully crafted
cultural artifacts we may have to be more modest in drawing correlations between
text and actual historical practice, but we stand to learn something significant
about the views and inclinations of those who created those depictions.[63]

In the case of rabbinic literature, attention to the literary construction of the
sacrificial process and to the textual choices made by the authors in verbally representing sacrificial actions is particularly important, for a simple reason: the rabbis already worked within a given and predetermined sacrificial system. The entire
array of "building-blocks" of which rabbinic sacrificial discourse consists—the
types of sacrificial substances, the occasions on which different substances are
offered and the combinations in which they are offered, the specific actions
required vis-à-vis the different substances, the basic taxonomies of different
sacrifices—all those are dictated by the expansive sacrificial legislation of the

---

61. For examples of the tendency to represent only one component of the sacrificial process in a
given artistic work, see David Frankfurter, "Egyptian Religion and the Problem of the Category 'Sacrifice,'" in Knust and Várhelyi, *Ancient Mediterranean Sacrifice*, 75–93; Jaś Elsner, "Sacrifice in Late Roman
Art," in *Greek and Roman Animal Sacrifice: Ancient Victims, Modern Observers*, ed. Christopher A.
Faraone and Fred S. Naiden (New York: Cambridge University Press, 2012), 120–63.

62. Two articles that appear side by side in one collected volume on ancient sacrifice, one on Greek
comedy and the other on Greek tragedy, make it abundantly clear how radically different the depiction
of sacrifice in these two genres is. See James Redfield, "Animal Sacrifice in Comedy: An Alternative
Point of View," and Albert Henrichs, "Animal Sacrifice in Greek Tragedy: Ritual, Metaphor, Problematizations," in Faraone and Naiden, *Greek and Roman Animal Sacrifice*, 167–79 and 180–94 respectively.

63. In this methodology I take my cue primarily from biblical scholars who have grappled with
textual representations of ritual. See Saul Olyan, *Rites and Rank: Hierarchy in Biblical Representations
of Cult* (Princeton: Princeton University Press, 2000), esp. 13–14; William Gilders, *Blood Ritual in the
Hebrew Bible: Meaning and Power* (Baltimore: Johns Hopkins University Press, 2004), esp. 8–11; James
W. Watts, *Ritual and Rhetoric in Leviticus: From Sacrifice to Scripture* (New York: Cambridge University
Press), esp. 27–36.

Pentateuch, chiefly Leviticus 1–7 and Numbers 28–29. While the rabbis do add details, definitions, and subclassifications to each of those building-blocks, they do not integrate any new types of offerings or activities into the biblical picture.[64] Thus, rabbinic depictions of sacrificial processes lend themselves neither to semantic analysis (in which every component of the process is read for its symbolic significance, à la Victor Turner's works on ritual[65]) nor to grammatical analysis (which examines the possible combinations of different components, à la Frits Staal's works on ritual[66]), since both the "semantic" elements and the "grammatical" structures are prescribed by the biblical sources. However, I propose, rabbinic texts do lend themselves to *discourse* analysis: their representations of sacrifices are put forth through a series of literary and rhetorical choices, and these choices amount to certain claims about the nature and purpose of different sacrificial procedures.

Discourse analysis is the main tool we have at our disposal when we venture to understand early rabbinic conceptions of and approaches toward sacrifice, since Tannaitic literature contains practically no explicit reflections on questions such as "What is sacrifice?" and "Why is sacrifice important?" Within the greater landscape of this literature, this is not at all unusual: it is the rabbis' ordinary mode of operation to engage with biblically ordained practices through the prism of "how" rather than through the prism of "why," or put differently, to think *with* the biblical injunctions rather than *about* them.[67] Specifically in the context of sacrifice, the rabbis are in direct continuity with the priestly authors from whose texts they depart, who provide comprehensive instructions for sacrifice but nothing resembling an explanation of these instructions. Yet, as James Watts compellingly argued, much can be understood about how the priestly authors wanted to portray sacrifices and how they wanted their audience to think of their value and benefit by looking at aspects of presentation and arrangement in their texts. It is significant, for example, that the priestly authors chose to begin their sacrificial manual of Leviticus 1–7 by speaking of the burnt offering (*'olah*), which is an offering given in its entirety to God with no portions given to the priests or owners, thereby presenting it as the paradigmatic sacrificial gift; it is also significant that the first set of instructions is directed to the Israelites as a people and not to the

---

64. As shown by Naphtali S. Meshel, *The "Grammar" of Sacrifice: A Generativistic Study of the Israelite Sacrificial System in the Priestly Writings* (New York: Oxford University Press, 2014).

65. For example, Victor Turner, *The Forest of Symbols: Aspects of Ndembu Ritual* (Ithaca: Cornell University Press, 1967). For symbolic explanations of the biblical priestly cult, see Mary Douglas, *Leviticus as Literature* (Oxford: Oxford University Press, 1999); Klawans, *Purity, Sacrifice, and the Temple,* 49–74.

66. Frits Staal, "The Meaninglessness of Ritual," *Numen* 26, no. 1 (1979): 2–22.

67. I thank Ishay Rosen-Zvi for this insight.

priests, despite the fact that it is the priests who are to carry out the instructions.[68] Similarly, as I will show, insights into the rabbis' approach to sacrifices and into the ideology guiding their portrayal of sacrifices can be gleaned from sensitivity to choices of wording, order, and perspective: it makes a difference whether one describes a sacrificial event from the point of view of the performing priest or from the point of view of the laypeople watching it; it makes a difference whether a particular component of the ritual is described in detail, mentioned in brief, or ignored altogether; and it makes a difference whether the consumption of a sacrificial offering by fire is described as the production of "a pleasing odor to the Lord" or as allowing the altar to "eat" the offering. The significance of such choices and others will be explored in the chapters that follow.

My main area of interest in this book, then, is the discourse that the rabbis construct around the sacrificial process—that is, around the different ritual *actions* that comprise "sacrifice" as a composite procedure. To be sure, there is much more to the Tannaitic sacrificial corpus than discussion of the procedure of sacrifice. It contains many discussions regarding sacrificial substances (how to choose them, what rules apply to them once they have been chosen, what quantities of what substances are required, what qualifies and disqualifies various animals for sacrifice, etc.); it addresses questions of hierarchy and primacy between different offerings; and it dedicates much attention to circumstances in which obligations to bring certain offerings are created, enforced, or dismissed. However, it is specifically in regard to the actions that comprise the sacrificial process that the rabbis introduce what I consider to be the most innovative and revolutionary aspect of their legislation: a discourse on the *validity* of sacrifices. At the core of this discourse stands the notion that specific performances of the sacrificial process can either "count" or "not count" as a sacrifice, depending on an array of factors that have to do primarily with the relations between the different actions of which the process consists. To that end, the rabbis reflect in great detail on different configurations in which one or more of the actions is omitted, misperformed, or compromised. Furthermore, the rabbis integrate in their discussions of sacrificial actions a dimension that is completely absent from biblical and Second Temple accounts of sacrifice: a dimension of intention and mental disposition.

In introducing categories of accidents and aberrations to the sacrificial discourse, the rabbis place certain components of the process at the center and others at the periphery, and they cluster together certain elements of the procedure while establishing a divide between other elements. The texts in which the rabbis dissect and reconfigure the different components of the sacrificial process in order to assess what makes for a valid sacrifice and what does not are effectively guided by the question of *how sacrifice works*: what sequence of activities counts as "sacrifice"

68. Watts, *Ritual and Rhetoric*, 57–60, 71–73.

and what sequence of activities is something other than sacrifice. In this respect, the rabbinic discourse on the sacrificial process uniquely allows us to reconstruct the underlying logic that the rabbis identify in the sequence of sacrificial actions, and thereby to uncover a rabbinic *theory* of sacrifice.

However, since I seek to understand the role that sacrifice plays in the early rabbis' conceptual and ideological world, not only as a self-contained ritual process but also as part of a greater picture of Torah-guided piety, I find it equally important to examine the ways in which rabbinic texts connect sacrifice with society and with identity. This connection is drawn primarily in textual units that discuss "congregational offerings," that is, offerings made on behalf of the entire people of Israel rather than by individuals or households. Some of these units are in the form of technical legislative debates, presenting casuistic rulings and taxonomical arguments; other units, however, are in the form of ritual narratives, providing poetic act-by-act accounts of the ways in which certain congregational sacrifices are carried out on specific occasions. It is in these textual units, as I will show, that the rabbis utilize sacrifice to define group boundaries, to reflect on the relations between collective and individual, and ultimately to construct a social and political vision. In other words, if Tannaitic discourse on the validity of sacrificial processes helps us reconstruct a rabbinic *theory* of sacrifice, Tannaitic discourse on congregational offerings helps us reconstruct a rabbinic *ethos* of sacrifice. These two aspects of the Tannaitic sacrificial vision—a theory of sacrifice as a ritual process and an ethos of sacrifice as religious and social practice—stand at the center of the inquiry presented in this book.

OVERVIEW OF THE BOOK

My primary goal in this book is to offer a rich and nuanced (although by no means comprehensive) picture of early rabbinic approaches to sacrifice as a ritual practice. I set out on this goal guided by the conviction that sacrifice and temple cult were an inseparable part of the rabbinic cultural landscape, and thus that an exploration of this topic—which occupies a significant amount of the early rabbinic textual creation—is crucial for reconstructing the intellectual and conceptual world of the rabbis. To achieve this goal, I ask not what the rabbis say *about* sacrifice but rather what they do *with* sacrifice: this book therefore focuses specifically on seemingly technical legal-ritual material and not on explicit statements on the value or meaning of sacrifice (which are, to begin with, very few in number in the Tannaitic corpus). The five chapters of the book present analyses of different key themes in the Tannaitic discourse of sacrifice, each charting an aspect of the sacrificial cult in which the rabbis present notable innovations, as I will outline below.

In utilizing rabbinic legal-ritual material to reconstruct an intellectual history, this book also seeks to make a methodological intervention in the study of early

Judaism: through its analyses, it argues that the clear-cut division that is often taken for granted between rabbinic "thought" (philosophy or theology) and rabbinic *halakhah* ("law" or "conduct") is a misguided one, and that rabbinic *halakhah* is in fact a critical site for uncovering and understanding the rabbis' views on various existential and religious issues.[69] Accordingly, each of the book's five chapters not only describes the principles and paradigms that the rabbis establish in their sacrificial discourse, but also ventures to connect those principles and paradigms to larger ideological and cultural trends, which resonate in different configurations between the different chapters.

Furthermore, I maintain that the incorporation of legal-ritual rabbinic material into our account of rabbinic culture has implications beyond the narrow scholarly field of early Judaism, and stands to impact the broader study of religion in late antiquity. The topic of sacrifice is a particularly instructive case in point, since transformations of sacrifice—both as an idea and as a practice—in the Mediterranean region in the course of the first five centuries of the Common Era are among the most defining traits of "late antiquity" as a historical epoch.[70] The rabbis, as a minority group within a minority group, probably have not been instrumental in bringing forth the wide-ranging political and economic changes that led to the decline of sacrifice in late antiquity. But they were, for all intents and purposes, one out of several specialized elites who formed a theoretical discourse on sacrifices, offering new perspectives on an old set of customs at a time of great political and religious upheaval. In this regard, the rabbis are comparable to other late ancient authors who engaged with the topic of sacrifice—Justin and Tertullian, Cyprian and Clement, Porphyry and Iamblichus, Julian and Sallustius—and the rabbis' sacrificial corpus must be taken into consideration if we attempt to speak about transformations of sacrifice as a mode of religiosity in late antiquity. Such consideration is the purpose of the conclusion, which builds on the analyses presented in the previous chapters in order to integrate the rabbinic theory of sacrifice and the rabbinic ethos of sacrifice into a broader cultural and historical context.

The first two chapters of the book discuss the rabbinic construction of the sacrificial process, that is, the ways in which the rabbis understand the different actions whose sequence comprises a valid sacrifice. The point of departure of these two chapters is the biblical model of sacrifice, which is an interactive model in essence: biblical accounts of sacrifice fundamentally rely on the notion that sacrifice is a vector of communication between the offerer and the deity, both of whom

---

69. See also Mira Balberg, *Purity, Body, and Self in Early Rabbinic Literature* (Berkeley and Los Angeles: University of California Press, 2014), 183–84.

70. See, for example, Scott Bradbury, "Julian's Pagan Revival and the Decline of Blood Sacrifice," *Phoenix* 49, no. 4 (1995): 331–56; Stroumsa, *The End of Sacrifice*; Richard Lim, "Christianization, Secularization, and the Transformation of Public Life," in *Companion to Late Antiquity*, ed. Philip Rousseau (Oxford: Wiley-Blackwell, 2012), 497–511.

manifest their presence and agency in the process in different symbolic ways. In contrast, I argue, the rabbis reconfigure the sacrificial process in a way that effectively eliminates both the giver and the receiver. Thus they substitute a vertical paradigm of sacrifice, centered on a human-divine axis, with a horizontal paradigm of sacrifice, centered on the collective of "Israel" and its constitution and formation through accurately performed sacrificial procedures.

Chapter 1, "Missing Persons," focuses on the marginalization of the giver, the one who brings the offering, in the sacrificial process. The first part of the chapter works to show that while the rabbis put immense emphasis on intention, will, and mental disposition in their legislation in general and in their sacrificial legislation in particular, they systematically deem the intention and will of the giver (the "owner" in rabbinic terms) inconsequential in determining the validity of the sacrifice. For the rabbis, the only person whose intentions are capable of affecting the offering is the officiating priest: I argue that this is because the rabbis maintain that intentions are of legal consequence only when they accompany a consequential action, and they do not take any of the actions performed by the owner—such as purchasing the offering, bringing the offering to the sanctuary, delivering it to the priests, and so on—to be constitutive of the sacrificial process itself. In the second part of the chapter, I show that the rabbis not only dismiss the giver's mental agency in the sacrificial process, but also undermine the quintessential physical gesture that marks the owner's agency in this process. Whereas the Priestly Code asserts that every sacrifice commences with the owner laying his[71] hands on the animal's head before it is slaughtered, the rabbis determine that certain offerings do not call for this gesture, that certain offerers may not perform this gesture, and most importantly, that in any case the sacrifice is valid even if the owner did not lay his hands on the offering. Thus, the rabbis effectively obviate the giver's presence in the sacrificial process.

Chapter 2, "The Work of Blood," shows that the rabbis redefined the biblical sacrificial process by centering it almost exclusively on one substance: blood. Rabbinic texts identify four activities related to blood—slaughter, receiving the blood in a vessel, walking the blood to the altar, and tossing the blood on the altar—and determine that these four activities make or break the sacrifice as a whole. Thereby, the activities that follow the tossing of blood, namely, the consumption of the offering either by fire or by human beings, are bracketed as an addendum to the ritual rather than as a critical component of it. The implications of this reframing of the sacrificial process are far-reaching: in determining that nothing actually has to be burned on the altar for the sacrifice to be valid, the rabbis altogether reject

71. Throughout the book I use masculine pronouns when discussing biblical and rabbinic sacrificial legislation. This is not necessarily an indication that the issue at hand pertains to men alone, but rather it is a reflection of the original language of the texts, whose imagined subject is always male.

the notion that the deity has to "receive" anything when a sacrifice is being performed. They thus put forth a new understanding of sacrifice as a religious activity, defined not by interaction but by what they call "permission": the work of blood is a procedure for turning prohibited substances into usable substances, and this procedure, when performed accurately and correctly, is tantamount to the attainment of atonement. I argue that by developing this noninteractive model the rabbis both make a claim about what sacrifice is not (a channel of communication between individual and deity) and make a claim about what sacrifice is (the ultimate example of a perfect religious action, which serves to construct, bolster, and express communal piety).

Chapter 3, "Sacrifice as One," discusses the rabbinic construction of a taxonomy of "congregational offerings" as opposed to "individual offerings," and the rabbis' use of this taxonomy to create a clear sacrificial hierarchy, guided by a profound collectivistic ideology. While the distinction between individual and congregational offerings has its roots in the Hebrew Bible, the rabbis present a novel interpretation of this distinction by prohibiting any kind of private funding for congregational offerings. They insist that congregational offerings must be attained strictly and exclusively through the half-shekel tribute to the temple that each member of the community must pay annually. Congregational sacrifices are thus portrayed in rabbinic texts as expressions of a unified, collective agency of the people as a whole, and their portrayal as such serves both to reject the prevalent Hellenistic and Roman model of euergetism (that is, benefactions of wealthy individuals) and to paint an idyllic picture of religious and social solidarity. Moreover, the rabbis present congregational offerings not only as belonging to everyone but also as efficacious for everyone, such that in various contexts congregational offerings override and even supersede individual offerings. Through their discourse on congregational sacrifices, I argue, the rabbis channel the language and imagery of the temple's cult toward a new vision of a Jewish political and religious utopia.

Chapter 4, "Three Hundred Passovers," brings together the themes discussed in the previous chapters by looking closely at one intriguing test case: the Passover sacrifice. In this complex and multifaceted ritual, whose exact structure and type are contested and obscure already in the biblical corpus, the various concerns and innovations of rabbinic sacrificial legislation converge in a particularly instructive and rich way. Two sets of disputes underlie the rabbinic discussions and controversies regarding the Passover sacrifice: First, is the Passover an individual or congregational sacrifice? And second, does the essence of the Passover sacrifice lie in the blood or in the meat? These two disputes are closely intertwined in rabbinic discussions, and point toward more fundamental questions regarding the significance and function of the Passover sacrifice. In the first part of the chapter, I show that rabbinic texts present a strong tendency to collectivize the Passover sacrifice, and to consider it—formally or informally—as a congregational offering, despite the fact that it is funded and consumed by individuals. In the second part of the chapter, I trace a persistent position within rabbinic texts that underplays the consumption component of the Passover offering and places all the emphasis on the manipulation of the offering's blood. I show that the inherent polymorphism and ambiguous nature of the Passover sacrifice turn it in a microlaboratory for examining the rabbinic sacrificial vision in all its complexity.

In chapter 5, "Ordinary Miracles," I turn to the unique literary genre of ritual narrative, which is peculiar to the Mishnah. Ritual narratives, which provide a vivid and affective play-by-play description of ritual performances either in or in adjacency to the temple, serve to construct an idealized picture of both correct practice and correct relation to practice not through casuistic legislation, but through the semblance of an eyewitness account. The chapter focuses on two expansive ritual narratives that pertain specifically to sacrificial procedures in the temple: the account of the daily morning ritual in tractate Tamid and, less prominently, the account of the Day of Atonement ritual in tractate Yoma. Through these narratives, I explore how sacrifices are shaped and presented in this unique genre, and whether and how these narratives resonate with the sacrificial vision discussed in previous chapters. At the same time, I also examine how sacrifice as a theme and trope serves the greater arc of these narratives in their effort to mythicize the temple as the marker of a golden age. My analyses of these narratives show a systematic emphasis on the mundane and routine over the exceptional or prestigious. Whereas cultic moments that could be perceived as occasions for hierophany (revelation of the divine) are underplayed significantly in mishnaic ritual narratives, sisyphic and technical cultic labors are highlighted and extolled. Furthermore, the Mishnah (primarily in tractate Tamid) repeatedly subdivides and multiplies the priestly labor in the temple, insisting that every sacrificial activity is performed by several priests rather than by one identifiable priestly figure. Thus, these tractates divert the audience's attention from both the substances and the individuals involved in sacrifice, and direct its attention instead to the actions themselves and to the collective dimension of worship. Through this mode of presenting the temple as an arena in which the ordinary is extraordinary and the mundane is sublime, the rabbis further promote a religious vision focused on correctness of action, perfection of performance, and communal solidarity.

Finally, the conclusion, titled "The End of Sacrifice, Revisited," builds on the analyses presented in the book's chapters to integrate the rabbinic sacrificial corpus into the transreligious and transregional story of the gradual decline and ultimate demise of sacrifice in the course of the first millennium c.e. Guided by the premise that Jews' engagement both in sacrificial practices and in sacrificial discourse cannot be understood in isolation from a broader imperial intellectual and political network, I open the conclusion with the following question: What would the story of "the end of sacrifice" and of the religious transformations of late antiquity look like if we took into account the rabbinic legal-ritual corpus, which is usually ignored altogether in such discussions? I suggest that a serious consideration of this corpus allows us to identify important correspondences between rabbinic ideas and developments and contemporaneous Greek, Roman, and early Christian ideas and developments, and that these correspondences go well beyond the paradigm of "substitution" according to which sacrifices were progressively replaced with alternative forms of worship. I show that the discursive persistence of sacrifice in Jewish literature and art despite the inapplicability of sacrificial practice to the audience's lives, the elaborate theory of sacrifice that the rabbis construct in defiance of earlier biblical precepts, and the utilization of sacrifice in creating an idealized public religion are all manners in which the rabbis participate in, contribute to, and appropriate existing ancient and late ancient conversations on sacrifice. Thus, I contend, the rabbinic sacrificial corpus makes a powerful case for the importance of incorporating not only Jewish literature, but specifically Jewish technical-legal literature, into the study of religion and culture in late antiquity.

1

Missing Persons

In biblical narrative, the practice of sacrifice is almost as old as humankind itself. The very first sacrificial acts in the Bible, those of Cain and Abel, who decided to share portions of their harvest and flocks with God, are described not only as self-initiated (rather than expected or required), but also as intuitive. For a human being who is in relationship with a deity, the story presupposes, the occasional offering of some of one's property to the deity is an integral part of the interaction, and the acceptance—or in Cain's case, rejection—of this property by the deity is what constitutes this interaction as mutual and reciprocal.

The story of Cain and Abel is commonly attributed to the Yahwist (J) source of the Pentateuch, which repeatedly depicts ancestral figures such as Noah, Abraham, Isaac, and Jacob as spontaneously performing sacrifices at key moments during their life dramas. Other biblical sources and strata present somewhat different perspectives on sacrifice as a religious practice.[1] The Deuteronomic Code (D) emphasizes the critical importance of performing sacrifices only in the one centralized shrine, "the place that the Lord will choose," thus constructing sacrifice as a public act that requires a preplanned pilgrimage rather than as a private and spontaneous act, but nonetheless continues to portray sacrifice as the ultimate way in which one communicates with the deity—whether communicating joy and gratitude or fear

---

1. For two of the most comprehensive studies on sacrifice in the Hebrew Bible, see Roland de Vaux, *Studies in Old Testament Sacrifice* (Cardiff: University of Wales Press, 1964); Gary A. Anderson, *Sacrifices and Offerings in Ancient Israel: Studies in Their Social and Political Importance* (Atlanta: Scholars Press, 1988). More recently, see David Janzen, *The Social Meanings of Sacrifice in the Hebrew Bible: A Study of Four Writings* (Berlin: Walter de Gruyter, 2004).

and supplication. Similarly, the books associated with the "Deuteronomistic History" (Joshua, Judges, Samuel, and Kings) describe kings, warriors, and laypeople as offering sacrifices both in times of crisis or distress and in times of victory and celebration, their sacrifices always accompanying words of prayer. The Priestly Code (P), by far the biblical source that engages most extensively with sacrificial practices, is concerned more with the appropriate procedures for the performance of sacrifice than with the religious experiences or mind-sets that it conveys, procedures that for this code include a specialized personnel and a wide array of ritual requirements. However, P is clear that different sacrifices are used as certified modes of approaching the deity and managing his presence among his people, either by enticing him to dwell among them or by staving off his anger and preventing his destructive departure.[2] Finally, in the Psalms the experience of making an offering to God in his temple is related as almost ecstatic in nature, and is put forth as the activity that gives the Psalmic liturgy both meaning and efficacy.[3]

Despite the fact that different biblical passages refer to different kinds of sacrifices, in different settings and for different purposes, one can safely generalize that the very enterprise of performing a sacrifice is portrayed in the Hebrew Bible as a form of interaction between the offerer and the deity. Baruch Levine succinctly summarized the role of sacrifice in Israelite society as follows: "Like other ancient Near Eastern cults, that of the Jerusalem temple and of other [cultic] centers represented a complex of dynamic acts aimed at securing certain responses from the deity relevant to vital concerns of current urgency."[4] We may debate about how different biblical authors understood the manner in which sacrifices actually work to secure responses from the deity—whether they saw animal or grain offerings as physically pleasing and desirable to God or saw them primarily as symbolic expressions of subordination and humility[5]—but it is evident that sacrifice is construed in the biblical corpus as functioning *within a relationship*. Regardless of the type, participants, mood, or circumstances of the sacrifice, the basic paradigm is identical: on one end an offerer (either an individual or a group), on the other end God, and in between—allowing for the communication or transformation that the

---

2. For an astute account of sacrifice as attaining different goals vis-à-vis the deity, see John Dunnill, *Covenant and Sacrifice in the Letter to the Hebrews* (New York: Cambridge University Press, 1992), 64–111.

3. On the description of sacrificial worship in the Psalms, see Eyal Regev, "Offerings of Righteousness: Visiting the Temple and Bringing Sacrifices as a Religious Experience in the Psalms" [Heb.], *Tarbitz* 73, no. 3 (2004): 365–86.

4. Baruch Levine, *In the Presence of the Lord: A Study of Cult and Some Cultic Terms in Ancient Israel* (Leiden: Brill, 1974), 41.

5. Such, for example, is the view of Moshe Halbertal (who is clearly influenced here by Moses Maimonides). See Halbertal, *On Sacrifice*, 7–36. Other examples for this approach are discussed in Gilders, *Blood Ritual*, 2–5. For a suggestion of the symbolic dimensions of Israelite sacrifice, see Klawans, *Purity, Sacrifice, and the Temple*, 49–73.

offerer is seeking—a sacrificial substance (animal, vegetable, etc.) and an altar.[6] This interactive paradigm is commonly viewed as the universal governing logic of sacrifice as a transcultural and transhistorical phenomenon, as put by Fritz Graf: "Man, located between animal below and god above, makes use of the animal that is subject to his will and ownership in order to communicate with the gods who are not at his free disposition."[7]

The pertinence of both addresser (offerer) and addressee (deity) to the sacrificial process is so patent in the Hebrew Bible[8] that it is hard to imagine how the definitive role of either of those parties can be undermined in a literature that relies so heavily on the biblical corpus, such as the Tannaitic literature. Nevertheless, in this chapter and the next I endeavor to show that the rabbis transformed the concept of sacrifice and the workings of the sacrificial process in a way that marginalized both the giver and the receiver to the point of inconsequentiality. This marginalization, to be clear, is never enacted through explicit statements on the essence or workings of sacrifices, but rather through dozens of small and seemingly technical rulings on the specifics of sacrificial processes, and through intricate rhetorical edifices in which some aspects of sacrifice are highlighted and others obfuscated. As a result, the rabbinic sacrificial paradigm is notably different from the biblical one insofar as its governing logic is not that of interaction, and the framework that gives it meaning is not that of a relationship: rather than appearing as a vector of communication between individual and deity, sacrifice in rabbinic texts is constructed as a self-contained transaction for which neither side is necessary. This chapter focuses on the marginalization of the individual offerer ("the owner" in rabbinic terms) in the Tannaitic construction of sacrifice, whereas the next chapter explores the rabbinic redefinition of the sacrificial process itself and the resultant marginalization of the "receiver" within the sacrificial picture.

It is important to stress at the outset that in their move away from the relational framework of sacrifice, and in their strong focus on the sacrificial procedure itself to the point of bracketing the procedure's presumed addresser and addressee, the rabbis unquestionably take their main cues from the biblical Priestly Code. The priestly model of sacrifice has been described already by Julius Wellhausen, one of the founding fathers of modern biblical criticism, as rigid, impersonal, and highly

---

6. There are, of course, multiple biblical texts (especially in the books of the Prophets) that describe sacrifice as futile and as accomplishing nothing in relation to the deity. However, as Klawans rightly observed, these texts do not present a rejection of sacrifice as such, but merely of the practice of making sacrifices while committing moral atrocities. See Klawans, *Purity, Sacrifice, and the Temple*, 75–100.

7. Fritz Graf, "One Generation after Burkert and Girard: Where are the Great Theories?," in Faraone and Naiden, *Greek and Roman Animal Sacrifice*, 41.

8. The same applies to Greek sacrifice, as shown extensively by Fred S. Naiden, *Smoke Signals for the Gods: Ancient Greek Sacrifice from the Archaic to the Roman Periods* (New York: Oxford University Press, 2013), 3–130.

structured, a model that differs radically from the intimate and interactive forms of sacrifice described in earlier biblical sources. According to Wellhausen, the concentration of the cult in the time of King Josiah turned sacrifice from a spontaneous ritual that could be carried out anywhere and anytime to a standardized procedure performed by authorized priests, and thus severed it from the owners' natural course of life and effectively made them dispensable.[9] Whereas Wellhausen identified this feature of the Priestly Code with the postexilic historical circumstances of its creation, Israel Knohl (following in the footsteps of Yehezkel Kaufman) described the Priestly Code in somewhat similar terms but attributed those traits to a specific theological agenda. According to Knohl, the authors of the Priestly Code eradicated from their accounts of sacrifice any indication of prayer, supplication, or expression of emotion on the side of the offerers, as well as any reference to the personal or communal circumstances in which sacrifices are offered. This eradication reflects the priestly authors' overarching view of God as existing beyond the reach and comprehension of human beings, as a transcendent entity that can never be approached directly.[10] Both Wellhausen and Knohl somewhat overstated their cases, and chose to ignore or dismiss priestly rhetoric and imageries that do present sacrifice as a communicative and reciprocal process.[11] But they were undoubtedly right that compared to other biblical sources the Priestly Code generally downplays the interactive dimension of sacrifice and shifts the focus from the individual offerer to the priests who perform the procedure. In this respect as well as in others, the rabbis' sacrificial legislation can be seen as a continuation of the priestly model of sacrifice rather than as a divergence from it.

Nevertheless, I argue that a closer look at rabbinic sacrificial legislation reveals that the rejection of the interactive model and the marginalization of the giver in this legislation is much more thorough and purposeful than it is in the Priestly Code. Furthermore, the rabbis' tendency to push the owner out of the sacrificial scene is most evident especially in the junctures in which the rabbis present inno-

---

9. See Julius Wellhausen, *Prolegomena to the History of Israel*, trans. J. Sutherland Black and Allan Menzies (Edinburgh: Adam & Charles Black, 1885), 55–82.

10. Israel Knohl, *The Sanctuary of Silence: A Study of the Priestly Strata in the Pentateuch* [Heb.] (Jerusalem: Magnes Press, 1993), 120–55.

11. The recurring priestly reference to various offerings as "a pleasing odor unto the Lord" stands in the way of Knohl's reading of the priestly deity as entirely transcendent and as unmoved by offerings, and Knohl's claim that this phrase is just an atrophied residue of "cultic vocabulary" that does not reflect the priestly view (*The Sanctuary of Silence*, 128) is very unconvincing. Similarly, the priestly description of divine fire as consuming the offerings on the day of the inauguration of the tabernacle, as well as the description that immediately follows of divine fire consuming two priests who made an offering in an unauthorized manner (Leviticus 9:22–10:2), clearly suggests that Yahweh—even if in a nonanthropomorphic fashion—actually receives the sacrifices and responds to them. While the priestly deity certainly does not *need* the offerings, he unquestionably expects them, approves or disapproves of them, and interacts with the people through them.

vations or departures from the Priestly Code—that is, in the moments in which they break from the biblical blueprint rather than follow it. One such juncture is the rabbis' incorporation of thoughts and intentions into the sacrificial process as critical elements in assessing the validity of sacrifices, a notion that has no precedent in the Priestly Code; another juncture is the rabbis' rulings regarding the stage of the sacrificial ritual in which the owner lays his hands on the animal's head, rulings that noticeably deviate from the biblical texts on which they build. It is on these two junctures that this chapter will focus.

In the first part of this chapter, I discuss the role of intention, will, and state of mind in the rabbinic sacrificial system, and argue that the subjective mind-set of the owner vis-à-vis the offering is of surprisingly little consequence when it comes to assessing the validity of the sacrificial process—that is, to determining whether the process is considered to have been successfully completed or needs to be repeated. The disregard for the owner's state of mind is noteworthy not only in light of the rabbis' greater tendency to see intention and will as crucial components in the fulfillment or transgression of commandments, but especially in light of the fact that the intentions and thoughts *of the priests* play a critical role in assessing the validity of sacrifices.

In the second part of the chapter, I argue that the rabbis significantly restrict not only the subjective agency of the offerer but also his objective agency, that is, his actual participation in the sacrificial process. The ritual in which the owner lays his hands on the sacrificial animal prior to its slaughter, which in the Priestly Code seems to be a critical and indispensable component of the sacrificial process, is regarded in rabbinic texts either as desirable but inconsequential or as downright eliminable, but never as instrumental to the sacrificial process. The dismissal of hand laying, which effectively makes the offerer's presence and participation in the sacrifice optional or even redundant, is the most manifest expression of what I identify as a broad rabbinic rejection of the interactive model I described above. By way of conclusion to this chapter, I venture to explain the conceptual and ideational frameworks that motivated the marginalization of the owner, and more broadly the rejection of the interactive model, in the rabbinic sacrificial system.

INTENTIONS THAT (DON'T) MATTER

One of the unmistakable trademarks of rabbinic legislation, in almost every area, is unprecedented emphasis on state of mind and intention.[12] While the distinction

---

12. See Howard Eilberg-Schwartz, *The Human Will in Judaism: The Mishnah's Philosophy of Intention* (Atlanta: Scholars Press, 1986); Balberg, *Purity, Body, and Self,* 74–95; Oriel Neuwirth, "Between Intention and Action: An Ethical and Theological Analysis of the Conception of Mitzvah in Rabbinic Literature" [Heb.] (PhD diss., Bar-Ilan University, 2012).

between transgressions committed deliberately and transgressions committed erroneously certainly has some biblical roots,[13] the rabbis overwhelmingly present thoughts and plans as decisive and oftentimes determining factors in the assessment of legal and ritual situations. Thus we find in the Mishnah the notion that a commandment fulfilled without proper "direction of the heart" is not considered to be fulfilled,[14] that a murderer is judged based on whom he intended to kill rather than on whom he actually killed,[15] that a plan to use an object suffices to make it susceptible to impurity,[16] and so forth. It only stands to reason that a ritual such as sacrifice, which is construed so unequivocally as an expression of piety, devotion, and reverence in biblical texts, would be portrayed in rabbinic legislation as a process in which the owner's state of mind is of crucial importance. Indeed, this expectation is reasonable not only in light of the biblical model, but also in light of the common sacrificial norms in the Graeco-Roman world more broadly: as Fred Naiden showed, the most critical component of sacrifice in ancient Greece, without which it would be seen not only as incomplete but as utterly worthless, was the prayer of the offerer at the commencement of the sacrifice, which had to be perceived by the gods as genuine.[17] Contrary to what one could expect, however, Tannaitic texts make the point that the offerer's intentions and mind-set have no bearing on the validity of the sacrifice.

To preempt any confusion or misunderstanding, it is necessary to establish very clearly the terms of the discussion that follows: the question of the *validity* of a particular sacrifice, with which I am concerned here, is wholly disparate from the question of whether this sacrifice is worthwhile or accepted approvingly by the deity. When the rabbis determine that a sacrifice is valid (*kasher*) or invalid (*pasul*) they assess only whether or not the sacrifice was performed correctly, in accordance with the required protocol: this can be decided exclusively by examining the manner in which the sacrifice took place and not by recourse to the deity's presumed predilections and reactions, which can only be assumed but never known. Of course, one could make a leap and maintain that declaring a sacrifice "invalid" effectively means that the inappropriate performance of the sacrifice makes God repudiate it,[18] but it is important to note that the rabbis themselves never present the categories of valid/invalid sacrifices in these terms. Rather, they present these categories in purely procedural terms, such that the questions guiding the categorization are simply (a) whether or not the offering may be consumed (by priests,

---

13. See Exodus 21:12–14.

14. For example, M. Berakhot 2.1; M. Rosh hashanah 3.7; M. Megillah 2.2 (all Mishnah citations according to ed. Albeck).

15. M. Sanhedrin 9.2.

16. M. Kelim 25.9.

17. Naiden, *Smoke Signals*, 82–130.

18. Such is the interpretation suggested by Eilberg-Schwartz, *The Human Will*, 149–59.

the owners, or the fire on the altar) and (b) whether or not the sacrifice must be repeated.

There is, famously, a long-standing notion in biblical and postbiblical tradition that sacrifices offered by morally corrupt people, or performed without appropriate pious disposition, are undesirable and even repugnant to God.[19] This idea surely resonated with the rabbis, and is indeed echoed in several Tannaitic passages that present obedience and reverence as what makes God approve of sacrifices:[20] thus, for example, tractate Menahot of the Mishnah concludes with the proclamation that it does not matter whether one brings a substantial animal offering or a meager grain offering "as long as one directs one's heart to Heaven."[21] However, divine approval is never conflated in rabbinic texts with validity: the latter is discussed in legal-ritual texts as a function of the sacrificial process itself and never as a function of the purpose of the sacrifice or the ethical standing of the offerer, whereas the former is presented in markedly moralistic or homiletic traditions that refer explicitly to the will and reactions of God. My argument, then, should not be understood as a wholesale assertion that "the rabbis don't care about the offerer's intentions"; rather, what I argue is that the rabbis do not assign importance to the offerer's intentions *in assessing the ritual validity of sacrifices.*[22]

It is especially in light of the notion that sacrifices must be offered with a pure heart and out of genuine piety that the rabbis' disregard for the offerer's intention in considering the validity of sacrifices is all the more conspicuous. Not only do the rabbis have no qualms about presenting thoughts and intentions as constitutive of legal actions and situations in other ritual arenas, but they even assign crucial importance to intentions and thoughts in the sacrificial process itself—but not to the intentions and thoughts of the offerer (to whom they refer as "owner"). In what follows, I demonstrate and discuss three aspects of the inconsequentiality of the owner's intentions in rabbinic sacrificial legislation: the role (or lack thereof) of the owner's will in the sacrificial process, the mental designation of the offering for appropriate purposes, and the ability of wrongful thoughts and plans to disqualify the offering.

---

19. See Klawans, *Purity, Sacrifice, and the Temple,* 75–100.

20. See, for example, T. Menahot 7.9 (all Tosefta citations of Order Qodashim according to ed. Tsukermandel). Cf. Sifre Numbers 143 (ed. Horovitz 191), Sifre zutta Numbers 28:2 (ed. Horovitz 322).

21. M. Menahot 13.11. Cf. Sifra nedavah 7.9.7 (ed. Finkelstein 65). See also Neuwirth, *Between Intention and Action,* 250–53.

22. In this regard I disagree with the analysis presented by Naftali Goldstein, which conflates questions of desirability and questions of validity in the assessment of sacrifices. See Naftali Goldstein, "Worship at the Temple in Jerusalem: Rabbinic Interpretation and Influence" [Heb.] (PhD diss., Hebrew University, 1977), 1–53.

They coerce him until he says, "I will it":
The inconsequentiality of the owner's will

As I noted above, the prevalent biblical pattern of sacrifice is one in which an individual or group offers something (mostly animals, sometimes grain or vegetables, and rarely a human being[23]) of his/its own property to the deity by burning all of it or parts of it on an altar. Various sentiments or situations can motivate such an offering: gratitude for past favors, an attempt to win favor so as to succeed in a future enterprise, repentance over misdoings, or a desire to honor the deity during a festival, celebration, or pilgrimage. Another common biblical pattern of sacrifice is the conditional vow (*neder*), in which one makes a commitment to offer something to the deity on the condition that the deity fills his or her request. Whereas nonpriestly biblical texts present mainly the abovementioned patterns of sacrifice, which are distinctly voluntary in nature, the Priestly Code also prescribes different obligatory sacrifices, which must be offered to atone for sin, to affect purification, as a required part of calendrical rituals, or as mandatory gifts to the priesthood.[24] The Priestly Code does maintain, however, the concept of voluntary offerings presented in accordance with the offerer's will, which can come in the form of either a burnt offering (*'olah*) or a well-being offering (*shelamim*).[25]

The Tannaitic sacrificial system does not deviate from the Priestly Code in acknowledging voluntary offerings (which it titles, following the Priestly terminology, *neder* and *nedavah*, "votive offering" and "freewill offering" respectively[26]) alongside obligatory offerings. It does, however, present an innovative take on the mechanism of voluntary offerings. For the rabbis, one's very *decision* to bring an offering to the temple by and by creates a debt that one has to pay. The underlying principle here is the notion that a verbal statement to the "High" (i.e., to the realm of the sacred) is equivalent to an actual transaction with a layperson (*'amirati le-gavoha ki-mesirati le-hediot*):[27] thus, as soon as one promises to give a portion of one's property to the temple, one is effectively in possession of something that is no longer one's own. Maintaining this principle, the rabbis significantly undermine the priestly distinction between "votive offering" and "freewill offering" as the two possible types of voluntary offerings. Whereas in the Priestly Code a votive offering is made in fulfillment of a previous conditional promise ("if this happens . . . I will give this or that to

23. On the debate regarding the prevalence of human sacrifice in the Hebrew Bible and in biblical Israel, see Levenson, *The Death and Resurrection of the Beloved Son*, 3–24.

24. See Leviticus 4–5, 14–16, 23; Numbers 28–29.

25. Leviticus 7:16, 19:5, 22:21; Numbers 15:3; Ezekiel 46:12.

26. I am following the translations and definitions proposed by Jacob Milgrom, *Leviticus 1–16: A New Translation with Introduction and Commentary* (New York: Doubleday, 1991), 419–20.

27. M. Qiddushin 1.6.

God"),[28] and a freewill offering is a spontaneous gift given of one's own accord, in rabbinic legislation both voluntary and freewill offerings are forms of payment of a debt generated by a previous promise.[29] The only difference between the two is that a votive offering pertains to a general promise to give something to the temple ("I will give a burnt offering"), whereas a freewill offering pertains to a promise to give a specific substance to the temple ("I will bring this particular sheep as a burnt offering").[30] Both types of promises, however, generate a concrete debt to the temple, which is treated and managed like any other debt: first, if the owner dies before he delivers the offering he promised, his heirs are liable to deliver that offering to the temple in his stead[31]; second and more important for our purposes, if the owner fails to bring the offering he promised in a timely manner, the temple treasurers or their emissaries have every right to come and mortgage other pieces of the owner's property so as to force him to bring the promised offering.[32]

The rabbis, then, significantly transform the concept of voluntary offering: they take it to mean not that one actually *brings* an offering to the temple of one's own free will, but rather that one willingly creates for oneself an *obligation* to bring an offering to the temple. This obligation, once created, obviates any further mental dispositions on the side of the owner, such that—rather paradoxically—a freewill offering can be brought under coercion. The paradoxicality of this arrangement did not escape the rabbis, who were aware of the incommensurability between the biblical ethos of voluntary wholehearted sacrifice and the notion that one can be forced to bring an offering, as we see in the following comment:

> Even though no atonement can be attained for [a person] until he comes to will it (*'ad she-yitratze*), for it was said "according to his will" (*li-retzono*, Leviticus 1:3), they coerce him until he says, "I will it" (*kofin 'oto 'ad she-yomar rotze 'ani*).[33]

28. As pointed out by Cartledge, the Hebrew Bible does not seem to contain any examples of dedicative vows that are not conditional in nature, perhaps with the exception of the Nazarite vow in Numbers 6 (in which a person effectively dedicates himself or herself). See Tony W. Cartledge, *Vows in the Hebrew Bible and the Ancient Near East* (Sheffield: JSOT Press, 1992), 11–35. However, some scholars maintain that the Nazariteship, too, is conditional in nature; see Zeev Weisman, "The Nazariteship in the Hebrew Bible: Its Types and its Origins" [Heb.], *Tarbitz* 36 (1967): 207–20.

29. There are some narrative anecdotes in rabbinic texts describing conditional vows (e.g., M. Nazir 3.6; T. 'Arakhin 3.1), but the conditional element is never mentioned in Tannaitic legal accounts on the workings of votive offerings.

30. See M. 'Arakhin 8.7. Several rabbinic sources do mention the possibility of officially dedicating the animal to the altar only *after* it has been brought to the temple (see BT Pesaḥim 66b, BT Nedarim 9b, and possibly also T. Ḥullin 2.17), but for the most part this option is rendered unacceptable.

31. T. 'Arakhin 3.14–15.

32. M. 'Arakhin 5.6; cf. 6.3.

33. M. 'Arakhin 5.6; cf. Sifra nedavah 3.3.15 (ed. Finkelstein 31). All translations of rabbinic sources in the book are mine, unless noted otherwise.

While in its biblical usage the word *ratzon* means "acceptance" or "satisfaction," and accordingly the phrase *li-retzono* means "so that one be accepted" (by the deity), in rabbinic Hebrew *ratzon* means "will" or "desire," and the phrase *li-retzono* is interpreted to mean "in accordance with one's will."[34] Thus, whereas in the biblical text the offerer's willingness to bring the offering seems to be assumed but is never overtly stated, in the rabbinic reading this willingness is stipulated in the very instructions regarding sacrifice, but the rabbis consciously circumvent it in their assertion that one can be forced into willing something. The Mishnah's explicit admission that sacrifices *should,* strictly speaking, be performed only in accordance with the offerer's will, and that only through a very loose definition of "will" can one reconcile this notion with the coercive mechanism of mortgaging property, powerfully indicates that the rabbis did not take their own legislative move here for granted.

This legislative move—namely, the idea that the "voluntary" component of voluntary offerings is not the delivery of the offering itself but the initiation of an obligation to do so—is significant not only because it introduces the practice of coercion to the sacrificial realm but also because it redefines the owner's part within the sacrificial ritual. Whereas in the biblical tradition the key aspect of the owner's participation in the sacrifice is the *delivery and presentation* of the offering at the temple,[35] in rabbinic legislation the key aspect of the owner's participation in the sacrifice—to some extent the only consequential aspect, as I will argue later on—is the *decision* to bring an offering. This decision, which can be made months or years before the offering is actually delivered, is indeed a manifestation of the owner's mental agency, which is powerful enough to create a very real debt:[36] but here, effectively, is where the owner's mental agency ends. One's volition, which generates for one the obligation to bring an offering in the first place, is utterly insignificant when it comes to the delivery and presentation of the offering in actuality.

The appropriate taxonomy for the rabbinic sacrificial system is thus not a distinction between voluntary and obligatory offerings, but rather a distinction between three different types of obligatory offerings. There are sacrificial obligations generated by the offering itself (if an animal is the firstborn of its mother, or the tenth in a flock, it belongs to the temple by its very essence); by circumstances (either calendrical circumstances or circumstances of personal or communal transgression or impurity); and by verbal promises that serve as monetary transactions for all intents and pur-

---

34. See Avi Hurvitz, *Between Language and Language: The History of Biblical Language in the Second Temple Period* [Heb.] (Jerusalem: Bialik Institute, 1972), 73–78; see also Yonatan Sagiv, "Studies in Early Rabbinic Hermeneutics as Reflected in Selected Chapters in the Sifra" [Heb.] (PhD diss., Hebrew University, 2009), 129–30.

35. On the centrality of presentation in ancient Near Eastern sacrificial rituals, see Tzvi Abusch, "Sacrifice in Mesopotamia," in *Sacrifice in Religious Experience,* ed. Albert I. Baumgarten (Leiden: Brill, 2002), 39–48.

36. See also Eilberg-Schwartz, *The Human Will,* 147–49.

poses. In none of these cases can the sacrificial process be viewed as a channel through which the owner is willfully giving something to the deity: rather, the process is construed as a channel through which God retrieves *what is already his.* The paradigm is not one of interaction or communication, but rather of a wrong being made right.

While Tannaitic texts are explicit that the owner's sincere and genuine will is not requisite for the successful delivery of votive and freewill offerings, they do not make an unequivocal statement on whether a certain mind-set on the owner's part is necessary for purification and reparation offerings. The Mishnah ascertains that unlike votive and freewill offerings, purification and reparation offerings cannot be claimed by force (that is, one's property is not mortgaged if one fails to deliver them, nor are one's heirs liable for them).[37] On the face of it, this discrepancy could be understood as indicating that the validity of purification and reparation sacrifices does depend on the owner's willful state of mind: however, it is more plausible to explain it as reflecting the distinct nature of these sacrifices. Whereas votive and freewill sacrifices are generated by a promise pertaining to one's *property,* purification and reparation sacrifices are generated by circumstances that pertain to one's *person* (moral or ritual transgression or impurity): therefore, they cannot be fulfilled by anyone except for that person, and cannot be addressed by taking a different piece of one's property. By way of analogy, we could say that purification and reparation offerings function more like an apology than like a payment of debt (this is not to say that such offerings should be understood as sacrificial forms of apology to the deity—their function is much more multifaceted and complex—but only that their mechanism is comparable).

But does the "apology," if we follow this analogy, have to be sincere? Must purification and reparation offerings be accompanied by a particular mind-set at the time of delivery to be considered valid? While Tannaitic texts do not address this question directly, one passage in the Mishnah seems to make a point of saying, albeit through silence, that a remorseful state of mind—that is, genuine identification of one with the offering one is delivering—is *not* a condition for the efficacy of purification and reparation offerings:

> A purification offering (*ḥattat*) and a reparation offering of certainty[38] (*'asham vadai*) atone. Death and the Day of Atonement atone along with repentance (*teshuvah*). Repentance atones for minor transgressions and for [breaches of] positive and negative commandments, but for major [transgressions] it suspends judgment until the Day of Atonement comes and atones.[39]

37. M. 'Arakhin 5.6; T. 'Arakhin 3.15.

38. This term refers to a reparation offering brought when one knows for a fact that he or she transgressed the law, as opposed to a "reparation offering of uncertainty" (*'asham talui*), which is brought when one only suspects that he or she transgressed the law.

39. M. Yoma 8.8.

The requirement for repentance is conspicuously missing from the Mishnah's comment on purification and reparation offerings. While repentance has an atoning power of its own, according to this passage, and it is emphatically necessary when alternative modes of atonement (death or the ascetic practices of the Day of Atonement) are relied upon, it is not said to be necessary when one offers the prescribed offerings: those seem to be considered efficacious in and of themselves. It is of course possible that repentance is assumed in the very action of bringing an offering, whereas it cannot be assumed in passive modes of atonement such as death and the Day of Atonement[40]; but the rhetoric of the Mishnah avoids associating the sacrificial path with the repentance path, and keeps them entirely disparate. Here the Mishnah markedly differs from other Tannaitic texts, the Tosefta and the Sifra, which stipulate that purification and reparation offerings affect atonement only for those who have repented.[41] While these passages do not pertain directly to the ritual issue of validity (that is, whether the sacrifice needs to be repeated), but rather to acceptability or efficacy, it is noteworthy that the mishnaic author here chose to bracket the owner's state of mind as noninstrumental to the sacrificial process: this choice reflects, I propose, a broader trend in the rabbis' approach to the owner's role in sacrificial settings.[42]

The rabbis' general disregard for the owner's will and mind-set in the sacrificial process would not be noteworthy if the rabbis always maintained a separation between the legal validity of an action and the intentions behind it, such that thoughts are restricted to the discursive realm of piety and ethics and the legal-ritual realm consists only of concrete and empirical facts. But this is not the case: the rabbinic position is that mind-sets and mental dispositions *can,* in fact, make or break legal reality. For example, two people in the same place and at the same time can physically hear the sound of the *shofar,* but only one who "directed his heart" (*kiven libo*) is actually considered to have fulfilled the ritual obligation of

40. This is Rashi's interpretation of the Mishnah in BT Yoma 85b d"h *ḥattat;* see also Saul Lieberman, *Tosefta ki-peshuta Mo'ed,* vol. 4 (New York: Jewish Theological Seminary, 1962), 825.

41. While T. Kippurim 4.5 repeats the phrasing of the Mishnah with only slight modifications, toward the end of the chapter in the Tosefta appears the statement "Purification offering and reparation offering and death and the Day of Atonement—all of those do not atone without repentance" (T. Kippurim 4.9; all Tosefta citations of Order Mo'ed according to ed. Lieberman). Cf. Sifra Emor 11.14.1 (ed. Weiss 102a); BT Shevu'ot 13a.

42. Possible additional evidence for the rabbinic dismissal of proper intention when it comes to purification offerings is the tradition found in M. Gittin 5.5 (= 'Eduyot 7.9), according to which stolen purification offerings, contrary to what one could expect, effect atonement for those who bring them. However, since this tradition is rather cryptic and could be interpreted in multiple ways, I hesitate to see it as another indication of the tendency to which I am pointing. On this passage, see Sagit Mor and Ronen Ahituv, "Sacrifice through Sin: The Place of Values in Respect to Sacrifices in Talmudic Literature" [Heb.], *Molad* 16 (2006): 40–60.

hearing the *shofar*.[43] The one who heard the sound without fully intending to do so, in contrast, must make a point of hearing it again—this time with proper intention—so as to fulfill the obligation. The fact that the rabbis explicitly say that one can bring an offering without wishing to do so, and this does not compromise the sacrifice itself, then, should at least give us pause. This pause is significantly extended when we turn to see that proper intentions and mind-sets *are* considered by the rabbis to determine the validity of sacrifices—but these determining intentions are apparently not those of the owner.

Whose thought is it, anyway?

Tractate Zevaḥim of the Mishnah, which commences the Order of Holies (Qodashim) and discusses the various intricacies of animal sacrifices, curiously begins not by describing the actions that should be applied to animal offerings, but rather by delineating appropriate and inappropriate mind-sets vis-à-vis those offerings. The first chapter of the tractate introduces the principle that all offerings must be slaughtered "for their sake" (*li-sheman*): that is, as the sacrifice is taking place the animal in question must be consciously intended as a specific type of offering (burnt offering, purification offering, well-being offering, etc.) in order to count as having been appropriately offered. If the animal was wrongly designated, then the sacrifice did not fulfill the obligation of the owner.[44] For example, if a person is under obligation to bring a purification offering to the temple and brings a bird for this purpose, but the bird is slaughtered without being actively *intended* as a purification offering (or is intended as a different kind of offering), then the sacrificial obligation of the person in question is still standing, and his or her purification is incomplete. While the Mishnah does not state explicitly who is the person on whom this designation depends—that is, which of the various participants in the sacrificial process is empowered to intend an offering as one type of offering and not another and thereby determine the sacrifice's validity—the Tosefta presents an unequivocal stance on this question:

> In any case (*le-'olam*) everything follows the slaughterer (*'aḥar ha-shoḥet*), for if the slaughterer intends [to designate the offering] for a purification offering and the owners intend [to designate the offering] for a burnt offering, [or] if the slaughterer

43. M. Rosh hashanah 3.7.

44. M. Zevaḥim 1.1; cf. M. Menaḥot 1.1. The rabbis distinguish between two kinds of offerings in regard to this requirement: for most offerings, if they were sacrificed with the wrong designation (or without designation) they are still acceptable, but the owners are not seen as having fulfilled their obligation and must bring an offering again. For the Passover offering and purification offerings (and according to one opinion, also for reparation offerings), a missing or wrongful designation actually disqualifies them altogether, such that they must be incinerated and cannot be consumed. See also M. Zevaḥim 1.3.

intends [to designate the offering] for a burnt offering and the owners intend [to designate the offering] for a purification offering—in any case everything follows the slaughterer.[45]

The Tosefta makes it clear that the intentions of the person slaughtering the offering override the intentions of the owner in any case: in other words, the wrongful designation that may void the offering is that of the *slaughterer*, not of the owner (unless the slaughterer and the owner are the same person, which is possible). Let us illustrate this with an example: a woman brought two birds to the temple in order to complete the process of purification after childbirth, and intended for one bird to be sacrificed as a burnt offering and the other as a purification offering, as prescribed in Leviticus 12:8. The priest who slaughtered the two birds, however, made a mistake and slaughtered both birds with the (spoken or silent) intention that they both be offered as burnt offerings. In such a case, the sacrifice is void, and the woman is not considered to have completed her purification process, even though her own intentions regarding those birds were commensurate with the law. In contrast, if the woman mistakenly intended for both birds to be offered as burnt offerings, but the priest correctly designated one as a burnt offering and one as a purification offering, the sacrifice is completely valid and the woman is now pure. The slaughterer's ability to impact the sacrifice is thus not only for better, by correctly designating an offering that the owner may have incorrectly designated otherwise, but also for worse: in either case, the owner's intention regarding the offering is inconsequential in determining what the offering is and whether it fulfilled its purpose.[46]

The second, third, and fourth chapters of tractate Zevaḥim address the effect of wrongful intentions regarding the time and place in which a sacrificial substance is to be consumed, intentions that, as I will elaborate in the next section, can disqualify an offering even if the sacrificial process itself was flawless. After four full chapters in which the Mishnah discusses the detrimental impact of inappropriate intentions on the validity of sacrifices, it concludes with a list of additional intentions that are required during the performance of sacrifice. In this concluding list the Mishnah supplements its previous instructions regarding "negative intentions" (that is, how wrongful intentions invalidate the sacrifice) with instructions regarding "positive intentions" (that is, what one should actively have in mind when performing a sacrifice):

An offering (*zevaḥ*) is [to be] slaughtered (*nizbaḥ*) for the sake of six things [that is, with the following six elements in mind]: for the sake of the [particular type of] offering, for the sake of the offerer [that is, the owner], for the sake of The Name [of

46. A similar point on the priests' ability to compromise offerings appears in a series of Tannaitic homilies on Numbers 18:1, "You and your sons alone shall bear responsibility for offenses connected with the priesthood." See Sifre Numbers 116 (ed. Horovitz 130).

God], for the sake of fire (*'ishim*), for the sake of odor (*reaḥ*), for the sake of pleasing (*niḥoaḥ*), and purification and reparation offerings—for the sake of [a particular] sin. R. Yose said: even if he had none of these in mind (*be-libo*), [the sacrifice] is valid, for it is a stipulation of the court that thought only follows the officiant (*she-'ein ha-maḥshavah holekhet 'ela 'aḥar ha-'oved*).[47]

At the basis of this passage stands the biblical verse "It is a burnt offering (*'olah*), an offering by fire (*'ishe*), of pleasing odor (*reaḥ niḥoaḥ*) to the Lord" (Leviticus 1:13), which the rabbis take as a paradigm for the constituent elements of sacrifice. Interestingly, the rabbis interpret these constituent elements as mental in essence, that is, as a set of intentions vis-à-vis the offering that must be actively present during the sacrifice: the offering must be designated as a particular type of offering (such as "burnt offering" in the verse), must be designated to be burned by fire so as to produce fragrant smoke and to please God, and of course be designated specifically for God. To the five elements in the verse the rabbis add that the offering must also be consciously associated with a particular owner so as to be valid, and with a particular transgression if the offering is an atoning one.[48] The question that immediately emerges from this passage is, who is doing the "intending"?—that is, who is the one on whose appropriate designations the validity of the sacrifice depends: is it the owner or the officiating priest? Since the anonymous Mishnah unhelpfully uses a passive form, "an offering is [to be] offered," and thus leaves this question unanswered, we need to turn to R. Yose's contesting statement in order to decipher the anonymous ruling in the first part of the passage.

As the structure of the passage indicates, R. Yose disagrees with the anonymous Mishnah about something, but there are two ways of understanding what it is that he disagrees about. One possibility is that he disagrees regarding the requirement of appropriate mental designation altogether: he says that "even if he had none of these in mind (*be-libo*), [the sacrifice] is valid" to convey that as long as the person at hand (whoever that may be) did not have inappropriate intentions, he does not need to have active appropriate intentions to ensure the validity of the offering. This is the interpretation proposed in the Babylonian Talmud and accordingly by most traditional commentators,[49] but this reading is difficult to uphold, since it renders the last clause, "for thought only follows the officiant," senseless: if R. Yose thinks that thought does not matter at all, what difference does it make whom it "follows"—that is, whose thought determines the ritual results? Unless one reads

47. M. Zevaḥim 4.6; cf. Sifra nedavah 14.17.2 (ed. Finkelstein 105–6).

48. It is not clear whether those six elements need to be verbally stated or merely thought of; see the discussion in Sagiv, "Studies in Early Rabbinic Hermeneutics," 90–91. However, the term "in his heart/mind" (*be-libo*) later on indicates that the appropriate intentions discussed in this passage are seen as primarily mental and not as a matter of ritual pronunciation.

49. BT Zevaḥim 2b.

the last clause as an independent summative statement, unrelated to what precedes it[50] (which is problematic against the subordinating preposition "for"), this interpretation is quite weak. Alternatively, another possibility is that R. Yose disagrees with the anonymous Mishnah not on the principle but on the identity of the person whose intentions are consequential: he contends that X (the one to whom the anonymous Mishnah ostensibly refers) does not affect the offering, but rather "thought only follows the *officiant*." Such a reading, which seems to be more compatible with the structure and grammar of the passage, suggests that the anonymous Mishnah—in contrast to R. Yose—assigns the power of "thought" not to the officiating priest but to someone else. Who could this "someone else" be?

On the face of it, if R. Yose sees the decisive "thought" as that of the officiating priest, then the disputing anonymous Mishnah must be understood as referring to the owner: this is indeed the interpretation suggested by Maimonides in his commentary on the Mishnah. Louis Finkelstein, however, suggested a different, and in my view highly compelling, interpretation for this passage. According to Finkelstein, R. Yose's comment should be read as contrasting the officiant (*'oved*, that is, the priest who ritually handles the blood and suet of the animal) with the slaughterer (*shoḥet*, the one who kills the animal).[51] While the person who performs the slaughter and the officiating priest who handles its parts thereafter can, in theory, be the same person, it is quite possible for them to be two different people—in fact, the slaughterer does not have to be a priest at all (although he usually is).[52] The anonymous Mishnah's position, then, is not that the owner must have proper intentions vis-à-vis the offering, but rather that the slaughterer (who may be the owner himself, but certainly does not have to be) must have them.

Finkelstein bases his reading primarily on the passage in the Tosefta that I quoted above. The Tosefta quotes the mishnaic passage beginning "an offering is to be offered for the sake of six things" in full, and immediately follows it with the comment that "in any case everything follows the slaughterer (*'aḥar ha-shoḥet*)."[53] The juxtaposition of R. Yose's ruling that "everything follows the officiant" to the Tosefta's unattributed ruling that "everything follows the slaughterer" can be taken as indicating that these are two conflicting positions: in other words, that the position that "everything follows the slaughterer" is in fact the anonymous opinion with which R. Yose disagrees. Further support for this reading can be found in the

50. As proposed by Goldstein, "Worship at the Temple in Jerusalem," 6–20.

51. Louis Finkelstein, *Sifra on Leviticus,* vol. 4 (New York: Jewish Theological Seminary Press, 1990), 88.

52. M. Zevaḥim 3.1. Sources from the Second Temple period usually refer exclusively to the priests as those who slaughter the offerings; see Adolf Büchler, *Die Priester und der Cultus im letzten Jahrzehnt des Tempelbestandes* (Vienna: Israel-Theol. Lehranstalt, 1895), 137–40.

53. T. Zevaḥim 5.13.

fact that the anonymous Mishnah uses the word *nizbaḥ*, which literally means "slaughtered," to refer to the phase in which the six proper intentions are required.

It is possible to argue that R. Yose's statement "Everything follows the officiant" and the Tosefta's statement "Everything follows the slaughterer" are ultimately identical in meaning, and that the anonymous Tosefta simply adopts R. Yose's position while rendering it in different words. However, the unusual noun *'oved* specifically indicates that the person in question is a priest, since the term *'avodah* (literally "work," but here in the sense of "worship") pertains exclusively to the work of priests in the temple.[54] It therefore seems purposefully to exclude those who perform nondistinctly priestly activities, such as slaughter,[55] and it is thus most plausible that the anonymous Mishnah (in contrast to R. Yose) does point to the slaughterer as the significant "intender" in the sacrificial process. If we accept this reading, then whether according to the anonymous Mishnah or according to R. Yose there is no question that the intentions of the owner are of no consequence to the validity of the sacrifice—unless the owner also happens to be the slaughterer, which is possible but not necessary.[56] Even if the slaughterer does happen to be the owner, it is pronouncedly not in his capacity as owner that his state of mind is of consequence. The Mishnah, however, is admittedly vague on this issue, and an alternative reading that points to the owner as the one on whose intentions the validity of the offering depends cannot be downright rejected.

Whether we consider the ruling that thought only follows the officiant or the slaughterer, but not the owner, as unanimously accepted or as contested, the implications of this ruling are far-reaching. It suggests that the owner may have completely inappropriate intentions regarding his sacrifice: he may think of offering it to another deity or of consuming it whole without burning the suet on the altar, or he may not even be aware of why and to whom he is sacrificing. All of this is inconsequential, since only the one(s) performing the sacrificial actions have any impact on their result. R. Yose's reference to this ruling as "a stipulation of the court" (*tenai beit din*) suggests that it may have been conceived specifically as a corrective measure for possible ritual mishaps—so as to ensure that sacrifices not be

---

54. For example, M. Zevaḥim 12.1: the term "fitting (*ra'ui*) for 'avodah" clearly means here "fitting for the work reserved for adequate priests," whereas slaughter can be performed by anyone.

55. See also M. Ḥullin 2.7.

56. As Gilders pointed out (*Blood Ritual,* 63, 156), in biblical (mainly priestly) accounts of sacrifice the identity of the slaughterer seems to be insignificant, but it is fairly clear that the owner is usually taken to be the slaughterer. In Greek and Roman cults, in contrast, slaughter was usually considered lowly work and was performed by slaves and not by owners or priests; see Ingvild Saelid Gilhus, *Animals, Gods, and Humans: Changing Attitudes to Animals in Greek, Roman, and Early Christian Ideas* (New York: Routledge, 2006), 116.

disqualified because of the misguided intentions of ill-informed (or ill-intentioned) individuals.[57]

Disqualifying intentions and the redefinition of "offerer"

The detrimental effect of inappropriate intentions and thoughts on the validity of sacrifices is particularly manifest in the rabbis' elaborate legislation on handling offerings in the wrong time (*ḥutz li-zemano*) or in the wrong place (*ḥutz li-meqomo*). One of the most striking innovations in rabbinic sacrificial legislation is that if one merely *plans* to perform certain sacrificial actions outside the designated time frame or designated sacred precincts, the offering at hand is disqualified, and the sacrifice is declared invalid, *as if* these forbidden actions were actually performed. Here too, as we shall see, the prerogative of invalidating sacrifices through wrongful plans is reserved exclusively for those who perform the slaughter and handle the blood, and emphatically not for the owners. In order to understand the importance of this legislative development, it is necessary to delve briefly into the rabbinic interpretation of "wrongful time" and "wrongful place" in sacrifices.

Chapters 6 and 7 of the book of Leviticus, which constitute a priestly manual of the various types of animal and grain offerings, include repeated warnings that offerings classified as "holy of holies" (*qodesh qodashim,* that is, sacrifices reserved for the priests alone) must be consumed by the priests only within the precincts of the tabernacle, in "a holy place."[58] No such restriction on the place of consumption is mentioned in regard to offerings consumed by the owners (which the rabbis refer to as "light holies," *qodashim qalim*), but here we do find a restriction on time: Leviticus 7:12–18 asserts that the owners may eat of the sacrificial meat only within a limited time frame—in the same day if the offering is one of thanksgiving, or within three days if it is a votive or freewill offering. After the designated time has passed, the meat is considered *piggul* (roughly translatable as "foul"), and if the owner consumes this meat, not only is the owner said to "bear guilt,"[59] but the sacrifice itself is considered void: "If any of the flesh of your offering of well-being is eaten on the third day, it shall not be acceptable (*lo yeratze*), nor shall it be credited to the one who offers it (*lo yeḥashev lo*)."[60]

---

57. The term "stipulation of the court" usually appears in rabbinic literature to denote a legal convention that is assumed to be effective even when not explicitly stated, and is meant to circumvent potential social mishaps or injustices: see, for example, M. Demai 7.3; M. Sheqalim 7.6; M. Kettubot 4.7–12.

58. Leviticus 6:9–10, 19; 7:6.

59. The rabbis interpret this "bearing of guilt" as punishment by extirpation (*karet*), although nothing in the verse suggests this. Perhaps they were influenced by the following verses (Leviticus 7:19–21), which prescribe this punishment to anyone who partakes in sacrificial meat while ritually impure.

60. Leviticus 7:18.

The ruling in this verse introduced a hermeneutic conundrum for the rabbis: they did not see how a sacrificial process that had already been completed could be voided three days after the fact. Guided by the view (on which I will elaborate in the next chapter) that an offering can only be disqualified during the process of slaughter and manipulation of blood, and that the consumption of the meat is not a part of the sacrificial process itself, the rabbis had to explain how the manner of eating can invalidate an already valid sacrifice. Their solution was that what disqualifies the offering is not its *actual* illegitimate consumption but the *plan* to consume the meat illegitimately if one bears such a plan in mind during the sacrificial process—that is, during the slaughter and manipulation of blood. This idea is stated most clearly in the Midrash Sifra to Leviticus:

> R. Aqiva said: I infer [from the verse] "If any of the flesh of your sacrifice of well-being is eaten on the third day, it shall not be acceptable" [that] if he ate of it on the third day it shall be disqualified. But can one say so? If it had been rendered valid, can it now again become invalid? . . . Thus Scripture says, "Nor shall it be credited to the one who offers it (*ha-maqriv 'oto*)"—it is disqualified at the time of offering (*haqravah*), not on the third day.[61]

R. Aqiva emphatically rejects the possibility of retroactive invalidation of sacrifice. It is impossible, he contends, to declare an offering disqualified after its sacrifice has been performed: whatever disqualified the offering had to have taken place "at the time of offering," during the sacrificial process itself. The anonymous Sifra supplements R. Aqiva's statement with a clarification: "The offering is disqualified through thought (*be-mahshavah*), and it is not disqualified on the third day." A sacrifice is not invalidated when one consumes the offering after the designated time (by this point it is too late to invalidate it, since the sacrifice is complete): rather, it is invalidated when one *thinks* of consuming the offering after the designated time.

This interpretation of Leviticus 7:18 as referring to "the time of offering" recalibrates the entire biblical category of *piggul:* for the rabbis, *piggul* is not meat left uneaten after the designated time has passed—such meat actually acquires the name *notar,* "remaining," which is its own category—but an offering that one *planned* to consume after its designated time. Accordingly, eating *piggul* (meat from an offering disqualified through wrongful plan) and eating *notar* (meat left from a legitimate offering after the designated time) are two separate and different transgressions.[62] In addition, the rabbis apply the principle of "disqualifying intention" to space as well as to time: they maintain that one disqualifies an offering by

61. Sifra tzav 8.12.1 (ed. Weiss 36a); cf. BT Zevaḥim 29a; and see Sagiv, "Studies in Early Rabbinic Hermeneutics," 92–104.

62. For example, M. 'Orlah 2.16; M. Zevaḥim 4.5; M. Menaḥot 11.8; M. Me'ilah 1.2–4.

merely planning to consume its meat outside the permitted place, in the same way that one disqualifies it by planning to consume the meat after the designated time (in the case of unlawful place, however, no punishment of extirpation is involved). Curiously, the rabbis restrict the principle that wrongful plan suffices to disqualify offerings to unlawful times and places alone: intentions to misuse offerings in other ways (for instance, to eat their suet, to feed them to impure persons, etc.) do not disqualify the offerings at hand in and of themselves.[63] Various conjectures, which are beyond the scope of this discussion, can be proposed as to why only intentions related to time and place are so potent in rabbinic legislation.[64] Here, however, I wish to focus specifically on the identity of the "intender" who is capable of disqualifying offerings through wrongful plans.

Who, then, is the one whose plan of consumption in an unlawful time or place disqualifies the offering? As we recall, the biblical verses that discuss the prohibition of consumption after the designated time refer squarely to the owner: these verses are specifically concerned with well-being offerings, which are eaten by the laypeople who bring them. It seems only reasonable, then, that if the owner is the one who actually eats, it would be the owner whose wrongful *plan* to eat disqualifies the sacrifice. This, however, is not the case: rather, Tannaitic sources are unequivocal that only those performing the sacrificial actions of slaughtering and blood manipulation can disqualify the offering through wrongful intentions. The notion that the owners' plans regarding eating have no legal repercussions even though they are the ones who actually eat the sacrificial meat is rather peculiar,[65] and indeed in the Babylonian Talmud we find an echo of a contesting view, according to which the owners are capable of generating *piggul* through their intentions:[66] but this is a lone minority position that has no real trace in Tannaitic legislation.[67]

---

63. M. Zevaḥim 3.3–6.

64. For some attempts at explanation, see Eilberg-Schwartz, *The Human Will*, 149–55; McClymond, "Don't Cry over Spilled Blood."

65. Indeed, several scholars automatically assumed that the Mishnah's highlighting of intentions in the sacrificial process pertains to the owner and not to the officiating priest, despite the texts' statements to the contrary. See, for example, Jacob Neusner, *Judaism: The Evidence of the Mishnah* (Atlanta: Scholars Press, 1988), 271–72; Petropoulou, *Animal Sacrifice*, 129. Goldstein, while aware that the Mishnah as it stands before us systematically refers to the priest and not to the owner in its discussions of *piggul*, attempted—unconvincingly, in my view—to argue that an earlier rabbinic position did consider the owners as capable of defiling a sacrifice through wrongful intention. See Goldstein, "Worship at the Temple in Jerusalem," 24–53.

66. See BT Zevaḥim 47a and BT Ḥullin 38b.

67. In one homily in the Sifra we encounter the assumption that the slaughterer is also the owner: "R. Eliezer says: Force your ear (*kof 'oznekha*) to hear that one who slaughters *his* offering (*mi-zivḥo*) in order to eat on the third day, to him the [words] 'it shall not be acceptable' refer" (Sifra tzav 8.12.1, ed. Weiss 36a). This assumption leaves open the possibility that for this tanna, the one who "plans" must also be the one who will eventually eat.

The early rabbis' position that the priest/slaughterer is the only one capable of disqualifying offerings through intentions is expressed especially clearly in an anonymous homily in the Sifra on the sentence "nor shall it be credited to the one who offers it" in Leviticus 7:18. Although the biblical ruling unquestionably refers to the owner of the offering, the homilist explains the phrase "the one who offers it" (*ha-maqriv 'oto*) as referring to the priest who physically performs the sacrifice (*ha-kohen ha-maqriv*)—thereby transforming the meaning of the word "offerer" altogether: from a term describing the layperson who brings an offering, it comes to describe the priest who handles the blood and flesh of the offering.[68]

Moreover, since the rabbis assign the ability to disqualify an offering to the one performing the sacrifice and not to the owner, they effectively sever the connection between the owner's consumption and the categories of "wrongful time/place" altogether. *Piggul* thus turns in Tannaitic legislation from a category pertaining strictly to the consumption of meat (in which the owner partakes) to a category that encompasses other sacrificial practices that are performed exclusively by the priests—namely, tossing of blood and burning of suet. That is to say, one can turn an offering into a *piggul* not only by planning to eat of it after the designated time but also by planning to handle the parts that are not eaten, the blood and the suet, after the designated time. Accordingly, the category of *piggul* applies in Tannaitic legislation not only to well-being offerings, which are eaten by the owners, but also to offerings eaten only by the priests and even more astoundingly to offerings that are not eaten at all but are burned whole on the altar.[69] The same goes for plans regarding unlawful place: one can disqualify an offering not only by planning to consume it outside the sacred precincts, but also by planning to burn it or toss its blood in the wrong place. The expansion of the categories of "outside its time" and "outside its place" beyond consumption of meat thus further shifts the focus from the owners to the priests.

How are we to understand the rabbinic view that only the priests or slaughterers are capable of disqualifying offerings through their intentions, even though the biblical verse on which this idea hinges clearly speaks of the owners? The key to answering this question can be found, I propose, in the statement attributed to R. Aqiva in the Sifra: "[The offering] is disqualified *at the time of offering* and not on the third day." The underlying principle here is that wrongful intention must accompany a concrete sacrificial action: "thought" about what one would do with an offering has no power to affect the offering when one is sitting in one's living room, but only when one is actively handling the offering in question. The same principle is made plain in the Mishnah, in which wrongful intention is always

---

68. Sifra tzav 8.12.2 (ed. Weiss 36a); cf. Sifra tzav 11.15.3 (ed. Weiss 39d). See also Sagiv, "Studies in Early Rabbinic Hermeneutics," 99–100.

69. As elaborated in Sifra tzav 8.12.6–7 (ed. Weiss 36b–c).

described as pertinent to a particular sacrificial activity. The repeated formula in the Mishnah is "one who does X in order to do Y," when Y is always an action that comes after X in the sacrificial protocol: for example, one "slaughters in order to [that is, with the intention to] toss the blood outside," or one "tosses the blood in order to consume the flesh after its time."[70] The rabbis, then, do not see intentions or thoughts in a Cartesian manner as free-floating cerebral phenomena—as cogently noted by Ishay Rosen-Zvi—but rather as *components of actions,* and thoughts are only of legal consequence when they constitute components of action and not in and of themselves.[71] Unlike Rosen-Zvi, however, I do not think that actions and intentions are identical or interchangeable in Tannaitic literature: as we saw, the rabbis do not claim that any kind of wrongful intention is tantamount to the equivalent wrongful action. Rather, in different ritual realms intentions play varying roles in assessing the results of the actions of which they are part. Grasping this crucial dimension of the rabbinic perception of thoughts and intentions more broadly, it becomes clearer why only those performing the sacrificial actions are capable of disqualifying sacrifices through unlawful intentions: for the rabbis one actually has to handle the offering before one can plan to mishandle it.

Having established that, it is also evident why, as I showed in the two previous sections, the owners' will and mind-set do not impact the validity of the offering: since the owners are not the ones who actively perform the sacrifice, whatever thoughts they have (or do not have) are not accompanied by concrete actions and therefore have no ritual consequences. However, herein exactly lies the rabbis' radical move: not in maintaining that intentions without actions are inconsequential, but in maintaining that the *owners' actions vis-à-vis the offering are inconsequential.* Since the rabbis mention only the slaughter and treatment of blood and suet in discussing sacrifices, it is easy to forget that there are actually various activities that precede the slaughter: first, the sacrificial animal (or grain offering) has to be physically brought to the temple and presented before the priests. In Greek and Roman sacrifices, the procession of offerers and offerings to the temple was perhaps the most extravagant and noticeable part of the entire sacrificial ritual,[72] and as Saul Lieberman noted, one lone mishnaic account actually depicts a festive procession to the Jerusalem temple highly reminiscent of Hellenistic practices.[73] Second and perhaps more importantly, the Priestly Code prescribes rituals in

---

70. M. Zevaḥim 2.2–3.

71. Rosen-Zvi, "The Mishnaic Mental Revolution."

72. See, for example, Jan N. Bremmer, *Greek Religion* (Cambridge: Cambridge University Press, 1999), 39–40; Mary Beard, John North, and Simon R. F. Price, *Religions of Rome*, vol. 1, *A History* (Cambridge: Cambridge University Press, 1998), 36; John Scheid, *An Introduction to Roman Religion*, trans. Janet Llyod (Bloomington: Indiana University Press), 82–83.

73. See M. Bikkurim 3.3; and Saul Lieberman, *Greek in Jewish Palestine/Hellenism in Jewish Palestine* (New York: Jewish Theological Seminary, 1994), 146.

which the owner expresses his relation to the offering, either by laying his hands on the animal's head (*semikhah*) or by "swinging" the offering along with the priest (*tenufah*). These activities could very well be perceived as sacrificial actions par excellence, during which appropriate intention (or the lack thereof) on the side of the owner would be considered to affect the validity of the offering. It is only reasonable to expect that if correct designation of the offering is required during the time of slaughter, it would also be required during the time of hand laying. The rabbis, however, do not consider the activities of the owner to be a decisive part of the sacrificial process—indeed in the next section we will see that they treat them as altogether dispensable—and therefore also do not assign importance to the owner's intentions.

The rabbinic exclusion of the owners from the sacrificial process should not be understood in terms of favoring priests over laypeople (which would be atypical for the rabbis): as I will show in greater detail in the next chapter, the rabbis consider some actions that can be performed by laypeople, such as slaughter, to be a critical part of the sacrificial process, and some actions that can be performed only by priests, such as burning of suet, as negligible. Rather, I argue that the exclusion of the owners should be viewed as part of a broader reframing of sacrifice as a legal and ritual concept. This reframing of the sacrificial process such that some activities are emphasized and others marginalized creates, I contend, a new and unique rabbinic model of sacrifice: this model is guided not by an interactive paradigm, in which an individual approaches a deity, but by a procedural paradigm, in which a commandment is fulfilled through a set of correct ritual actions. In addition, the marginalization of the owner in the sacrificial process reflects a tendency among the rabbis to conceive of sacrifice as a collective enterprise rather than as an individual enterprise. Before further developing my argument regarding this new model of sacrifice, to which I shall return at the end of this chapter, I turn to demonstrating that the rabbis not only limited the ritual efficacy of the owner's intentions, but also significantly limited the actual participation of the owner in the sacrificial ritual.

TO LAY HANDS OR NOT TO LAY HANDS?

Above I argued that the rabbis' disregard for the owners' intentions and mind-sets in determining the validity of the sacrificial process should be understood in light of their more overarching view of intention as a component of action: since the owners do not perform what the rabbis perceive as consequential sacrificial actions, they are also not empowered to form consequential sacrificial intentions. This, to be sure, is not because the owners perform no actions at all during the sacrificial process, but because the actions that they do perform are without ritual repercussions. To develop and demonstrate this point further, in what follows

I discuss the most quintessential sacrificial action of the owner, namely, the laying of hands (*semikhah*) on the offered animal's head, and I show a strong inclination within rabbinic legislation to dismiss this practice as merely optional and, in some cases, to eliminate it altogether.

As the Priestly Code's accounts of the different types of animal sacrifices make evident, all forms of sacrifice commence in the exact same way: the owner brings forth the animal to the entrance of the sanctuary, lays his hands on its head, and then (he or someone else) slaughters it.[74] The variation among the different types of offerings comes into play only after the slaughter, and is manifested in the ways in which the blood is handled and the meat and/or suet are burned; but the owner's initial actions are always identical, and their pinnacle is the laying of hands. Scholars widely disagree on the meaning and function of hand laying, some suggesting that it signals ownership, others that it serves to transfer one's sins to the animal, and yet others that it is a way of setting the animal as a substitute for oneself:[75] what remains undisputed, however, is that the laying of hands is seen in the Priestly Code as critical to the attainment of the sacrifice's purpose vis-à-vis the owner. This view is expressed especially lucidly in Leviticus 1:3–4:

> If the offering is a burnt offering from the herd, he shall offer a male without blemish; he shall bring it to the entrance of the Tent of Meeting, for acceptance on his behalf (*li-retzono*) before the Lord. He shall lay his hand on the head of the burnt offering, and it shall be acceptable on his behalf as atonement for him (*ve-nirtza lo lekhaper 'alav*).

As Jacob Milgrom explains, the repetition of the root *r-tz-h,* "to accept," twice in these verses, once in regard to the unblemished animal and once in regard to the laying of hands, makes it clear that both of these conditions are essential for the acceptance of the offering.[76] Moreover, the use of the converted perfect form *ve-nirtza,* "and it shall be acceptable," indicates that the laying of hands is effectively what *makes* the sacrifice acceptable. Indeed, the laying of hands seems to serve as a ritualized expression of the owner's position as the raison d'être of the entire sacrifice, as the one who initiates it and as the one who hopes to benefit from it.

In Tannaitic literature, in contrast, the status of hand laying is much more ambiguous. On the one hand, several Tannaitic texts mention that certain offerings "require hand laying" (*te'unim semikhah*),[77] and specific references to hand

---

74. Leviticus 1:3–5; 3:1–2; 4:4, 15, 24, 27–29. It should be mentioned that this does not apply to bird offerings, probably because of the physical inability to lay hands on a bird of small size.

75. For a comprehensive discussion of the different interpretations of hand laying, see Milgrom, *Leviticus 1–16,* 150–53.

76. Milgrom, *Leviticus 1–16,* 153.

77. For example, M. Zevaḥim 10.2; Menaḥot 5.7.

laying also appear in narrative-like accounts of sacrificial rituals.[78] On the other hand, as I will show, various passages across Tannaitic literature make the point that the absence of hand laying does not compromise the validity of the sacrifice, and moreover, that for some offerings and for some offerers hand laying does not apply in the first place. There thus seems to be an overall ambivalence among the rabbis regarding the pertinence of this practice to the sacrificial process, an ambivalence that according to one cluster of traditions can be traced far back to the nascence of the rabbinic movement. According to a famous passage in tractate Ḥagigah of the Mishnah, the question of whether "to lay hands" (*lismokh*) or "not to lay hands" was an enduring bone of contention among the five "Pairs" that are considered to have been the protorabbinic leaders during the Second Temple period. The controversy regarding hand laying is identified in the Tosefta as the first—and for a long time, the only—controversy ever to divide the rabbis.[79] While the exact meaning and topic of this "first controversy" is obscure, it is evident that for the rabbis, broadly speaking, hand laying was not straightforwardly conceived as integral to the sacrificial process, as it is in the Priestly Code. In what follows I will first explain the controversy of the Pairs as pertaining directly to the question of the owner's participation in the sacrificial process, and then argue that despite the seeming victory of those supporting the practice of hand laying, a closer look reveals that this practice was significantly limited, both in its occurrence and in its ritual repercussions, in later Tannaitic legislation.

The "first controversy"

In the midst of tractate Ḥagigah, which is generally concerned with regulations for pilgrimage and specifically with pilgrimage offerings, we find a rather terse and cryptic account of an enduring disagreement among the earliest sages mentioned in rabbinic literature, who are known as "the Pairs." The disagreement is related in medias res, without a hint of the exact context or meaning of the positions presented:

> Yose ben Yoezer says [that one should] not lay hands, Yose ben Yohanan says [that one should] lay hands.
> Yehoshua ben Peraḥya says [that one should] not lay hands, Nitai[80] the Arbelite says [that one should] lay hands.
> Yehudah ben Tabai says [that one should] not lay hands, Shimon ben Shetaḥ says [that one should] lay hands.
> Shemaʿaya says [that one should] lay hands, Avtalion says [that one should not] lay hands.

---

78. For example, M. Yoma 3.8, 4.2, 6.2; M. Tamid 7.3; M. Negaʿim 14.8.
79. T. Ḥagigah 2.8; cf. PT Ḥagigah 2.2, 77d.
80. In MSS of the Mishnah and in MS Leiden of the Palestinian Talmud: Mattai.

Hillel and Menaḥem did not disagree. Menaḥem left, Shammai entered. Shammai says [that one should] not lay hands, Hillel says [that one should] lay hands.[81]

The passage is obscure, and it is not at all clear what it is that the Pairs disagree about: if the controversy is read in the plainest way possible, it appears to concern the general practice of laying hands on the sacrificial victim's head, with one party in each pair actually dismissing this practice altogether and one party claiming that it should be maintained.[82] Such an interpretation is not entirely impossible: indeed there is some evidence, as I will show later on, that at least some of the rabbis found the practice of hand laying in its broadest sense to be expendable, and it could be argued that their position is a direct continuation of the same position among the Pairs. However, it is quite difficult to assume that one of each pair advised a wholesale rejection of a practice that is explicitly mandated in biblical law. The ongoing controversy is thus more readily understood in the context in which it appears in the Mishnah, which concerns feast offerings (*hagigah*) brought to the temple by pilgrims, usually on festivals.[83] The question at hand seems to be not whether to lay hands or not to lay hands on offerings in general, but rather only whether to lay hands on feast offerings during pilgrimage or not. What, then, is the particular issue with pilgrims' feast offerings that (according to the objectors) precludes hand laying?

The Tosefta explains the controversy of the Pairs as pertaining specifically to pilgrimage offerings made during festival days (*yom tov*) in which labor is prohibited, and therefore as guided by the assumption that hand laying is a form of labor. According to those who instruct "not to lay hands" the festival labor prohibition trumps the sacrificial protocol, while according to those who instruct "to lay hands" the sacrificial protocol trumps the festival labor prohibition.[84] This line of

---

81. M. Ḥagigah 2.2.

82. Some attempts have been made to interpret the term *semikhah* as pertaining to other practices, such as the ordination of rabbis or the offering of tithes, but none of them can be sustained, as noted by Hanokh Albeck, *The Six Orders of the Mishnah: Mo'ed* [Heb.] (Jerusalem: Bialik Institute, 1952), 511; see also Lieberman, *Tosefta ki-peshuta Mo'ed*, 5:1300.

83. On feast offerings, see Henshke, *Festival Joy*, 24–85.

84. T. Ḥagigah 2.10. The Tosefta's interpretation rests directly on the passage that immediately follows in the Mishnah, in which the House of Shammai and the House of Hillel disagree on whether one can offer burnt offerings and lay hands on them on the festival day. At the core of the controversy stands the notion that slaughter for the sake of eating is permitted on festival days, but not for any other purpose: since well-being offerings are eaten by the owners, the disciples of the House of Shammai permit their sacrifice on festival days, but prohibit burnt offerings (however, cf. Sifra Emor 12.15.5, ed. Weiss 102c; and see Henshke, *Festival Joy*, 61–65). This led the Tosefta to interpret the controversy regarding hand laying as pertaining to the labor prohibition on festivals as well.

explanation is followed in the Talmuds,[85] but as several scholars noted, there is really no reason why laying of hands would be considered as labor, and this explanation is altogether unconvincing.[86] Rather, it seems that the "not to lay hands" party objected to the custom of laying hands on offerings brought to Jerusalem during festival pilgrimages not because of the sacred nature of the festival day, but because of something about these offerings as such. In other words, the problem is not the *time* in which those offerings are brought (festival), but rather the *setting* in which those offerings are brought (pilgrimage). What stands behind this objection?

E. E. Hallewy argued that the Pairs' dispute regarding the laying of hands was just a decoy for what was really at stake for the two disputing factions: the mass participation of laypeople in temple life during festivals. According to Hallewy, laypeople were only inclined to bring offerings insofar as they knew that they would be able to lay their hands on them and thereby actively participate in the sacrificial process, and so by prohibiting hand laying those who were of this persuasion actually hoped to minimize the number of people who brought sacrifices to the temple altogether. Their hope was to restore to Jerusalem some of the "sanctity of the festival" that was lost, in Hallewy's view, in the raucous and boisterous disorder of thousands of people bringing their offerings.[87] In contrast, those who upheld the practice of hand laying were of the view that such lay participation was critical to a sense of communal solidarity and to the joy of the festival.[88] Hallewy based his argument almost entirely on an anecdote in the Palestinian Talmud, in which it is told that after the House of Shammai prevailed and hand laying was prohibited, the temple court became "desolate" (*shomemet*), which eventually led

---

85. In the Talmuds, the laying of hands is explained to be a form of "riding" on the animal, since one ostensibly uses all his force when doing so (BT Ḥagigah 16b; PT Ḥagigah 2.2, 77d). However, riding itself is prohibited only on account of *shevut* (that is, not because the activity itself is considered a violation of the Sabbath or festival, but to maintain the sanctified day as a day of rest), and a renowned rabbinic principle asserts that *shevut* prohibitions do not apply to the realm of the temple at all; see the discussion of this principle in Yitzhak Gilat, *Studies in the Development of Halakha* [Heb.] (Ramat Gan: Bar Ilan University Press, 2001), 87–108. The Talmud's explanation is thus quite weak, and in truth, the notion that hand laying is prohibited on account of *shevut* appears nowhere in rabbinic literature except in an attempt to account for the controversy of the Pairs.

86. See Elimelech E. Hallewy, "The First Controversy" [Heb.], *Tarbitz* 28, no. 2 (1959): 154–57; Henshke, *Festival Joy*, 134–37.

87. Hallewy, "The First Controversy," 157.

88. The controversy regarding the inclusion of the "masses" in temple life is often characterized as a quintessential Pharisees-Sadducees controversy; see Israel Knohl, "Participation of the People in Temple Worship: Second Temple Sectarian Conflict and the Biblical Tradition" [Heb.], *Tarbitz* 60, no. 2 (1991): 139–46.

one rabbi to overturn the prohibition and to allow hand laying.[89] There is, however, a substantial leap between maintaining that this "desolation" was the result of the prohibition and asserting, as Hallewy does, that this was the *purpose* of the prohibition. I thus have qualms about the tenability of Hallewy's historical reconstruction, but I do believe that his identification of a connection between lay participation and hand laying is correct at its core.[90]

Whereas Hallewy identified the controversy regarding hand laying as a disguise for the question of the "respectability" of the temple, David Henshke explained this controversy as an expression of a dispute regarding the very nature of feast offering as a sacrificial category: namely, whether this offering was to be considered a congregational offering (*qorban tzibur*) or an individual offering (*qorban yaḥid*).[91] I will expand on congregational and individual offerings in chapter 3, but for the purposes of this discussion suffice it to know that the rabbis use the category of "individual offerings" to denote offerings given by private persons for thanksgiving, atonement, reparation, or any other personal goals, whereas "congregational offerings" are offerings that are incumbent upon the congregation as a whole, either on specific circumstances or on specific times of the year. At the basis of Henshke's reading lies a mishnaic ruling according to which hand laying applies only to individual offerings (with some exceptions, as I will discuss below), not to congregational offerings.[92] Henshke suggested that the objection to hand laying on feast offerings derived from a view of such offerings as congregational offerings.[93] This view, according to Henshke, rests on the fact that the obligation to provide feast offerings at festivals applies to the congregation as a whole and does not pertain only to specific individuals, even though each individual acquires the offering of his own funds.[94]

I think Henshke is correct in his reconstruction of a rabbinic controversy regarding the classification of feast offerings as congregational or individual, as well as in his suggestion that it is this controversy that stands at the core of the

---

89. PT Betza 2.4, 61c (= PT Ḥagigah 2.3, 78a); note that the "desolation" of the court is not mentioned in the Tosefta version of this narrative (T. Ḥagigah 2.11), nor in the Babylonian version (BT Betza 20b).

90. For a different (albeit unconvincing) explanation of the controversy regarding hand laying as reflective of a broader controversy regarding lay participation in the sacrificial process, see Bruce Chilton, *The Temple of Jesus: His Sacrificial Program within a Cultural History of Sacrifice* (University Park: Pennsylvania State University Press, 1992), 103–11.

91. Henshke, *Festival Joy*, 140–47.

92. M. Menaḥot 9.7.

93. Indeed, T. Temurah 1.17 explicitly identifies feast offerings as congregational offerings.

94. In this regard, feast offerings are equivalent to Passover offerings, to which hand laying does not apply, and which similarly constitute an obligation for the entire congregation even though each individual (or group) delivers them separately. Indeed, the Passover offering is classified in some rabbinic texts as a congregational offering and in others as individual, and Henshke suggests that a similar duality was at play for feast offerings. See my detailed discussion in chapter 4.

Pairs' disagreement on hand laying. I wish to argue, however, that the question of hand laying is not a by-product of a technical controversy regarding the classification of offerings, but rather a facet of the deeper question that underlies this controversy: the question of the agency of the individual owner vis-à-vis his sacrifice. Throughout rabbinic literature, the term "congregational offering" primarily refers to an offering that is provided by collective funds and is made on behalf of all of the congregation and not on behalf of one person or a small group of persons.[95] The classification of feast offerings, which are funded by and brought on behalf of individuals or families, as "congregational" is a rather bold interpretive move that cannot be seen as a mere comment on the nature of these offerings but must be understood as a way of emphatically dismissing the importance of individual offerers within the sacrificial system. When individual offerings are collapsed into a larger "congregational" offering, each individual offerer is rendered inconsequential in and of himself, and meaningful only as part of the collective. Indeed Henshke points in this direction, noting that those who classify feast offerings as congregational "obliterate the personal dimension of the pilgrimage and its offerings . . . [such that] when [an individual] performs the pilgrimage and sacrifices . . . [his offerings] are but an anonymous contribution to the public celebration."[96] Henshke assumes that some rabbis obliterated the personal dimension of feast offerings—expressed among other things in the laying of hands—because they classified them as congregational: in contrast, I propose that feast offerings were classified by some rabbis as congregational *in order* to obliterate their personal dimension and to bracket the owner's agency. In other words, those who ruled against hand laying on feast offerings did not necessarily set out to limit the number of laypeople participating in the sacrificial feasts, as Hallewy claimed, but rather to limit their *significance*. They wished to make the point that it is not the individual offerer who defines the offering and gives it meaning, but rather something else—in this case, evidently, the collective.

Those acquainted with rabbinic conventions of ruling know well that if the position that calls for hand laying is associated with the name of Hillel, and the opposing opinion is associated with the name of Shammai, then it is almost necessarily the former position that eventually prevails. The Tosefta relates the victory of the Hillelites—and of the custom of hand laying—in a very dramatic fashion, describing how disciples of the House of Shammai attempted to establish the law in accordance with their view, but one of the disciples of the House of Shammai who "knew that the law is according to the House of Hillel in every place" pre-

95. See Tzvi Arye Steinfeld, "On the Definition of Individual and Congregational Offerings," in *Shoshanat Yaakov: Jewish and Iranian Studies in Honor of Yaakov Elman,* ed. Shai Secunda and Steven Fine (Leiden: Brill, 2012), 1–28.

96. Henshke, *Festival Joy,* 146 (my translation).

vented that from happening. This disciple placed multiple goats and sheep in the temple court and said, "Whoever needs to bring burnt offerings and well-being offerings should come and take and lay his hands," and the people followed suit. On that day, the Tosefta concludes, "the law was established according to the house of Hillel and no one questioned this."[97] On the face of it, then, the "official" line of the rabbis encourages participation of laypeople in the sacrificial process and embraces the practice of hand laying. However, if we examine the treatment of hand laying beyond the context of feast offerings, we can identify a systematic attempt to restrict both the prevalence and the significance of this practice, an attempt that suggests that certain reservations regarding lay participation in the sacrificial process may have continued to inform the rabbis long after the controversy of the Pairs was ostensibly resolved.

"Remainders of the commandment": The dispensability of hand laying

While the enduring controversy of the Pairs regarding hand laying seems to pertain to one specific type of offerings, namely, to feast offerings, anonymous rabbinic traditions assert that there are also other types of offerings to which hand laying does not apply. I already mentioned that congregational offerings are said not to require hand laying, an understandable ruling considering the fact that such sacrifices ostensibly have no "owner" (although some congregational offerings—and according to one tradition, all of them—are said to require hand laying by the officiating priest).[98] More conspicuously, the Mishnah rules that three kinds of individual offerings—firstborns, animal tithes, and the Passover offering—do not require hand laying.[99] Unlike in the case of feast offerings, regarding these three offerings there does not seem to be any disagreement, and their exclusion from the practice of hand laying appears to be uncontested.

The ruling that hand laying does not apply to firstborns, tithes, and the Passover is curious: in essence, all three are well-being offerings (*shelamim*), in which

---

97. T. Ḥagigah 2.11.

98. M. Menaḥot 9.7 mentions that even though "all congregational offerings do not include hand laying," there are a few exceptions to this rule, including the bull offered to atone for a violation of all the commandments, the scapegoat of the Day of Atonement, and according to R. Shimon, also goats offered to atone for idol worship: in all those cases the priest lays his hands on the sacrificial animal. One mishnaic passage (M. Tamid 7.3) even mentions a practice of hand laying on the daily offering (*tamid*), which is perhaps the ultimate example of a congregational offering. This mishnaic passage may be in keeping with a view expressed in the Mekhilta demilu'im, according to which there is an analogy between the offerings that the priests make for their own sake and all other congregational sacrifices: "In the same way that [the priests'] offerings require hand laying, so congregational offerings require hand laying, and in the same way that he [the priest] lays his hands on his own offerings, so he lays them on congregational offerings" (Sifra tzav Mekhilta demilu'im 1.13, ed. Weiss 41c).

99. M. Menaḥot 9.7.

the meat is eaten by the owners (priests in the case of firstborn animals, lay owners in the case of tithes and the Passover), and well-being offerings are explicitly said in Leviticus 3 to require hand laying by the owner. Why, then, are these three kinds of offerings excluded? In the Sifra, their exclusion is presented as deriving from the possessive form "*his* offering" (*qorbano*) in Leviticus 3:2 and 3:8: "He shall lay his hands on the head of his offering and slaughter it at the entrance of the Tent of Meeting."[100] As in many of the exacting readings of the Sifra, it is not entirely clear how the alleged emphasis "*his* offering" is supposed to lead the interpreter to the targeted halakhic conclusion.[101] The medieval commentator Shlomo b. Aderet (1235–1310) suggested that the possessive is meant to indicate that only offerings that the owner brings of his own accord require hand laying, and since those three are mandatory offerings, hand laying does not apply to them.[102] This commentator admits, however, that this reading is difficult considering the fact that purification and reparation offerings are also obligatory but still require hand laying. An alternative route was taken by Yehudah Aryeh Leib Alter (1847–1905) in his commentary *Sefat Emet*, in which he claimed that firstborns and tithes cannot be considered "one's own" offerings, since their sacrificial nature is inherent in them and is not a result of the owner's sanctification: the firstborn is sacred because it is the first offspring of its mother, and the tithe is sacred because it is the tenth animal of a flock. Alas, this leaves open the question of the Passover, which has no intrinsic sanctity until it is designated to be offered: here the commentator suggests that perhaps the Passover cannot be considered "one's own" because every person has to offer it.[103]

It is not my intention to determine which, if any, of these explanations actually captures the logic behind the exclusion of those three kinds of offerings from hand laying, or indeed whether there was a coherent logic to this rabbinic ruling in the first place. It is quite possible that the rabbis simply registered the fact that hand laying is not explicitly mentioned in regard to these three offerings in the Pentateuch, and this sufficed to conclude that hand laying does not apply to them. Rather, my purpose is only to show that there is no one self-evident reason that three subcategories of well-being offerings do not require hand laying. This restrictive view of hand laying as pertaining only to some offerings and not to others seems to be a rabbinic innovation, which does not follow on any apparent biblical cues. At the core of this restrictive view stands, I contend, a rabbinic understanding of hand laying as an independent subritual that is not integral to the sacrificial process as such, but functions merely as an addendum to it. This view makes it

---

100. Sifra nedavah 13.17.4–6 (ed. Finkelstein 103); cf. BT Menaḥot 92b.
101. As discussed at length in Yadin-Israel, *Scripture and Tradition*, 9–72.
102. Hidushei haRashbah on BT Menaḥot 93a (Warsaw: Bamberg, 1861).
103. Sefat Emet on Qodashim (Warsaw, 1925).

possible for the rabbis to determine that in some sacrifices this addendum is not in order,[104] and thereby to reveal their view that the owner's participation in the sacrificial ritual is not a component of the sacrifice itself, but rather its own separate procedure—and indeed not a requisite one.

In accordance with their view that hand laying is not an inherent component in the sacrificial process but rather an independent ritual appendix, the rabbis limit not only the category of offerings to which this practice applies, but also the category of persons to whom this practice applies. One mishnaic passage asserts that hand laying pertains only to adult, free, able-bodied, Jewish males:

> All lay their hands (*hakol somkhin*), except for the deaf, the mentally inept, the minor, the blind, the gentile, and the slave, and the emissary (*shaliaḥ*), and the woman.[105]

While it is not at all unusual for the rabbis to limit agency in different legal arenas only to adult-free-able-Jewish males,[106] and in this regard this list is in keeping with their general tendency, it should be noted that there is no full congruity between the persons to whom hand laying applies and the persons who partake in the sacrificial system. Most noticeably, women are excluded here from hand laying even though women are not only allowed to bring offerings but in some cases required to do so (for example, after childbirth).[107] Slaves are mentioned in the Mishnah alongside women as persons who are required to bring offerings in certain situations, even though their master may be the one paying for them.[108] The question of whether offerings made by gentiles are to be accepted was apparently hotly debated during the Second Temple period, and there does seem to be some residue of resistance to gentile offerings in much later rabbinic literature,[109] but the unequivocal position in the Mishnah is that gentiles are allowed to offer voluntary offerings if they wish to do so.[110] There are thus at least three categories of persons who partake in the sacrificial system but are excluded from hand laying, which again indicates that the rabbis did not consider hand laying—the ultimate token of

---

104. See also M. Temurah 3.4.

105. M. Menaḥot 9.8.

106. See, for example, M. Megillah 2.4; M. Ḥagigah 1.1; M. Gittin 2.5; M. Parah 5.4, and many others.

107. See Leviticus 12:6–8, 15:28–30. In truth, the rabbis assume that women's mandatory offerings always take the form of bird offerings (as evident in Mishnah Qinnim), which do not require hand laying; but women's offerings are certainly not restricted to bird offerings.

108. M. Nega'im 14.12.

109. See Israel Knohl, "Acceptance of Offerings from Gentiles" [Heb.], *Tarbitz* 48, nos. 3–4 (1979): 341–45; Daniel R. Schwartz, *Studies in the Jewish Background of Christianity* (Tübingen: J. C. B. Mohr, 1992), 102–16.

110. For example, M. Sheqalim 1.5, 7.6.

the owner's participation—to be an inextricable part of the sacrificial process, but a ritual unto itself, subject to its own rules and restrictions.[111] The most striking facet of the rabbinic bracketing of hand laying as separate from the sacrificial procedure, however, is the ruling that even when hand laying is officially required, that is, when the offering and the offerer fit the criteria discussed above, hand laying is nonetheless *inconsequential*. Simply put, even when hand laying is in order it does not really matter whether it was performed or not. The Mishnah defines the laying of hands as "remainders of the commandment" (*sheyare mitzvah*),[112] a term used to indicate that a particular action is formally a part of the process required for the proper fulfillment of a commandment, but the commandment is nonetheless considered fulfilled even if this action was omitted. The laying of hands by the owner thus has no impact on the validity of the sacrifice itself. The view that hand laying is not instrumental to the completion of the sacrificial process is introduced multiple times in the Sifra, which comments in regard to various types of offerings that "even though one did not lay his hands" (*'af 'al pi she-lo samakh*), the sacrifice is valid.[113]

Unlike Hallewy, I do not suppose that the rabbis who minimized and marginalized the practice of hand laying in the manners discussed so far were averse to the custom itself and advocated its eradication (whether in theory or in actuality). Deeming a ritual inconsequential is not necessarily tantamount to discouraging one from performing this ritual, and indeed one tradition mentions that even those to whom hand laying technically does not apply are welcome to lay their hand on their offerings if they desire to do so.[114] Moreover, one passage in the Sifra states quite clearly that the owners are actually frowned upon if they did not lay their hands on the offering:

> [On Leviticus 1:4, "He shall lay his hand on the head of the burnt offering, and it shall be acceptable in his behalf as atonement for him"] Since we have found that there is no atonement except in blood, why does scripture say, "And he shall lay his hand . . . and it shall be acceptable?" This is to teach that if one made the laying of hands a remainder of the commandment, it is as though he did not atone.[115]

111. The exclusion of deaf, mentally inept, and minors from the list is unsurprising, since those three are usually considered not to be obligated to perform any commandments. The exclusion of the blind could be understood as practical in nature (a blind person may not be able to perform hand laying), although there is a minority opinion according to which blind persons are exempt from commandments altogether (BT Qiddushin 31a; Baba Qamma 87a). The exclusion of the emissary (*shaliaḥ*) is somewhat curious considering the staple rabbinic rule that "one's emissary is like oneself," but can be explained if the laying of hands is understood as representing the direct agency of the owner.

112. M. Menaḥot 9.8.

113. Regarding burnt offerings: Sifra nedavah 3.4.8, 5.7.7 (ed. Finkelstein 34, 55); regarding well-being offerings: Sifra nedavah 14.17.1, 14.19.1 (ed. Finkelstein 105, 112); regarding purification offerings: Sifra ḥovah 4.6.7 (ed. Finkelstein 146); regarding reparation offerings: Sifra tzav 4.8.4 (ed. Weiss 33d).

114. Sifra nedavah 2.2.2 (ed. Finkelstein 20); BT Ḥagigah 16b.

115. Sifra nedavah 3.4.10 (ed. Finkelstein 35); cf. M. Nega'im 14.4.

This anonymous homily powerfully expresses the incongruity to which I alluded at the beginning of this chapter, between sacrifice as a manifestation of the owner's piety and sacrifice as a self-contained ritual assessed according to the correctness of the actions of which it is comprised. The homilist acknowledges that the laying of hands in itself has no impact on the validity of the process: only the manipulation of blood, in the rabbis' view, has the power to effect atonement. Nevertheless, the lack of piety demonstrated by the fact that the owner did not take the trouble to lay his hands compromises the religious integrity of the process to such extent that it is as though the sacrifice was not efficacious at all. Interestingly, here the term "remainders of the commandments," which in the Mishnah serves to define the laying of hands, serves to define the owner's flawed attitude to this practice: he *makes* the laying of hands a "remainder of the commandment" by taking it lightly. The Sifra thus emphasizes that while the laying of hands is not critical to the successful completion of the sacrificial process, it ought to be regarded as though it is. The word *ke'ilu*, "as though," is the key here: it encapsulates the gap between ritual reality, in which the owner's actions are inconsequential, and religious ethos, in which they are all that matters. This gap is even more pronounced in the version of the same homily in the Babylonian Talmud, which concludes with the words "It is as though he did not atone, *but he atoned*" (*ke'ilu lo kiper ve-kiper*).[116] It is important to bear in mind, however, that it is the rabbis who impose this distinction between ritual reality and religious ethos, between validity and piety, in the first place. Had the rabbis wished to say that the absence of hand laying voids the offering altogether, nothing would have stood in their way—just as they were completely capable of saying that lack of proper intentions on the side of the owner invalidates the offering, but chose not to say so. This choice to bracket the ritual agency of the owner, which cannot in any way be taken as a straightforward interpretive reading of the Pentateuch, opens a window to the rabbis' greater conception of sacrifice.

If the rabbis did not scorn the owner's actual participation in the sacrificial process, then, why did they dismiss the laying of hands—and more broadly, all other components of the owner's physical and mental involvement in the sacrifice—as ritually insignificant? I propose that behind this interpretive-legislative decision stands a rejection of the notion that sacrifice is a channel through which an individual approaches the deity and communicates with him. Sacrifice, the rabbis seem to be saying, is not a form of interaction: while it could be read as a manifestation of piety and reverence, it is not piety and reverence that make or break it, but rather the correct performance of blood-related ritual actions. The owner is thus excluded from the sacrificial picture in order to make the point that

---

116. BT Yoma 5a; BT Zevaḥim 6a; BT Menaḥot 93b; this is also the version in the printed editions of the Sifra.

while the sacrifice is offered *for* him, it is not offered *by* him—not simply in the sense that he is dependent upon the officiating priest but more broadly in the sense that he has no control at all over the efficacy and validity of the offering. Furthermore, in bracketing hand laying as an expandable part of the ritual the rabbis significantly diminish the apparent differences between individual and congregational sacrifices, thereby allowing the former to be conceived of or even transformed into the latter. This tendency to champion collective worship over individual worship is, as I will demonstrate later in the book, very dominant in rabbinic sacrificial legislation. By way of conclusion to this chapter, I will suggest a few speculations on the perceptions and concerns that may have animated this rejection of the communicative model—and thereby the marginalization of the owner—in the Tannaitic sacrificial legislation.

THE MARGINALIZATION OF THE OFFERER AND THE RABBINIC SACRIFICIAL VISION

I began this chapter by describing the biblical model of sacrifice as relational in nature: it is a model in which the offering is a vector of communication between the giver (owner) and a receiver (deity), and it is defined and represented as enabling and establishing a connection between those two entities. I then showed that in Tannaitic legislation the "giver" is systematically construed as inconsequential in the sacrificial process. Of course, the rabbis do maintain that offerings must *have* owners: the very act of sacrifice must commence with the owner specifically dedicating a portion of his property to the temple, and moreover, an offering without owners—that is, a sacrificial animal whose owner died, or that the owner of which is unknown—cannot be offered at all and must be incinerated.[117] But the owner's actions and dispositions, I argued, have no impact on the efficacy and validity of the sacrifice itself, and thereby the sacrificial procedure in its rabbinic construction cannot be seen as a form of direct interaction between the owner and the deity, since the owner is effectively absent from the scene (and may very well, as I will mention shortly, be *actually* absent from the scene).

The rabbis' marginalization of the owner in the sacrificial process cannot be understood simply as a continuation of the same trend in the Priestly Code, despite the fact that the Priestly Code does construe sacrifice in a more impersonal manner than earlier biblical sources, and does put heightened emphasis on the priests rather than on the owners. The unique features of the rabbinic sacrificial legislation that I discussed in this chapter strongly indicate that the rabbis operated with a distinct and independent agenda that goes well beyond the biblical infrastructure. When the rabbis question the necessity of hand laying on the sacrificial

117. See, for example, M. Pesaḥim 6.6, 7.9, 8.2; M. Temurah 4.1.

animal's head and in some cases eliminate it, they are not working *with* the biblical text but *against* it: they declare a ritual that is clearly pertinent to the priestly understanding of the sacrificial procedure to be expendable. As Martha Himmelfarb noted, "It is noteworthy that P requires lay participation in the process of sacrifice. This practice stands in contrast to that of other ancient cults in which priests performed rituals out of view of the laity."[118] The rabbis' notion that lay participation is not crucial for the validity of the offering is thus not a derivative of the priestly spirit of sacrifice but rather a rejection of a central tenet of it. Similarly, when the rabbis read the word "the offerer" in Leviticus 7:18 as pertaining to the priest and not to the owner, they consciously interpret the priestly text against its own logic and context, in order to promote a particular view of what the sacrificial process is and who is included in and excluded from it. Finally, the rabbinic position that it is the priest's intentions vis-à-vis the sacrifice, rather than the owner's intentions, that make the sacrifice valid or invalid, cannot be viewed as adopting a priestly paradigm—for the simple reason that in the priestly paradigm intentions are of no consequence whatsoever. It is the rabbis who choose to incorporate intentions into their view of the correct sacrificial procedure in the first place, and at the same time to assert that the owner's intentions are not instrumental to the procedure. I thus contend that while there are certainly avenues of continuity between the sacrificial vision of the Priestly Code and the sacrificial vision of the rabbis, the rabbis' legislation still presents notable innovations and significant departures from the biblical traditions on which it builds.

If the marginalization of the owner in rabbinic sacrificial legislation is indeed innovative, what stands behind this innovation? One possibility is to explain the bracketing of the owner in strictly pragmatic terms. Simply put, the rabbis realized that the owners cannot always be physically present when sacrifices are performed on their behalf. The anomaly of the Judean sacrificial system, in which there is only one temple in one location, makes what every Greek or Roman or Egyptian can do relatively easily—go over to the local temple with an offering in one's hand—extremely complicated. Therefore, a highly common practice among Jews outside Jerusalem (as described both in Second Temple literature and in rabbinic literature) was to send money to the temple, and to have other people buy and deliver an offering on one's behalf.[119] It is quite likely that in light of this

---

118. Martha Himmelfarb, "'Found Written in the Book of Moses: Priests in the Era of Torah," in *Was 70 CE a Watershed in Jewish History? On Jews and Judaism before and after the Destruction of the Second Temple,* ed. Daniel R. Schwartz, Zeev Weiss, and Ruth A. Clements (Leiden: Brill, 2012), 30.

119. The evidence for this common practice is discussed by James B. Rives, "Animal Sacrifice and Political Identity in Rome and Judea," *in Jews and Christians in the First and Second Centuries: How to Write Their History,* ed. Peter J. Tomson and Joshua Schwartz (Leiden: Brill, 2014), 110–18. Indications for the practice of "sending" an offering from overseas without being physically present can also be found in M. Sheqalim 7.7 and M. Gittin 3.3.

reality the rabbis or their predecessors figured that the owner as such cannot be considered instrumental to the sacrificial process. This problem is of course irrelevant to the Priestly Code, which describes a completely different cultic reality with the movable Tent of Meeting at its center, or to other biblical texts that do not assume a centralized temple at all.

To this we may add that perhaps the owner's involvement was dismissed not only because it was often unfeasible, but also because it could potentially be problematic. When a person delivers an offering, one can never be sure for what or for whom exactly this person is offering: for example, as Philo comments, there seems to have been some ambiguity (perhaps a purposeful one) about whether the offerings made daily in the Jerusalem temple "for the emperor" were offerings to Yahweh for the health and prosperity (*huper soterias*) of the emperor, or offerings directed to the emperor as a deity-like entity.[120] Especially in light of the fact that the rabbis did not exclude non-Jews from partaking in the sacrificial system, it is possible that they (or, again, their predecessors) developed the mechanism that "everything follows the slaughterer/officiant" as a religious safety-valve of sorts, made to ensure that worship in the temple is never compromised by improper or misguided predilection of lay offerers.

Either or both of these practical considerations may have informed the rabbis in their textual construction of sacrifice, and it is quite possible that the roots of the legal mechanisms that effectively obviate the owner's agency date back to the time and circumstances of the Jerusalem temple. However, even if the perception that the owner is inconsequential to the sacrificial process emerged as a result of concrete ritual and religious challenges, it is my contention that in the Tannaitic literary creation this perception functions within a more comprehensive theological and ideological edifice. As I will show in the next chapter, the rabbis marginalized not only the components of the offering in which the *giver* manifests his presence and agency, but also, quite astoundingly, the parts in which the *receiver* ostensibly manifests his presence—that is, the burning of the sacrificial meat or suet on the altar. The rabbis redefined the sacrificial practice as consisting exclusively of blood-related activities, thereby severing the ritual representations both of the addresser and of the addressee from their portrayal of sacrifice.

When the elimination of the act of giving (presentation before God) is taken together with the elimination of the act of receiving (burning and production of smoke), what emerges is a new picture of sacrifice, both vis-à-vis the Bible and vis-à-vis the greater Mediterranean landscape, which is decidedly not relational and not interactive. In other words, the rabbis seem to be saying through their elaborate sacrificial legislation that sacrifice is not an efficacious way through which an

120. Philo, *The Embassy to Gaius* 355–57 (ed. Yonge 789); cf. Flavius Josephus, *Against Apion* 2.6 (ed. Whiston 798).

individual can approach the deity but rather a self-contained process assessed only by its own correctness. This, I cannot stress strongly enough, does not mean that they thought that sacrifices were worthless or "barbaric" or obsolete, but rather that they considered their value in terms of an accurate and scrupulous fulfillment of ritual duty and not in terms of attaining direct contact with God.[121] Furthermore, as chapter 3 will show, the rabbis perceived this ritual duty as collective in essence, and therefore emphasized and heralded the collective and congregational dimensions of sacrifice while downplaying and minimizing its individual dimensions. In the following chapters I will argue that the noninteractive model that the rabbis devised derives to some extent from a theological agenda—namely, from the rejection of the notion that God is pleased or persuaded by material substances—but also, and in my view more importantly, from an attempt to promote an idealized vision of Israelite sacrifice as a perfected manifestation of a collective reverence for the law and of a communal sense of solidarity.

---

121. This is roughly the manner in which Wellhausen, without much sympathy, describes the Priestly Code's idea of sacrifice: "If formerly the sacrifice had taken its complexion from the quality of the occasion which led to it, it now had essentially but one uniform purpose—to be a medium of worship. . . . A manifoldness of rites took the place of individualising occasions; technique was the main thing, and strict fidelity to rubric" (*Prolegomena*, 78). I believe that this reading is heavily influenced by the Mishnah, which Wellhausen takes as faithfully representing the cultic life of the Second Temple. Unlike Wellhausen, however, I do not see the rabbinic emphasis on procedure as indicative of a religion of "shells" devoid of a "soul," but rather as reflecting a sustained, passionate, self-standing religious vision with its own integrity.

2

The Work of Blood

In the previous chapter, I showed that the components of the sacrificial ritual in which the prominent actor is the owner—namely, the components of procession, presentation, and hand laying—receive very little attention in rabbinic legislation, and are emphatically without impact in determining the validity and efficacy of the sacrificial process. The rabbis, I have argued, bracket those parts as ritually inconsequential and as effectively detachable from the sacrifice "itself" insofar as sacrifice is perceived as a meaningful legal activity. To borrow a term from performance theorist Richard Schechner, the owner's actions are construed by the rabbis as "proto-performance": they are "the source or impulse that gives rise to the performance"[1] (in this case, the sacrificial process), since without the owner's initiative or obligation no sacrifice would take place, but the owner has no role in the performance per se. The owner, one could say, is comparable to a donor who funds a lecture series at a university, but neither delivers the lectures herself nor is she, necessarily, present when the lectures are delivered. When, then, does the actual sacrificial performance begin, according to the rabbis, and what does it entail? Put differently, what actions constitute sacrifice "itself" in Tannaitic legislation?

The rabbis, in their usual manner of scrutinizing legal and ritual protocols down to their most minute details and accounting for every possible scenario through which various halakhic activities can unfold, notably construct the sacrificial process as consisting of several separate actions and underscore multiple ritual junctures within the process. However, when one turns to look at the literary attention given to these different actions, and more importantly, to the rabbis' own

---

1. Richard Schechner, *Performance Studies: An Introduction* (New York: Routledge, 2013), 226.

assertions on the workings and function of the different actions, it becomes immediately clear that the rabbis put the entire weight of the sacrificial process on one specific subset of actions—those having to do with the blood of sacrificial animals. This set of actions, which commences with the slaughter of the animal and concludes with the application of its blood on the altar, is emphasized in Tannaitic texts as the heart of the sacrificial process, as the only phase in which intentions and mind-sets are of consequence, and most strikingly, as a phase capable of obviating all the other sacrificial actions that antecede it. The consumption of the sacrificial flesh and suet, either by humans or by fire, is marked in rabbinic legislation as ritually marginal and can be defined—again utilizing Schechner's terminology—as an "aftermath" of the performance. The rabbis' construction of sacrifice as tantamount to the manipulation of blood, which I contend to be unprecedented in earlier texts, is the topic of this chapter.

My purpose in this chapter is to examine and analyze the Tannaitic construction of the manipulation of blood as encapsulating the sacrificial process in its entirety, and to propose some implications of this interpretive move for understanding the rabbinic textual sacrificial project more broadly. I thus venture to account both for the "negative" dimension of the rabbis' emphasis on blood—that is, what is pushed to the side as a result of the positioning of blood at the center—and for the "positive" dimension of this emphasis—that is, what function and effect the rabbis assign to blood and why. I will argue that the combination of the negative and positive dimensions of blood manipulation as construed by the rabbis amounts to an innovative theory of sacrifice as a ritual procedure, insofar as it eliminates from this procedure what is traditionally thought of as its most stable and important component: the receiver. The rabbis do, of course, acknowledge that parts of the offerings are designated for "the altar," but they very patently make the point that the validity of sacrifice does not depend on whether or not "the altar" received its due share or not. Rather, the dominant position in Tannaitic texts equates consumption "by the altar" (i.e., burning) and consumption by humans (i.e., eating) as two forms of the same activity, and treats both forms of activity as at least partially expendable.

My account of the rabbinic theory of sacrifice in this chapter thus serves to complete the picture I presented in the previous chapter: whereas in chapter 1 I argued that the rabbis construed sacrifice as a process *without addresser* by eliminating the agency of the offerer, in this chapter I argue that they construed it as a process *without addressee* by redefining the actions of which the core of sacrifice is comprised. Both aspects of the rabbinic recomposition of sacrifice work together, I propose, toward a new model of sacrifice, which is distinctly, as I already mentioned, not a model of vertical communication—a way of conveying something to the deity—but a model of procedural perfection.

In the first part of this chapter, I explain the rabbinic principles of what I title here "the work of blood" and demonstrate how the sacrificial process is redefined by the rabbis—in terms of both the substances it involves and the actions of which it consists—so that its validity depends primarily on the manipulation of blood. I give special attention to the rabbis' repositioning of ritual burning at the periphery of the sacrificial process, which effectively obliterates the requirement for divine acceptance of the offering. In the second part, I turn to explore the "positive" function assigned to blood in Tannaitic texts. I show that blood is strongly associated with two functions: atonement (*kapparah*) and permission (*hatarah*). The former is concerned with forgiveness of sins and ritual cleansing; the latter is a procedure for allowing the consumption of sacrificial goods. I argue that these two functions converge insofar as for the rabbis correct procedure is tantamount to atonement, and the value of sacrifice lies not in the substances it involves but in the accuracy of the actions applied to them. In the final part of the chapter, I venture to synthesize the analysis proposed here and in the previous chapter toward a more comprehensive reconstruction of a rabbinic theory of sacrifice.

BLOOD AT THE CENTER

Since animal sacrifices in the biblical tradition necessarily involve slaughter (that is, the animal cannot be strangled or burned alive), they also necessarily involve the shedding of blood. The role and significance of the blood emitted during sacrifice, however, vary widely among different biblical accounts of and instructions for sacrifice. In the JE traditions of the Pentateuch, references to the sacrifices made by ancestral figures make no mention of blood whatsoever: the one exception to this rule is the account of the covenant ritual in Exodus 24, in which sacrificial blood is used to ratify the covenant between Yahweh and the Israelites, but does not seem to constitute part of the sacrificial procedure itself.[2] In Deuteronomy, only a single verse refers to the treatment of blood in the sacrificial process: "Present your burnt offerings on the altar of the Lord your God, both the meat and the blood. The blood of your sacrifices must be poured on the altar of the Lord your God, but you may eat the meat" (Deuteronomy 12:27). While this verse gives no explanation of the import or efficacy of blood within the sacrificial ritual, it does indicate that the blood is seen as part of the sacrificial substances, both in

---

2. On the role of blood in the covenant ritual of Exodus 24, see Ronald Hendel, "Sacrifice as a Cultural System: The Ritual Symbolism of Exodus 24, 3–8," *Zeitschrift für die alttestamentliche Wissenschaft* 101, no. 3 (1989): 366–90; Gilders, *Blood Ritual*, 38–43; David Biale, *Blood and Belief: The Circulation of a Symbol between Jews and Christians* (Berkeley and Los Angeles: University of California Press, 2007), 39–43.

referring to burnt offerings as consisting of "meat and blood" (*ha-basar ve-ha-dam*), and in stipulating that the blood is applied to the altar (and not poured on the ground, as it is in nonsacrificial slaughter).[3] It is only in the Priestly and Holiness Codes (and in texts such as Ezekiel and Chronicles that reflect strong priestly influence) that blood features prominently in sacrificial rituals and is actually proposed to be of critical importance within the process. However, even within the priestly legislation we must distinguish between references to burnt offerings and well-being offerings, in which the blood is simply said to be poured "on and around the altar" (*'al ha-mizbeah saviv*),[4] and references to purification offerings, in which blood is carefully sprinkled against the curtain (*parokhet*) and smeared on the horns of the altar.[5] In the latter case, blood indisputably serves a concrete and distinct ritual function (as Jacob Milgrom put it, it functions as a "detergent" of sorts[6]), whereas in the former case blood seems to be applied to the altar simply as one component of the sacrificial animal.[7]

To be clear, there is no question that in the Priestly Code (and to some extent in other ancient religious traditions[8]) blood is a remarkably potent and powerful substance that can be used to effect purification, to sanctify persons and objects, and even to ward off powers of destruction.[9] It should be noted, however, that not every slaughter of an animal in order to use its blood for ritual purposes is neces-

3. Two additional texts pertaining to the Deuteronomic tradition seem to convey a similar concern with the application of blood to the altar: 1 Samuel 14:32–35 and 2 Kings 16:11–15. However, the exact meaning of the former text is uncertain, and it may just be referring to the prohibition on eating blood (see Gilders, *Blood Ritual*, 54–57), whereas the latter text may be of priestly provenance (52–54).

4. Leviticus 1:5, 3:2. For a recent discussion of the meaning of this phrase, see Naphtali S. Meshel, "The Form and Function of Biblical Blood Ritual," *Vetus Testamentum* 63 (2013): 1–14.

5. Leviticus 4:6–7 and passim; 16:14–20.

6. Jacob Milgrom, "Israel's Sanctuary: The Priestly 'Picture of Dorian Gray,'" *Revue Biblique* 83 (1976): 390–99; on this concept, see Noam Zohar, "Repentance and Purification: The Significance and Semantics of חטאת in the Pentateuch," *Journal of Biblical Literature* 107, no. 4 (1988): 609–18; Ray Gane, *Cult and Character: Purification Offerings, Day of Atonement, and Theodicy* (Winona Lake, IN: Eisenbrauns, 2005), 163–97.

7. See Gilders, *Blood Ritual*, 70–78. Consider also David P. Wright's claim that the concept of a blood-centered purification offering is a unique priestly hybrid of earlier models of burnt offering (in which blood has no unique significance) and purification rites unrelated to sacrifice. See Wright, "Ritual Theory, Ritual Texts," 202–5.

8. On the importance of blood in Greek sacrificial rituals, see Stanley K. Stowers, "On the Comparison of Blood in Greek and Israelite Ritual," in *Ḥesed ve-emet: Studies in Honor of Ernest S. Frerichs*, ed. Jodi Magness and Seymour Gitin (Atlanta: Scholars Press, 1998), 179–96.

9. I am referring here specifically to the account in Exodus 12:21–23 in which the blood on the doorposts is said to keep "the destroyer" (*mashhit*) away from the houses of the Israelites in Egypt. In his study on festivals in the Pentateuch, Shimon Gesundheit has convincingly shown that this tradition is priestly in origin and cannot be attributed, as previously claimed, to the J or E sources. See Shimon Gesundheit, *Three Times a Year: Studies on Festival Legislation in the Pentateuch* (Tübingen: Mohr Siebeck, 2012), 58–67.

sarily a sacrifice: for example, the bird used for the purification of the leper in Leviticus 14:2–7 and the red cow used for elimination of corpse impurity in Numbers 19:2–8 are slaughtered outside the tabernacle and are not brought to an altar, and as such cannot be considered "sacrifices" per se. In order for a ritual killing of an animal to fall under the biblical category of sacrifice (*qorban, 'olah,* etc.), one activity must ineluctably be present: burning of the entire animal or part of it on an altar. As Christian Eberhart demonstrated, reference to burning on an altar is the only common denominator of all biblical accounts of sacrifice, regardless of their provenance.[10] Even in the Priestly Code, sacrifices are repeatedly said to produce "an offering by fire, a pleasing odor to the Lord" (*'ishe reah nihoah la-Yahweh*). This rhetoric makes it evident that insofar as sacrifice was seen by priestly authors as an act of transferring something to the domain of God (as suggested by the fact that the Hebrew verb *hiqriv,* "made an offering," literally means "brought near"), the actual transferring meant burning and, perhaps more significantly, the production of smoke.[11] William Gilders, in his thorough study on blood ritual in the Hebrew Bible, similarly pointed that in priestly accounts of sacrifice the component of burning is as prominent as the component of blood manipulation, if not more so.[12]

Similarly, while the application of blood to the altar is certainly mentioned in references to the performance of sacrifices in Second Temple literature, it is always mentioned alongside burning,[13] and in several texts the application of blood is depicted as emphatically marginal to the burning of flesh or suet and to the production of smoke. As Himmelfarb has shown, sacrificial instructions in the Aramaic Testament of Levi and in the book of Jubilees stress mainly the importance of frankincense and incense, which are burned along with the offering to produce a pleasant odor.[14] Moreover, blood is portrayed in those texts primarily as a substance of which one ought to beware—both of eating it and of having it stain one's

10. Christian A. Eberhart, "A Neglected Feature of Sacrifice in the Hebrew Bible: Remarks on the Burning Rite on the Altar," *Harvard Theological Review* 97, no. 4 (2004): 485–93.

11. Christian A. Eberhart, "Sacrifice? Holy Smokes! Reflections on Cult Terminology for Understanding Sacrifice in the Hebrew Bible," in *Ritual and Metaphor: Sacrifice in the Bible,* ed. Christian A. Eberhart (Atlanta: Society of Biblical Literature, 2011), 17–32.

12. Gilders, *Blood Ritual,* 95, 138.

13. In most of the references to sacrifice in the Dead Sea Scrolls, the manipulation of blood and the burning of meat or suet are mentioned alongside each other, as is the case in the biblical model on which these texts rely. This is especially notable in the Temple Scroll's treatment of sacrifices, but also in CD IV.2; 4Q214 fr. 2; 4Q156; Genesis Apocryphon VII.

14. Martha Himmelfarb, "Earthly Sacrifice and Heavenly Incense: The Law of the Priesthood in *Aramaic Levi* and *Jubilees,*" in *Heavenly Realms and Earthly Realities in Late Antique Religions,* ed. Ra'anan S. Boustan and Annette Yoshiko Reed (New York: Cambridge University Press, 2004), 103–22.

clothes—rather than as a particularly ritually efficacious substance.[15] This emphasis on burning and aroma in biblical and postbiblical depictions of sacrifice is in
full keeping with sacrificial language and imagery in the ancient Greek and Hellenistic world: the Greek verb *thuein*, "to sacrifice," literally means "to make
smoke,"[16] and both visual and textual accounts of sacrifice from the ancient Mediterranean unequivocally describe smoke and smell as what is effectively given to
the gods.[17]

There is, however, one passage in the book of Jubilees that emphatically ties
together the dangers involved in the inappropriate use of blood with its sacrificial
potency: "And you, command the children of Israel not to eat any blood, so that
their names and seed might be before the Lord God always. . . . They shall keep it
for their generations, so that they might make supplication on your behalf with
blood before the altar."[18] Here blood is described as an instrument through which
the Children of Israel approach the deity, an instrument that can be effective only
when they also refrain from eating blood.[19] The root of this view, according to
which the blood applied to the altar is in and of itself what effects atonement for
the offerer, lies in one famous (and very obscure) biblical verse: "For the life of the
flesh is in the blood; and I have given it to you for making atonement for your lives
on the altar; for, as life, it is the blood that makes atonement (*ki ha-dam hu ba-
nefesh yekhaper*)."[20] While Gilders convincingly made the case that this lone verse
(commonly attributed to the Holiness Code) cannot be used wholesale to account
for the function of blood in the Hebrew Bible,[21] the notion of sacrificial blood as
the agent of atonement does seem to have had lingering resonance in postbiblical
literature, both in the book of Jubilees and in several rabbinic traditions that
declare plainly that "there is no atonement except in blood."[22] This notion is perhaps most emphasized and developed in the Letter to the Hebrews, in which Jesus

15. See Jubilees 21 (ed. Charlesworth vol. 2, 95–96); *Aramaic Levi Document* 25–32, in Henryk
Drawnel, *An Aramaic Wisdom Text from Qumran: A New Interpretation of the Levi Document* (Leiden:
Brill, 2004), 132–34. See also Cana Werman, "The Rules of Consuming and Covering the Blood in the
Priestly Halakha and the Halakha of the Sages" [Heb.], *Tarbitz* 63 (1994): 173–83.

16. See Christopher A. Faraone and Fred S. Naiden, "Introduction," in Faraone and Naiden, *Greek
and Roman Animal Sacrifice*, 2.

17. See Gilhus, *Animals, Gods, and Humans*, 115, 143; Graf, "One Generation after Burkert and
Girard," 47; Naiden, *Smoke Signals*, 3–38.

18. Jubilees 6.13–14 (ed. Charlesworth vol. 2, 67).

19. See William K. Gilders, "Blood and Covenant: Interpretive Elaboration on Genesis 9.4–6 in
the Book of Jubilees," in *Journal for the Study of the Pseudepigrapha* 15 (2006): 83–118. Cf. Biale, *Blood
and Belief*, 47–51.

20. Leviticus 17:11.

21. Gilders, *Blood Ritual*, 12–25.

22. Sifra nedavah 3.4.9–10 (ed. Finkelstein 34–35); T. Zevaḥim 8.17; BT Yoma 5a; BT Zevaḥim 6a;
BT Menaḥot 93b.

is depicted as a high priest who atones for the sins of Israel once and for all through his very own blood.[23]

There is certainly a biblical basis, then, for the rabbis' heightened attention to blood within the sacrificial process. But a close look at Tannaitic sacrificial legislation reveals that the rabbis do not simply underscore that the treatment of blood is the most efficacious part of the sacrificial process, but rather construe the treatment of blood as the sacrificial process per se. They both expand the ritual component of the manipulation of blood from a single action to a series of actions, and make the point that the manipulation of blood is the most critical and determining part in assessing the validity of sacrifices. Some rabbis even maintain that the sacrificial flesh is secondary in importance to the blood, and that a sacrifice may be considered complete and valid even with no flesh at hand. Most strikingly, the act of burning, which in prerabbinic traditions is portrayed as the most definitive action in the sacrificial process, is relegated in Tannaitic legislation to the category of "remainders of the commandment." This figuration of the treatment of blood as the be-all and end-all of sacrifice, which I now turn to demonstrate, opens a window to key aspects of the rabbis' sacrificial vision.

The fourfold work of blood

In the previous chapter I discussed the rabbinic notion that an offering can be disqualified if the one(s) performing the sacrificial actions devised inappropriate intentions vis-à-vis this offering while performing those actions. When we turn to examine this mechanism of disqualification through thought more closely, it becomes evident that there are only four actions during which intention is consequential enough to disqualify the offering.[24] These actions are (1) the slaughter of the sacrificial animal (*shekhitah*), (2) the reception of the blood of the slaughtered animal in a vessel (*qabalah*), (3) walking with the vessel of blood from the place of slaughter to the altar (*holakhah*), and (4) tossing of the blood on the altar (*zeriqah*).[25] These four activities are referred to in later Talmudic texts as "the four works" (*'arba 'avodot*), and in medieval commentaries they are referred to as "the work of blood" (*'avodat ha-dam*), a term that I will also use in this chapter. As Tannaitic texts repeatedly indicate, these four works are the core of the sacrificial process, and, at least to some extent, they *are* the sacrificial process.

---

23. Especially Hebrews 5:1–10, 7:1–28, 9:1–10:27.

24. For example, M. Zevaḥim 1.4, 2.3.

25. Rabbinic texts use the word "tossing" (*zeriqah*) as a generic term for all manners of application of blood to the altar: sprinkling, smearing, and so on. As Noam Zohar pointed out, while the Priestly Code prescribes different manners of blood manipulation for different kinds of offerings, rabbinic texts significantly underplay the differences between ritual instructions for different types of offerings. See Zohar, "Purification Offering," 50–56.

The anonymous view in the Mishnah is that each of these four activities is a separate critical juncture during the sacrificial process, and that all four are of the same status when it comes to disqualifying the sacrifice through wrongful intentions or actions—that is, all four works have the same ritual repercussions and import. However, the Mishnah also reports a minority opinion attributed to R. Shimon, according to which the act of walking with the blood cannot really be seen as "work" (specifically because one can imagine a sacrificial scenario in which the slaughter is performed right by the altar and no walking is necessary), and accordingly one cannot disqualify an offering while walking the blood.[26] Another Tannaitic tradition attributes to R. Aqiva the view that offerings cannot be disqualified through thought during the stage of their reception in a vessel.[27] Although these traditions were rejected by the redactors of the Mishnah, they do indicate that the rabbis were at least partially aware that the second and third sacrificial "works" are to some extent an artificial construction.

By incorporating both "receiving" and "'walking" into the work of blood, the rabbis expanded the biblical ritual of blood manipulation from a single activity (namely, the application of blood to the altar) to a prolonged multiphased procedure. Another facet of this expansion is the placement of slaughter alongside the other components of blood manipulation, such that it is assigned the same import and ritual power as the other three actions. In the Priestly Code, slaughter is separate from manipulation of blood insofar as the latter must be performed by a priest, and the former can apparently be performed by anyone, and can therefore be seen as less ritually significant than the application of blood and burning of suet/meat.[28] In Tannaitic texts, in contrast, slaughter is mentioned alongside the other works as equally potent in terms of its repercussions, and is thus construed as part of the extended manipulation of blood.[29] As I will show later in this chapter, it is the burning of suet and meat, which in the Priestly Code features alongside the manipulation of blood, that gets recast as a marginal and significantly less consequential activity by the rabbis.

The unique standing of the fourfold work of blood over and above other components of the sacrificial ritual is manifest, first and foremost, in the fact that this stage of the ritual has the power to invalidate the following stages—and thereby the sacrifice as a whole—through intentions and thoughts. The sacrificial process can be roughly divided into three stages: delivery (of the living animal to the sanc-

26. M. Zevaḥim 1.4. Cf. Sifra tzav 8.12.5 (ed. Weiss 36b).

27. T. Zevaḥim 1.8; Sifra nedavah 4.4.5 (ed. Finkelstein 37). See the discussion in Sagiv, "Studies in Early Rabbinic Hermeneutics," 63–71.

28. See Gilders, *Blood Ritual*, 89, 107.

29. Although, as I mentioned in the previous chapter, M. Zevaḥim 4.6 may attest to a different position: it is possible that R. Yose's statement that "everything follows the officiant" is meant to reject the view that slaughter is as consequential as the other works of blood.

tuary), transformation (which involves slaughter and manipulation of blood), and distribution (of the meat and suet among those who will consume them). During the first stage, which consists of choosing the animal, bringing it to the sanctuary, and laying one's hands on it, the owner is the main actor: as we have seen, this stage is essentially without ritual repercussions at all in the sense that the owner's actions are without consequence for the validity of the sacrifice (although the sacrifice is of course considered invalid if there are inherent flaws in the animal itself). The second stage, which commences with the act of slaughter that transforms the living animal into blood and meat, consists of the fourfold work of blood. This stage is critical and exceptional insofar as two levels of "correctness" are required in its course. First, the blood-related actions themselves must be performed correctly (that is, the blood must be applied in the right places, by a pure priest, received in an appropriate vessel, etc.). Second, the blood-related actions must be performed with correct intentions vis-à-vis the sacrificial substances—the blood itself, the meat, and the suet.[30] Put differently, the offering is disqualified in the second stage if it involves inappropriate intentions regarding the third stage (but also inappropriate intentions regarding the last component of the second stage, the tossing of blood).[31] Finally, in the third stage, which consists of burning and eating, the owners and/or priests are liable if the meat or suet is handled incorrectly; but at this point wrongful thoughts are no longer consequential. We see, then, that the second stage, during which the blood is handled, is of clear primacy within the sacrificial process, since it encapsulates the third stage: *in performing blood-related activities physically, the performer also performs meat-related activities mentally.* Thereby, the work of blood can be seen as effectively entailing the entire sacrificial process, to such an extent that some rabbis, as I will show, actually determine that a sacrifice is valid even if the third stage was never performed at all.

The primacy of the work of blood within the sacrificial process is manifest not only in the notion that intentions formed during this stage can invalidate the sacrifice, but also in the view that the completion of the work of blood is ritually tantamount to the completion of the sacrifice as whole. A recurring rabbinic position is that if a person must provide an offering in order to change his ritual

---

30. There are several rabbinic sources that define the category of disqualifying intention in a much more restricted way, as applying only to offerings made on the external altar or as requiring commensurability between the location of wrongful intention and the location of wrongful action; see M. Zevaḥim 4.4; T. Zevaḥim 5.4; Sifra tzav 8.13. 5–6 (ed. Weiss 37c). However, these specific restrictions do not resonate beyond these sources.

31. The tossing of blood is the only one of the four "works" that can be both the *subject* of inappropriate intention and the *opportunity* for inappropriate intention: one can disqualify an offering both by intending to act wrongfully while tossing the blood *and* by intending to toss the blood wrongfully. In the language of T. Zevaḥim 3.8, "The tossing of blood generates *piggul* and is subject to *piggul* (*mefagelet u-mitpagelet*)."

status—for example, to transition from a state of impurity to a state of purity, or to fulfill a Nazarite vow—his ritual transformation is effective immediately after the blood has been tossed. There is no need for the person in question to wait until the meat and suet are consumed before resuming his or her regular activities.[32] Interestingly, some rabbis even maintain that one fulfilled one's obligation to partake in the Passover offering if one was merely capable of partaking in it when the blood was tossed. As I will discuss at greater length in chapter 4, these rabbis assert that if one was ritually pure when the blood of the Passover offering was tossed and later became impure, then even though he may not eat of the sacrificial meat (which is the essence of the laypeople's obligation in regard to the Passover offering), he is not required to perform a "second Passover," that is, to repeat the sacrifice.[33] The successful completion of the work of blood, then, ritually functions as the completion of the sacrificial process in its entirety.

Finally, a particularly instructive example of the rabbis' positioning of the work of blood as the most definitive point in the sacrificial process can be found in the purity requirements of the priests. The priests, as emphasized in Leviticus 22:1–9, must be ritually pure in order to partake in sacrificial meat. On its face, this simply means that they must be ritually pure when they actually sit down to eat the meat: but the Mishnah determines that priests who plan to eat of the offerings must be ritually pure already at the point at which the blood of these offerings is tossed: "Even if he was impure during the tossing of blood and pure during the burning of suet, he does not partake in the meat, for it was said (Leviticus 7:33), 'The son of Aaron who offers the blood and the fat of the well-being offering shall have the right thigh as his share.'"[34] In its context, this biblical verse asserts that only the priest who actually performs the sacrifice is entitled to receive a portion of the offering, but the rabbis infer from it that *any* priest who wants to partake in an offering, and not just the specific priest who performs the sacrifice, must be pure when the blood is tossed. The priest's participation in the third stage is thus determined by his status in the second stage, during the work of blood.

By positioning the work of blood as the most decisive component of the sacrificial process the rabbis also redefine the essence of the offering itself, and shift the focus from the consumable parts of the animal—the meat and the suet—to the blood, such that the latter rather than the former is positioned as the key sacrificial substance. It is to the relation between blood and meat in Tannaitic sacrificial legislation that I now turn.

---

32. See M. Karetot 2.1; Sifre zutta Numbers 6.20 (ed. Horovitz 246; cf. M. Nazir 6.9).
33. T. Pisḥa 7.5–6, 12.
34. M. Zevaḥim 12.1.

Meat vs. blood

Sacrifice, as a process that consists of multiple actions that must be performed accurately and cautiously, holds within it the opportunity for numerous accidents and mishaps, and much of the rabbis' sacrificial legislation accounts for such possible accidents and their impact (or lack thereof) on the validity of sacrifices.[35] By the term "accidents" I am referring not to procedural mistakes (for example, performing sacrificial actions in the wrong order, in the wrong manner, or with wrongful intentions) that render the sacrifice void, but rather to occurrences that compromise the sacrificial substances themselves such that it is unclear whether the sacrificial procedure can even be carried out. This latter type of accidents pertains to three main scenarios: (1) a sacrificial substance was taken out of the precincts of the temple; (2) a sacrificial substance contracted impurity; and (3) a sacrificial substance was partially or entirely lost. Accidents that take place during the delivery stage of the sacrifice—for example, when the intended sacrificial animal is lost, severely wounded, or turns out to be unfit for sacrifice—of course preclude the possibility of sacrifice altogether; but when the accident takes place after the slaughter, that is, after the animal has already been transformed into blood and meat/suet, one is confronted with the question of whether and how to proceed with the sacrificial process. This question is the topic of one of the central controversies in rabbinic sacrificial legislation, which is related most clearly in the following passage:[36]

> R. Eliezer says: If there is no blood, there is no meat; but even though there is no meat, there is blood. R. Yehoshua says: If there is no blood, there is no meat, and if there is no meat, there is no blood.
>
> How so? If the blood became impure or was spilled or got outside the precincts, the meat shall be [left out until it is] deformed (te'ubar tzurato), and then shall be incinerated. If the meat became impure or got out of the precincts, R. Eliezer says: [The priest] should toss the blood; and R. Yehoshua says: He should not toss the blood. And if he did toss the blood, whether intentionally or erroneously, R. Yehoshua concedes that the [offering] was made acceptable (hurtzah).[37]

According to R. Eliezer, while sacrifice consists both of blood and of meat, only the former is absolutely vital for the completion of the sacrificial process. Therefore, if the blood was compromised in such a way that it cannot be tossed on the altar, the meat is unusable and must be incinerated. However, if the meat was compromised in such a way that it cannot be burned or eaten, one can still toss the blood, and the sacrifice is rendered acceptable. R. Yehoshua, in contrast, maintains that there is

---

35. See also McClymond, "Don't Cry over Spilled Blood."

36. See also Sifre Deuteronomy 78 (ed. Finkelstein 143); and cf. T. Menahot 4.5 and M. Menahot 3.4. This controversy is discussed extensively in BT Pesahim 77a–78a; BT Zevahim 104a; BT Menahot 26a.

37. T. Zevahim 4.1.

mutual dependence between the meat and the blood, and that either one of them is of no value without the other: accordingly, if the blood is intact and the meat is missing one cannot toss the blood. It should be noted that in this passage R. Eliezer and R. Yehoshua subsume under the category of "meat" both the part that is eaten by the owners or the priests and the suet ('*emorim* or *ḥalavim*) that is burned on the altar, a point to which I will return later on.

R. Yehoshua's opinion coheres much more squarely with biblical accounts of sacrifice, in which the meat is of critical importance alongside the blood. Indeed, in the Tosefta passage that follows, R. Yehoshua supplies a biblical verse to prove his point:

> R. Yehoshua says: Behold, [Scripture] says, "Present your burnt offerings on the altar of the Lord your God, *both the meat and the blood*" (Deuteronomy 12:27a)—[this indicates that] if there is no blood there is no meat, and if there is no meat there is no blood.
>
> R. Eliezer said to him: Behold, [Scripture] says, "The blood of your offerings must be poured on the altar of the Lord your God" (Deuteronomy 12:27b)—[this indicates that] this takes place even if there is no meat. How then do I uphold "both the meat and the blood?"—[Scripture] analogizes meat to blood. In the same way that blood is tossed, so the meat is tossed [on the altar].[38]

R. Eliezer emphatically downplays the role of meat in the sacrificial process, arguing that it is secondary to blood and is equivalent to it only in terms of manner of handling (a rather wild interpretive move, since no biblical text refers to the arrangement of meat on the altar in terms of "tossing") and not in terms of importance or indispensability. This position, I contend, is an extreme version of the general Tannaitic view of the work of blood as the most definitive and consequential part of the sacrificial ritual, which we have seen above. R. Eliezer takes this view to the next step, and transforms it into a bold pragmatic ruling: he asserts that if the work of blood essentially captures the entire sacrificial process, then the rest of the sacrificial process can actually be dispensed with. This dispensation is of course given only in case the meat cannot be offered and not in case the meat is available and fit for sacrifice, but the underlying logic of the dispensation reflects a more general consideration of the meat component of sacrifice as ancillary. The Tofesta's concluding comment, "And if he did toss the blood, whether intentionally or erroneously, R. Yehoshua concedes that the [offering] was made acceptable," indicates that while R. Yehoshua does not go as far as dismissing the role of meat in the sacrificial process altogether, he does fundamentally subscribe to this logic too.[39] Although he maintains that one should initially refrain from tossing blood

---

38. T. Zevaḥim 4.2.

39. Note that R. Yehoshua does not require the entire amount of meat to be available in order to toss the blood, but only a token amount of an olive-volume; see T. Zevaḥim 4.3.

when the meat cannot be offered, he admits that if one did it anyway then after the fact the sacrifice is accepted: the offerer is not culpable, and the sacrifice need not be repeated.[40] That is, even for R. Yehoshua an offering that consists solely of blood without any meat *is still a valid offering*. Interestingly, in the Sifra the only opinion mentioned in regard to the relations between blood and meat is R. Eliezer's: his view is presented anonymously as the only authoritative position on the matter, and there is no trace of a disputing position.[41]

The notion that correct treatment of the blood effectively completes the sacrificial process resonates beyond the question of availability of meat. One notable example of this notion can be found in the mishnaic instructions regarding bird offerings. Leviticus 1:14–17 describes a rather elaborate procedure that must be carried out when one offers a bird on the altar: "The priest shall bring it to the altar, wring off the head and burn it on the altar; its blood shall be drained out on the side of the altar. He is to remove the crop and the feathers and throw them down east of the altar where the ashes are. He shall tear it open by the wings, not dividing it completely, and then the priest shall burn it on the wood that is burning on the altar." The Mishnah repeats these instructions and adds to them (mentioning also that the bird's intestines should be removed and that it should be sprinkled with salt),[42] but then proceeds to clarify: "Even if he did not remove the crop or the feathers or the intestines that come out with [the crop] and did not sprinkle it with salt, whatever he changed about [the manner of handling the offering]—once he has drained its blood, [the sacrifice] is valid."[43] The ritual instructions at hand pertain to a bird sacrificed as a burnt offering (*'olah*), yet the Mishnah relegates the actual burning part to the margins of the process: while it does not explicitly say that the burning component is of no importance, it claims that the sacrifice is valid even if the burning takes place in complete violation of biblical instructions. The successful manipulation of blood marks the successful completion of the sacrifice.

Perhaps the most extreme version of the identification of sacrifice with blood and blood alone appears in a couple of statements attributed to R. Yehudah, for whom not only does the loss of blood prohibit the continuation of the sacrificial process, but the loss of blood is identical in its repercussions to the loss of the sacrificial animal itself. This view is manifest in R. Yehudah's ruling regarding the

---

40. The *huf'al* passive form of the word *hurtzah* indicates that the offering in this case is not accepted but is *made* acceptable through an external mechanism, in this case probably by the frontlet rosette (*tziz*) of the high priest's headdress. The rabbis interpret the statement that the rosette is meant to "take away any sins arising from the holies . . . so as to win acceptance for them [i.e., the People of Israel] before the Lord" (Exodus 28:38) to mean that the rosette serves as a safety valve in case of ritual accidents. See M. Pesaḥim 7.7; M. Menaḥot 3.3.

41. Sifra nedavah 4.5.12 (ed. Finkelstein 40).

42. M. Zevaḥim 6.5.

43. M. Zevaḥim 6.6.

purgation ritual of the Day of Atonement, a ritual that requires two goats, one of which is offered as purification offering and the other of which is sent away to the wilderness. The anonymous Mishnah states that the two goats are mutually dependent, such that if one goat of the pair died (after it had already been designated to be either sacrificed or sent away), the other one cannot be used, and a whole new pair must be chosen. To this ruling R. Yehudah adds: "If the blood [of the sacrificial goat] was spilled, the sent-away goat shall die; if the sent-away goat died, the blood shall be spilled."[44] Whereas the anonymous Mishnah, when addressing the possibility of the sacrificial goat's blood being accidentally spilled during the process, simply states that other blood must be provided instead,[45] R. Yehudah insists that the blood is tantamount to the animal itself, and if the blood of the animal that was designated originally is not available the whole ritual must start anew. Correspondingly, if the animal designated to be sent away died, then the blood of the sacrificial goat must be spilled and cannot be used. R. Yehudah does not make a similar ruling regarding the loss of sacrificial meat or suet, even though those also play a role in the sacrificial procedure: for him a sacrificial animal is essentially a repository of sacrificial blood.

Another tradition attributed to R. Yehudah strongly resonates with the one above in stating that the loss of blood undoes the entire sacrificial procedure, even if it is already under way. This tradition concerns disqualified offerings that accidentally end up on the altar: the rule in this case is that if an offering was disqualified during the sacrificial process (as opposed to before it, as in the case of animals not fit for sacrifice), and its meat or suet was mistakenly placed on the altar, they cannot be taken off the altar and must nonetheless be burned on it.[46] R. Yehudah, in contrast, submits that there is an exception to this rule: if the offering was disqualified because the blood was spilled or got out of the precincts, or if it was slaughtered during nighttime, then even if the meat or suet is already on the altar it must be removed.[47] In pairing an animal slaughtered in a forbidden manner (which renders it unusable) with meat whose corresponding blood was acciden-

44. M. Yoma 6.1. The rite of the two goats on the Day of Atonement is essentially similar to the rite of the two birds in the purification of the leper, during which one bird is killed and the other is sent away (Leviticus 14:2–8). In M. Nega'im 14.5 the ruling "If the blood [of the slaughtered bird] was spilled, the sent-away bird shall die; if the sent-away bird died, the blood shall be spilled" appears anonymously, and is not attributed to a particular sage. It stands to reason, then, that R. Yehudah imported this ruling from the context of purification from leprosy to the context of the Day of Atonement. It should be noted, however, that the slaughtered bird in the leper's purification ritual is not a sacrificial offering: it has no function except to produce blood in which the living bird is then dipped, which is not the case for the purification goat of the Day of Atonement.

45. M. Yoma 5.7.

46. M. Zevaḥim 9.1–2.

47. M. Zevaḥim 9.2; cf. Sifra tzav 1.1.7 (ed. Weiss 29a) and BT Zevaḥim 84a.

tally lost, R. Yehudah makes the point that meat without blood cannot even remotely be seen as a sacrificial offering. He insists that if there is no blood, animal parts that would otherwise constitute a fully acceptable offering must be removed from the altar in the same way that animal wool or horns must be removed from the altar: they are simply not a sacrificial substance.[48]

In placing such strong emphasis on blood and on the manipulation of blood, the sources I have discussed so far seem to divide both the sacrificial substances and the sacrificial process into a binary of blood as opposed to nonblood, and assert the primacy of the former over the latter. Nevertheless, we must not forget that the category of "nonblood" consists of two different subcomponents: parts consumed by humans and parts burned whole on the altar that are ostensibly designated for the deity. Regardless of the type of offering, the suet, which consists of "the internal organs and all the fat that is connected to them, both kidneys with the fat on them near the loins, and the long lobe of the liver,"[49] is always burned in its entirety. In case the offering at hand is a burnt offering, all of the animal's flesh, and not just the suet, is burned whole on the altar. For the rabbis, however, the distinction between meat and suet, between the portion of humans and the portion of the deity, is of little consequence, and the two are discussed jointly and interchangeably in contrastive relation to blood. Thus, R. Yehoshua, who, as we saw, maintains that "if there is no meat there is no blood," clarifies that the blood can be tossed as long as there is a sufficient amount either of meat (*basar*) or of suet (*ḥelev*), but there is no need for both:[50] "If the meat became impure but the suet is intact, he may toss the blood for the suet; if the suet became impure but the meat is intact, he may toss the blood for the meat."[51] In what follows, I will argue that this interchangeability of human consumption and divine consumption, and the positioning of both as secondary to the treatment of blood, amount to a radical transformation in the concept of sacrifice as we are accustomed to thinking of it: fundamentally, the rabbis turn sacrifice into a process without a receiver.

"Consumption by the altar" as a sacrificial aftermath

As I mentioned above, the rabbis effectively divide the sacrificial process into three stages: the delivery stage, in which the main actor is the owner and which I defined earlier as "proto-performance"; the transformation stage, which revolves around blood and bears most if not all of the weight of the sacrificial process; and the

---

48. M. Zevaḥim 9.5.

49. Leviticus 3:3–4.

50. T. Zevaḥim 4.3; cf. T. Pisḥa 6.3–4.

51. T. Pisḥa 6.4. The one exception to this rule is the Passover offering, in which the blood cannot be tossed unless there is a sufficient amount of edible meat, since this particular type of offering is designated primarily for eating.

distribution stage, which consists of burning (*haqtrara*) on the altar and eating (*'akhilah*) by priests or owners. The classification of burning and eating into the same subgroup of actions, actions that can be compromised during the second stage through wrongful thoughts, is evident in the multiple passages in which the rabbis parallel inappropriate manners of burning with inappropriate manners of eating and always assess them identically. To take but three examples:[52]

> This is the rule: one who slaughters or receives or walks or tosses [the blood] [with the intention of] eating something that is customary to eat or burning something that is customary to burn, [if he planned to eat or burn it] outside its place—it is disqualified, but there is no [punishment of] extirpation. [If he planned to eat or burn it] outside its time—it is foul (*piggul*), and one is liable to be extirpated on account of it.[53]

> One who slaughters [with the intention of] eating something that is not customary to eat or [with the intention of] burning something that is not customary to burn— the sacrifice is valid, but R. Eliezer disqualifies it. One who slaughters [with the intention of] eating something that is customary to eat [in a wrongful manner] or [with the intention of] burning something that is customary to burn [in a wrongful manner]—[if the wrongful intention pertains to a quantity of] less than the volume of an olive, the sacrifice is valid.[54]

> One who slaughters an [animal] offering [with the intention of] eating half an olive-volume of its meat outside and half an olive-volume of its meat inside, or [with the intention of] burning half an olive-volume of its suet outside and half an olive-volume of its suet inside—the offering is valid. One who slaughters an [animal] offering [with the intention of] eating an olive-volume of its meat today and an olive-volume of its meat tomorrow, or [with the intention of] burning an olive-volume of its suet today and an olive-volume of its suet tomorrow, whether he thought of [wrongful] time before thinking of [wrongful] place or thought of [wrongful] place before thinking of [wrongful] time, the sacrifice is invalid but there is no [punishment of] extirpation.[55]

There is certainly a clear logic behind the rabbinic pairing of eating and burning. To begin, there is an overlap between burning and eating in terms of the substances involved: while the suet is always burned on the altar, the meat is sometimes burned on the altar along with the suet and sometimes eaten by human beings. Accordingly, as we have seen, the rabbis assume a certain interchangeability between meat and suet, and thereby also between the actions that pertain to them. Moreover, both burning and eating amount to the eventual elimination of

---

52. For additional examples, see M. Zevaḥim 2.2, 2.5, 6.7; T. Zevaḥim 2.1, 2.9, 2.11–17.
53. M. Zevaḥim 2.3.
54. M. Zevaḥim 3.3.
55. T. Zevaḥim 2.12.

the sacrificial animal, such that both can be seen as forms of consumption. Indeed, one rabbinic source explicitly refers to both human and divine consumption as forms of "eating," comparing "eating by human beings and eating by the altar" (ʾakhilah la-ʾadam ve-ʾakhilah la-mizbeaḥ).[56]

The use of the term "eating" both in relation to persons and in relation to the altar is not merely a semantic play: it reflects a fundamental rabbinic view of the third stage of the sacrificial process as a stage of distribution of sacrificial "goods" between different beneficiaries. These "goods" include the meat, the hide, and the suet, and the beneficiaries are the priests, the owners, and "the altar" (mizbeaḥ). It is noteworthy that the rabbis use an animate object, the altar, to denote the nonhuman beneficiary of the sacrificial process, rather than referring to this nonhuman participant as "God" or "Heaven" or "the High."[57] This word choice indicates that the rabbis were reluctant to portray the deity as physically benefiting from sacrificial offerings, a point to which I will return shortly; however, they were certainly not the first ones to use the word "altar" in this manner and context. In 1 Corinthians 10:18 Paul refers to offerings as shared between the people of Israel and "the altar" (tou thusiasteriou), thus suggesting that this may have been a common way of denoting the deity's presence in the sacrificial scene.[58]

Different distribution plans exist for different kinds of offerings. For example, when well-being offerings are made, the altar receives the suet, the priests receive a portion of the meat (the breast and the thigh), and the owners receive most of the meat and the hide. When burnt offerings are made, the altar receives the meat and the suet, the priests receive the hide, and the owners receive nothing. When a high priest makes a purification offering, the altar receives the suet, but the owner and the other priests receive nothing, since the meat and hide are incinerated.[59] In these and other distribution plans the altar is only one of three beneficiaries, and emphatically not more important than the other two. As one passage in the Tosefta puts it, "The power of the altar is greater than the power of the priests [in some cases], and the power of the priests is greater than the power of the altar [in other cases]. . . . The power of the priests is greater than the power of Israel [in some cases], and the power of Israel is greater than the power of the priests [in other cases]."[60]

56. Sifra tzav 8.12.6 (ed. Weiss 36c).

57. With one exception: in M. Sheqalim 6.6 the divine recipient is referred to as "the Name" (ha-shem) rather than as "the altar." The tradition in this passage is attributed to the priests, and perhaps this unique terminology was characteristic of priestly circles.

58. See Wendell L. Willis, Idol Meat in Corinth: The Pauline Argument in 1 Corinthians 8 and 10 (Atlanta: Scholars Press, 1985), 185–87. For another rabbinic passage that portrays the altar as consuming offerings (here acerbically as "abolishing the property of Israel"), see T. Sukkah 4.13.

59. M. Zevaḥim 12.2–3.

60. T. Zevaḥim 5.3.

There are, then, certain clear analogies between meat and suet and between burning and eating, and the rabbinic decision to cluster the two together does not initially strike one as odd. What does call for attention, however, is the sharp divide between the work of blood on the one hand and the burning of suet on the other hand, such that the former is construed as the ultimate critical juncture within the sacrificial process, and the latter is construed as the aftermath of the process. Upon a closer look at biblical accounts of sacrifice, the act of burning seems to be associated much more closely with the work of blood than with eating by priests or owners. First, both the application of blood and the burning of suet or meat take place *on the altar,* as opposed to eating, which takes place at a remote location.[61] Second, both suet and blood are substances completely prohibited for human consumption, and as such can be seen as the exclusive portion of the deity; their pairing is thus as natural as the pairing of suet and meat, if not more so.[62] Third, in biblical sources the burning of suet, like the tossing of blood, must be performed in order to allow for subsequent human consumption: burning is depicted as a precondition for human consumption rather than as a parallel of human consumption.[63] Fourth and most important, burning functions in biblical and postbiblical accounts of sacrifice as *the emblematic sacrificial activity,* which cannot be said of human eating.[64] Since God is often associated with fire, the consumption of suet or meat by fire is interpreted in biblical texts as a sign of divine acceptance,[65] and the production of smoke is repeatedly described as "pleasing to the Lord." Thus, when the rabbis determine that intentions of improper consumption that are devised during the time of offering (*haqravah*) disqualify the sacrifice, one could easily expect that the burning of suet would fall under the category of "offering" rather than under the category of consumption.

When the rabbis classify burning alongside eating, then, rather than alongside the manipulation of blood, they relegate this action from the center of the sacrificial process to its periphery. This relegation is effected in rabbinic legislation not only through the rhetorical analogization of burning to eating, but much more blatantly, also through the explicit position that burning is simply not crucial to the completion of the sacrificial process. We have already seen that according to R. Yehoshua, one can toss the blood and thereby complete the sacrificial process

---

61. Indeed in T. Zevaḥim 11.4 and 11.7 blood is analogized to suet in this respect, as they are both designated for the altar; see below.

62. See Leviticus 7:22–27, and accordingly the discussions in M. Karetot 3.1–2, 4.1–2.

63. See Leviticus 7:28–33 and 1 Samuel 2:12–17.

64. The only exception to this rule is the showbread, which is wholly consumed by the priests (Leviticus 24:5–9) and does not entail burning. The Priestly Code does not refer to it as an "offering" but does regard it as "holy of holies."

65. As made evident in Leviticus 9:22–24, Judges 13:15–20, 1 Kings 18:36–39, 1 Chronicles 21:26, and 2 Chronicles 7:1–3; see Milgrom, *Leviticus 1–16,* 590–91.

successfully even if there is no suet remaining for burning, as long as some meat is left (whereas according to R. Eliezer, neither suet nor meat is necessary). In several other passages it is stated plainly that an offering is valid even if its suet has not been burned,[66] and that "burning does not hinder (me'akevet) atonement."[67] One tradition in the Tosefta goes so far as to refer to the burning of suet as "remainders of the commandment" (sheyare mitzvah)—a term that we saw in the previous chapter applied to the laying of hands by the owner.[68] This is of course not to say that there are no strict rules and stipulations regarding the time, place, and manner in which burning is to be performed (in the same way that there are strict rules regarding the way sacrificial eating is to be performed), but it is to say that the rabbis place the act of burning, the most manifest expression of the physical giving of the offering to the deity, at the margins of the sacrificial process. Burning, for the rabbis, is a way of deriving benefit from an offering whose ritual treatment is already complete, rather than the definitive component of the ritual treatment. This interpretive and legislative move is particularly remarkable in light of the predominance and centrality of burning in biblical literature.

What could have led the rabbis to dismiss what is arguably the pinnacle of the sacrificial ritual as mere "remainders of the commandment"? How can the production of fragrant smoke, which is explicitly said to be "pleasing to the Lord," be regarded as dispensable? The answer that immediately presents itself is that the rabbis strove to underplay the burning on the altar exactly *because* biblical texts describe it as sensually pleasing to God. Like various others ancient authors, the rabbis vehemently rejected the notion that the deity desires offerings for his physical pleasure or derives any concrete benefit from them.[69] While one cannot say that the rabbis generally shirked anthropomorphism,[70] they clearly thought that attributing to God an actual penchant for meat is ridiculous and demeaning, and attempted to explain the "pleasing" aspect of sacrifices in a different fashion. Thus, for example, the Tosefta quotes a series of verses from Psalm 50 that dismiss the idea that God actually benefits from human sacrificial gifts, and concludes that the only value in such gifts is the proclamation of faith they entail:

66. T. Zevaḥim 1.1.

67. Sifra tzav 8.12.4 (ed. Weiss 36b); cf. Sifre Deuteronomy 129 (ed. Finkelstein 186).

68. T. Zevaḥim 12.7.

69. On philosophical arguments against the view that the gods derive benefit from sacrifices, see Daniel C. Ullucci, *The Christian Rejection of Animal Sacrifice* (New York: Oxford University Press, 2012), 31–64. I shall expand on this point in the conclusion.

70. On anthropomorphism in rabbinic literature, see Yair Lorberbaum's helpful survey in "Anthropomorphisms in Early Rabbinic Literature: Maimonides and Modern Scholarship," in *Traditions of Maimonideanism,* ed. Carlos Fraenkel (Leiden: Brill, 2009), 313–53; see also Shamma Friedman, "Anthropomorphism and Its Eradication," in *Iconoclasm and Iconoclash: Struggle for Religious Identity,* ed. Willem J. van Asselt, Paul van Geest, Daniela Müller, and Theo Salemink (Leiden: Brill, 2007), 157–78.

"If I were hungry, I would not tell you, for the world and all that is in it is mine: Do I eat the flesh of bulls, or drink the blood of goats?" (Psalm 50:12)—Is there any hunger before Him? And moreover, [God] said: If there was hunger before me, would the lamb that you offer in the morning and the lamb that you offer in the afternoon be enough for me? And even if they were enough for me, would I place my nourishment in your hands? Rather I said to you (Psalm 50:13): "Offer to God a sacrifice of thanksgiving" (todah)—so that you would acknowledge me (tehe mode bi)—"and pay your vows to the Most High" (ibid).[71]

The Tosefta presents a creative wordplay on the word todah, which in the biblical verse refers to a sacrifice of thanksgiving, but the root of which more generally conveys acknowledgment or admission, and thereby asserts that sacrifices are essentially channels through which the offerer conveys his reverence toward God. Another midrashic passage makes a similar point using the same biblical verses, and concludes that God's pleasure derives not from the fragrance of meat but from the obedience of his people—"since I spoke and my will was done."[72] Particularly daring is one tradition according to which it is not God's will that is being fulfilled through sacrifice, but rather the offerer's will: simply put, it is human beings who wish to make sacrifices, and God allows them to do so but certainly does not desire it.[73]

It is quite possible, then, to explain the rabbis' trivialization of burning as part of their discomfort with the idea that the purpose of sacrifice is to give sensual pleasure to the deity. Yet it should be observed that in classifying burning on the altar alongside eating and not alongside the work of blood the anthropomorphic problem is in some ways exacerbated rather than resolved. Although the rabbis describe "the altar" rather than the deity as receiving the meat or the suet, they nonetheless position God (through his inanimate placeholder) among those who partake in the offering. One rabbinic tradition goes so far as to present the altar as God's "table," imploring that one should provide burnt offerings alongside well-being offerings "so that your table would not be full while your Maker's table is empty."[74] Instead of presenting burning as a manifestation of God's approval that allows for human consumption, the rabbis present it as an *equivalent* of human consumption. I thus contend that the rabbis' relegation of burning to a sacrificial aftermath reflects a rejection not simply of the anthropomorphic view of sacrifice, but of the broader view of sacrifice as a mode of communication with the deity.

Burning, as I mentioned above, is not only the channel through which offerings are delivered to the deity; it is also an emblematic signal that the deity received the

---

71. T. Menaḥot 7.9. Cf. Sifre zutta Numbers 28:2 (ed. Horovitz 322).

72. Sifre Numbers 107, 118 (ed. Horovitz 110, 140).

73. Sifre Numbers 143 (ed. Horovitz 191–92). See also Sagiv, "Studies in Early Rabbinic Hermeneutics," 120–30.

74. Mekhilta deRabbi Ishmael Mishpatim 20 (ed. Horovitz-Rabin 333).

offering. When the rabbis make the point that burning is not critical to the validity of sacrifice they effectively reject the notion that the deity is somehow present in the sacrificial scene and actively accepts the offering.[75] Furthermore, while rabbinic sacrifice, like biblical and other ancient sacrifice, is fundamentally a process in which something is transferred to the domain "of the High," for the rabbis the success of the process is determined by the actions of which the transferring itself consists, and emphatically not by the ultimate reception of the transferred object. The reception of the sacrificed object, whether by humans or by "the altar" is certainly a desirable outcome, but the process of transfer is complete and valid even if no one actually received the object, and even if at the end of the process there was no object left to receive. The marginalization of burning in rabbinic sacrificial legislation, then, can be seen as part of a broader rabbinic attempt to construct a noninteractive model of sacrifice, as I proposed in the previous chapter: in the same way that the rabbis place the addresser at the periphery of the sacrificial process, so they place the addressee at the periphery of the sacrificial process.[76]

But what do the rabbis propose instead of an interactive model? If neither the owner's intentions nor the deity's reception and approval matter, what *does* matter in sacrifice? In what follows I will show that the rabbis conceive of sacrifice not as a mode of interaction but as a mode of *transformation,* both of the offerer and of the offering. The rabbis, however, construe this transformation as a self-contained process whose value and validity do not depend on the products that the transformation generates but on the correctness of the transformation procedure itself. In other words, the rabbis shift the weight of sacrifice as a religious ritual from objects to actions.

BLOOD AND SACRIFICIAL TRANSFORMATION

So far I have discussed the rabbinic emphasis on the work of blood mainly in terms of what it excludes, namely, the initial delivery of the animal by the owner

75. The idea that the deity appears during the sacrificial process was prominent not only in ancient polytheistic religions, as shown by Frankfurter ("Egyptian Religion," 83–85), but can also be traced in the Hebrew Bible and in Second Temple literature. See Simeon Chavel, "A Kingdom of Priests and Its Earthen Altars in Exodus 19–24," *Vetus Testamentum* 65 (2015): 160–222; Michael Schneider, *The Appearance of the High Priest: Theophany, Apotheosis, and Binitarian Theology from the Priestly Tradition of the Second Temple Period through Ancient Jewish Mysticism* [Heb.] (Los Angeles: Cherub Press, 2012).

76. In his dissertation on reciprocity in biblical and Judean notions of sacrifice Aaron Glaim similarly claims that rabbinic texts do not present a reciprocal understanding of sacrifice. See Aaron Glaim, "Reciprocity, Sacrifice, and Salvation in Judean Religion at the Turn of the Era" (PhD diss., Brown University, 2014), 243–89. However, Glaim's argument is made mainly out of silence, as he (rightly) claims not to identify any reciprocal language in rabbinic texts. My aim is to show that the rabbis make a series of legislative and rhetorical choices specifically to *reject* a model of reciprocity, and a model of interaction more broadly.

on the one hand and the reception of the meat or suet by the deity or the priests on the other hand. To some extent this presentation of the work of blood in a negative fashion—that is, in terms of what it is not—is appropriate: as I have proposed, the rabbis seem to be distinctly interested in underplaying the importance of the "addresser" and the "addressee" in the sacrificial process so as to reject the notion that sacrifice is a channel of direct interaction with the deity. When both these components are bracketed, the work of blood is all that is left. However, rabbinic texts make it clear that the work of blood functions so prominently in the sacrificial process not only because of what it is not but also because of what it is: a mechanism of transformation. Sacrifice, the rabbis indicate, is a vehicle for changing something into something else, and this desired change can be attained only through blood and through no other sacrificial substance. The purpose of this section is to explore the "positive" dimension of the work of blood: to examine who or what undergoes change in the course of sacrifice through the vehicle of blood, and how the rabbis understood and conceptualized the workings and meaning of this change.

In approaching blood as a mechanism of transformation, that is, in focusing on what blood *does* within the sacrificial process, I am deliberately setting aside the question of what blood *signifies* for the rabbis. Blood is indisputably one of the most potent and charged semiotic objects across cultures, whose symbolic range is almost infinite. In the words of Caroline Bynum, blood is often described as capable of evoking "elemental opposites such as life and death, fertility and violence, nurture and blight."[77] I do not doubt that in the world of the rabbis, as in the world of their predecessors, blood had powerful connotations of kinship, covenant, initiation, pollution, birth, battle, and many other things, and that those connotations may have played consciously or unconsciously into their perceptions of sacrifice. Nevertheless, the rabbinic sacrificial corpus is completely devoid of allusions to the symbolic dimensions of blood. In fact, blood as such is of remarkably little interest for the rabbis: as Noam Zohar correctly observed, Tannaitic texts actually downplay the transformative power of blood as a substance and focus on the correctness of the actions pertaining to blood, that is, on its praxis. Their concern is with processes and procedures, with what is done *to* blood and what is done *through* blood.[78] Since my aim here is to reconstruct a theory of sacrifice through the very practice-oriented accounts in Tannaitic literature, I avoid projecting onto these accounts a set of cultural ciphers that may or may not underlie them, and instead I venture to understand the blood rituals of the rabbis as they are presented, namely, as procedures that enable change. The question of *why* blood ena-

---

77. Caroline Walker Bynum, *Wonderful Blood: Theology and Practice in Late Medieval Northern Germany and Beyond* (Philadelphia: University of Pennsylvania Press, 2007), 17.

78. Zohar, "Purification Offering," 21–77.

bles change is one that I cannot answer except by leaping into unfounded conjectures; but rabbinic texts do offer some answers to the questions of *what* change blood enables and how.

Rabbinic texts explain the transformative workings of blood in the sacrificial process through two different models. One model, which rests on the concept of atonement (*kapparah*), suggests that blood enables a transformation of the offerer; the other model, which rests on the concept of permission (*hatarah*), suggests that blood enables the transformation of the offering. The former is concerned with forgiveness of sins and ritual cleansing; the latter is concerned with the ability to consume sacrificial goods. Despite the fact that the rabbis do not straightforwardly integrate the two models, I contend that the two are not only not mutually exclusive, but also entirely congruent with one another. Moreover, I propose that it is exactly at the intersection of these two models that the key to the rabbinic theory of sacrifice lies.

Blood as agent of atonement

Blood features in some form or other in all the sacrifices that are introduced in Leviticus 1–5, but it is unquestionably most prominent and central in the type of sacrifice that constitutes a distinct priestly innovation—the sacrifice referred to as *ḥattat*, often translated as either "purification offering" or "sin offering."[79] This sacrifice, which involves careful sprinkling of blood on the curtain of the sanctuary (*parokhet*) and on the altar, is required of individuals or groups who committed transgressions, and also as part of purification rituals following bodily impurity. The designated purpose of this sacrifice is conveyed through the root *kpr,* whose exact meaning and etymology are disputed but which clearly connotes making a wrong right: reestablishing or reenabling persons, spaces, or objects that were previously disenabled within the sacred sphere. While the root *kpr* is perhaps most accurately translated as "to expiate" or "to effect purgation" in the biblical context,[80] here I utilize the more common translation "to atone," since this translation better reflects the rabbis' generic use of the verb *kipper* and the noun *kapparah* to denote any action taken to repair a previous misdeed or offense.

The description of the *ḥattat* offering in Leviticus 4 certainly highlights the role of blood more than descriptions of other sacrifices, but it does not necessarily suggest that it is strictly the blood that serves to attain atonement: rather, atonement is presented as the outcome of the completion of the sacrifice as a whole, including the burning component.[81] It is only in Leviticus 16, which describes the process of

---

79. On *ḥattat* as priestly innovation, see Watts, *Ritual and Rhetoric,* 79–85.

80. See Milgrom, *Leviticus 1–16,* 1079–84.

81. Cf. Leviticus 1:4, in which "atonement" is not associated with blood at all, but rather with the owner's laying of hands on the animal.

the purification of the tabernacle, that the function of atonement is associated exclusively with blood. However, the most overarching statement regarding the role of blood in the sacrificial process, which in all likelihood informs the rabbinic approach, appears in Leviticus 17:11, which provides a rationale for the prohibition on consumption of blood: "For the life of the flesh is in the blood; and I have given it to you for making atonement for your lives on the altar; for, as life, it is the blood that makes atonement." This verse, commonly attributed to the Holiness Code, goes one step beyond the priestly texts in proclaiming that blood *as such* effects atonement in any and every sacrificial context, not merely in rituals specifically designated for purification or purgation. Put differently, Leviticus 17:11 asserts that all forms of sacrifice are modes of atonement, and in all forms of sacrifice atonement is attained through blood.

Examination of Tannaitic texts (and even more so of Amoraic texts) reveals that the principle put forth in Leviticus 17:11 is pervasive in the rabbinic construal of sacrifice. Beyond the explicit statement that "there is no atonement except in blood,"[82] in several passages the correctness and completeness of the work of blood is assessed using the phrases "He [the priest] atoned" or "He did not atone," thus indicating that proper treatment of the blood is tantamount to the attainment of atonement. This pertains, to be sure, not only to contexts in which atonement is the proclaimed purpose of the ritual, such as the annual purgation of the sanctuary,[83] but to all sacrificial settings and to all types of offerings.[84] Indeed, the rabbis often speak of the function of all sacrifices, regardless of their type or designated purpose, in terms of atonement.[85] We already encountered two examples of this tendency in the previous chapter. First, when the Mishnah explains why it is legitimate to mortgage one's property if one failed to deliver an offering, it proclaims, "Even though no atonement can be attained for him (*'ein mitkaper lo*) until he comes to will it, they coerce him until he says 'I will it.'"[86] As we may recall, mortgaging applies exclusively to votive and freewill offerings, and not to purification and reparation offerings, whose manifest purpose is atonement: nonetheless, the rabbis assess the acceptability and efficacy of such offerings through the concept of atonement. Similarly, the statement that one who did not lay his hands on the animal's head "is considered as though he did not atone" indicates that offerings are evaluated across the board as modes of atonement.[87] As we will see in

---

82. T. Zevaḥim 8.17; Sifra nedavah 3.4.9–10 (ed. Finkelstein 34–35); BT Yoma 5a; BT Zevaḥim 6a; BT Menaḥot 93b.

83. For example, T. Kippurim 3.8; Sifra Aḥare mot 4.4.2 (ed. Weiss 81d).

84. M. Zevaḥim 4.1–2.

85. For example, T. Sheqalim 1.6; T. Baba Qamma 7.6; Mekhilta deRabbi Ishamel Yitro 10 (ed. Horovitz-Rabin 240).

86. M. 'Arakhin 5.6. Cf. Sifra nedavah 3.3.15 (ed. Finkelstein 31).

87. Sifra nedavah 3.4.10 (ed. Finkelstein 35). Cf. M. Nega'im 14.4.

chapter 4, even the Passover offering is presented in rabbinic texts as entailing a component of atonement, and its blood is said to be tossed "for the sake" of each individual participant.[88]

If the rabbis identify the work of blood as the vehicle through which atonement is attained, and if they conceive of the purpose of all sacrifices primarily and perhaps exclusively as the attainment of atonement for the offerer(s), it is rather unsurprising that all sacrificial elements except for the work of blood are rendered expandable by the rabbis. Since neither burning nor eating nor hand laying "hinder[s] the atonement,"[89] which depends only on the correct and complete treatment of blood, we see why these elements can be relegated, in the rabbinic framework, to the status of "remainders of the commandment."

The rabbis' tendency to reconfigure all sacrifice in terms of atonement, and correspondingly the entirety of the sacrificial procedure in terms of the work of blood, are particularly noteworthy in light of a parallel phenomenon in a new sacrificial tradition that was forming, approximately at the same period as rabbinic legislation, in the works of early Christian writers. For the disciples of Jesus, who lived in a world in which sacrifice was a dominant practice and a fundamental religious category, sacrifice was the most readily available epistemological framework through which to interpret their Lord's death. In the apt words of George Heyman, "If Jesus' death was predicted by the Scriptures, then his death must be considered part of a greater divine plan. That a person's death could be considered 'useful' or 'effective' was one of the major rationales that allowed it to be understood as a 'sacrifice.'"[90] Colored by the specific circumstances of Jesus's violent death, the very concept of sacrifice in early Christian writings came to be heavily centered on blood,[91] and was gradually redefined predominantly in terms of atonement.

In the letters of Paul, Jesus's presentation as sacrifice operates primarily along the lines of a communion—that is, a sacrificial meal (*koinōnia*) in which members of a community partake—a metaphor that still places emphasis on aspects of consumption rather than on the efficacy of blood per se.[92] Paul's reference to Jesus as the Passover offering (*to pascha hēmōn*) in 1 Corinthians 5:7–8 invokes a clear connotation of a shared feast: "For our paschal lamb, Christ, has been sacrificed. Therefore, let us keep our feast (*eortazōmen*)." The verb *eortazō* strongly connotes

---

88. For example, T. Pisḥa 7.7–13.

89. Sifra tzav 8.12.4 (ed. Weiss 36b); cf. Sifre Deuteronomy 129 (ed. Finkelstein 186).

90. George Heyman, *The Power of Sacrifice: Roman and Christian Discourses in Conflict* (Washington, DC: Catholic University of America Press, 2007), 122–23.

91. One notable exception is the depiction of Jesus as *pharmakon* or scapegoat. See Jennifer K. Berenson Maclean, "Barabbas, the Scapegoat Ritual, and the Development of the Passion Narrative," *Harvard Theological Review* 100, no. 3 (2007): 309–34.

92. 1 Corinthians 10:16–20. See Willis, *Idol Meat in Corinth*, 184–86; Heyman, *The Power of Sacrifice*, 111–17.

the communal sharing of food and drink on festive occasions,[93] and more specifically a sacrificial banquet, in which meat is shared after a portion of the animal has been offered to the deity.[94] When Paul refers specifically to Jesus's blood, he usually speaks of it as a sealer of a covenant rather than as a sacrificial substance. Thus, for example, in 1 Corinthians 11:25: "In the same way he took the cup, after supper, saying, 'This cup is the new covenant (*diathēkē*) in my blood.'" Jesus's blood is identically regarded as "the blood of the new covenant" in the Synoptic Gospels,[95] thereby paralleling the blood of the "old covenant"—that is, the blood that recurrently appears in Hebrew Bible covenant narratives, from Genesis 15 through Exodus 24, as ratifying the mutual commitment between God and Israel. The notion that Jesus's blood is the means through which the community of his followers was established is reiterated in Acts 20:28: "Be shepherds of the church of God, which he acquired (*periepoiēsato*) with his own blood."

In the Last Supper account in the Gospel of Matthew, however, we find an additional dimension to the notion of Jesus's blood as "blood of the covenant": it is said to be "poured out for many *for the forgiveness of sins*."[96] The association of Jesus's blood with the function of atonement casts Jesus's sacrifice specifically as *ḥattat* (purification/sin offering), the blood of which effects ritual cleansing—of the sanctuary and of the offerer.[97] This idea can be traced, although not with certainty, already in 2 Corinthians 5:21: "He made him who knew no sin to be sin for us (*hamartian huper hēmōn*)." Since the word *hamartia* is used in the Septuagint both to denote sin (*ḥet*) and to denote the purification offering that is made on account of sin (*ḥattat*), it is quite possible to read this verse as "he made him who knew no sin into a *sin offering*."[98] The notion that it is specifically Jesus's blood that effects atonement is echoed in Romans 3:25, in which Jesus is described as "*hilasterion* through his blood." The word *hilasterion* is regularly used in the Septuagint to denote the *kapporet*, the cover of the Ark of the Covenant on which blood is sprin-

---

93. See, for example, LXX to 1 Samuel 30:16, "eating and drinking and feasting" (*esthiontes kai pinontes kai eortazontes*).

94. For example, Psalm 42:4: "How I used to go with the crowd, and led them to the house of God, with the voice of joy and praise, a multitude keeping a holy day" (*hogeg*, LXX: *eortazontos*).

95. Matthew 28:26; Mark 14:24; Luke 22:20. Contrast this with John 6:53–55, in which the blood and flesh are compared with manna and regarded as a substance of life.

96. Matthew 28:26.

97. Here I agree with Noam Zohar ("Purification and Repentance") in his contention with Milgrom, who claims that purification offerings pertain to the sanctuary alone and not to the persons who offer them.

98. Cf. Romans 8.3. This understanding of Jesus's death as him "turning" into a purification offering is probably inspired by the Septuagint to Isaiah 53:10, "You make his life [an offering for] sin (*tasim 'asham nafsho*)": *dōte peri hamartias hē psuchē humōn*. Consider, however, the vehement objections to tracing an atonement theology in the letters of Paul raised by Bradley H. McLean, "The Absence of Atoning Sacrifice in Paul's Soteriology," *New Testament Studies* 38, no. 4 (1992): 531–53.

kled during the purification rituals of the Day of Atonement. Jesus is thus depicted here as a place of atonement rather than as an offering of atonement, but his blood is clearly assigned an atoning function.[99]

Jesus's blood becomes a highly prominent motif in later books of the New Testament, and appears time and again as the transformative substance that brought about (and will eventually bring again) a new era for humankind. In the Johannine books, which develop the notion of Jesus as "the lamb of God who takes away the sin of the world,"[100] Jesus's blood is described as purifying and cleansing,[101] but also as empowering and as establishing a new triumphant community;[102] in other texts, Jesus's blood is referred to as sanctifying,[103] as bringing peace,[104] and as redeeming.[105] No New Testament text, however, positions blood at the very center of its theological claim to the same extent as the Letter to the Hebrews.[106] Whereas in other texts references to Jesus's blood lend themselves, at least in principle, to a symbolic reading (that is, as referring more generally to Jesus's life rather than to his actual physical blood[107]), the Letter to the Hebrews leaves very little room for doubt that Jesus's blood *as such* functioned exactly like the blood of sacrificial animals, and thereby became the ultimate sacrifice to end all sacrifices.[108]

The Letter to the Hebrews, which creates an elaborate sacrificial paradigm in which Jesus is both the high priest and the sacrificial victim, builds heavily on the imagery of the Day of Atonement ritual as described in Leviticus 16.[109] This particular sacrificial ritual, in which the high priest goes into the inner sanctum, and which cannot be carried out "without blood," is contrasted in Hebrews 9:6–11 with mundane sacrifices and gifts, which "deal only with food and drink and various lustrations."[110] For this author, the only substance that makes sacrifice—any sacrifice—efficacious is blood, and therefore Jesus's ultimate entry into the Holy of

99. See Daniel Stökl Ben Ezra, *The Impact of Yom Kippur on Early Christianity* (Tübingen: Mohr Siebeck, 2003), 197–203; Heyman, *The Power of Sacrifice*, 120–22.

100. John 1:29.

101. 1 John 1:7; Revelation 1:5, 7:14.

102. Revelation 5:9, 12:11.

103. 1 Peter 1:19.

104. Colossians 1:20.

105. Ephesians 1:7.

106. For general background on the letter, its provenance, its name, and its dating, see Harold W. Attridge, *Hebrews: A Commentary on the Epistle to the Hebrews* (Minneapolis: Augsburg Press, 1989), 1–26.

107. As argued by McLean, "The Absence of Atoning Sacrifice."

108. According to Dunnill, the author's main purpose is to unite all the different kinds of sacrificial interactions with the deity into a single model. See Dunnill, *Covenant and Sacrifice in the Letter to the Hebrews*, 239–56.

109. See Stökl Ben Ezra, *The Impact of Yom Kippur*, 180–97.

110. Hebrews 9:10.

Holies, "not with the blood of goats and calves, but with his own blood,"[111] attains eternal redemption. Later in the same chapter, the author accounts in detail why blood is crucial not only for atonement and purification but also for the formation of a covenant (both of which comprise, in his view, the redemption enabled through Jesus's death), and concludes: "Indeed, under the law almost everything is purified with blood, and without the shedding of blood there is no forgiveness of sins."[112] For our purposes, it is important to note that the components of burning, smoke, and consumption of meat are entirely absent from Hebrews' portrayal of sacrifice: in fact, toward the end of the letter the author insists that what makes Jesus's sacrifice the ultimate one is that there is no edible component to it.[113] "Real" sacrifice is configured in this text as consisting of blood and blood alone.

The emphasis on Jesus's blood as a transformative substance that sanctifies, purifies, and atones for those who have faith in him, and accordingly as the only form of "true" efficacious sacrifice, is reiterated and developed in various texts from the second century. Both in the *Epistle of Barnabas* and in Justin's *Dialogue with Trypho* this idea is invoked specifically to dismiss the Israelite/Jewish sacrificial cult (which both authors explicitly mention to have ceased). The *Epistle of Barnabas* closely echoes Hebrews when stating, "For it was for this reason that the Lord endured to deliver up his flesh to corruption, that we should be sanctified by the remission of sin, that is, by his sprinkled blood."[114] Similarly, Justin writes, "[We] no longer were purified by the blood of goats and of sheep, or by the ashes of an heifer, or by the offerings of fine flour, but by faith through the blood of Christ,"[115] and he dismisses the blood of the old covenant—that of circumcision— as obsolete now that "the blood of salvation" has been shed.[116]

What are we to make of the fact that around the same time two communities that inherited biblical tropes and concepts of sacrifice reconfigured the very idea of this ritual in comparable ways, largely dismissing—unlike their Jewish predecessors or their Greek and Roman contemporaries—all elements except for blood and all associations except for atonement? It is tempting to imagine a direct connection between the blood discourse of early Christian texts and the blood discourse of the rabbinic sacrificial corpus: to suggest that the rabbis developed their emphasis on atonement through correct blood praxis as a response to the notion of the ultimate efficacy of Jesus's blood, or to suggest that the author of Hebrews and his readership were familiar with some protorabbinic sacrificial legislation

111. Hebrews 9:12.
112. Hebrews 9:22. See Biale, *Blood and Belief,* 54–57.
113. Hebrews 13:10–12.
114. Barnabas 5:1, in Kirsopp Lake, *The Apostolic Fathers,* vol. 1 (London: Heinemann, 1912), 355.
115. *Dialogue with Trypho,* 13, in Alexander Roberts, James Donaldson, and Arthur Cleveland Coxe, eds., *Ante-Nicene Fathers,* vol. 1 (New York: Scribner Books, 1903), 200.
116. *Dialogue with Trypho,* 24 (*Ante-Nicene Fathers,* 1:206).

that signaled the work of blood as the only consequential part of the ritual. Such direct connection, however, is highly unlikely. What is more likely is that rabbinic and early Christian writings reflect broader theological and soteriological approaches that converged around the theme of sacrifice. On a theological level, both Jewish and Christian authors (like Greek and Roman philosophers) had strong reservations regarding the reciprocal model of sacrifice, and they distanced sacrifice from "meat and smoke" to assert the difference between their sacrifice and the sacrifice practiced by "idol worshippers."[117] On a soteriological level, Jews and Christians of the first centuries both shared, as Gary Anderson has convincingly shown, acute awareness of sin and of the ongoing corrupt state of humankind, and continuously attempted to devise active ways to overcome it.[118] In utilizing the biblical framework of purification/sin offering to redefine sacrifice as a whole, thereby centering sacrifice almost entirely on blood and not on edible goods, both the rabbis and early Christian authors found ways to maintain the idea of sacrifice while reinventing it to serve their own interpretive needs.[119]

The rabbinic emphasis on blood as a vehicle of atonement and on atonement as the ultimate purpose of all forms of sacrifice, and the resonance between the rabbinic reconfiguration of sacrifice and early Christian reconfigurations of sacrifice, help us understand more fully what motivated the rabbis to place blood at the center of their sacrificial paradigm and to push all other elements to the margins. It was not only their aversion to the notion that the deity is appeased or compelled by edible substances, but also their view of the eradication of sin as the most urgent task of the individual and the collective alike. Nevertheless, while we may now have an answer to the question of what function blood serves in the rabbinic view of sacrifice and why this function is so important, we have yet to see *how* blood serves this function.

Above I argued that for the rabbis, sacrifice is not a mode of interaction with the deity, and that their legislation amounts to a construction of sacrifice as a process without giver and without receiver. But if blood stands at the center of the

117. See Ullucci, *The Christian Rejection of Animal Sacrifice*; and my discussion in the conclusion.

118. Gary A. Anderson, *Sin: A History* (New Haven: Yale University Press, 2009). See also, from a different perspective, Ishay Rosen-Zvi, *Demonic Desires: "Yetzer Hara" and the Problem of Evil in Late Antiquity* (Philadelphia: University of Pennsylvania Press, 2011).

119. As also pointed out by Biale, *Blood and Belief*, 44–80; and by Ra'anan Boustan and Annette Yoshiko Reed, "Introduction: Blood and the Boundaries of Jewish and Christian Identities in Late Antiquity," *Henoch* 30, no. 2 (2008): 7–20. To this we may add the fact that in ancient mystery cults, particularly in the cult of Mithras and of Magna Mater, blood played a key role in the initiation and sanctification of the participants: for denizens of the eastern Mediterranean region, in which these cults were widely popular, this may have been another influential factor in the reconfiguration of blood as the center and essence of sacrifice. See Mary Beard, John North, and Simon F. R. Price, *Religions of Rome*, vol. 2 (Cambridge: Cambridge University Press, 1998), 160–62.

sacrificial process, and if blood is what allows for the transformation of the offerer (namely, the attainment of atonement), is blood itself not a mode of interaction? In other words, is blood not something that is *given* to the deity and thereby, when received, establishes communication between the offerer and God? How does blood effect atonement, in the rabbis' view, if not as a substance that is somehow desirable or efficacious in its own right? To address these questions, let us now turn to understand the status of blood compared to other sacrificial substances.

Is blood an offering?

Biblical texts are notably vague on the question of whether blood is an offering in itself, that is, whether it is to be counted among the things that the deity receives through the sacrificial transaction. The fact that blood is always tossed on the altar does suggest that blood is in some way transferred to the deity,[120] but as Gilders has pointed out, it is possible to interpret the placement of blood on the altar not as an act of giving but as an act of returning to God something that belongs to him in the first place. Especially if one upholds the notion expressed in Leviticus 17:11 that blood is the force of life, then blood is understood in the priestly framework as the divine component of the animal, which is not offered by human beings but rather *claimed back* at the time of sacrifice.[121] However, since blood functions in biblical texts also as a ritual detergent, as a sealer of covenants, and as a tool of sanctification, the possibilities of interpretation for the application of blood on the altar are many, and are not necessarily consistent across different biblical texts.

The biblical ambiguity on whether blood is part of the sacrificial transaction or is wholly separate from it persists in rabbinic texts. On the one hand, the tossing of blood on the altar is classified alongside burning and eating as an element of the sacrificial process that can be affected by wrongful intentions, thus indicating that the tossing of blood is part of the "distribution" stage.[122] On the other hand, unlike meat and suet, blood is not subject to *piggul,* that is, to disqualification through wrongful intentions.[123] When the Mishnah describes the distribution of "goods" among the different beneficiaries it does not mention blood among those goods, and includes only meat, suet, and hide;[124] but the Tosefta and the Sifra do classify blood alongside suet as a portion that is allocated to the altar: "A burnt offering is

120. See McClymond, *Beyond Sacred Violence,* 111–21, who classifies blood as "liquid offering"; for a more text-based discussion, see Meshel, "The Form and Function of Biblical Blood Ritual."
121. Gilders, *Blood Ritual,* 70–78.
122. M. Zevaḥim 2.2; T. Zevaḥim 3.8.
123. M. Zevaḥim 4.3.
124. M. Zevaḥim 4.4. However, M. Zevaḥim 10.3 refers to both blood and suet as "holies of holies" (*qodshe qodashim*). This is a highly irregular usage of the term "holies of holies," which generally refers to types of offerings rather than to animal parts, and in this respect this passage is aberrant not only within the Mishnah but more widely in rabbinic literature.

entirely for the High, and its hide for the priests. Holies of holies [that is, purification and reparation offerings]—the blood and the suet are for the altar, and the meat and the hide for the priests. Light Holies—the blood and the suet are for the altar, and the meat and the hide for the owners."[125] It is thus difficult to identify an unequivocal rabbinic position on whether blood is part of the offering or functions separately from other sacrificial substances, and it seems that there was ambivalence or disagreement among the rabbis on this issue.

We do have a strong indication, however, that even rabbis who classified blood alongside other sacrificial substances identified a qualitative difference between blood on the one hand and edible and burnable substances on the other hand, and maintained that blood does not function like other "goods" that are distributed among the beneficiaries. An anonymous ruling in tractate Ḥullin of the Mishnah asserts that unlike all other sacrificial substances (meat, suet, wine, grain, oil, incense, and even hides) the category of me'ilah, "misuse of sacred items," does not apply to blood.[126] That is to say, if one used sacrificial blood to fertilize one's garden, for example, he would not be required to pay a fine, nor would he be subject to punishment in the same way that he would be if he used sacrificial meat, suet, or wine. The fact that blood is used in the process of sacrifice, then, does not confer a status of sanctity upon it. A ruling in tractate Me'ilah, attributed to R. Shimon,[127] does make the category of "misuse" applicable to blood, but specifies that blood is an anomaly within the sacrificial system: unlike all other substances, blood is "treated leniently at the beginning and stringently at the end."[128] Curiously, blood is not subject to me'ilah before it is tossed on the altar, but only after it has been tossed and has trickled through the hollow pipes underneath the altar down to the Qidron Valley—only at that point are those who misuse it subject to punishment and fine.[129] This position suggests that blood does not bear any sanctity by virtue of being part of the sacrificial animal, or by virtue of being designated for the altar: rather, it gains sanctity only as a result of the sacrificial process, after it has been used to fill a particular function in the procedure.[130]

Examination of parallel Tosefta passages reveals that the two traditions in the Mishnah reflect two opposing Tannaitic positions on the status of blood within the

---

125. T. Zevaḥim 11.4, 7; cf. Sifra nedavah 13.16.2 (ed. Finkelstein 99). Another possible evidence of the view of blood as part of the offering is a homily that reads the word "my offering" (qorbani) in Numbers 28:2 as referring to blood; see Sifre Numbers 142 and Sifre zutta Numbers 28:2 (ed. Horovitz 188, 322). However, since the homilist here attempts to provide a sacrificial referent for every word in the verse, it is not certain how literally one should take this reading.

126. M. Ḥullin 8.6; cf. M. Me'ilah 1–2.

127. In the printed editions of the Mishnah: R. Ishmael.

128. M. Me'ilah 3.3.

129. Also M. Yoma 5.6.; cf. M. Middot 3.2.

130. I thank Yair Furstenberg for this insight.

sacrificial system. According to the Tosefta, the view that blood is subject to *me'ilah* after it has been tossed is associated with R. Meir and R. Shimon, whereas for the Sages (*hakhamim*) this category is not applicable to blood at all.[131] In stating that one cannot misuse blood the way one misuses other sacrificial substances, the Sages in the Tosefta (and the anonymous Mishnah) emphatically make the point that blood is not a sacred substance and is therefore not part of what is distributed or "given" to the deity. However, even the view according to which one does incur punishment for misusing blood makes the same point by turning the ordinary mechanism of *me'ilah* on its head: as a rule, one is guilty of *me'ilah* if one uses a sacred item before its sacral treatment is complete.[132] In saying that this category applies to blood only after it was ritually used, those who uphold this position effectively say that the sanctity of blood is not inherent, but acquired through the procedure.

The view that sacrificial blood is not inherently sacred resonates in a Tosefta tradition regarding the consumption of blood. According to R. Yehudah, if a person consumes the blood of an animal dedicated as a sacrificial offering, he is liable twice: once for consuming blood and once for illicitly consuming a sacred substance. The Sages, in contrast, rule that this person is liable only for the consumption of blood (as he would be if he consumed the blood of a nonconsecrated animal). However, if one consumes the suet of a consecrated animal, the Sages too maintain that he is liable both for eating suet and for eating a sacred substance.[133] The position of the Sages here is commensurate with the position of the Sages regarding *me'ilah*: blood, they insist, is not equivalent to other parts of the offering and cannot be seen as an offering to God in itself. R. Yehudah's contesting position, which is dismissed in the Tosefta and not even mentioned in the Mishnah, attests that the Sages' opinion was not the only view on the matter, but it is certainly the one that prevailed in the redacted texts.

We may conclude, then, that while the rabbis (or some of them) acknowledged the correspondence between blood and other sacrificial substances in general, and blood and suet in particular, they made a point of establishing a categorical difference between blood and all other substances nonetheless. Both blood and suet are placed on the altar, but whereas suet *belongs* to the altar and those who misuse it are actively taking something that is not their own, blood does not seem to belong to anyone, at least not initially: it is part of the sacrificial transaction, but it is not sacrificial property as such. Even according to the view that blood ultimately becomes the property of the temple such that it is possible to misuse it, the appropriation of blood and the conferral of a sacred status upon it occur only after the

131. T. Kippurim 3.2; T. Zevahim 6.9; T. Me'ilah 1.16.
132. M. Me'ilah 2.1–9.
133. T. Hullin 7.11–12.

blood plays its part in the sacrificial process. Underlying these rulings, I propose, is the notion that blood is not desirable or consequential in the sacrificial setting in and of itself, but rather its value lies in the procedural function that it fills.

What, then, is the procedural function that blood fills? Above we saw that the rabbis defined blood as the vehicle of atonement, but in what capacity does it serve to attain atonement? If the rabbis reject the idea that blood is of value in and of itself, how does the placement of blood on the altar allow the transformation of the sinful or impure state of the offerer? While the rabbis do not present a direct answer to the second and third questions, they do put forth an innovative answer to the first question: they maintain that blood functions as *permitter,* that is, as the facilitator that allows the distribution of all other substances among the participants. Whereas the concept of atonement focuses on the transformation of the offerer through the sacrificial process, the concept of permission focuses on the offering and on the transformation of its constituent parts from a state of unusability to a state of usability. Let me first lay out the model of "permission" in greater detail, and then attempt to reconcile it with the model of atonement.

Blood as "permitter"

In the previous chapter I discussed the category of *piggul,* which the rabbis interpret as an offering made with the thought of consumption (by fire or by persons) after the designated time. After introducing this principle, the Mishnah makes the point that thought regarding inappropriate time suffices to generate *piggul* (and thereby a punishment of extirpation) only if in every other respect the work of blood was performed correctly. The phrase used to denote the correct treatment of blood is "the permitter was brought forth according to its ordinance" (*qarav ha-matir ke-mitzvato*).[134] As this repeated phrase indicates, the function of blood within the sacrificial process is one of "permitting," or perhaps more literally "unbinding": it makes substances previously prohibited for use legitimate for use, either by human beings or by the altar. The following passage exemplifies this idea clearly:

> The blood of a burnt offering permits (*matir*) its meat for the altar and its hide for the priests. The blood of a burnt bird offering permits its meat for the altar. The blood of a bird purification offering permits its meat for the priests. The blood of incinerated bulls and incinerated goats permits their suet to be offered.[135]

As this passage and others similar to it explain, the application of sacrificial blood to the altar removes the invisible fence from around the sanctified animal's parts and allows them to be distributed between the different beneficiaries. This invisible fence is the restriction placed upon the sacrificial animal and its respective

---

134. M. Zevaḥim 2.3–4, 6.7; cf. T. Zevaḥim 2.4–8, 5.1–2, 7.13–15.
135. M. Zevaḥim 2.4.

parts once it was consecrated, whether by birth (in the case of tithes and first-borns), by a vow, or by being brought into the temple. To be clear, we must not understand the procedure of "permitting" or "unbinding" as tantamount to desac-ralization. Even after the blood has been tossed, the substances in question are still considered sacred, and there are clear restrictions as to who may use them and how. Some of the substances also remain subject to me'ilah (that is, warrant a fine and punishment if they are misused) even after the tossing of blood, depending on the type of offering.[136] But even use within the sacred realm is considered in rab-binic legislation as requiring a transformation of the sacred substances, which is here effected by blood.

Sacrifice, then, is constructed by the rabbis as a self-contained and self-referring process: it consists of an initial transformation into unusability and then a trans-formation back into usability, albeit a modified and restricted manner of usability. This mechanism of dual transformation is expressed nicely in a homily in the Sifra on the treatment of grain offerings (which, as I will show in the next section, oper-ate according to the same principle as animal offerings). According to Leviticus 6:15–16, after a handful of the grain offering is burned on the altar the priests may consume the rest of the offering, but their portion must remain unleavened (mat-zot te'akhel). The homilist vocalizes the word matzot, "unleavened," as mitzvot, "ordinances," and uses this reading to explain the paradigm of sacrifice as effec-tively a process of re-permitting: "Since the [offering] was permitted [for con-sumption] and was then prohibited and then became permitted again, is it possi-ble that it should return to its [initial state of] permissibility (le-heterah ha-rishon)?—Scripture tells you 'it shall be eaten [according to the] ordinance.'"[137] This homily and more broadly the rabbinic concept of "permitter" help us define the ritual function of each of the three stages of the sacrificial process that I identi-fied above. The delivery stage is set in motion once the animal is consecrated and thereby forbidden for use, and continues until the animal is slaughtered; the trans-formation stage is the process through which the prohibition resulting from con-secration is removed; and the distribution stage ensues as a result of the successful completion of the transformation stage such that the animal in its new form is again permitted, but can be used only "according to the ordinance."

The rabbinic presentation of sacrifice as a self-contained process of transition from usability to unusability to usability again is not striking in itself. In a sense, one could say that this fundamental paradigm can be identified almost universally as the structure of most sacrificial processes, as observed by Henri Hubert and Marcel Mauss.[138] What I do find remarkable about this rabbinic construction of

---

136. M. Me'ilah 2.1–9.
137. Sifra tzav 2.2.9 (ed. Weiss 30d).
138. Hubert and Mauss, Sacrifice, 19–49.

sacrifice, however, is the notion that the deity himself depends on the process of "permitting" in order to consume his share. One who reads the sacrificial instructions in the book of Leviticus would expect that blood and suet would function together as "permitters," and that the allocation of God's share to the altar would be cast as what allows for consecutive consumption by humans. The notion that humans may eat or drink only after giving to the deities their due portions is pervasive in various cultures and underlies common customs like the offering of first-fruits or first portion of the new crops.[139] But the rabbis emphasize that it is not the offering to God that renders the sacrificial goods permitted: rather it is specifically the work of blood that makes sacrificial goods permitted, and not only for humans—but also for God himself! The placement of sacrificial parts on the altar, in this scheme, is not the epitome of the process of consecration, as Hubert and Mauss would describe it,[140] but rather already an indication that the prohibition deriving from consecration has been lifted.

For the rabbis, then, "permission" is not tantamount to fair and appropriate distribution, but rather denotes undoing an existing prohibition so that distribution can begin in the first place. Although the rabbis never explain why blood in particular fills this function, we may suggest a plausible biblical foundation for this view: the strict prohibition against consumption of blood, and the insistence that since blood is prohibited for human beings it must be placed on the altar, powerfully present the placement of blood on the altar as what renders the consumption of the meat legitimate.[141] It is thus not surprising that the rabbis identify the work of blood as prerequisite to the permissibility of consumption more broadly, whether by humans or by fire: blood must be appropriately and carefully put away before any "eating" can take place.

Let us note, however, that whereas the model of permission suggests that the work of blood is a necessary condition for proceeding with the sacrificial process, the model of atonement suggests that the work of blood is the only part of the sacrificial process that matters, and presents blood as the only substance that actually needs to be present for the sacrifice to be valid. The model of permission construes sacrifice as a self-contained process, defined only from within itself (the usable becomes unusable and then usable again); the model of atonement construes sacrifice as a channel through which human beings can overcome

139. This is most evident in the ritual offering of the first crop of grain ('omer) and the firstfruits (bikkurim) in Leviticus 23:12–18, but also in the law regarding fourth-year fruits (Leviticus 19:23–25) and firstborn animals and humans (Exodus 13:11–13). For similar practices in the Greek and Roman world, see Theodora Suk Fong Jim, *Sharing with the Gods: Aparchai and Dekatai in Ancient Greece* (New York: Oxford University Press, 2014); John Scheid, "Roman Animal Sacrifice and the System of Being," in Faraone and Naiden, *Greek and Roman Animal Sacrifice*, 84–98.

140. Hubert and Mauss, *Sacrifice*, 26–28.

141. Leviticus 17:10–15; Deuteronomy 12:22–27.

transgression, sin, and iniquity. Are these two models completely incongruent? Do they represent two opposing and conflicting approaches to sacrifice, or can they be reconciled? An interesting tradition in the Palestinian Talmud does identify these models as conflicting, and associates each model with a different disciple of R. Yoḥanan. R. Abahu in the name of R. Yoḥanan defines blood as "atonement for the soul (*kapparat nefesh*) alone," whereas R. Ḥiyya in the name of R. Yoḥanan defines it as "extirpation for the soul (*karet nefesh*) alone."[142] The former maintains that blood is crucial for transformation of the offerer; the latter maintains that blood is crucial only insofar as it hinders consumption, as consumption of blood warrants extirpation.

Nevertheless, I would like to propose that at least in the Tannaitic view, these two models are entirely consistent with each other, because *permission and atonement are one and the same* for the rabbis. Put differently, in the rabbinic sacrificial vision atonement is attained through the correct procedure for putting away blood: it is not a function of the blood itself, which is of no inherent sanctity, but of the actions and intentions that are applied to it as it is handled. This emphasis on actions rather than on substances, and the definition of religious rehabilitation and transformation in terms of performance "according to the ordinance," are key for understanding the rabbinic theory of sacrifice. Before delving further into this idea, it is necessary to complete the picture presented so far with a brief discussion of ostensibly "bloodless" sacrifices, that is, grain offerings.

The paradigm of blood in grain offerings

My discussion of the treatment of blood as front and center in the rabbinic sacrificial process may have generated the impression that the only type of sacrifice that the rabbis consider in their legislative and interpretive works is animal sacrifice. This is certainly not the case: an entire mishnaic tractate by the name of Menaḥot (offerings) is dedicated to a whole host of vegetable and grain offerings mentioned in the Priestly Code, including semolina offerings, the weekly showbread, wine and oil offerings, the offering of the first grain (*'omer*), and others. However, even a cursory look at tractate Menaḥot suffices to show that large parts of this tractate are simply a replication of tractate Zevaḥim, the tractate dedicated to animal offerings, with the names of specific offerings and components of offerings replaced to fit the new context.[143] The wording and order of much of the two tractates (both in the Mishnah and in the Tosefta) are almost identical, and more importantly, the operational principles that guide the two tractates are identical: the rabbis apply all

142. PT Yoma 5.8, 43a.
143. See, for example, the following parallels: M. Zevaḥim 1.1 and Menaḥot 1.1; M. Zevaḥim 2.1 and Menaḥot 1.2; M. Zevaḥim 2.2–3 and Menaḥot 2.3; M. Zevaḥim 2.4–5 and Menaḥot 1.3–4; M. Zevaḥim 3.3 and Menaḥot 3.1.

the categories that pertain to animal offerings to grain offerings (and to some extent also to wine and oil offerings[144]). Thus, the sacrificial process pertaining to grain offerings can be divided into three stages, equivalent to the three stages pertaining to animal offerings: (1) preparation and delivery of the portion of grain by the owner; (2) manipulation of a "handful" (*qometz*) of the offering designated to be burned on the altar by the priest, and (3) consumption of the remaining offering by the priests.[145] As in the case of animal offerings, it is the second stage that the rabbis deem to be the most—and in effect, the only—consequential part of the ritual.

The second stage of the sacrificial process for grain offerings is the removal of a handful of semolina over which oil was poured (as described in Leviticus 2:1–10) and its burning on the altar. In the Mishnah, this stage is subdivided into four constitutive activities, clearly patterned after the fourfold work of blood: removal of the handful from the rest of the offering, placement of the handful in a vessel, walking the handful to the altar, and burning it on the altar.[146] The introduction of the second and third "works" here is so artificial that it leaves no doubt that the paradigm of animal offerings was haphazardly copied to the context of grain offerings: the biblical description makes it very clear that the portion removed from the offering is contained in the priest's hand and not in a vessel, and there is clearly no need to "walk" the handful anywhere, since the removal of the handful is explicitly said to be performed by the altar.[147] Modeled after the work of blood in animal offerings, the series of actions pertaining to the handful in grain offerings is discussed as capable of disqualifying the offering if performed with wrongful intentions. Thus, a grain offering whose handful was removed (or "received" or "walked" or burned) with the thought of consuming the offering in an unlawful time or place is disqualified.[148] Like blood in animal offerings, the handful in grain offerings is referred to as "permitter" (*matir*), and the correct treatment of the handful is regarded as "bringing forth the permitter according to its ordinance" (*qarav ha-matir ke-mitzvato*).[149] Perhaps the most manifest example of the complete analogy between animal offerings and grain offerings in rabbinic sources is the appearance

144. However, wine and oil offerings are fundamentally different from grain offerings insofar as they normally accompany other (grain or animal) offerings and do not stand alone; accordingly they are subordinate to the laws governing the offering they are complementing.

145. Note that offerings brought by priests are burned whole on the altar and are not consumed by the priests at all; the paradigm of three stages and "permitting" thus cannot be applied to them, which attests to the limitation of the blood paradigm's application to grain offerings.

146. M. Menaḥot 1.4.

147. Leviticus 2:8.

148. M. Menaḥot 1.1–2.1. Some offerings are disqualified also if their handful was removed when the offering was designated mistakenly (not for "its sake").

149. M. Menaḥot 1.3–4.

of R. Eliezer and R. Yehoshua's controversy regarding meat and blood in the context of grain offerings:

R. Eliezer says: If there is no blood, there is no meat; but even though there is no meat, there is blood.

R. Yehoshua says: If there is no blood, there is no meat, and if there is no meat, there is no blood.[150]

R. Yose said: I see [more merit in] the words of R. Eliezer, who said: If there is no handful (*qometz*), there are no remainders (*shirayim*), but even though there are no remainders, there is a handful— than in the words of R. Yehoshua, who said: If there is no handful, there are no remainders, and if there are no remainders, there is no handful.[151]

As in the case of meat and blood, R. Eliezer maintains that as long as the "permitter" is present the consumable substance (here the "remainders" eaten by the priests) is dispensable, whereas R. Yehoshua maintains that the two are mutually dependent. While the general question of relations between sacrificial components is certainly relevant to all types of offerings, the identical phrasing and styling of the two controversies clearly demonstrate that the rabbis constructed animal and grain offerings as operationally and conceptually identical.

The artificial import of the blood paradigm to the context of grain offerings becomes particularly evident in light of the rabbinic uncertainty regarding the exact status and function of the handful. On the one hand, the handful is akin to suet in animal offerings insofar as it is the deity's portion that is burned on the altar; on the other hand, the rabbis make it akin to blood in animal offerings insofar as it functions as a permitter. The handful thus performs double duty in grain offerings as both the portion of the deity and the transformative element that allows each one of the participants—including the deity—to receive their portions. In and of itself this dual function of the handful is completely logical: as I mentioned above, it is only reasonable to assume that human consumption is made possible only after the deity receives his portion, and therefore that the application of this portion to the altar is effectively what renders the rest of the offering usable. However, since in animal sacrifices there is insistent distinction between blood, which allows for consumption, and suet, whose consumption depends on blood, Tannaitic sources present certain ambivalence on whether the handful is more like blood or more like suet.[152] This ambivalence reveals both the extent to which the rabbis considered the work of blood as the paradigmatic

150. T. Zevaḥim 4.1.

151. T. Menaḥot 4.5. Cf. M. Menaḥot 3.3–4; Sifra nedavah 9.10.11 (ed. Finkelstein 74). As in the case of the meat/blood controversy, the Sifra relates anonymously and without contestation only the position attributed to R. Eliezer.

152. See Sifra nedavah 9.10.11 (ed. Finkelstein 74); Sifra tzav 8.13.8 (ed. Weiss 37a); M. Zevaḥim 4.3; M. Meʿilah 2.9; T. Zevaḥim 5.3.

sacrificial ritual, and the limitations and difficulties pertinent to their attempt to impose this sacrificial paradigm across the board.[153]

THE WORK OF BLOOD AND
THE PERFECTION OF ACTION

My purpose in this chapter was to demonstrate and explore the centrality of blood in the rabbinic construction of the sacrificial process, and to argue that the rabbis considered the work of blood as an encapsulation of the sacrificial process as a whole. In placing the work of blood at the center, I have shown, the rabbis significantly marginalize what could otherwise be considered the determining element of the sacrificial process: the burning of meat or suet on the altar that marks the deity's participation in or acceptance of the offering. In the rabbinic scheme, the correct treatment of blood releases the sacrificial meat and suet from the prohibition imposed upon them by consecration, and consecutively allows the different participants to partake in their portion. Within this scheme, the "altar," the deity's placeholder, is presented not as the main addressee on whose acceptance of the offering the consumption of the other participants depends, but as a participant equal to the others whose own consumption depends exclusively on the successful work of blood.

As we have seen, the rabbis define the work of blood in two different and seemingly incongruent ways. On the one hand, the work of blood is presented as a mere technical procedure that enables the transition of sacrificial substances into a state of usability, such that it ostensibly serves something other than itself. On the other hand, the work of blood is identified with the attainment of atonement, which is put forth as the main, if not the only, purpose of the sacrificial ritual. What is more, the attainment of atonement is emphatically not dependent on any other substance except for blood. In other words, the work of blood is geared to make meat and suet available for consumption, but the rabbis make clear that the sacrifice is valid even if the meat or suet were never consumed: that which serves the rest of the ritual is in fact the heart of the ritual, and the one substance that has no inherent value is the only substance that truly matters.

I propose that this apparent conundrum leads us directly to the core of the rabbinic theory of sacrifice, namely, that the rabbis locate the essence, efficacy, and value of sacrifice in the correct performance of actions and not in the transaction of goods. While the rabbis certainly subscribe to the notion that sacrifice is in

153. M. Menaḥot 1.3 adds the burning of frankincense on the altar to the list of activities that can be disqualified through intention (apparently a controversial position, as related in M. Menaḥot 2.1). It is possible that the triad of burning the handful, eating, and burning frankincense was put forth in an effort to imitate the triad of tossing the blood, eating the meat, and burning the suet in animal sacrifices.

essence a transaction in which material goods are transferred to the domain of the High, they use their legislation to make the point that the validity and success of sacrifice do not depend on any of these material goods. Moreover, they do not even depend on the intentions and dispositions of the giving party or the receiving party, but rather only *on getting the procedure done right*. To prevent any misunderstanding, it is not that the rabbis have no stakes in sacrifice as a religious practice and paradigm, or that they seek to trivialize it: they have the highest stakes in sacrifice, as they maintain that it is a critical tool for the forgiveness of sins and achievement of an equilibrium between Israel and their God. But the rabbis define the proper way to handle those stakes in a very specific way, as hinging on perfect performance of four blood-related activities.

How are we to understand the rabbis' focus on correctness of actions rather than on reception of objects, and their replacement of a paradigm of giving and receiving with a paradigm of self-contained ritual procedure? One possible direction for answering this question has to do with the specific historical context in which the Tannaitic texts were compiled—namely, after the destruction of the Jerusalem temple. While we do not have any concrete evidence that Jews in Palestine or outside of it performed sacrificial rituals outside the temple in the rabbinic period,[154] the rabbis certainly consider it a possibility, if only a hypothetical one, that Jews would do so.[155] Their unequivocal position is that any vow to make a sacrifice outside the temple is void, and that any ritual slaughter conducted outside the temple cannot be considered sacrifice.[156] If we consider the rabbinic emphasis on the correctness of sacrificial actions and particularly on the actions pertaining to blood in light of the insistence that sacrifice outside the temple is invalid, it is certainly conceivable that the rabbis placed so much weight on the precision of the work of blood in order to preclude the possibility of independent sacrificial activities (whether real or imagined). By making the point that the designation of an animal for God and the burning of its parts on an altar do not a sacrifice make, the rabbis may have attempted to confine the practice of sacrifice strictly to the now-nonexistent realm of the centralized temple.

Another way of approaching the rabbinic focus on correctness of action rather than on the giving-receiving dynamic is to attribute it to the rabbis' theological-philosophical conviction that human beings cannot interact with God in the same way they interact with each other. Put differently, the rabbinic sacrificial legislation

---

154. On this topic, see Brown, *Temple and Sacrifice in Rabbinic Judaism*, 20–24; Guttmann, "The End of the Jewish Sacrificial Cult."

155. See M. Menaḥot 13.10; M. Ḥullin 2.10.

156. As stated most explicitly in T. Ḥullin 2.25–27. One curious exception to this rule is the temple of Onias in Leontopolis (*miqdash ḥonio*), which is discussed in M. Menaḥot 13.10. On the temple in Leontopolis and its unique position, see Daniel R. Schwartz, "The Jews of Egypt between the Temple of Onias, the Temple of Jerusalem, and Heaven" [Heb.], *Zion* 62, no. 1 (1997): 5–22.

can be read as a rejection of the common view expressed in the old Greek proverb *dora theous peithei*, "Gifts persuade the gods."[157] As I mentioned above, various midrashic texts vehemently reject the notion that God stands to benefit in any way from gifts provided by humans, or that the meat and suet he is offered have any value for him, and it seems reasonable to read the rabbinic sacrificial legislation in the same light. By dismissing the actual distribution of the sacrificial goods as the mere aftermath of the sacrificial process and as inconsequential to its validity, the rabbis powerfully express the view that the delivered objects are not desirable in and of themselves. As I will show in greater detail in the conclusion, the rabbis align in this view with many Greek, Roman, and early Christian authors who mocked and condemned the notion that sacrifice is a mode of exchange with divine beings.

However, let us note that while the midrashic tradition I quoted above locates the purpose and significance of sacrifice in the attitude of the *offerer*—"so that you will acknowledge me"—the legal sources I have examined so far marginalize not only the role of the receiver in the sacrificial process, but also the role of the giver. That is to say, sacrifice is not calibrated in Tannaitic legislation as depending on the offerer's piety and genuine desire to give something to God, but as dependent strictly on the actions of the officiants. What the rabbis develop is not a competing communicative model of sacrifice, in which what is "really" delivered is not animal parts but a sense of gratitude or devotion,[158] but rather a noncommunicative model altogether. The essence of this noncommunicative model can be summarized as what anthropologists Caroline Humphrey and James Laidlaw titled "the ritual commitment": right actions done in the right order with the right state of mind.[159]

Some readers may find this description of the rabbis' approach to sacrifice disconcerting, perhaps even demeaning. They may infer from my account that the rabbis are concerned only with accurate procedure and not with intimate interaction with God, only with technical details and not with sincerity of emotion, which could resonate with age-old characterizations of Jews as operating according to the letter and not the spirit of the law, and with stereotypes about rabbinic Judaism as punctilious and soulless. Let me assure you that nothing could be further from my intentions here. First, since I do not subscribe to the notion that contemplative and interiorized religiosity is somehow superior to a practice-based and externalized religiosity, I certainly do not maintain that the rabbis' emphasis on correct action is to be either looked down upon or apologized for. Second and more important, it would be misguided to construe the rabbis' bottom line, following my analysis,

---

157. For a discussion of this notion, see Jim, *Sharing with the Gods*, 60–67.

158. As proposed by Halbertal, *On Sacrifice*, 24–29.

159. Caroline Humphrey and James Laidlaw, *The Archetypal Actions of Ritual: A Theory of Ritual Illustrated by the Jain Rite of Worship* (New York: Oxford University Press, 1994), 88–110.

in terms of the "emptiness" or "meaninglessness" of sacrifice. To say that sacrifice is defined by perfect performance is not to rob this ritual of philosophical and religious content: on the contrary, it is to flesh out its philosophical and religious content.

To clarify this last sentence, let me reiterate that I see the Tannaitic legal creation as an intellectual project, which seeks not only to "tell people what to do" but to grapple, through the medium of casuistic rulings, with various religious, social, and philosophical questions. If my account of the rabbinic approach to sacrifice were narrowed down to a normative injunction, and this injunction was "Just get that blood on the altar correctly and don't mess it up, as none of this really matters" this would indeed be a bit disappointing. But if we see the rabbinic sacrificial project as an attempt to understand what sacrifice is and how it operates, what makes it efficacious and what are the necessary conditions for its successful completion, what emerges from the rabbis' legislation is a thoughtful answer to these questions. Like the theories of many philosophers and theologians, the rabbinic theory of sacrifice rejects the notion that sacrifice works in a reciprocal manner and is a channel for the material satisfaction of the deity, but unlike other philosophers and theologians, the rabbis do not resort to allegory or metonymy or custom or pragmatism to explain why sacrifice is valuable. Rather, their theory is that sacrifice has transformative power *because* it manifests perfect and attentive performance of required actions. In the rabbinic theory of sacrifice, correct action is not the empty vessel that remained when sacrifice lost its content and value: rather, correct action *is* the content and *is* the value that the rabbis promote through their sacrificial legislation.

The rabbis' sacrificial project, then, is not simply to reframe sacrifice as devoid of problematic anthropomorphic or reciprocal connotations, but to establish sacrifice primarily as a manifestation of commitment to accurate and scrupulous performance of the law. Sacrifice accomplishes atonement not because God enjoys the smell, as proclaimed in Genesis 8:21, but because it is done according to "its ordinance." In this regard, sacrifice is not fundamentally different from other areas of rabbinic legislation: as shown by Tzvi Novick, emphasis on procedural accuracy in the fulfillment of commandments is a staple of Tannaitic texts,[160] and as I have argued elsewhere, the kind of subject that the Mishnah cultivates and promotes is one whose every action is defined by an attempt to follow the law down to its minute details.[161] But sacrifice stands out within rabbinic legislation insofar as the form of this ritual and the biblical language associated with it are fundamentally material, sensual, and interactive. In other words, as a ritual in which edible sub-

---

160. Tzvi Novick, *What Is Good and What God Demands: Normative Structures in Tannaitic Literature* (Leiden: Brill, 2010).

161. Balberg, *Purity, Body, and Self,* 175–79.

stances are transferred from the owner to the altar, sacrifice resists a strictly procedural interpretation perhaps more than any other halakhic praxis. The rabbis' efforts to subordinate sacrifice to their religious ideology of accurate performance and adherence to the law thus require thorough recalibration of the elements, sequence, and rhetoric of this ritual, and thereby attest to the depth of the rabbis' commitment to this ideology.

Moreover, I propose that it is exactly because of the palpable gap between the biblical rhetoric of material efficacy of sacrifices (appeasing, pleasing, cleansing, etc.) and the rabbinic ethos of correctness of action that sacrifice remained such a significant and potent topic for the rabbis even when sacrifices were no longer actively performed. This gap presented them with an opportunity to tie together the language of efficacy, transformation, and proximity to the sacred with the ideals of accurate observance, carefully formed intentions, and legal erudition, and with an opportunity to translate the former into the latter. Sacrifice thus became the ultimate playing field on which the force and vision of rabbinic *halakhah* could be displayed in the most powerful and convincing manner.

3

Sacrifice as One

The biblical book of Leviticus, which details the desired nature of the priestly sacrificial cult through a highly systematic and comprehensive set of instructions, begins its survey of the different types of sacrifices as follows:

> The Lord summoned Moses and spoke to him from the Tent of Meeting, saying: "Speak to the people of Israel and say to them: 'When any of you bring an offering of livestock to the Lord, you shall bring your offering from the herd or from the flock. If the offering is a burnt offering from the herd, he shall offer a male without blemish; he shall bring it to the entrance of the Tent of Meeting, for acceptance in his behalf before the Lord. He shall lay his hand on the head of the burnt offering, and it shall be acceptable in his behalf as atonement for him.'"[1]

Two rhetorical choices are notable in this opening passage. First, the authors (or redactors) chose to begin with the burnt offering (*'olah*), an offering that is consumed by fire in its entirety, and neither priests nor owners eat of it. Second, this passage makes the point that offerings are brought forth by *individuals.* In his work on persuasive techniques in the book of Leviticus, James Watts has rightfully noted that the choice to commence the pericope with the one type of offering of which the priests receive no edible parts helps portray the sacrificial cult as a whole as a mode of selfless giving to the deity rather than as a source of income for the priests.[2] I would like to add to Watts's observation that the choice to describe sacrifice as fundamentally an individual act, initiated and led by "any person from

---

1. Leviticus 1:1–4 (NRSV translation, with slight modifications).
2. Watts, *Ritual and Rhetoric,* 71–73.

among you," enhances the persuasive force of the priestly text by presenting the delivery of offerings as something that laypeople themselves desire. Sacrificial worship is constructed in the first chapters of Leviticus not as sanctioned by an authoritative elite, but as a spontaneous act of piety that the priests are merely helping the people carry out. This opening sets the stage for the entire priestly sacrificial scheme, establishing sacrifice primarily as a channel through which individual human beings can approach the deity—whether for purposes of thanks-giving, atonement, reparation, or any other goal—in accordance with their own will. Indeed, the primary meaning of the root *qrb*, from which the word *qorban*, "offering," stems, is "to approach."

Although the first five chapters of Leviticus make a point of presenting the dif-ferent types of offerings as brought forth by "a person" (*'adam* or *nefesh*), thereby establishing the paradigmatic sacrifice as an individual act, the Priestly Code men-tions multiple offerings that are incumbent upon the congregation as a whole. These offerings range from the two daily burnt offerings to the slew of burnt offer-ings, purification offerings, and wine and grain offerings made on Sabbaths and during festivals to special offerings made in exceptional circumstances—for exam-ple, if the entire congregation sinned or for the inauguration of the tabernacle. It should be noted that the notion of obligatory collective offerings is unique to the priestly school: in the JE sources of the Pentateuch, as well as in D and in the Deu-teronomic History, offerings are described as brought by individuals or by fami-lies, and no reference is made to offerings brought by "the people" as such. How-ever, even in the priestly texts it is not indicated how mandated congregational offerings differ from individual offerings except that the responsibility to deliver them is collective in nature: aside from that fact, the procedures, purposes, and desired results of all sacrifices seem to be identical regardless of who is sacrificing and for whose sake.[3] It is fair to say, then, that the paradigmatic priestly sacrifice is an individual one, but that on particular occasions the entire congregation func-tions as an individual and brings forth a communal offering.[4]

In this chapter I argue that various early rabbinic sources reveal a sustained effort to overturn the priestly picture and to present congregational offerings, rather than individual offerings, as the paradigmatic mode of sacrificial worship. For the rabbis, congregational offerings are not only made *on behalf* of the com-munity as a whole but are actively made *by* the entire community as a corporate

3. As Naphtali Meshel has shown, some recurring features of congregational offerings are found in biblical literature (for example, congregational offerings are always of male animals), but those fea-tures are not unique to congregational offerings and appear in certain kinds of individual offerings as well, depending on other factors. See Meshel, *The "Grammar" of Sacrifice.*

4. On the interchangeability of individual and collective in biblical culture, see Henry Wheeler Robinson, *Corporate Personality in Ancient Israel* (Philadelphia: Fortress Press, 1973).

entity, since every single member of the community must participate in their funding. Thereby, in the rabbis' presentation, congregational offerings are not a collective variation on individual offerings, but rather the contrary: individual offerings are pale shadows or partial versions of congregational offerings.

Whereas in the Priestly Code there is neither a designated terminology that distinguishes offerings made by individuals from offerings made collectively, nor any indication that the two are categorically different from one another, in rabbinic texts the classification of offerings as either congregational (*qorbanot tzibur*) or individual (*qorbanot yaḥid*) is one of the foundations of the entire discourse on sacrifice.[5] Several rabbinic passages attempt to present an elaborate taxonomy of congregational versus individual offerings, and to delineate a list of traits that distinguish the former from the latter. A cursory look at these passages, however, suffices to show that this taxonomic enterprise is less than fully successful: the multiple exceptions to almost every rule laid out in those passages, which are acknowledged by the rabbis themselves, divulge the fact that the biblical sources do not really lend themselves to this type of hard and fast categorization. For example, the Mishnah states that only congregational sacrifices can be performed on the Sabbath, and only congregational sacrifices can be performed in a state of ritual impurity, but this statement is immediately followed by examples of certain individual sacrifices that also override the Sabbath and can be performed in a state of impurity; in the Tosefta this statement is also met with examples of various congregational sacrifices that do not override the Sabbath and cannot be made in a state of impurity.[6] Similarly, the Mishnah's ruling that individual offerings require the owner to lay his hands on the animal's head, whereas congregational offerings do not require this, is immediately supplemented with a list of numerous exceptions to both these rules.[7] More critically, in some cases it is not even

---

5. It is quite possible that this rabbinic categorization is influenced by the centrality of the categories of *sacra privata* and *sacra publica* in Roman religion. In the context of Roman religion, this distinction had immediate implications in terms of who conducts the ritual (whether or not a priest is involved, and what type of priest), where the ritual takes place (in a state-run temple, in a local shrine, or at home), and even, to some extent, which gods are invoked (as some gods, such as the Penates and the Lares, pertain to private household sacrifices only). For specific discussions on public and private sacrifices in Roman religion, see David G. Orr, "Roman Domestic Religion: The Evidence of Household Shrines," in *Aufstieg und Niedergang der römischen Welt* II.16.2: *Religion* (*Heidentum: Römische Religion, Allgemeines*), ed. Wolfgang Haase (Berlin and New York: Walter de Gruyter, 1978), 1557–91; Eric M. Orlin, *Temples, Religion, and Politics in the Roman Republic* (Leiden: Brill, 1997); Scheid, *An Introduction to Roman Religion*, 41–127; Michele Renee Saltzman, "The End of Public Sacrifice: Changing Definitions of Sacrifice in Post-Constantinian Rome and Italy," in Knust and Várhelyi, *Ancient Mediterranean Sacrifice*, 167–83.

6. M. Temurah 2.1; T. Temurah 1.17–18.

7. M. Menaḥot 9.7; however, cf. Sifra tzav (Mekhilta demilu'im) 1.13 (ed. Weiss 41c), according to which all offerings, including congregational offerings, require hand laying.

entirely clear which offerings are to be subsumed under which category, since different texts introduce different and competing systems of classification.[8]

The many incongruities and controversies surrounding the rabbinic classification of offerings as congregational or individual reveal, indeed, that the attempt at clear differentiation between those two categories is somewhat foreign to the biblical texts on which the rabbis rely; but they also reveal how critically important this differentiation was for the rabbis. At the core of these somewhat forced rabbinic attempts to chart out clear differences between congregational and individual offerings stands an assumption that the distinction between those two types of offerings is qualitative rather than quantitative: that is, that congregational offerings are not simply offerings that happen to have many addressers rather than a single addresser, but rather they are offerings that are subject to completely separate sets of rules and are delivered and handled according to a unique protocol. The rabbinic insistence on such qualitative distinction is guided, I contend, by an underlying perception of hierarchy within the sacrificial system, in which congregational sacrifices are inherently superior to individual ones, and by a view that the superiority of the former must be manifested in their manner of performance. My purpose in this chapter is to examine the rabbinic construction of congregational offerings as categorically different from individual offerings, and the interpretive and legislative tools used to assert the former's supremacy over the latter, in order to uncover some of the ideological convictions that animate the rabbinic sacrificial vision.

In the first part of this chapter, I discuss the innovative rabbinic notion that congregational sacrifices may be procured only through public funds, that is, the funds collected through the annual half-shekel tribute to the temple. As I will show, the vehement rejection of any individual funding of congregational sacrifices—a rejection that has no trace in earlier Jewish writings and in all likelihood was not effective during the times of the temple—serves the rabbis to construct the Jewish cultic system as the diametrical opposition of the Hellenistic-Roman cultic system, which relies heavily on euergetism (donations of private benefactors for civic and state purposes). In the second part of the chapter, I turn to examine rabbinic traditions that emphasize the power, value, and preferred status of congregational offerings over that of individual offerings. Operating on the principle that "Israel" as a congregation is a single corporate body, the rabbis construct the realm of individual sacrifices as entailed in and to some extent even superseded by the realm of congregational sacrifices. The most radical manifestation of this notion is the idea that even sacrifices made by individuals for individuals, such as the Passover sacrifice, should be considered congregational sacrifices, which I will discuss briefly here

8. The various incongruities and disputes regarding the classification of individual vs. congregational offerings were recently explored in detail by Steinfeld, "On the Definition of Individual and Congregational Offerings."

and continue to develop in the next chapter. I conclude this chapter with several observations on the meaning and function of the rabbinic ethos of collective cult in the historical context of the Roman Empire of the late second and early third centuries C.E.

THE ANNUAL HALF-SHEKEL TRIBUTE AND THE COLLECTIVIZATION OF THE CULT

Various biblical sources describe particular events or circumstances in which the people were asked—or required—to donate money toward the upkeep of the temple. The most foundational example of such public participation in the funding of the cult is the story of the establishment of the tabernacle in the wilderness, in which each one of the Israelites "whose heart prompts him to give" is asked to donate gold, silver, wood, skins, gems, oil for lamps, and any other materials necessary for the building of the tabernacle.[9] These donations are then supplemented with mandatory half-shekel payments that all Israelites are required to give as "ransom" (*kofer*) for their lives, an arrangement required specifically toward the census conducted upon the departure from Sinai, and guided by the pervasive biblical view that a census poses mortal danger for the people.[10] According to the book of Kings, donations toward the restoration and upkeep of the temple were also solicited by King Jehoash during his reign,[11] and similar voluntary donations are mentioned in regard to the establishment of the temple of Solomon in the book of Chronicles and in regard to the establishment of the Second Temple in the book of Ezra.[12] In all these cases, it should be noted, funds collected from the people are not utilized toward the sacrificial cult but rather for the physical establishment or maintenance of the sanctuary. As for the offerings themselves, the Priestly Code mentions several offerings that are to be provided by the people of Israel as such, but does not mention how those offerings are to be procured.[13] According to the book of Ezekiel, it is the prince (*nasi*) who is responsible for providing "burnt offerings, grain offerings, and drink offerings, at the festivals, the new moons, and the sabbaths, all the appointed festivals of the house of Israel,"[14] and this notion is echoed in the book of Chronicles, in which the kings and their officers are unfailingly those providing the offerings on cultic occasions.[15]

9. Exodus 25:1–8.
10. Exodus 30:11–16; cf. 2 Samuel 24:1–17.
11. 2 Kings 12:5–17.
12. 1 Chronicles 29:6–9; Ezra 8:17–34.
13. For example, Leviticus 4:14, 9:3, 16:5, 23:9–20; Numbers 28:1–30.
14. Ezekiel 45:17.
15. 2 Chronicles 29:20–25, 30:24, 31:3, 35:7–9.

It is only in the book of Nehemiah, which recounts the establishment and solid-ification of the Judean community that returned from Babylonia to the region of Judah (then the Persian province Yehud) in the fifth century B.C.E., that the idea of a publicly funded sacrificial cult is first introduced in the Bible. Nehemiah relates in detail the pledge (*'amanah*) agreed upon by the community of returners, as part of which the members of the community make an obligation "to pay yearly one-third of a shekel for the service of the house of our God: for the rows of bread, the regular grain offering, the regular burnt offering, [the offerings for] the sabbaths, the new moons, the appointed festivals, the sacred things, and the sin offerings to make atonement for Israel, and for all the work of the house of our God."[16] This pledge stands in certain tension with the account in the book of Ezra, according to which the Persian king Darius agreed to provide all the necessary offerings for the newly erected temple in Jerusalem himself,[17] and it is difficult to know whether one of the accounts (or both of them) present an idealized picture either of the community or of its relations with the Persian king, or whether, as suggested by Jacob Liver, the community had to make this arrangement because the Persian kings failed to make good on this promise.[18] Either way, Liver has convincingly shown that textual accounts from both the Persian and the Hellenistic periods regularly mention kings and rulers as providing the calendrical offerings for the Jerusalem temple, as was indeed the custom throughout the ancient Mediterra-nean world.[19]

Sources from the Roman period, in contrast, introduce a Jewish custom of pay-ing annually a half-shekel mandatory tribute to the Jerusalem temple, a custom that seems to be based on a crossing of the onetime half-shekel ransom payment in the book of Exodus with the annual third-shekel donation in the book of Nehe-miah.[20] While it is not entirely clear what this tribute was used to procure, one passage in Josephus's *Against Apion* does mention offerings purchased at the "com-munal expense of all the Jews" (*ex impensa communi omnium Iudaeorum*), which suggests that by this point annual donations were used, among other things,

---

16. Nehemiah 10:32–33.

17. Ezra 6:8–10.

18. Jacob Liver, "The Edict of the Half-Shekel" [Heb.], in *The Yehezkel Kaufman Jubilee Volume,* ed. Menahem Haran (Jerusalem: Magnes Press, 1961), 54–67.

19. Liver, "The Edict of the Half-Shekel." For evidence of this practice, see 2 Maccabees 3.3; Josephus, *Antiquities of the Jews* 12.3.3 (ed. Whiston 317). Josephus's account of the reign of Herod (*An-tiquities of the Jews* 15.11.6, ed. Whiston 425) presents a similar picture.

20. Philo, *On the Special Laws* 1.76–78 (ed. Yonge 541); Josephus, *Antiquities of the Jews* 3.8.2 (ed. Whiston 91), 18.9.1 (ed. Whiston 497); *Wars of the Jews* 7.6.6 (ed. Whiston 761); Matthew 17:24–27. The custom is also documented in Roman sources discussing the *fiscus iudaicus*—an annual tribute to the temple of Jupiter that Jews throughout the empire were forced to pay after the destruction of the Jerusalem temple (see below).

toward the sacrificial cult itself.[21] This corresponds with the picture portrayed in tractate Sheqalim of the Mishnah and its parallel in the Tosefta, which describe in great detail the workings of the mandatory half-shekel annual tribute. According to the mishnaic account, the funds collected through the half-shekel donations were used to procure "daily offerings and festival offerings and their libations and the two loaves of bread and the showbread and all the congregational offerings" as well as to fund various other temple expenses, such as wages for temple craftsmen and experts.[22] In addition, those public funds are said to have been used to maintain "the aqueduct and the town walls and its towers and all the needs of the town (i.e., Jerusalem)."[23] Although the Mishnah's description of the collection procedure of the shekels is clearly idealized and cannot be taken at face value as historically reliable, it certainly reflects a custom that was actively practiced at the end of the Second Temple period. Unfortunately, there is no way of knowing how widely accepted this custom was and what percent of the Jewish population actively participated in it: it seems that at least some Jewish groups, such as the Dead Sea Sect and the disciples of Jesus, were quite averse to paying this tribute.[24] But one way or another, for Jews living in the Roman period—unlike in earlier periods—there has already been an established identification of public worship with public funds.

Rejection of private funding for congregational offerings

While the custom of funding the cult through annual tributes clearly has its roots in the Second Temple period, there is one component of the rabbinic legislation regarding the annual tribute to the temple that has no precedent in earlier texts: the rabbis prohibit the funding of congregational offerings through any means *except* for the annual tribute. That is to say, they rule out the possibility that congregational offerings or temple needs be provided fully or in part by wealthy individuals, which was a common practice throughout the Mediterranean world.[25] As a rule, in Hellenistic and Roman cities public sacrifices were to be procured through public funds: in the words of the second-century Roman grammarian

---

21. Josephus, *Against Apion* 2.6 (ed. Whiston 798); this portion of the work unfortunately survived only in the Latin translation.

22. M. Sheqalim 4.1.

23. M. Sheqalim 4.2.

24. See Jacob Liver, "The Half-Shekel in Scrolls of the Judean Desert Sect" [Heb.], *Tarbitz* 31, no. 1 (1962): 18–22; David Flusser, "The Half-Shekel in the Gospel and among the Judean Desert Sect" [Heb.], *Tarbitz* 31, no. 2 (1962): 150–56; Sara Mandell, "Who Paid the Temple Tax When the Jews Were under Roman Rule?," *Harvard Theological Review* 77, no. 2 (1984): 223–32; Chilton, *The Temple of Jesus*, 129–30; Yoram Erder, "Second Temple Period Sectarian Polemic Concerning the Half-Shekel Commandment in Light of Early Karaite Halakhah" [Heb.], *Meghillot* 8–9 (2010): 3–28.

25. For multiple examples of this custom, see Petropoulou, *Animal Sacrifice*, 76–91; Naiden, *Smoke Signals*, 183–201.

Sextus Pompeius Festus, "public sacred things from the public expense" (*publica sacra quae publico sumptu*).[26] These public funds could be either sacred (specifically, the treasuries of temples) or civic, but as Scott Bradbury has pointed out, both of these types of resources usually fell short of covering the cultic expenses of the city in full, and therefore these funds were almost always supplemented with donations of private benefactors.[27]

By vehemently rejecting the possibility of using private donations for public worship, the rabbis transform a practice that was evidently established as a means to an end—a way of procuring sacrificial needs with no other sources of funding available—into a manifestation of a collectivistic ideology: they maintain that since congregational sacrifices are for everyone they must also be provided by everyone, and "by everyone" necessarily means "by no one in particular." Thus, for example, the Sifre to the book of Numbers comments on the various components of daily offerings:

> "My offering, the food for my offering by fire, my pleasing odor, you shall take care to offer (*tishmeru*) to me at its appointed time" (Numbers 28:2). My offering—this is the blood; food—this is the suet; . . . my fire—these are the handfuls [of fine flour] and frankincense; my pleasing odor—these are the cornets of showbread; you [pl.] shall take care to offer—[this is to indicate] that *he may only bring [those] from the appropriation of the chamber* [i.e., from the donated coins collected in the temple chamber].[28]

The same verse is interpreted in the Sifre zutta to the book of Numbers as teaching explicitly that "the daily offerings come from the congregation and not from individuals" (*ve-lo mi-shel yeḥidim*), a reading that this midrash applies to other types of congregational offerings as well.[29]

There is no extant nonrabbinic evidence that such rejection of congregational offerings brought by individuals was at play during the Second Temple period. As I mentioned, texts from the Persian and Hellenistic periods indicate that it was customary for kings and rulers to donate congregational offerings to the temple, and the only objection to this practice seems to have emerged in the time of the Great Revolt—not because the donations in question were of individuals, but because they were of foreigners.[30] However, one rabbinic text, the Scholion to the Scroll of Fasts (Megillat Ta'anit), projects this prohibition back into the times of the

26. Sextus Pompeius Festus, *De verborum significatu quae supersunt cum Pauli epitome*, ed. Wallace M. Lindsay (Stuttgart: B. G. Teubner, 1997), 284.

27. Bradbury, "Julian's Pagan Revival," 348.

28. Sifre Numbers 142 (ed. Horovitz 188).

29. Sifre zutta Numbers 28:2 (ed. Horovitz 322). Cf. Sifre Zutta Numbers 15:2, 19:2 (ed. Horovitz 280, 300).

30. Josephus, *Wars of the Jews* 2.17.2 (ed. Whiston 624).

Jerusalem temple and presents it as a bone of contention between the Sadducees and the "Sages" (usually but problematically identified with the Pharisees[31]). The Scroll of Fasts is a Second Temple period text that relates a list of days on which one must not mourn, and is traditionally accompanied by a Scholion (which was compiled during the Talmudic period) that provides explanations of the different days in the list. In a comment on the first appointed time mentioned in the scroll— the first eight days of Nisan, in which "the daily offering was established" ('*itoqam temida*)—the Scholion relates the following:

> "The daily offering was established"—For the Sadducees used to say: one brings daily offerings from [the property] of individuals, this one brings them for one week and that one brings them for two weeks and another brings them for thirty days. And what did they say [that is, on what did they base this]?—They said: Scripture says, "You [sing.] shall offer (*ta'ase*) the one lamb in the morning" (Numbers 28:4). The Sages told them: you are not permitted to do so, for congregational offerings are only from all of Israel, as it was said: "Command the Israelites my offering . . . you [pl.] shall take care (*tishmeru*) to offer to me at its appointed time" (Numbers 28:2)—[this is to indicate] that [congregational offerings] must all be brought from the appropriation of the chamber [i.e., from the annual tribute].[32]

According to the Scholion, the edict regarding a mandatory half-shekel tribute was issued in correspondence with the Sages' position that individuals may not fund congregational offerings, and the time of year in which the Sages eventually prevailed was marked with an eight-day-long festival to mark the "establishment of the daily offering." While it is generally agreed that the appointed time mentioned in the original Scroll has nothing to do with the debate on the funding of congregational offerings,[33] scholars do tend to accept the Scholion's account of a controversy between the Sages/Pharisees and the Sadducees on this matter as historically reliable, and see it as an expression of the Sadducees' elitism as opposed to the Pharisees' commitment to egalitarianism and desire to increase public participation in temple life.[34] I am rather skeptical that a text compiled in the fifth or

---

31. For a recent discussion of the identification of the rabbis with the Pharisees, see Annette Yoshiko Reed, "When Did Rabbis Become Pharisees? Reflections on Christian Evidence for Post-70 Judaism," in *Envisioning Judaism: Essays in Honor of Peter Schäfer on the Occasion of His Seventieth Birthday*, ed. Ra'anan S. Boustan, Klaus Herrmann, Reimund Leicht, Annette Yoshiko Reed, and Giuseppe Veltri, vol. 2 (Tübingen: Mohr Siebeck, 2013), 859–96.

32. My translation of MS Parma version of the Scholion as reconstructed by Vered Noam, *Megillat Ta'anit: Versions, Interpretation, History* [Heb.] (Jerusalem: Yad Ben Zvi, 2003) 55–57. Cf. BT Menaḥot 65a.

33. On different interpretations of the original date, see Noam, *Megillat Ta'anit*, 65–69.

34. See Albeck, *The Six Orders of the Mishnah: Mo'ed*, 184; Moshe Beer, "The Sects and the Half-Shekel" [Heb.], *Tarbitz* 31, no. 3 (1962): 298–99; Eyal Regev, *The Sadducees and Their Law: Religion and Society in the Second Temple Period* [Heb.] (Jerusalem: Yad Ben Zvi, 2005), 132–39; Noam, *Megillat Ta'anit*, 172. See also Knohl, "Participation of the People in Temple Worship."

sixth century reliably reflects events that took place hundreds of years earlier, and am inclined to see the Scholion as projecting a rabbinic innovation back into the Second Temple period, as it does on several other occasions. My purpose here, however, is not to determine how far back the rabbis' rejection of individual funding for congregational offerings can be traced, but rather to understand the implications of this rejection within the rabbinic sacrificial vision more broadly.

One central implication of the rabbinic (or protorabbinic) ruling that individuals may not provide for congregational sacrificial needs is a restriction on one of the most quintessential forms of piety in the ancient world: the gift to the temple.[35] Seth Schwartz has argued that donations of wealthy benefactors for the greater good of the public were generally treated with suspicion among Jewish communities of the Second Temple period (a point to which I will return below), but "the provision of sacrifices and votive gifts to the temple were likely, though not absolutely certain, to be admired."[36] To a limited extent, the rabbis preserve a sense of appreciation for such benefactions, as shown in several anecdotes on wealthy individuals who donated lavish gifts to the temple and were mentioned "in praise" (li-shevah). It should be noted, however, that the few gifts mentioned in these anecdotes are of a completely superfluous and merely decorative nature: golden handles for the tools used in the Day of Atonement ritual, a golden tablet on which the oath of the adulteress woman is written, golden "lots" for the two goats of the Day of Atonement, and so forth.[37] Anecdotes about actual sacrificial gifts, or about substantial monetary donations to the temple funds, are completely missing from Tannaitic sources. The rabbis, of course, acknowledge that individuals may be inclined to donate gifts—whether goods or money—to the temple, and do not say that such gifts should be rejected altogether: but as I will show momentarily, they develop an intricate mechanism to ensure that individual gifts are never used for congregational worship as such.

Although the ideal of all congregational offerings being funded strictly by the annual tribute appears in all Tannaitic compilations, there is a traceable difference between the different compilations in the ways this ideal is introduced and negotiated. The Tosefta and the Tannaitic midrashim present a relatively soft version of this principle and allow room for more gray areas and exceptions, maintaining the

---

35. For but a few examples, see Folkert T. van Straten, "Gifts for the Gods," in *Faith, Hope, and Worship: Aspects of Religious Mentality in the Ancient World,* ed. Henk S. Versnel (Leiden: Brill, 1981), 65–150; Orlin, *Temples, Religion, and Politics in the Roman Republic,* 11–75; Dominic Janes, *God and Gold in Late Antiquity* (Cambridge: Cambridge University Press, 1998).

36. Seth Schwartz, *Were the Jews a Mediterranean Society?* (Princeton: Princeton University Press, 2009), 106.

37. M. Yoma 3.9–10; see also T. Sheqalim 2.6; T. Kippurim 1.21–22. On gifts to the temple in rabbinic sources, see Gregg Gardner, "Giving to the Poor in Early Rabbinic Judaism" (PhD diss., Princeton University, 2009), 183–90.

notion that purely public funding is the ideal but noting that it is not always the reality.[38] The Mishnah, on the other hand, is unequivocal that individuals may never fund any congregational offerings and upholds this principle fiercely. The following example illustrates this well:

> Those who guard uncultivated plants (*sefiḥim*) in the seventh year take their wages from the appropriation of the chamber. R. Yose says: If one wishes, he may volunteer to guard them for free. They told him: [But] you too admit that [congregational offerings] may only be brought from [the property] of the congregation![39]

The issue at hand is the two annual grain offerings—the *'omer*, which is offered after the first day of Passover, and the two loaves, which are offered during the Festival of Weeks—both of which, according to the Mishnah, are congregational offerings and are paid for by the annual tribute. In the seventh year, in which tilling of the land is prohibited, these two offerings are prepared using grain plants that grew on their own, which are of course very sought after and hard to come by: for this reason, it is necessary to appoint guards who will protect those uncultivated grains from thieves and animals. According to the anonymous Mishnah, those guards are paid from the public temple funds, since their work is instrumental for the preparation of congregational offerings. When R. Yose proposes that one should be allowed to guard those voluntarily if one wishes to do so, the anonymous—and thereby, authoritative—response is that this conflicts with the idea that congregational offerings must be funded strictly by the congregation. According to the logic of the anonymous Mishnah, if one guards those plants without compensation it is as though he is their owner, and thereby congregational offerings would seem as though they are brought from the property of an individual. In the Tosefta, in contrast, the controversy is presented a bit differently:

> The guards of uncultivated plants in seventh years and jubilee years, so as to use them for offering the *'omer* and the two loaves, take their wages from the appropriation of the chamber . . . and if one wants to volunteer, they do not heed him. R. Yose says: If one wants to volunteer, he may volunteer, as long as he delivers [the grains] to the congregation.[40]

Although the Tosefta, like the Mishnah, presents R. Yose's opinion as a minority position opposed to an anonymous ruling, the final retort of the anonymous Mishnah, "you too admit that they may only be brought from [the property] of the congregation," does not appear in the Tosefta, and so R. Yose's position is not forcefully rejected, as it is in the Mishnah. Furthermore, the Tosefta presents the

---

38. See Sifre Numbers 72 (ed. Horovitz 67); and cf. BT Yoma 3a–b; Sifre zutta Numbers 9.5 (ed. Horovitz 258–59); and cf. BT Ḥagigah 6b.

39. M. Sheqalim 4.1.

40. T. Menaḥot 10.22.

arrangement suggested by R. Yose as allowing for a transition or middle ground between individual and congregational offerings: one may bring something of his own property but give it to the congregation and thereby turn it into a congregational offering. This arrangement of "delivery" to the congregation is mentioned in the Tosefta in three additional contexts, and in all three this notion is mentioned anonymously, without any contesting position alongside it.[41]

In the Mishnah, in contrast, the arrangement of "delivery to the congregation" is not mentioned even a single time. Rather, the Mishnah relates only one procedure through which individual donations to the temple can be utilized for public needs: they are to be sold (although still within the precincts of the temple), and the proceeds from the sale are then to be allocated to the "upkeep of the house" (*bedeq ha-bayit*)—that is, to the maintenance of the temple and *not* to the sacrificial worship itself. For example, if one dedicated to the temple sacrificial substances such as oil and wine, those cannot be used for congregational offerings. Rather, they must be sold to individuals who wish to use them for their own individual offerings, and then the money paid by those individuals will be readdressed to the upkeep of the temple.[42] Similarly, in a case that one dedicated male animals that are fit to be offered as burnt offerings, R. Eliezer rules that those animals must be sold to individuals, and then the money is to be transferred to the upkeep of the temple. Conversely, R. Yehoshua maintains that those animals themselves must be offered on the altar, but not as congregational offerings but as individual offerings on behalf of the dedicator.[43] A particularly complex mechanism is devised in the Mishnah for things that cannot be used for any purpose except for congregational offerings, a category under which only incense or the components of incense seem to fall.[44] Such substances, if donated by individuals, are to be given to the temple's craftsmen as wages, and then repurchased from them (using temple funds) so that the craftsmen are left with money and the temple treasurers with the sacrificial substance.[45]

41. See T. Sheqalim 2.7; T. Menaḥot 6.17; T. Kippurim 1.23 (cf. M. Yoma 3.7). In addition to these rulings, the Tosefta also describes the offering of wood mentioned in Nehemiah 10:35 in the following way: "When the members of the *golah* [that is, the Judean community in the restoration period] ascended [to Judea] they did not find wood in the [temple's] chamber, and those [people] stood and volunteered wood of their own [property] and delivered it to the congregation" (T. Ta'aniyot 3.5; cf. *Megillat Ta'anit* to the fifteenth of Av, ed. Noam 217–22). In the Babylonian Talmud's version of this tradition (BT Ta'anit 28a) the phrase "and delivered them to the congregation" is missing in all the manuscripts.

42. M. Sheqalim 4.8; cf. Sifra ḥova 12.21.6 (ed. Finkelstein 210).

43. M. Sheqalim 4.7; cf. T. Sheqalim 2.10; BT Zevaḥim 103b.

44. As explained in BT Karetot 6a and PT Yoma 5:1, 42b (= PT Sheqalim 4:3, 48b).

45. M. Sheqalim 4.6. The Mishnah presents a controversy between R. Aqiva and Ben Azzai regarding the exact way in which this transaction is carried out, but the principle is the same for both.

The principle introduced in the Mishnah, then, is that individual gifts to the temple—with the exclusion of purely decorative gifts—must be transformed into money and allocated as the temple's treasurers see fit, such that it is impossible to associate the giver with the gift. By selling whatever individual donors give, the gift is standardized into the form of currency and thereby unrecognizably swallowed in a greater repository of money over which the donor has no control (the Mishnah's reference to this procedure as one in which the money "falls" to the upkeep of the temple powerfully captures this). Thereby, the rabbis ensure a complete disconnection between any specific individual and the communal sacrificial worship in the temple, marking all aspects of congregational worship as provided *by no one in particular.* Put differently, the rabbis insist that congregational sacrifices are made "by everyone" not only insofar as they represent the public in its entirety, but also to the strict exclusion of the possibility that any one person (or family, for that matter) is associated with them.

Perhaps the most extreme version of the rabbinic prohibition on the funding of congregational offerings by individuals can be found in the Mishnah's discussion of the priests' obligation to pay the annual half-shekel tribute. While the anonymous Mishnah's position is that priests are obligated to pay the half-shekel tribute like everyone else, it does mention that if priests fail to do so, their property is not to be forcefully mortgaged (unlike the property of others who fail to pay) "on account of peaceful ways" (*mipne darkhei shalom*).[46] The Mishnah then presents one tradition according to which at least some rabbis maintained that the priests are in fact exempt from this tribute: "R. Yehudah said: Ben Bukhri testified in Yavneh [that] any priest who pays the [half] shekel does not sin."[47] Underlying Ben Bukhri's statement is the notion that priests are not required to pay the tribute, and therefore the only relevant question is whether they are *allowed* to pay it. Ben Bukhri's negative formulation "any priest who pays the [half] shekel does *not* sin" strongly suggests that there were some who thought that donating to the temple's public funds when one is not obligated to do so *is* a sin, since if one is not required to pay the tribute his donation is in effect a private gift, not a contribution to a public fund. In this implied view, supplementation of the congregational funds with an unwarranted individual donation is not only not recognized favorably as a benefaction, but is in fact rebuked as a transgression.[48] Echoing this view, the Bab-

46. M. Sheqalim 1.3.
47. M. Sheqalim 1.4.
48. Later in the same passage (M. Sheqalim 1.4) Yoḥanan Ben Zakkai is quoted as saying that while the priests must pay the annual tribute, they exempt themselves by saying that if they participate in the funding of offerings they will not be able to eat of them, since the offerings of priests must be burned whole and not be eaten (Leviticus 6:23). According to this reading, the implicit "sin" of priests who pay the tribute is not in offering individual funds for congregational offerings, but in consuming offerings that are effectively "theirs."

ylonian Talmud goes so far as to say that if a congregational offering was partially funded by individual voluntary donations, the offering is to be seen as a nonconsecrated substance (*ḥullin*) that one is prohibited from bringing to the temple.[49]

The ideal temple as ideal society: Anti-euergetism and collectivism

Wherefrom emerged the rabbinic vision of congregational sacrifices as completely dissociated from any individual donors? As I mentioned above, this vision does not cohere with extant evidence on the workings of the temple and the sacrificial system in the Second Temple period, nor does it cohere with what we know of sacrifices and temples throughout the ancient Mediterranean world. I propose that it is exactly this incongruity with the prevalent model in the Hellenistic and Roman world that can serve to explain, at least in part, the rabbinic resistance to individuals providing congregational cultic needs. As Seth Schwartz showed in his study on Jewish responses to euergetism to which I alluded above, one can identify a lingering thread of Jewish resistance to this social arrangement and to the expectation of reciprocity it entails, in which the beneficiaries are held in the benefactor's debt indefinitely. This resistance is explained by Schwartz not only as due to Jews' discomfort with the favors of foreign rulers and aristocrats that generate obligations of fealty and loyalty, but also as due to the incompatibility of euergetism with the biblical ethos of solidarity, equality, and the community as one corporate body.[50]

Following in the footsteps of Schwartz, I propose that the Tannaitic insistence that congregational worship is funded strictly by the public and never by wealthy individuals reflects an ideological rejection of the euergetistic model, and an effort to construct the temple as a social and religious utopia, relying purely on communal solidarity. This effort, I wish to emphasize, is literary in nature: the rabbis are utilizing the no-longer-existing temple as what Ishay Rosen-Zvi called "a privileged site" to imagine what they deem to be an ideal society. The temple is used here, as in other mishnaic contexts noted by Rosen-Zvi, for "a revival of a distant past which is dramatized in the present . . . as part of a conscious effort of an elite group to create and to preserve collective identity through discursive means within the political limitations in which they operate."[51]

The following anecdote from tractate Sheqalim of the Mishnah serves particularly well to demonstrate the rabbis' utilization of an idealized temple to present an anti-euergetistic social and religious model:

---

49. Unless (here the Talmud echoes the Tosefta) the volunteer fully and wholeheartedly "delivered his donation to the congregation." BT Menaḥot 21b; BT ʿArakhin 4a.

50. Schwartz, *Were the Jews a Mediterranean Society?* 25–33.

51. Rosen-Zvi, "The Body and the Temple," 81 (my translation).

[A member] of the House of Rabban Gamaliel would enter [the chamber of the temple] with his [half] shekel between his fingers, and fling it in front of the collector, and the collector would intentfully (*mitkaven*) push it into the basket.[52]

"The House of Rabban Gamaliel" mentioned here refers to the patriarchal dynasty, although it is unclear whether the ambiguous epithet "of the House of (*shel beit*) Rabban Gamaliel" pertains only to the patriarchs (*nesi'im*) themselves, to every member of the family, or to a representative of the patriarchal family as a whole. Either way, the custom described here is intriguing: a member of the "first family," who according to the rabbinic depiction was both wealthy and in a position of leadership, made a point of donating his/their mandatory half-shekel right before the coins in the chamber would be collected into baskets and put to use. The practice was meant to ensure that the coin donated by the patriarch or his family would be among those put to use immediately, such that it would be used to procure the congregational sacrifices that stand at the top of the temple treasury's priorities of expenditure. This anecdote perfectly captures the anti-euergetistic vision that the early rabbis developed through the theme of the annual tribute to the temple: the wealthiest and most powerful in the Jewish community give exactly the same as everyone else in terms of quantity—a mere half-shekel—but in giving this standard tribute they demonstrate greater piety and alacrity than everyone else, thereby presenting their leadership position as resting on religious merit and not on financial resources.

Particularly interesting in regard to the rejection of euergetism is the Mishnah's comment on a practice of donating anonymously to the temple, which is equated with a practice of donating anonymously to the poor. The Mishnah mentions that there were two chambers in the temple, one called "the chamber of the discrete" (*lishkat ḥasha'im*) and the other called "the chamber of vessels" (*lishkat ha-kelim*). The former was a repository of charity: those who "fear sin" would throw money into it so as to sustain the poor.[53] The latter was a repository for artifacts that could potentially be used in the temple: "Anyone who would volunteer [to contribute] a vessel would throw it in there, and once every thirty days the treasurers would open it, and they would leave every vessel that they deemed necessary for the upkeep of the temple, and the rest would be sold for their worth and [the proceedings] would be allocated to the upkeep of the temple."[54] This passage, which ties together donations to the poor with donations to the temple, further enhances the rabbis' depiction of the temple as a social and religious utopia by portraying it as maintaining not only the cult but also a system of public welfare. More impor-

52. M. Sheqalim 3.3.
53. The Mishnah specifically refers to "poor [persons] of prominent families" (*benei tovim*), presumably because they are the ones who would be most ashamed to receive charity openly. On this phrase, see Gardner, "Giving to the Poor," 114 n. 62, 125–27.
54. M. Sheqalim 5.6.

tantly for our purposes, this passage equates a manner of giving to the poor anonymously with a manner of donating to the temple anonymously. The benefits of this discrete arrangement are perfectly understandable in the context of gifts to the poor (as such anonymous donations save the poor person the shame and embarrassment of receiving money directly);[55] but in the context of the temple this manner of giving, whether it ever was practiced or not, seems to manifest an anti-euergetistic approach, in which one does *not* want his gifts to be recognized as his own and does *not* desire the honors that gift giving to the temple usually entails.

The rabbis thus utilize the notion that public worship is funded strictly by public resources to construct an idyllic picture of Jewish/Judean cult as guided by values of egalitarianism, communal piety, and solidarity. However, by presenting a novel legislative interpretation of this paradigm, according to which individuals are emphatically *prohibited* from funding congregational offerings, the rabbis generate a social and religious model profoundly opposed to the Hellenistic-Roman one. This model can be understood accordingly as a form of cultural resistance, since the rabbis present the (imaginary) Jewish society not only as fundamentally disparate from—and better than—surrounding societies, but also as nondependent on the graces of foreign rulers and aristocrats.

Furthermore, it is perhaps unsurprising that the rabbis chose to center this idyllic picture specifically on the annual half-shekel tribute to the temple: this tribute was of symbolic significance in the relations between Jews and the Roman Empire, since in the aftermath of the Great Revolt it was transformed into the notorious "Jewish tax" (*fiscus iudaicus*).[56] This tax, which was levied by the emperor Vespasian on all Jews throughout the empire, required that the same amount that used to be paid annually to the now-destroyed Jerusalem temple (two denarii or two drachmas) be paid toward the restoration of the temple of Jupiter Capitolinus in Rome, which was burned in 69 C.E.[57] The tax continued to be collected, however, even after the temple of Jupiter was rededicated in 75 C.E.—apparently well into the third or fourth century—and at least for the first twenty years (during the time of Domitian) was said to have been enforced in a particularly harsh manner.[58] Read against

55. Such anonymous giving is emphatically praised as the noblest form of charity in Amoraic sources: see BT Baba Batra 10b; BT Ḥagigah 5a; BT Kettubot 67b. Interestingly, the rabbis devise an institution of communal funds for charity, which are also a form of anonymous giving; see Gardner, "Giving to the Poor," 49–62, 91–95.

56. I thank Alexei Sivertsev for this insight.

57. While various Roman texts mention this tax, the two sources that explicitly connect the newly levied tax with the tribute previously paid to the temple are Josephus, *Wars of the Jews* 7.6.6 (ed. Whiston 761) and Cassius Dio, *Roman History* 65.7.2 (ed. Cary 271). For discussion of these sources, see Marius Heemstra, *The Fiscus Judaicus and the Parting of the Ways* (Tübingen: Mohr Siebeck, 2010), 9–23.

58. See Martin Goodman, "Nerva, the Fiscus Judaicus, and Jewish Identity," *Journal of Roman Studies* 79 (1989): 40–44.

this historical context, the rabbis' insistence on the tribute to the temple as the only channel through which participation in the collective Jewish cult is possible can be understood as a subversion of the Roman paradigm: the tax levied by the emperor to humiliate and penalize the Jews was reappropriated by the rabbis as a marker of solidarity, religious unity, and autonomy.

On one level, then, the rabbinic construction of the temple as publicly funded can be read as a textual exercise in what anthropologist James Scott titled "the art of not being governed."[59] But on another level, I propose, the rabbinic elimination of individuals (qua individuals) from the realm of congregational worship reflects a deep-seated collectivistic ideology in which the group—in this case the people of Israel—supersedes its constitutive individuals.[60] In other words, the rabbis promote a view of the congregation as an entity that both encompasses and overrides individuals, and therefore also of congregational worship as a setting in which individuals may not be identifiable as such (or as Little League coaches would put it, "There is no I in team").

This collectivistic ideology also accounts, I contend, for the mishnaic ruling that gentiles may not partake in the annual half-shekel tribute, and that if they do attempt to pay the tribute their payment is to be rejected.[61] This ruling cannot be explained by the fact that gentiles are not obligated to pay the tribute, and therefore their payment is auxiliary, since the same passage specifies that even though women, slaves, and minors are exempt from paying the tribute, if they offer the payment it is to be accepted. This ruling also cannot be explained as part of a general prohibition to engage gentiles in the temple cult, since rabbinic literature mentions various sacrificial avenues open to gentiles who wish to worship in the Jerusalem temple.[62] Rather, I believe this ruling derives from a particularistic view of "the congregation" as consisting exclusively of Jews, which in turn leads to the view that offerings partially funded by non-Jews categorically cannot be seen as congregational. Individuals can contribute to public funds only insofar as they are absorbed by the public entity and encapsulated in it, and since gentiles cannot, in the rabbis' view, blend into the corporate entity of Israel, they cannot partake in congregational worship. In what follows, I turn to show that the rabbis' collectivis-

---

59. James C. Scott, *The Art of Not Being Governed: An Anarchist History of Upland Southeast Asia* (New Haven: Yale University Press, 2010).

60. According to Charlotte Fonrobert, there is an overarching tendency in Tannaitic literature to promote a collectivistic and anti-individualistic model of identity; see Charlotte E. Fonrobert, "'Humanity Was Created as an Individual': Synechdocal Individuality in the Mishnah as a Jewish Response to Romanization," in *The Individual in the Religions of the Ancient Mediterranean*, ed. Jörg Rüpke (New York: Oxford University Press, 2013), 489–521.

61. M. Sheqalim 1.5.

62. See, in addition to M. Sheqalim 1.5, also M. Sheqalim 7.6; and see Knohl, "Acceptance of Offerings from Gentiles"; Schwartz, *Studies in the Jewish Background of Christianity*, 102–16.

tic ideology led them not only to redefine the workings of congregational sacrifices, but also to remap the relations between individual sacrifices and congregational sacrifices.

CONGREGATIONAL SACRIFICES ABOVE AND BEYOND INDIVIDUAL SACRIFICES

Congregational offerings as means of all-encompassing atonement

Although the rabbinic vision of the annual half-shekel tribute is thoroughly idealized, this vision does take into account the possibility that some people may resist the obligation to pay the required sum at the designated time. In such a case, the practice prescribed by the Mishnah is identical to the practice prescribed for individuals who made a vow but failed to deliver the offering to the temple[63]: a portion of the property of those who retard their payment, equivalent in its value to the sum they owe, is mortgaged and taken away until they pay.[64] How does this practice of forcing people to contribute to the temple against their will square with the biblical ethos of donations (and sacrifices) made in the spirit of generosity and out of genuine piety?[65] Tosefta Sheqalim proposes a creative explanation for this seeming tension between free will and coercion, using the following parable:

> To what can this [the practice of mortgaging the property of people who fail to pay the half-shekel] be compared? To a person who was afflicted with a wound in his leg, and a physician binds him down and cuts his flesh in order to heal him. Thus said the Holy One, blessed be He: mortgage [the people of] Israel for their shekels, so that congregational offerings be offered by them. For congregational offerings appease (*meratzin*) and atone (*mekhaprin*) between Israel and their father in heaven, as we found in the donation of shekels given by the Israelites in the wilderness: "You shall take the atonement money (*kesef ha-kippurim*) from the Israelites and shall designate it for the service of the Tent of Meeting" (Exodus 30:16).[66]

The Tosefta explains the practice of forcing individuals to partake in the congregational sacrifices through mandatory tribute as equivalent to a medical procedure: while the experience itself is unpleasant for the "patient," and thus she must be forcefully made to endure it, the unpleasantness is ultimately worthwhile for her, since it yields desirable results. Accordingly, in the same way that a patient eventually approves of the painful procedure she underwent, so do the people of Israel

---

63. M. 'Arakhin 5.6.
64. M. Sheqalim 1.3.
65. As emphasized, for example, in the depiction of donations for the establishment of the tabernacle in Exodus 25:2 and 35:5.
66. T. Sheqalim 1.6.

eventually approve of the tributes they were forced to pay, such that the mandatory tribute can be seen as willful in the greater scheme of things.[67]

Much can be said about this analogy of sacrifices to medical procedures, but here I wish to focus specifically on the Tosefta's proclamation that "congregational offerings appease and atone between Israel and their father in heaven." This statement, while seemingly inconspicuous, is quite radical insofar as it points distinctly to congregational offerings as pleasing and enabling atonement. In the biblical sacrificial system, it is evident that offerings "appease and atone" for whomever offers them, whether an individual or a community, depending on the exact circumstances. For example, Leviticus 4 presents four possible scenarios for the performance of a purification sacrifice (*hattat*), a sacrifice that must be made when a person or group unwittingly committed a transgression: purification sacrifice by an anointed priest, purification sacrifice by the entire congregation, purification sacrifice by a prince, and purification sacrifice by an individual. The congregational purification sacrifice is prescribed only for cases in which the people sinned *collectively*—for example, because they were all misled or misinformed about something—whereas individuals who sinned independently must bring their own offerings in order to effect atonement. Such individuals are not atoned for by a communal offering, simply because it is not the appropriate mode of atonement for them. In contrast, the Tosefta here highlights congregational sacrifices as *the* channel through which appeasement and atonement can be attained, without indicating that those can (and sometime must) be attained for individuals through their own sacrifices. In a bold exegetical move, the Tosefta turns the half-shekel payments collected toward the census in the wilderness from a onetime means of *ransom* to an ongoing means of *atonement*, presenting this fixed payment as capable of effecting atonement perpetually, regardless of the specific circumstances.

The Tosefta's presentation of congregational offerings as "appeasing and atoning" is better understood when read against the first chapter of Mishnah Shevu'ot. At the core of this chapter stands the biblical verse of Leviticus 5:3: "When one touches human uncleanness—any uncleanness by which one can become unclean—and is unaware of it, when he comes to know it, he shall be guilty." Building on this verse, the mishnaic chapter discusses various scenarios in which a person unknowingly exposed a sacred substance to impurity (for example, by entering the temple or consuming sacred food while impure). The Mishnah subdivides the general category of "unawareness" mentioned in the verse into four subcategories:[68]

1. Awareness in both the beginning and the end but not in the interim (e.g., a person knew he was impure before entering the temple, forgot about his

67. See also Lieberman, *Tosefta ki-peshuta Mo'ed*, 4:661.
68. M. Shevu'ot 1.1–4.

impurity while in the temple, and was then reminded and realized he transgressed)

2. Awareness in the beginning but not in the end (e.g., a person knew he was impure before entering the temple but then forgot about it, and did not realize he had transgressed, if at all, until long after the events)

3. Awareness in the end and not in the beginning (e.g., a person only realized he was impure after leaving the temple)

4. Awareness neither in the beginning nor in the end (e.g., a person never knew he was impure to begin with, and did not realize he had transgressed, if at all, until long after the events)

Whereas Leviticus 5 generally prescribes a reparation offering (*'asham*) for any case of "unawareness," the Mishnah prescribes it only for cases of the first and second categories listed above, that is, cases in which the person in question initially knew of the impurity at hand and then forgot about it.[69] In contrast, in cases in which one was not initially aware of the impurity at hand and discovered it only after coming into contact with the sacred (or did not find out about it at all), the rabbis assert that atonement is effected though congregational purification offerings—whether the goats brought at the beginning of each month, the goat offered on the Day of Atonement, or the goats offered at festivals. The Mishnah's insistence that individual reparation offerings are required only if the person in question was initially aware of the impurity can be viewed as part of a general Tannaitic tendency to highlight aspects of consciousness and subjectivity in definitions of sin and guilt, as cogently shown by Noam Zohar.[70] This tendency, however, does not explain why congregational offerings are said to atone in all other cases. If the rabbis maintain that sacrifices are required only if one failed on a mental level (knowing of impurity but forgetting about it), why claim that other sacrifices are needed when such mental failure did not take place?

A plausible explanation for this sacrificial "division of labor" in the Mishnah is that the rabbis registered the priestly distinction between atoning for a person (that is, ridding an individual of the weight or "debt" of transgression),[71] and atoning for the "holy" (that is, restoring the temple and the sancta to a state of purity).[72] They maintained that while only mental failure necessitates atonement for a person—through the means of individual reparation sacrifices—any impurity

---

69. M. Shevu'ot 1.2.

70. Zohar, "Purification Offering," 89–127.

71. On the priestly perception of sin as a weight that one carries, see Baruch J. Schwartz, "The Bearing of Sin in Priestly Literature," in *Pomegranates and Golden Bells: Studies in Biblical, Jewish, and Near Eastern Ritual, Law, and Literature in Honor of Jacob Milgrom*, ed. David P. Wright, David N. Freedman, and Avi Hurvitz (Winona Lake, IN: Eisenbrauns, 1995), 3–21; see also Anderson, *Sin*, 15–39.

72. See Milgrom, *Leviticus 1–16*, 443–56.

conveyed to the sancta necessitates a sacrifice so as to be cleared away, and this is the function of congregational sacrifices.[73] In other words, congregational sacrifices serve to correct damage where there is no culprit, in accordance with the dominant Tannaitic view that if one is not mentally responsible for the transgression, one cannot be held a culprit. Through the mechanism of congregational purification sacrifices, then, the congregation as a whole can maintain the sanctity of the temple even in the shadow of individual transgressions.

The idea that congregational sacrifices allow the community to maintain the purity of the sancta and thereby its religious well-being is already biblical in origin. But in the biblical scheme it is also evident that the individual who is at fault for the breach of purity is held culpable (and therefore must bring an offering) in *all* cases, regardless of his state of awareness. In the Mishnah, in contrast, the individual is responsible only when he knew of the possibility of transgression ahead of time, and he is otherwise exempt from an offering altogether. Thus the Mishnah constructs a relation between individual and congregational sacrifices that is very different from the biblical relation. In the Priestly Code the system of congregational sacrifices is a safety valve of sorts, operating alongside but separately from individual sacrifices: those who transgressed must always bring offerings, but there is a mechanism in place to maintain the purity of the sancta in case they delay, forget, refuse, and so forth. In the Mishnah, in contrast, congregational sacrifices *replace* individual sacrifices in every case in which the transgressor is not fully responsible in the rabbis' view. If the priestly paradigm is that one is responsible for any ritual damage that one has caused, the rabbinic paradigm is that one is responsible only for ritual damages that are one's own fault—but this does not mean that for the rabbis damages that are not one's fault can be dismissed as inconsequential: they are consequential, but they are taken care of by congregational sacrifices.

The Mishnah's notion that congregational sacrifices replace individual sacrifices whenever the transgressor is not mentally at fault has significant religious implications, as this notion forcefully stands against the alternative approach, namely, the approach that one is always potentially guilty of some transgression or other even if one does not know it. If one is to adopt the priestly approach that one is fully responsible for every transgression, whether he is aware that it took place or not, then it is only natural that one who attempts to adhere to a religious system with hundreds of minute details would always assume that he has done *something* wrong and that he must atone for it. A passage in tractate Karetot indicates that the compilers of the Mishnah were familiar with such an approach, and indeed sought to reject it. This passage concerns the offering known as "reparation offering of

---

73. This reading seems to be straightforward at least in respect to Leviticus 16:15–17, which refers to the purification offering of the Day of Atonement as "atoning [for] the sanctum" (*kapper 'et ha-qodesh*).

SACRIFICE AS ONE   129

uncertainty" ('asham talui), an offering that one is supposed to bring if one believes that he may have committed a transgression, but is not sure that he has indeed done so:

> R. Eliezer said: One may volunteer a reparation offering of uncertainty on any day and at any time that one wants, and it is called "the reparation offering of the pious" ('asham ḥasidim). They said about Baba b. Butta[74] that he would volunteer a reparation offering of uncertainty every day, except for one day after the Day of Atonement. He said: By this Abode [i.e., the temple]! If they would let me I would bring it, but they tell me, "Wait until you enter [a state of] doubt." But the Sages say: One does not bring a reparation offering of uncertainty except for things that are worthy of extirpation (karet) when done consciously, and [require] a purification offering when done erroneously.[75]

R. Eliezer's statement that "one may volunteer a reparation offering of uncertainty on any day and at any time that one wants" stems from the notion that any individual at any time is potentially guilty of some transgression: there is always a possibility that one did something wrong and does not know it, and the reparation offering of uncertainty serves as a form of insurance, in the spirit of "Better safe than sorry."[76] The Sages, in contrast, do not accept this insurance policy view, and maintain that a reparation offering of uncertainty may be brought only if one has a *specific* transgression that he may have committed in mind, and moreover, a transgression of a particular kind—one of the thirty-six transgressions the punishment for which is extirpation.[77]

I propose to read the first chapter of Mishnah Shevu'ot as geared exactly against the apprehensive state of mind that underlies the practice of "the reparation offering of the pious" described in Mishnah Karetot. Whereas "the Sages" in Karetot merely reject this practice as legally unfounded and unsound, the anonymous rulings in Shevu'ot present a concrete alternative to this practice: instead of bringing a just-in-case offering that one is not required to bring, one may rest assured that his transgression, if it indeed occurred, is taken care of by congregational sacrifices. Congregational sacrifices, then, are not simply a mechanism for ensuring the purity of the sancta: they are also a mechanism for ensuring the peace of mind of each individual.

Perhaps most striking in this regard is the comment that concludes this unit in Mishnah Shev'uot, which points to one congregational offering—the scapegoat

---

74. In the printed version: ben Butti.
75. M. Karetot 6.3.
76. See Zohar, "Purification Offering," 78–88. Knohl, however, assumes that this practice derives from perpetual existential guilt and not from fear of transgression. See Israel Knohl, "A Parashah Concerned with Accepting the Kingdom of Heaven," *Tarbitz* 53, no. 1 (1984): 25–26.
77. M. Karetot 1.1.

of the Day of Atonement—as capable of atoning for any and every form of transgression:

> And for the rest of the transgressions in the Torah [in addition to conveying impurity to the sancta, as discussed so far], the minor [transgressions] and the major ones, the [ones] done consciously (*zedonot*) and the [ones] done erroneously (*shegagot*), [the ones done] knowingly and [the ones done] unknowingly, [breaching of] positive commandments and [breaching of] negative commandments, [transgressions punishable by] extirpation and [transgressions punishable by] execution by a court—the scapegoat atones [for all of them].[78]

While the scapegoat of the Day of Atonement is not an offering per se insofar as it is not offered on the altar but sent away to the wilderness, it is still considered a congregational offering in rabbinic terms and is specifically said to be funded by the annual half-shekel tribute.[79] The scapegoat, according to this passage, does for any and every transgression what the purification offerings offered during different festivals do for cases of conveying impurity to the sancta without prior knowledge. However, this passage does not limit the atoning effect of the scapegoat only to cases in which transgressions were committed unknowingly, but extends it to every possible scenario of transgression.[80]

This all-inclusive depiction of the scapegoat's atoning function is particularly significant in light of the fact that the redactors of the Mishnah held that individual purification offerings pertain only to cases in which the transgression in question is punishable by extirpation and was committed erroneously, that is, to a rather limited pool of transgressions.[81] The scapegoat is thus presented here as the ultimate mechanism of atonement, covering both transgressions for which individual purification offerings can atone *and* transgressions for which they cannot atone. This does not, of course, obviate individual purification offerings altogether, and it is still the rabbinic assumption that one is obligated to bring such offerings if the circumstances of the transgression require it, but the strong rhetoric of the Mishnah does indicate that individual purification offerings are seen, at least to some extent, as auxiliary in nature.[82]

We are now in a better position to understand the Tosefta's statement that "congregational offerings appease and atone between Israel and their father in heaven," and to perceive what I believe to be a critical aspect of the rabbinic sacrificial ethos:

---

78. M. Shevu'ot 1.6.

79. M. Sheqalim 4.2.

80. In Leviticus 16, the scapegoat is described as *removing* all the iniquities of the Israelites from the camp, but not as atoning for them; see Milgrom, *Leviticus 1–16*, 1071–79.

81. For the list of transgressions to which purification offerings apply, see M. Karetot 1.1–2.

82. The auxiliary nature of individual purification offerings is also implied in M. Yoma 8.8, here not vis-à-vis congregational purification offerings but rather vis-à-vis repentance.

for the rabbis, congregational offerings are not simply a component of temple worship, but are the very reason on account of which the temple and the cult exist in the first place.

"It suffices for an individual to be lesser than the congregation": A rabbinic sacrificial hierarchy

Above we saw that congregational purification offerings are depicted both as capable of achieving what individual offerings can achieve and as accounting for more than individual offerings can achieve. However, the preferred and elevated status of congregational offerings over individual offerings can be traced in rabbinic depictions of other types of offerings as well. One prominent example is the mishnaic account of the manner in which congregational burnt offerings are to be managed. The second chapter of Mishnah Yoma elaborates in great detail how many priests were assigned, through a lottery, to carry the sacrificial animal's parts to the altar, a number that varies in accordance with the kind of animal that is being offered (nine priests for a lamb, eleven for a ram, and twenty-four for a bull).[83] At the end of the chapter we find the following comment: "To what does this apply? To congregational offerings, but in [what concerns] individual offerings, if one wants to offer, he offers."[84] This comment indicates that no process of lottery among the priests is required to decide who manages individual offerings, as well as that individual offerings can be carried out in whichever number of priests is interested and available. This ruling has, of course, a practical component to it: presumably there are too many individual offerings on a given day to assign multiple priests for the task, and it also cannot be predicted how many individual offerings will be delivered on a specific day. But the Mishnah's point that congregational offerings require a special and festive sacrificial protocol, whereas individual offerings do not, serves to create both a visible distinction and a discursive distinction between the two types of sacrifices: not only are congregational sacrifices and individual sacrifices performed differently,[85] but the exact manner of performance is also an important legislative issue in the case of the former and a nonissue in the case of the latter.

The mishnaic distinction between the ritualized and orchestrated manner of handling congregational offerings and the freestyle manner of handling individual offerings serves as a powerful indication that the rabbis work to create artificial differences between two types of sacrifices that are not actually inherently different

---

83. M. Yoma 2.5–7; cf. M. Tamid 4.3.
84. M. Yoma 2.7.
85. In BT Yoma 26a, the requirement for multiple priests in the handling of congregational offerings is explained by the verse "The glory of a king is a multitude of people" (Proverbs 14:28); cf. BT Sukkah 52b.

from one another. Put differently, since the sacrificial substances and procedures are effectively identical for both individual and congregational offerings, the distinctions between them are imposed, rather than revealed, in rabbinic sources, and are imposed specifically in order to pronounce the supremacy of congregational sacrifices over individual sacrifices. A particularly instructive example for such artificial imposition of difference, and thereby of the supremacy of congregational sacrifices, can be found in the following passage:

> A person may volunteer [to offer] a grain offering of sixty tenths [of an *'efah* of fine flour], and deliver it in one vessel. But if he said, "Sixty-one [tenths of an *'efah*] are upon me," he delivers sixty tenths in one vessel and one tenth in another vessel. This is because on the first day of the festival [i.e., Sukkot] that happens to take place on the Sabbath, the congregation brings sixty-one [tenths], and it suffices for an individual to be lesser than the congregation [in the amount of] one [tenth].[86]

Grain offerings of a "tenth" (*'isaron*) of fine flour are usually brought to the altar as accompaniment for animal offerings, but they can also be offered by individuals independently, as offerings in their own right. The minimal amount of a fine flour offering is one tenth, but the rabbis maintain that individuals may offer up to sixty tenths if they desire to do so.[87] This does not mean that one is prohibited from bringing more than sixty tenths, but rather that any amount greater than sixty— even by a single tenth—must be placed in a difference vessel and be treated as a separate offering. The reason provided in the Mishnah for this ruling is that sixty-one tenths is the maximal amount offered by the congregation. This amount of fine flour is offered when the first day of Sukkot happens to take place on the Sabbath, which results in a particularly large number of animal offerings and thereby of accompanying grain offerings.[88] Since the maximal amount of fine flour in a congregational offering is sixty-one tenths, the maximal amount of fine flour in an individual offering has to be less than that, in order to maintain the superiority of the congregation to the individual. This reasoning is later rejected by R. Shimon, who argues that the reason for this restriction is practical (more than sixty tenths of fine flour will not mix with oil thoroughly enough).[89] But whatever the "original" reason for the restriction of individuals' fine flour offering may be, it is notable that in order to explain this restriction the anonymous Mishnah utilizes the notion

86. M. Menaḥot 12.4.

87. M. Menaḥot 13.2.

88. On the first day of Sukkot the sacrificial protocol calls for thirteen bulls, each one of which is accompanied by three tenths of fine flours; for two rams, each of which is accompanied by two tenths of fine flour; and for fourteen lambs, each of which is accompanied by one tenth of fine flour (39+4+14 = 57). In addition, four additional lambs, each accompanied by one tenth of fine flour, are offered if the festival takes place on the Sabbath.

89. Cf. T. Menaḥot 12.8.

that congregational offerings must be different from—and superior to—individual offerings, and regards this notion as self-evident.

It is not difficult to explain why the rabbis hold congregational sacrifices in higher regard than individual sacrifices: certainly the very concept of an offering made for the sake of an entire community suggests that such an offering is more powerful and more potent than an offering made by individuals. The fact that most congregational sacrifices are associated with festivals and holy days similarly assigns them greater festivity and sanctity than mundane individual sacrifices. I propose, nonetheless, that the rabbis establish a clear sacrificial hierarchy in which congregational sacrifices surpass individual sacrifices—both in efficacy and in mode of performance—not only in order to make a statement about sacrifices, but also in order to make a statement about the relations between individual and community. The collectivistic ideology promoted by the rabbis, which leads them to portray congregational offerings as offered by everyone (through the half-shekel tribute) and therefore, emphatically, by no one in particular, also leads them to portray individual sacrifices as inferior to congregational sacrifices. Since all individuals are implicated in the congregation, and participate in the sacrificial cult insofar as they are constitutive of the congregation, individual participation loses some, if not much, of its independent religious value in the rabbinic reframing of sacrifice.

The notion that all individuals are implicated in the congregation, and therefore each and every person can be actively considered an owner and offerer of each congregational offering, is put forth especially vividly in tractate Ta'anit of the Mishnah, which discusses the institution of ma'amad ("post" or "office," but literally "standing up"). According to the Mishnah, each one of the twenty-four divisions of priests, which took turns serving in the temple, was matched with a ma'amad, a group of laypeople from among the locals of Jerusalem, who took turns being present at the temple while congregational sacrifices were made.[90] The laypeople of the ma'amad function in this setting as representatives of the entire people of Israel, and their role while present at the temple is simply to embody each and every member of the congregation as an owner of each and every congregational offering. The Mishnah asks rhetorically, "How can a person's offering be offered when he is not attending to it?"—thus asserting that congregational offerings should, in principle, be made in the presence of every person who partook in their funding, and that it is only because of technical difficulty that a small group of representatives stands in for the entirety of the congregation. This very institution of representation, however, manifests the principle that congregational offerings are, at their core, individual offerings—each individual is an owner of each

90. M. Ta'anit 4.2.

congregational offering—and accordingly, that individuals actively express their personal piety through their membership in the collective.

The most radical expression of the collectivistic tendency in the rabbinic construction of sacrifice can be traced in the identification of the Passover and pilgrimage offerings as congregational offerings. I will discuss this topic extensively in the next chapter, but for now suffice it to note that alongside texts that unequivocally classify these two offerings as individual offerings, we find several texts that classify one or both of them as congregational offerings. This is quite surprising, since the Passover and pilgrimage offerings—which are similar in form and function insofar as they mainly serve to constitute a feast for their offerers—do not meet the two basic criteria for congregational offerings: they are not funded *by* the public (but rather each household or group provides its own offering), and they are not offered *for* the public (but rather, again, for each household or group as its own unit).

On one level, these conflicting classifications seem to reflect a controversy about what makes a sacrifice congregational, its mode of obligation or its mode of performance: since the obligation to perform the Passover or pilgrimage is incumbent upon the people of Israel as a whole, it can be claimed that the respective offerings on those occasions are congregational in essence even if they are technically performed by individuals. On another level, however, the classification of these offerings as congregational seems to rely on a corporate view of the people of Israel, according to which a single sacrificial performance, if it is collectively sanctioned, is ritually akin to multiple sacrificial performances. This view is made explicit in a ruling attributed to R. Eliezer, according to which "if all the people of Israel have only a single Passover [lamb] they can all fulfill their obligation through it."[91] While the Pentateuch explicitly requires that each household provide its own lamb, this requirement is interpreted by R. Eliezer as auxiliary in nature, since a single Passover offering can accomplish for the Israelites the exact same thing that thousands of offerings can accomplish. R. Eliezer's position is guided by the view that if the Passover sacrifice must be performed by the people as such, then it must be performed by them *as a collective,* that is, as a single entity, and for a single entity a single sacrifice suffices. Individual Passover (and similarly, pilgrimage) offerings are not, according to this view, expressions of individual cultic agency, but rather multiple expressions of a collective cultic agency.

Reframing the sacrificial experience: Congregational
sacrifices as spectacles

The rabbinic attempt to establish a palpable, visible difference between congregational sacrifices and individual sacrifices is manifest not only in the insistence on

---

91. Mekhilta deRabbi Ishmael Bo 5 (ed. Horovitz-Rabin 17); cf. PT Pesaḥim 7.5, 34b; BT Pesaḥim 78b; BT Qiddushin 42a.

a different manner of performance, but also in the purposeful shaping of congregational sacrifices as *spectacles*.[92] In its narrative descriptions of two central rituals of congregational sacrifices—the daily morning sacrifice and the Day of Atonement sacrifice—the Mishnah makes a point of incorporating an audience into the sacrificial scene, occasionally referring to "the people" (*ha-ʿam*) as present and responsive in the ritual.

Thus, for example, in tractate Tamid of the Mishnah the rabbinic account of the rituals surrounding the daily burnt offering includes a component that has no trace in the priestly literature[93]—a blessing of "the people" by the officiating priests.[94] The "people" who are being blessed are clearly physically present in the temple, since the Mishnah mentions that they prostrate every time the priests blow the horn.[95] Particularly interesting in this regard is a comment according to which just before the priest in charge was about to offer incense—a ritual that must be performed with no one else in the sanctuary[96]—"the people departed" (*pershu ha-ʿam*).[97] This comment confounded the traditional commentators of the Mishnah, since presumably laypeople are prohibited from being in the sanctuary at all times and are restricted to the temple courts, and there is no reason why they should depart from the court while the incense is offered.[98] Therefore, commentators assumed that the term "people" is used here to refer to the priests who must leave the area between the hall and the altar during the offering of incense.[99] Such usage of the word "people," however, is highly irregular and improbable, and it seems more likely that the mishnaic author here wished to stress that "the people" were present and observing the sacrificial process: this author did so at the expense of coherence with standard ritual protocols.

Who are "the people" who were present at the temple during the ritual of the morning daily offering? One possibility is that this term refers to the members of the *maʿamad,* the representative group of laypeople matched with the division of the priests, but the Mishnah does not say so explicitly. Alternatively, the Mishnah

92. On the literary construction of rabbinic temple rituals as spectacles, see also Naftali S. Cohn, "The Ritual Narrative Genre in the Mishnah: The Invention of the Rabbinic Past in the Representation of Temple Ritual" (PhD diss., University of Pennsylvania, 2008), 146–59.

93. See Israel Knohl, "Between Voice and Silence: The Relations between Prayer and Temple Cult," *Journal of Biblical Literature* 115, no. 1 (1996): 17–30.

94. M. Tamid 5.1; and see my elaborate discussion in chapter 5.

95. M. Tamid 7.3.

96. Leviticus 16:17.

97. M. Tamid 6.3.

98. See Albeck, *The Six Orders of the Mishnah: Qodashim,* 429. Albeck mentions a passage in the Sifra (Aḥare mot 3.4.6, ed. Weiss 81d) that explicitly rejects the notion that the people must leave the court when incense is being offered.

99. See Maimonides and Obadiah of Berteniro's Mishnah commentaries, both of which seem to rely on M. Kelim 1.9.

may be referring to the people who happened to come to the temple that day in order to perform their own individual sacrifices, but again this is not specified in the text. Rather, the Mishnah makes it seem as though "the people" are present at the temple specifically *in order* to observe the daily offering, thereby depicting this ritual as inherently involving spectatorship, and depicting this spectatorship as a form of participation in the ritual on the congregation's end.

The role of "the people" as engaged spectators is emphasized even more in tractate Yoma of the Mishnah, which describes the various sacrificial procedures of the Day of Atonement, a day on which no one except for the high priest is sacrificing, and therefore there is no reason for any person to be present in the temple area except as a spectator. The rituals of the day are emphatically described as meant to be watched,[100] and one mishnaic passage even makes a point of saying that the spectators had to choose which of the rituals they wanted to watch, since there was more than one option:

> One who sees the high priest as he is reading [the Torah] cannot see the bull and the goat being burned, and one who sees the bull and the goat being burned cannot see the high priest as he is reading, not because one is not permitted [to do so], but rather because there was a long way [between the places in which these two rituals were performed] and they were both [performed] at the same time.[101]

Moreover, in the Day of Atonement rituals the presence of the people is not merely assumed, but in fact shapes and impacts particular components of the ritual. For example, the Mishnah mentions that when the high priest is washing and changing his garments (which he does five times during the day), a sheet of fine linen is put forth to hide him from the people.[102] In addition, the Mishnah stipulates that the prayer said by the high priest after he exits the inner sanctum must be short, "so as not to terrify Israel."[103] The picture underlying this stipulation is of a multitude of people anxiously waiting to see if the high priest will emerge alive from the inner sanctum, a place harboring the danger of death to anyone who enters it,[104] and the more time the high priest takes, the more the people start to panic. The high priest's prayer is thus specifically designed with the gazing eye of the people in mind.[105]

---

100. See M. Yoma 1.8: "The rooster's call would not come about until the court was filled with [the people of] Israel." This statement could be understood as referring either only to the Day of Atonement or to any day in the year.

101. M. Yoma 7.2.

102. M. Yoma 3.4, 3.6.

103. M. Yoma 5.1.

104. The same notion is reiterated in M. Yoma 7.4, in which it is mentioned that the high priest would conduct a feast at the end of the Day of Atonement in gratitude for having survived the endeavor.

105. The printed edition of the Mishnah also mentions that the people prostrated after hearing the name of God uttered by the high priest (M. Yoma 6.2 and in some editions also M. Yoma 3.8). However, the Mishnah's manuscripts do not include this comment.

The creators of the Mishnah, then, shape the two congregational offerings that they describe at length not only as belonging to everyone (since the entire public participates in their funding), and not only as efficacious for everyone, but also as accessible and visible to everyone. Thereby, the experience of making a pilgrimage to the temple in order to present one's own offerings, which in the book of Psalms is described as an experience of religious elation,[106] is replaced in the Mishnah with the experience of witnessing congregational sacrifices in the temple. Whereas the role of the owner in individual offerings is effectively eradicated in rabbinic legislation, as I showed in detail in chapter 1, the role of the "people" in congregational sacrifices is highlighted and played up, such that congregational worship comes to be seen as the quintessential and ultimate expression of the Jewish sacrificial cult. By way of conclusion to this chapter, I will suggest that we can gain further insights into the construction of congregational sacrifices in Tannaitic texts by examining the social and political context in which early rabbinic literature developed, and by considering the intricate relations between sacrifice and group identity in the first centuries of the Common Era.

CONGREGATIONAL SACRIFICES AND JEWISH IMPERIAL IDENTITY

The concept of congregational or communal offerings, made on behalf of the people as a collective, is by no means a rabbinic invention. As I mentioned at the beginning of this chapter, this notion is deeply rooted in biblical (primarily priestly) texts, and it is paralleled in the religious cultures of ancient Greece and Rome, in which communal sacrifices were regularly made for collective entities—from the city or *polis* to the entire empire.[107] What makes the rabbinic picture unique, I have argued, is not the institution of congregational offerings as such nor the reliance of such offerings on public funding, but rather (1) the insistence that these offerings never be provided by any identifiable individual but only by the people as a whole through a system of fixed and mandatory payments, and (2) the rhetorical elevation of congregational offerings above and beyond individual offerings. Both these tendencies, I suggested, are guided by a strong collectivistic ethos, through which the rabbis shape the mandatory funding of congregational offerings as a genuine form of cultic participation for each and every person in the congregation. While there are, of course, still avenues of individual sacrificial activity in rabbinic legislation—both

106. See Regev, "Offerings of Righteousness."
107. See, for example, Stanley Stowers, "Greeks Who Sacrifice and Those Who Do Not," in *The Social World of the First Christians: Essays in Honor of Wayne A. Meeks,* ed. L. Michael White and O. Larry Yarbrough (Philadelphia: Fortress Press, 1995), 293–333.

required and voluntary—the rabbis make the point that when one pays the tribute to the temple one is, in fact, seen as someone who actively brought an offering.

As the rabbis develop this interpretation of congregational sacrifices as fully and utterly communal—as made not only *for* everyone but also *by* everyone, such that each member of the community is an owner but no one member of the community can be *the* owner—they also create a communal paradigm that is fundamentally defined by sacrificial practice. In other words, the rabbinic notion that congregational offerings must be funded exclusively through the annual tribute to the temple, alongside the rulings that each and every free Jewish male (including priests!) must pay this tribute and that non-Jews are prohibited from paying this tribute, creates an equation between participation in the funding of congregational offerings and Jewishness itself. Congregational offerings in Tannaitic literature are therefore not merely one component of the worship in the temple: they are constructed as emblems of Jewish group identity, acquiring their efficacy through the cultic agency of every member of the group while unequivocally excluding anyone who is not a member.

The Mishnah's discussion of the collection of the temple tribute divides potential payers into four groups: those who must pay and whose property is mortgaged if they fail to do so, which includes "Levites and Israel[ites], converts, and freed slaves"; those who officially have to pay but are not forced to do so, namely, priests; those who do not have to pay, but whose payments are accepted if they offer them, which includes persons without full legal agency (women, slaves, and minors); and those whose payments are not accepted even if they venture to pay, under which category fall gentiles and Samaritans.[108] No criterion is suggested, however, as to what allows one to be considered an "Israel[ite]." Is it one's descent, or one's way of life? Are Jews by birth who do not self-identify as such among those whose property is mortgaged if they fail to pay? Are Jews by birth whom the rabbis identify as wayward or "heretical" required to pay? The Mishnah does not address these questions, thereby painting a somewhat idyllic picture (as it does throughout tractate Sheqalim), in which the question of who is to be counted among "Israel" for the purposes of the temple tribute is an unproblematic one.

While there is nothing unusual about the Tannaitic use of "Israel" as a straightforward category that requires no further explanation,[109] the unproblematized use of this inclusive term in regard to the temple tribute is particularly notable in light of our knowledge of the Roman counterpart of the half-shekel, the *fiscus iudaicus*. As Martin Goodman has shown, the Roman policy of levying a tax on all the Jews

108. M. Sheqalim 1.3–5.
109. On the binary division of "Israel" as opposed to "gentile" in rabbinic literature, see Ishay Rosen-Zvi and Adi Ophir, "*Goy*: Towards a Genealogy," *Dine Israel* 28 (2011): 69–122.

throughout the empire forced Roman officials to confront and debate the question of who ought to be considered a Jew for tax purposes, and ultimately to exempt from the tax Jews by descent who did not openly identify as such. In Goodman's concise words, "Nerva may have unwittingly taken a significant step toward the treatment of Jews in late antiquity more as a religion than as a nation."[110] Recently, Marius Heemstra has further bolstered Goodman's observations by arguing that the Roman *fiscus iudaicus* policy played a major role in the "parting of the ways" between Jews and Christians when the latter were officially exempt from the tax, and were thus identified by the empire as non-Jews.[111] If we consider the rabbinic discourse on congregational offerings against the background of the shifting boundaries and definitions of Jewishness in the first centuries of the Common Era, we may be able to gain a better understanding of the stakes that the rabbis had in depicting the collective cult as a manifestation of a perfectly cohesive and united ethno-religious entity.

When the rabbis shaped the temple tribute as a marker of communal identity, they tied together communal identity specifically with sacrificial activities: in the Tannaitic model, being part of "Israel" acquires a distinct meaning of being an offerer—through the mandatory tribute—of congregational offerings. Membership in the collective thus takes the form of membership in sacrifice: those by whom and for whom congregational sacrifices are made are affirmed by those sacrifices as one united community, embodying ideals of equality and solidarity. Moreover, in the rabbinic rhetoric congregational offerings are exactly what allows the survival of the community *as* a community: those offerings "appease and atone between Israel and their father in heaven," such that even if individuals from among the community sin, the collective as such remains intact. Congregational sacrifices, then, are presented by the rabbis not only as manifestations of communal identity but also as allowing the community to survive and regenerate.

The notion that shared sacrifices generate and solidify group boundaries and establish patterns of belonging and affinity is deeply engrained in the social reality of the ancient world. As Stanley Stowers has shown in detail, from archaic Greece to the Roman Empire sacrificial practices were so critical in the formation of relations of kinship and of communal associations that in all prominent forms of social organization "the criterion for membership was not birth but sacrifice."[112] From the basic unit of the household (*oikos*) through the larger unit of the clan (*genos*) to the most inclusive unit of the city (*polis*), participation in common sacrificial cult was the definitive maker and marker of membership. Since sacrifice

110. Goodman, "Nerva, the Fiscus Judaicus, and Jewish Identity," 40.
111. Heemstra, *The Fiscus Judaicus.*
112. Stowers, "Greeks Who Sacrifice," 311.

was seen as a quintessential familial activity,[113] occasions on which a group of people sacrificed together were seen as constitutive of this group of people as a family of sorts. This view of shared sacrifice as establishing relations of kinship among the participants remained highly influential in the Roman Empire throughout the first centuries of the Common Era, but, as Philippa Townsend has shown, during that period this notion went through significant transformations that were inextricably linked to the transformations of the concept and practice of sacrifice itself.[114] Sacrifice became a site through which aspects of particular versus universal identity were negotiated,[115] and through which the possibilities of forming new modes of kinship were brought to the fore. In particular, Townsend focuses on a theme developed in several early Christian works, according to which the sacrificial blood of Christ generated the Christians as a new race (*ethnos*). In Townsend's words, "The procreative powers of material sacrifice provide a physical, as well as spiritual, basis for the kinship of the Christian people, which serves to replace that of traditional descent through sexual production."[116]

The most instructive example of the use of sacrifice to establish new modes of kinship and to generate communal identities is the Roman imperial cult,[117] and particularly the cults of the Genius Augusti and Lares Augusti, in which the imperial family's ancestors and household gods were worshipped in the same way that each family's own ancestors and household gods were worshipped.[118] By establishing the imperial *gens* as an object of devotion across cities, regions, and languages, the Roman Empire effectively turned all its residents (at least those who did not resist this cult) into a single clan.[119] Moreover, in certain respects it was not only imperial sacrifices but sacrifice in general that functioned as a unifying mechanism in the Roman Empire. As James Rives observed, the very practice of sacrifice, for all its different versions and permutations, was conceived in the Roman Empire

---

113. See Peter Altman, *Festive Meals in Ancient Israel: Deuteronomy's Identity Politics in Their Ancient Near Eastern Context* (Berlin: Walter de Gruyter, 2011). Several mishnaic passages similarly retain the idea that sacrifice is essentially a family activity; for example, M. Ḥagigah 1.5: "If one has many eaters [that is, many household members] and few assets, he should bring [on a pilgrimage] many well-being offerings and few burnt offerings; [if one has] few eaters and many assets, he should bring many burnt offerings and few well-being offerings."

114. Philippa L. Townsend, "Another Race? Ethnicity, Universalism, and the Emergence of Christianity" (PhD diss., Princeton University, 2009), 208–76.

115. Townsend, "Another Race?," 217–40; see also Jeremy M. Schott, *Christianity, Empire, and the Making of Religion in Late Antiquity* (Philadelphia: University of Pennsylvania Press, 2008).

116. Townsend, "Another Race?," 248 (emphasis in the original).

117. For a helpful overview of the Roman imperial cult, see Simon R. F. Price, "Between Man and God: Sacrifice in the Roman Imperial Cult," *Journal of Roman Studies* 70 (1980): 28–43.

118. On the Lares Augusti and Genius Augusti, see J. Bert Lott, *The Neighborhoods of Augustan Rome* (New York: Cambridge University Press, 2004), 107–17.

119. On Christian resistance to the imperial cult, see Heyman, *The Power of Sacrifice*, 161–235.

as the closest thing to a unified imperial religion: "Because [sacrifice] was not clearly marked as either Greek or Roman in origin, it seemed universal. . . . Since some form of ritualized slaughter was already practiced among many of the peoples over whom the Romans established hegemony, it was readily available as a tool for cultural and political integration."[120] According to Rives, it was this exact view of sacrifice as a universal phenomenon—and as a universalizing and uniting tool—that led the emperor Trajan Decius to require every Roman citizen to perform a sacrifice in the presence of an imperial official in 249 C.E.: it was an attempt to interpolate every single individual across the empire into the collective imperial entity.[121] Sacrifice in the Roman Empire was the most immediate channel through which one could express one's pertinence to a greater collective, a topic to which I will return in the conclusion.[122]

It is perhaps not incidental that the rabbis developed a picture of congregational offerings as idealized manifestations of unity and solidarity at a time in which ethnic and religious identities and boundaries were going through rapid transformations, and in which those transformations were often deeply entangled in sacrificial discourse and sacrificial practice. Against the surge of ideas regarding one's ability to choose one's family and one's race, against universalizing ideals of "Greekness" or "Romanness,"[123] and against the changing definitions of Jewishness itself and the effort on the side of multiple actors to reconfigure its boundaries,[124] the rabbinic discourse on congregational offerings can be seen as an attempt to fantasize a stable and self-contained Jewish identity, generated by and affirmed through sacrifice. The temple is construed in this fantasy as the emblem of Jewish oneness, and communal sacrificial worship as an expression of complete consonance between each individual and the collective to which he belongs. As we shall see in the next chapter, the rabbinic collectivistic ethos, the view of sacrifice as a unifying mechanism, and the depiction of "Israel" as a cohesive entity that expresses its unity through sacrificial practices also play a definitive role in the rabbinic construction of the Passover sacrifice.

120. Rives, "Animal Sacrifice and Political Identity," 109.

121. James B. Rives, "The Decree of Decius and the Religion of the Empire," *Journal of Roman Studies* 89 (1999): 135–54.

122. Peter Herz explains the pervasiveness of sacrificial rituals in the Roman army in a similar way: "It would be appropriate to say that it was the emperors' main intention to achieve a religious Romanization of all soldiers without any regard to their origin or personal beliefs." See Peter Herz, "Sacrifice and Sacrificial Ceremonies in the Roman Imperial Army," in *Sacrifice in Religious Experience*, ed. Albert I. Baumgarten (Leiden: Brill, 2002), 85.

123. On the influence of universal notions of Greekness and Romanness in the eastern Roman Empire of the first centuries, see Nathanael J. Andrade, *Syrian Identity in the Graeco-Roman World* (Cambridge: Cambridge University Press, 2013), 245–340.

124. See Daniel Boyarin, *Border Lines: The Partition of Judaeo-Christianity* (Philadelphia: University of Pennsylvania Press, 2004), 37–85.

4

Three Hundred Passovers

One of the foundational myths of the rabbinic movement is the story of Hillel the Elder's appointment as patriarch.[1] As the story goes, one time the fourteenth of Nisan, the day on which the Passover sacrifice (henceforth the Passover[2]) is ritually performed, took place on the Sabbath. The people, or their leaders,[3] were confounded by the question, Which is to take precedence, the Sabbath (on which slaughter is prohibited) or the sacrifice? Should the sacrifice be postponed until after the Sabbath, or should the Sabbath be violated for the sake of the sacrifice? When Hillel the Elder is approached with this question, his initial cryptic response is "Do we have only one Passover a year that [may] override the Sabbath? We have more than three hundred[4] Passovers a year, and they [surely] override the Sabbath!" Seeing the confusion of his peers, he continues to explain:

1. T. Pisḥa 4.12–13. Cf. PT Pesaḥim 6:1, 33a; BT Pesaḥim 66a. For an excellent analysis of the different versions of this story, see Menachem Katz, "The Stories of Hillel's Appointment as Nasi in the Talmudic Literature: A Foundation Legend of the Jewish Scholars' World" [Heb.], Sidra 26 (2011): 81–116.

2. I chose to refer to the offering made on the fourteenth of Nisan as "the Passover," since this is the most accurate English rendering of the Hebrew term ha-pesaḥ. The Passover festival, it should be noted, is named after the offering and not vice versa.

3. In the Tosefta version it is not specified who raised the question before Hillel, but in the Palestinian and Babylonian Talmuds the conundrum is associated with the patriarchal family at the time, the sons of Betera. This association could be the result of a harmonizing interpretation of T. Pisḥa 4.13 with T. Sanhedrin 7.11.

4. In the Babylonian Talmud the version is "two hundred Passovers." In the Palestinian Talmud there is a discussion of whether the correct version is one hundred, two hundred, or three hundred.

The daily offering (*tamid*) is a congregational offering, and the Passover is a congregational offering. In the same way that the daily offering—as a congregational offering—overrides the Sabbath, so does the Passover—as a congregational offering—override the Sabbath.

Furthermore, it was said "at its appointed time" (*be-mo'ado*) regarding the daily offering (Numbers 28:2), and it was said "at its appointed time" regarding the Passover (Numbers 9:2). In the same way that the daily offering—about which it was said "at its appointed time"—overrides the Sabbath, so does the Passover—about which it was said "at its appointed time"—override the Sabbath.

Furthermore, this can be deduced a fortriori: If the daily offering, for which there is no [punishment of] extirpation [if one fails to perform it], overrides the Sabbath, does not logic require that the Passover, for which there is [a punishment of] extirpation [if one fails to perform it], would also override the Sabbath?

Furthermore, I have received [a tradition] from my masters that the Passover overrides the Sabbath.[5]

Whether it is Hillel's series of scriptural reasonings that convinces his peers or his conclusive statement that he is following an established teaching of his masters,[6] his ruling that the Passover overrides the Sabbath is fully endorsed, and the story concludes not only with a celebratory performance of the Passover but also with the appointment of Hillel as the legendary founder of the patriarchal dynasty.

This well-known story came to be so seminal within the rabbinic foundational mythology because it is seen as capturing the triumph of rabbinic hermeneutics: Hillel is depicted in this story as successfully utilizing the interpretive tools known as *middot*—rules of scriptural analogy and comparison—to reach a convincing and lasting legal decision.[7] Here, however, I wish to draw attention to the substance of the analogy put forth by Hillel rather than to the methods through which this analogy is laid out. A closer look reveals that the only equation that is immediately relevant to the question at hand, namely, whether the Passover overrides the Sabbath, is the appearance of the expression "at its appointed time" in the Pentateuch in regard to both the daily offering and the Passover. This scriptural resonance in itself suffices to support the claim that the time of these offerings is fixed in the calendar and should not be changed, and indeed in the Mekhilta, in which the story of Hillel does not appear, the repeated expression "at its appointed time" provides all the scriptural proof necessary for the ruling that the Passover,

---

5. Quoted according to the Tosefta (MS Vienna version).

6. Indeed in the Palestinian Talmud's version Hillel's arguments are all rejected, and only the received tradition carries weight with his interlocutors. In the Babylonian Talmud, in contrast, the received tradition is not mentioned at all in this part of the account, and only appears at a later point.

7. As recounted in T. Sanhedrin 7.11; on these interpretive tools, see David Daube, "Rabbinic Methods of Interpretation and Hellenistic Rhetoric," *Hebrew Union College Annual* 22 (1949): 239–64.

like the daily offering, overrides the Sabbath.[8] In the narrative, in contrast, Hillel attempts to establish a broader analogy: he wants to show that the Passover is comparable to the daily offering across the board, that is, that the two are fundamentally the same type of offering—so much so that one can say that there are multiple "Passovers" every year and not just one. It is not that these two different offerings are similar insofar as they share the trait of calendrical fixedness, but rather we can surmise that they share the trait of calendrical fixedness because they are similar. The very notion that these two offerings are generally comparable is far from being self-evident, and should in itself be appreciated for its boldness, since on the face of it no two offerings in the Israelite sacrificial system are more different: whereas the daily offering is a burnt offering, that is, an offering consumed in its entirety on the altar and in which human beings have no share, the Passover is primarily if not exclusively a meal, a feast shared among small groups of laypeople.

Interestingly enough, in arguing for an overarching analogy between the Passover and the daily offering, Hillel does not mention the most immediate and palpable similarity between those two offerings—the fact that they both require exactly the same type of animal: an unblemished yearling male lamb.[9] Rather, he curiously classifies both of them as "congregational offerings," an odd statement to make since, as I mentioned in the previous chapter, the Passover is brought by individuals for individuals and does not seem to qualify as a congregational offering at all.[10] Indeed, Hillel's comparison of the daily offering and the Passover as two kinds of congregational offerings is entirely missing from the rendition of this story in the Babylonian Talmud, a clear indication, as noted by Menachem Katz,[11] that the Babylonian adaptors of this tradition were uncomfortable with what seemed like a blatant contradiction of the Mishnah's identification of the Passover as an individual offering.[12]

I propose, then, that there is more at stake in this narrative then the specific ruling on whether or not the Passover should be performed on the Sabbath: the scriptural arguments attributed to Hillel are animated by the greater question of the role and status of the Passover sacrifice within the Israelite cultic system. By positioning the Passover alongside the daily offering, the ultimate marker of congregational worship, Hillel makes the point that the popular sacrificial feast, in which multitudes of people participate through eating and drinking, is as sacred and as constitutive of the cultic life as the daily ritual conducted by the priests in

---

8. Mekhilta deRabbi Ishmael Bo 5 (ed. Horovitz-Rabin 17).

9. Exodus 12:5; Numbers 28:3.

10. Lieberman (*Tosefta ki-peshuta Mo'ed,* 4:566–67) conjectured that the Tosefta did not actually intend to classify the Passover as a congregational offering in every respect, and that it used the term "congregational offering" very loosely.

11. Katz, "The Stories of Hillel's Appointment," 102 n. 74.

12. M. Menaḥot 9.7; see also T. Temurah 1.17; BT Yoma 51a.

which an offering is given in its entirety to God. This ruling resonates with another ruling attributed to the House of Hillel, according to which during pilgrimage festivals one is to spend on feast offerings—that is, offerings eaten by the owners— double the amount that one is to spend on burnt offerings (in contrast to the opin- ion of the House of Shammai, which requires spending the greater sum on burnt offerings).[13] Hillel and his school are thus depicted in rabbinic sources as priori- tizing public participation in the temple's life, and promoting an anthropocentric rather than a theocentric sacrificial vision.[14]

The story of Hillel and the Passover that took place on the Sabbath therefore functions in rabbinic lore as a story of a double triumph: the triumph of herme- neutical methods and the triumph of popular forms of piety.[15] But underlying this story is a fundamental question that had been engaging biblical interpreters for centuries before the rabbis and has continued to engage biblical interpreters for centuries after the rabbis: What *is* the Passover? An anomaly within the biblical sacrificial landscape, the Passover fails to fall under any clear-cut category. It has some characteristics of each one of the major sacrificial types (burnt offering, well- being offering, and purification offering), but does not fully cohere with any of them; it is both domestic and centralized, both private and public, both a meal and a purification rite; it is not clear whether the main obligation that it entails is to sacrifice or to eat; and it is not clear what its purpose is and what makes it effica- cious. The conflicting and ambiguous accounts of the Passover in the Pentateuch constitute a lingering interpretive problem for later readers who venture to pro- vide a systematic account of this ritual, but they also—as interpretive problems usually do—provide opportunities for interpreters to promote their own ritual and social agenda through their construction of the ritual. In the narrative we have seen above, Hillel reframes the Passover in the image of the daily burnt offering (and ignores features of the former that are clearly incongruent with the latter) in order to advocate not only for a certain ad-hoc ruling but also, as I argued, for a particular vision of the importance of massively attended sacrificial feasts. This chapter will show that the tradition regarding Hillel is but one example of the complex and multivalent rabbinic attempts to define, conceptualize, and analogize the Passover so as to determine its place and function in the sacrificial system, attempts in which sustained interpretive efforts converge with rabbinic views on the workings of sacrifices more broadly.

13. M. Ḥagigah 1.2.

14. As argued by Hallewy, "The First Controversy"; and Knohl, "Participation of the People in Temple Worship."

15. The championing of popular piety is especially evident in the second part of the story, in which the people devise by themselves, without being instructed, methods of bringing their knives to the temple without violating the Sabbath, thereby demonstrating Hillel's declaration that "if they are not prophets, they are sons of prophets."

Because the polymorphism and ambiguity of the Passover make it an especially pliable and malleable ritual category, this rabbinic construction of the Passover serves as an illuminating test case for the interpretive and legislative tendencies identified in the previous chapters. In particular, this chapter explores two central disputes regarding the nature of the Passover that loom large in rabbinic sources: first, a dispute about whether the Passover is an individual or a congregational offering, and second, a dispute about whether it is the tossing of blood or eating of meat that constitutes the most definitive action vis-à-vis the Passover. These two disputes, which in the case of the Passover are intertwined, help both to underscore the prominence of the legislative transformations in the rabbinic sacrificial discourse pointed to earlier, and to understand some of the greater ideational stakes involved in the construction of the Passover in early rabbinic literature.

ONE FOR ALL, ALL FOR ONE: THE PASSOVER BETWEEN INDIVIDUAL AND CONGREGATION

Chapter 12 in the book of Exodus, which relates the events of the night of the Israelites' departure from Egypt and the ritual instructions surrounding these events, is the locus classicus of the biblical commandment to perform a sacrifice called Passover (*pesaḥ*) annually on the fourteenth day of the first month. This chapter, however, poses a significant challenge for any exegete who wishes to root the custom of the Passover sacrifice in the night of the exodus, for the simple reason that the word "sacrifice" (*qorban*) is not mentioned in it even a single time. The Israelites are instructed to choose unblemished lambs, slaughter them, smear their blood on their door frames, roast the lambs thoroughly, and finally eat them "in haste" without leaving any remains. The blood of the lambs, it is indicated, will serve to mark the houses of the Israelites so as to prevent God from smiting their houses during the destructive rampage through Egypt.[16] There is no altar on which the blood is sprinkled and on which the suet is burned, and the slaughter and consumption of meat do not take place in a shrine or place of worship, but in private houses. The lambs thus seem to serve exclusively as a meal that sustains the Israelites during that long night and keeps them engaged in their homes.

Nevertheless, while there are no explicit sacrificial references in Exodus 12, the chapter contains several allusions to sacrificial practices—and oddly, to several different and incongruent sacrificial practices. As mentioned above, the requirement that the lambs all be yearling unblemished males (v. 5) corresponds with the instructions for the daily burnt offering in Numbers 28:1–5. The instruction not to

---

16. Exodus 12:13, 12:23. On the nature of the "destroyer" and the apotropaic function of the blood, see Levine, *In the Presence of the Lord*, 74–75; William H. C. Propp, *Exodus 1–18 with a New Translation and Commentary*, Anchor Bible 2 (New York: Doubleday, 1999), 434–39.

leave any meat uneaten until the morning and to burn the remainders (v. 10) corresponds with the instructions pertaining to well-being offerings, as does the use of the word zevaḥ (roughly translatable as "slain offering") in verse 27, a phrase used exclusively for offerings consumed by the owners.[17] Finally, the instruction to apply blood to the door frames using a bunch of hyssop (v. 22) is reminiscent of biblical purification rites such as the bird rite of the leper and the burning of the red cow.[18] Scholars assumed that these different configurations of the function of the Passover lamb are in part attributable to the different sources of the Pentateuch (although they widely disagreed on which sources are detectable in which verses).[19] Recent work by Shimon Gesundheit, however, has convincingly shown that the entire chapter can be safely attributed to the Priestly Code, with several different editorial hands at play.[20] The different calibrations of the Passover in ways associable with other types of offerings are better understood if one recognizes that the multilayered Passover pericope in Exodus 12 does not attempt to account for an existing *ritual,* but rather that the different hands working in this chapter are interpreting a cryptic *textual tradition.*[21] As Gesundheit has shown, the priestly authors of this chapter are responding to a terse base text that mentions a custom called "Passover" involving the roasting and consumption of lambs and the application of their blood to the door frames, and are attempting to find a sustained cultic language to make sense of this text. As a result, the picture of the Passover in Exodus 12 is polymorphous, ambiguous, and leaves open the question of whether the Passover qualifies as a sacrifice, and if so, what kind of sacrifice it is.

The question of whether the Passover is a sacrifice receives an affirmative answer in other biblical texts. The account in Numbers 9:1–14, which relates the Passover celebration in the first year in the wilderness and the inability of those who were ritually impure to participate in it, explicitly refers to the Passover as "the Lord's offering" (*qorban Yahweh*). In addition, the very stipulation that prohibits impure persons from participating in the ritual assumes that the Passover is subject to the same rules as other sacrifices. In Deuteronomy 16:1–7, the Israelites are fiercely prohibited from slaughtering the Passover anywhere except in "the place that the Lord will choose," which suggests that the Passover is comparable to

17. See Levine, *In the Presence of the Lord,* 46–52.

18. Leviticus 14:4; Numbers 19:6.

19. On the textual sources of Exodus 12, see Brevard S. Childs, *The Book of Exodus,* Old Testament Library (Louisville, KY: Westminster John Knox Press, [1974] 2004), 184–86; Knohl, *The Sanctuary of Silence,* 26–29; Propp, *Exodus 1–18,* 373–86.

20. Gesundheit, *Three Times a Year,* 46–146.

21. I thank Simeon Chavel for his many observations and insights regarding biblical accounts of the Passover.

other offerings.[22] Neither of these texts, however, mentions any specific sacrificial practices that apply to the Passover, such as the burning of suet or the application of blood to the altar. It is only in biblical texts from the Persian period that we encounter a full-on incorporation of the Passover into the sacrificial protocol: first, in specifying that the slaughter and the performance of the sacrificial ritual are performed by the priests and the Levites, and second and more important, in specifying that the blood of the lambs is tossed on the altar.[23]

From various accounts and descriptions of the Passover composed in the Hellenistic and Roman periods, it is evident that the sacrificial model presented in literature from the Persian period was generally upheld during the Second Temple period.[24] This model follows the Exodus pericope in terms of the date (the fourteenth of the first month at dusk), the type of animals fit for slaughter (lambs and goats only), and the manner of preparation (roasting without breaking the bones),[25] but adds both the requirement for performance in one centralized place (following Deuteronomy) and the standard sacrificial protocol of tossing of blood and burning of suet on the altar by the priests.[26] This amalgamated model for the Passover can be found in the book of Jubilees,[27] in the works of Josephus[28] and Philo of Alexandria,[29] and in the Mishnah and Tosefta,[30] and it is still the form of the Passover sacrifice conducted by the Samaritan community.[31] Nevertheless,

22. See Bernard M. Levinson, *Deuteronomy and the Hermeneutics of Legal Innovation* (New York: Oxford University Press, 1997), 53–97.

23. Ezra 6:19–20; 2 Chronicles 30:16, 35:10–11.

24. According to the Mishnah, however, the owners rather than the priests were the ones performing the slaughter (M. Pesaḥim 5.6; cf. the reference to the people bringing their own knives to the temple in T. Pisḥa 4.14). Philo similarly stresses that the owners and not the priests perform the slaughter (*Life of Moses* 2.224–25, ed. Yonge 511).

25. As opposed to the ritual instructions in Deuteronomy 16:1–7, according to which the Passover is slaughtered on the fifteenth rather than on the fourteenth, can be of either flock animals or cattle animals, and can be boiled rather than roasted.

26. While it is possible that certain Jewish communities (notably in Qumran and in Egypt) conducted the Passover sacrifice outside the Jerusalem temple, no evidence can be found for sacrificing in private households. For consideration of evidence from the Second Temple period, see Joseph Tabory, *The Passover Ritual throughout the Generations* [Heb.] (Tel Aviv: Ha-kibbutz ha-me'uhad, 1996), 78–92.

27. *Jubilees* 49 (ed. Charlesworth vol. 2, 140–42).

28. Flavius Josephus, *Antiquities of the Jews* 14.2.1–2, 17.9.3, 18.2.2, 20.5.3 (ed. Whiston 367, 465, 478, 531); *Wars of the Jews* 2.1.3, 2.12.1, 2.14.3, 5.3.1, 6.5.3, 6.9.3 (ed. Whiston 598, 612, 616, 701, 742, 749).

29. Philo, *Life of Moses* 2.224–25 (ed. Yonge 511); *On the Special Laws* 2.148 (ed. Yonge 582); see also Philo, *Questions and Answers on Exodus*, trans. Ralph Marcus (Cambridge, MA: Harvard University Press, 1953), 18–19.

30. See mainly M. Pesaḥim chapters 5–9 and corresponding chapters in the Tosefta.

31. The Samaritans, of course, conduct the sacrifice at their own sacred site on Mt. Gerizim, rather than in Jerusalem. On the Samaritan Passover, see Reinhard Pummer, "Samaritan Rituals and Customs," in *The Samaritans*, ed. Alan D. Crown (Tübingen: J.C.B. Mohr, 1989), 678–86.

while the rabbis had a more or less established picture of the practical manner in which the Passover is to be performed, their interpretive and legislative treatments of the Passover are animated by unresolved conceptual and hermeneutical questions regarding this unusual offering, and by recurring attempts to define its place and function within the sacrificial system in relation to other types of offerings.

On the face of it, the most immediate category under which the Passover can be subsumed is that of well-being offerings (*shelamim*), that is, offerings consumed by the owners with the exception of the blood and suet that are placed on the altar. Indeed, the rabbis acknowledge that in terms of the sacrificial protocol, the Passover is most closely identifiable—and to a certain extent even interchangeable— with unspecified well-being offerings.[32] There is, however, one critical incongruity between the Passover and standard well-being offerings: whereas well-being offerings are quintessentially voluntary in nature,[33] and are made by individuals in special circumstances, various biblical sources indicate that the Passover *must* be performed on its designated day as part of the calendrical requirements. In addition, whereas well-being offerings are free in form and any unblemished quadruped can be used for this purpose, the ritual instructions in Exodus 12 place severe restrictions on the type of animal that can be used as well as on its manner of preparation. In its calendrical fixity and in the exacting instructions regarding the type of animals, the Passover resembles the collective burnt offerings and purification offerings prescribed for various festivals much more than it resembles individual well-being offerings given in fulfillment of a vow or as a spontaneous expression of goodwill.

There are, in truth, two isolated priestly examples of obligatory well-being offerings in which the animal type is specified: in preparation for the inauguration of the tabernacle, the people are told to provide a ram and a bull for well-being offerings,[34] and in the instructions regarding the festival of Weeks, two lambs for well-being offerings are mentioned among the many other offerings of the day.[35] In principle, one could argue that the Passover is yet another example of an obligatory well-being offering like those two. However, unlike the two offerings mentioned above, and unlike other calendrical obligatory offerings, the Passover must be made by each and every household. The Passover is not a single sacrificial substance given on behalf of the people, but rather it necessarily entails the production of multiple sacrificial substances, each explicitly associated with specific

---

32. M. Pesaḥim 5.2, 9.2; M. Sheqalim 2.5.

33. Firstborns and tithes, although they could be considered obligatory well-being offerings, are of a different category than the Passover, since in these two cases the animals ostensibly never belonged to their offerers to begin with.

34. Leviticus 9:4.

35. Leviticus 23:19.

individuals. Both Josephus and rabbinic texts indicate that by the end of Second Temple period the Passover offerings were provided by clans (Greek: *phatria*, Hebrew: *ḥavurah*) whose makeup was flexible and did not necessarily align with households in the traditional sense,[36] but the notion that each person must have claim to one recognizable Passover offering is nonetheless maintained.

The Passover thus constitutes a strange aberration within the biblical sacrificial landscape. In functioning primarily as a meal—according to Exodus 12, exclusively as a meal—it resembles individual well-being offerings, but unlike them it is obligatory, fixed, and heavily sanctioned. The latter traits align it with mandatory calendrical offerings, but unlike them, the Passover does not take the form of a single collective offering but of multiple personal offerings. In addition, the fact that the Passover does not fall neatly under any established sacrificial category from among those listed in Leviticus 1–5 but constitutes a category unto itself opens the question of its exact purpose and function. The aberrant nature of the Passover poses a significant interpretive challenge for the rabbis, who are striving to create a clear and systematic sacrificial taxonomy, but it also provides them with an opportunity to mold the Passover in the ways most compelling to them. In what follows, I will show that the Passover serves in rabbinic legislation as a particularly potent discursive site for configuring the relations between individual and collective; in the next section, I will explore its potency for configuring the relations between meat and blood.

The Passover and the spectrum of collectivity

The fact that the biblical Passover sacrifice is ambiguously portrayed as both personal and collective, both an intimate domestic ritual and a communal centralized ritual, gave biblical interpreters who discussed the Passover notable liberty to shape it in the image of their own concerns and persuasions. Different interpreters highlight and stress aspects of the Passover that best serve their overall rhetorical purposes, and significantly marginalize the opposite aspects, such that different works present completely different accounts of this ritual. Thus, for example, the Passover pericope in Jubilees 49 emphasizes that the sacrifice is performed in a single place in the presence of all the people.[37] There is no hint of any activity taking place in private houses or in small groups, and even when accounting for the first Passover in Egypt, Jubilees mentions private houses only in the context of application of blood to the door frames.[38] This emphasis on collectivity corresponds with Jubilees' more overarching views of the covenantal relations between

---

36. See Josephus, *Wars of the Jews* 6.9.3 (ed. Whiston 749); M. Pesaḥim 7.13–8.7.

37. Jubilees 49:17–21 (ed. Charlesworth vol. 2, 141).

38. Jubilees 49:5–6 (ed. Charlesworth vol. 2, 140).

God and Israel as a communal and eternal entity.[39] In contrast, Philo of Alexandria stresses almost exclusively the individual aspect of the Passover ritual, and proclaims that when the Passover is offered, each household functions as a temple and each individual functions as a priest.[40] He treats the Passover as a manifestation of personal and spontaneous sentiments of thanksgiving, and significantly downplays its heavily centralized and ritualized components. Thereby, Philo promotes his own take on the Israelite cult as egalitarian and nonhierarchical, and on the people of Israel as exceptionally and genuinely pious.

While the literary genres used in rabbinic compilations are very different from those used in works such as Jubilees or Philo's treatises, I argue that the early rabbis similarly use the rhetorical and textual tools available to them—whether exegetical, legislative, or taxonomic tools—to prioritize one aspect of the Passover and to downplay the other. Furthermore, I argue that although rabbinic texts present a diversity of approaches to the relation between individual and collective aspects in the Passover sacrifice, a strong inclination can be identified in these texts toward the collective side. To begin exploring this relation, let us first examine the classification of the Passover within the rabbinic taxonomy of "congregational offerings" (qorbanot tzibur) versus "individual offerings" (qorbanot yahid).

Two passages in the Mishnah delineate various distinctions between congregational offerings and individual offerings. The first of the two, which I discussed in some detail in the first chapter, appears in tractate Menahot. This passage charts out a distinction between the two types of offerings specifically in regard to the practice of laying hands on the animal's head upon the slaughter, ruling that congregational offerings do not entail hand laying whereas individual offerings do.[41] This rule, however, has multiple exceptions on both ends: the Mishnah acknowledges that there are two congregational offerings that do entail hand laying (a bull offered following a communal transgression and the scapegoat of the Day of Atonement),[42] and there are also three individual offerings that do not entail hand laying: firstborns, tithes, and the Passover. This passage, then, explicitly lists the Passover as an individual offering. Within the rabbinic binary taxonomy, the classification of the Passover as an individual offering seems predictable, considering the fact that the Passover is lacking the one trait that, as I discussed in the previous chapter, is the fundamental requirement for all congregational offerings: it is not a

---

39. On the Passover in the book of Jubilees, see Michael Segal, *The Book of Jubilees: Rewritten Bible, Redaction, Ideology, and Theology* [Heb.] (Jerusalem: Magnes Press, 2008), 149–59, 160–69; Cana Werman and Ahron Shemesh, *Revealing the Hidden: Interpretation and Halakha in the Dead Sea Scrolls* [Heb.] (Jerusalem: Bialik Institute, 2011), 305–10.

40. Philo, *On the Special Laws* 2.148 (ed. Yonge 582); cf. *Questions and Answers on Exodus* 18–19.

41. M. Menahot 9.7.

42. R. Shimon adds a third exception, of goats offered as purification for communal idolatry.

publicly funded offering, but rather consists of multiple offerings provided by multiple individuals from their own private funds.

The second passage, which appears in tractate Temurah, lists a series of several traits that distinguish individual offerings from congregational offerings, such as the requirement to replace the offering if it was lost, the required sex of the sacrificial animals, and others. For our purposes, the relevant segment of this passage reads as follows:

> There is [a trait] of congregational offerings that does not apply to individual offerings, [which is] that congregational offerings override the Sabbath and impurity, whereas individual offerings override neither the Sabbath nor impurity.
>
> R. Meir said: But are not the pan-made grain offerings of the high priest and the bull [offered by the high priest] on the Day of Atonement individual offerings, and nonetheless they override the Sabbath and impurity? Rather, it is because their time is fixed.[43]

The anonymous tanna in the first part of the passage charts a clear-cut difference between individual and congregational offerings: whereas the former cannot be performed when the owners are in a state of ritual impurity (but rather they are postponed until the owners are purified), and cannot be performed on the Sabbath (but rather they are postponed until after the Sabbath), the latter are performed regardless of these conditions. Any reader who is remotely familiar with rules pertaining to the Passover would immediately register that the Passover—if it is considered an individual offering—is a blatant exception to this rule, since multiple rabbinic sources present an uncontested consensus that the Passover overrides both the Sabbath and impurity.[44] Tzvi Steinfeld has thus convincingly argued that the general principle put forth by the anonymous tanna here divulges a view according to which the Passover is not, in fact, an individual offering, but rather a congregational offering.[45]

R. Meir, in contrast, objects to the anonymous statement of the Mishnah, arguing that there are several cases of individual offerings that do override the Sabbath and impurity, and therefore that the anonymous Mishnah's generalization is incorrect: what determines whether an offering will override the Sabbath and impurity is not whether it is congregational or individual, but rather whether its time is fixed or flexible. What is noteworthy about R. Meir's objection is that the Passover, which serves as perfect example for his argument, is oddly not invoked.[46] This

---

43. M. Temurah 2.1 (2.2 in the Mishnah's manuscripts).

44. As will be discussed in greater detail below; for now, see M. Pesaḥim 6.1–6, 7.4–6.

45. Steinfeld, "On the Definition of Individual and Congregational Offerings," 40–44.

46. The Passover is not mentioned in any of the Mishnah's manuscripts, nor does it appear in the Mishnah of tractate Temurah in any of the manuscripts or printed editions of the Babylonian Talmud. However, in BT Yoma 50a R. Meir's objection includes the Passover in addition to the two other

oddity is enhanced in light of the fact that in the parallel Tosefta passage the counterexamples to the Mishnah's rule do include, alongside the two offerings of the high priest mentioned in the Mishnah, also the Passover as another example of an individual offering.[47]

The question arises, then, why the Passover is not mentioned in the Mishnah's version of R. Meir's objection. One could, of course, claim that this omission can be explained merely as a result of flawed transmission; but it can also be explained as reflecting a deliberate choice on either end. Perhaps the objection originally included the Passover (as is the case in the Tosefta), and the Passover was edited out in the Mishnah, since the redactor was not inclined to classify the Passover as an individual offering; alternatively, perhaps the original version did not include the Passover, and it was added in the Tosefta version in order to make it cohere with the view that the Passover is an individual offering. Either way, this omission may well indicate that either R. Meir himself (to the extent that we see the attribution as reliable) or the redactor of this mishnaic passage was disinclined to categorize the Passover as an individual offering.

While no hard and fast conclusions can be drawn from the silence of this passage regarding the Passover, when this silence is paired with the Tosefta's tradition regarding Hillel the Elder, with which I opened this chapter, there is reason to suspect that this passage silently subscribes to Hillel's explicit classification of the Passover as a congregational offering.[48] At the very least, it would not be far-fetched to surmise that the Passover is not mentioned in the Mishnah because its classification as an individual offering is a matter of contention. What stands behind this contention?

On one level, these two opposing modes of classification are the direct result of the anomaly of the Passover within the biblical sacrificial system, and of the rabbinic attempt to impose on the biblical sacrificial system a taxonomy that is essentially foreign to it. These conflicting classifications can be read as reflecting a scholastic disagreement on the question of what trait of a particular offering is most decisive for classifying it as individual or congregational: the manner in which it is funded, the manner in which it is performed, its calendrical fixity, and so forth. On another level, however, the classification of an offering as individual or congregational has very real stakes to it when it comes to assessing the nature of the obligations that this offering entails: whereas an individual offering is directly

---

offerings. Although R. Meir's opinion is prefaced with the word *tenan* in most of the manuscripts, indicating that it is a Mishnah quotation, it is probably a rendition of an extramishnaic teaching. See Ya'akov N. Epstein, *Introduction to the Text of the Mishnah* [Heb.] (Jerusalem: Magnes Press, 2000), 777; Steinfeld, "On the Definition of Individual and Congregational Offerings," 31 n. 2.

47. T. Temurah 1.17.

48. See also Steinfeld, "On the Definition of Individual and Congregational Offerings," 40–44.

incumbent upon a particular person, a congregational offering is incumbent upon the community as a corporate unit. Underlying the taxonomic question of what type of offering the Passover is, then, is the question of what constitutes—for every single person of Israel—a fulfillment of his obligation vis-à-vis the Passover.

As David Henshke has noted, when the Passover is classified as a congregational offering, it is by and by defined as a ritual obligation of the people of Israel as a collective, rather than of every individual or household separately.[49] Of course, it is the sacrificial offerings of individuals through which this collective obligation is fulfilled, but the collective obligation is considered fulfilled even if not every person in the community actively partakes in it. Such recalibration of the Passover has immediate practical implications for a situation in which a large portion of the community does not actively take the long journey to Jerusalem to participate in the Passover ritual in the temple—as we know to have been the case in the Second Temple period.[50] We can thus understand the rabbinic inclination to "collectivize" the Passover as a means of grappling with the discrepancy between the idealized biblical picture, in which every person participates in the Passover, and the reality, in which only a fraction of the Jewish population actually does so (a reality, it is worth noting, that is not explicitly addressed in Tannaitic sources). Declaring the Passover a congregational offering shifts the weight from the individual to the collective, and positions the performance of the Passover at its designated time by whichever number of people are doing so at the time as a *collective act,* in which every individual is automatically implicated.

Yet the rabbinic tendency to collectivize the Passover is discernible beyond the taxonomic question of whether this offering qualifies as congregational or individual, and attests to a deep-seated ideology that goes well beyond the practical question of what constitutes a fulfillment of the commandment regarding the Passover. A particularly instructive example for the collectivistic ethos guiding the rabbinic construction of the Passover can be found in the Mishnah's treatment of the impact of ritual impurity on the performance of the Passover. According to Numbers 9:1–14, the Passover—like all other sacrifices—cannot be performed in a state of ritual impurity, and those who are impure at the fixed time of the Passover (the fourteenth of the first month) cannot partake in it. For those who were unable to perform the Passover at the designated time because they were impure or on "a distant road," the fourteenth of the second month functions as a second chance or "makeup" opportunity to do so. The Mishnah, however, frames the biblical edict as pertaining only to a situation in which a minority of the congregation is ritually

49. Henshke, *Festival Joy,* 140–47.

50. As noted by Shmuel Safrai, "The Pilgrimage Commandment and Its Observance during the Second Temple Period" [Heb.], *Zion* 25, no. 2 (1960): 67–84.

impure, and rules that if the majority of the congregation is impure on the four-teenth of the first month, the Passover is to be carried out as planned:

> If the congregation (*qahal*) or the majority of it became impure, or if the priests were impure and the congregation was pure, [the Passover] should be performed in [a state of] impurity.
>
> If a minority of the congregation became impure, the pure ones perform the first [that is, perform the sacrifice on the fourteenth of the first month], and the impure ones perform the second [that is, perform the sacrifice on the fourteenth of the second month].[51]

The Mishnah's ruling is guided by the view that the Passover has to be performed at its designated time by the congregation *as such*, even if most or all of the congregation is impure. One way or another the majority of the people must sacrifice on the fourteenth of the first month—even if the priests themselves, who are attending to the sacrifice, are ritually impure.[52] In accordance with this view, the first Passover is referred to in the Tosefta as "congregational Passover" (*pesaḥ tzibbur*), and the second Passover, the "makeup" opportunity for those who were unable to perform the first Passover, is referred to as "individual Passover" (*pesaḥ yaḥid*).[53] The numerical majority of the congregation is equated here with the corporate entity that is the people as a whole. Through this ruling, the Mishnah effectively (though not explicitly) construes the Passover as a collective sacrifice, which is made by "the people" rather than by individuals or households.

The collectivization of the Passover is even more apparent in the parallel Tosefta passage, which addresses a situation in which there is no discernible majority, but rather half of the congregation is pure and half is impure. In such a case, the anonymous Tosefta rules that those who are impure will perform the Passover in the second month: that is, they will be subject to the same rule as a minority of impure persons, since they cannot be defined as a clear majority. In contrast, R. Shimon rules that since neither the pure half nor the impure half constitutes a majority, both groups shall be seen as majorities, and both will perform the Passover in the first month—but separately: "The pure shall perform [the Passover] by themselves and the impure shall perform [the Passover] by themselves." R. Shimon's suggestion is followed by an immediate objection:

> They said to him: One does not divide the congregation. Either everyone performs [the Passover] in [a state of] purity, or everyone performs it in [a state of] impurity.[54]

---

51. M. Pesaḥim 7.6.

52. This ruling, as pointed out and debated in T. Pisḥa 8.4–5, stands in stark opposition to the story related in 2 Chronicles 30, in which the Passover was postponed because the priests and Levites were impure.

53. T. Pisḥa 4.14.

54. T. Pisḥa 6.2. Cf. PT Pesaḥim 7:6, 34c; PT Horayot 1:6, 46b.

The assertion that "one does not divide the congregation" powerfully conveys the view that the Passover offering is not, in essence, an individual offering that many people perform at the same time, but a collective offering performed by the congregation as a congregation. Even the creation of two separate circles in which the Passover is offered is unacceptable for the anonymous voice in this passage, since it suggests an internal division of what must function as a single entity. Interestingly, in the Babylonian Talmud's rendition of this debate the phrase used repeatedly is not "one does not divide the congregation" ('ein ḥolqin 'et ha-tzibbur), as in the Tosefta, but rather "a congregational offering may not be divided" ('ein qorban tzibbur ḥaluq).[55] In the Mishnah, the phrase "a congregational offering may not be divided" is invoked when discussing congregational offerings that consist of several separate parts, such as the different hornets of the showbread, the two loaves of bread of the festival of Weeks, and so forth. Regarding such cases, R. Yehudah rules that if one part of the offering became impure, all other parts must be incinerated along with it, since "a congregational offering may not be divided."[56] The Babylonian Talmud uses the same phrase to object to two separate performances of the Passover sacrifice. In the Babylonian adaption of the Tannaitic tradition, then, not only is the Passover a congregational offering, but the many individual Passover offerings are conceptualized as components of a single sacrificial substance.[57]

The Babylonian Talmud's take on the Passover as a single offering consisting of multiple parts resonates with what is probably the most far-reaching Tannaitic expression of the tendency to collectivize the Passover. As I mentioned briefly in the previous chapter, a statement attributed to R. Eliezer asserts that a single Passover offering suffices to fulfill Israel's obligation:

> R. Eliezer says: From where do you infer that if all the people of Israel have only a single Passover [lamb] they can all fulfill their obligation through it? For it is said: "And all the assembled congregation of Israel (qehal 'adat benei yisr'ael) will slaughter it ('oto) at twilight" (Exodus 12:6).[58]

---

55. BT Pesaḥim 79a–80a. This phrase is also invoked in PT Pesaḥim 7:6, 34c and PT Horayot 1:6, 46b, but there it is not applied directly to the Passover but rather only invoked as a point of comparison. In the Palestinian Talmud the position is rendered as "one does not perform the Passover in half."

56. M. Menaḥot 2.2; cf. T. Menaḥot 3.2.

57. It is not inconceivable to read the Tosefta's statement in the same manner if we take the sentence "One does not divide the congregation" as shorthand for "One does not divide the congregation[al offering]." Since rabbinic texts often omit the word "offering" (qorban) when discussing different types of offerings, such a reading is certainly possible. I thank Azzan Yadin-Israel for this observation.

58. Mekhilta deRabbi Ishmael Bo 5 (ed. Horovitz-Rabin 17); cf. PT Pesaḥim 7.5, 34b; BT Pesaḥim 78b, Qiddushin 42a. In the Palestinian and Babylonian Talmuds this statement is attributed to R. Nathan (and in some of the versions in BT Qiddushin, to R. Yonatan).

Relying on the biblical reference to the Passover lamb in the singular form *'oto* in Exodus 12:6, which makes it seem as though the entire congregation is slaughtering a single lamb, R. Eliezer asserts that the Passover ritual, in essence, does not require more than a single offering. For R. Eliezer, there really is no fundamental difference between the Passover and other congregational offerings: it is not an obligation of multiple people that is fulfilled by multiple offerings, but rather an obligation of the community as a single corporate entity to perform a single sacrificial act. This sacrifice can be carried out through multiple lambs, but each one of those lambs is an instantiation of one communal offering. The oneness of the people is commensurate, in this picture, with the oneness of the offering.

R. Eliezer's statement, which effectively obliterates the individual dimension of the Passover altogether, can be seen as the most extreme point on a spectrum of collectivization on which several Tannaitic sources position the Passover. The different traditions that we have examined so far, which explicitly or implicitly classify the Passover as a congregational offering or at least subject it to a congregational protocol, can all be located along this spectrum. It is important to note, however, that even the two passages in the Mishnah and the Tosefta that classify the Passover as an individual offering still present a certain degree of collectivization locatable along this spectrum. Both these passages distinctly mention the Passover as an exception to the rules governing individual offerings (hand laying in Mishnah Menaḥot, Sabbath and impurity in Tosefta Temurah), thus positioning it outside the realm of individual offerings in the strictest sense.

In particular, the Mishnah's ruling that the Passover does not require hand laying serves, as I argued in the first chapter, as a way of minimizing the agency of individual owners and of dissociating the Passover from the particular person or group providing it.[59] The minimization of the owner's agency can be discerned in rabbinic sacrificial legislation more broadly, but in the case of the Passover the ruling regarding hand laying serves to configure the Passover, at least to some extent, as ritually comparable to congregational offerings. Especially in light of the fact that the sacrificial rite of the Passover involves more owner participation than any other individual sacrifice (since here it is distinctly the owners who perform the slaughter[60]), the rabbis' insistence that the clearest marker of individual ownership be absent from this rite is noteworthy. This absence makes the point that even though the sacrificial animal is provided from the owners' private funds and designated to feed them, it does not really *belong* to them, because it is part of a greater communal enterprise.

---

59. To be sure, the fact that the Passover is offered by a group and not by a single person has nothing to do with the fact that it does not require hand laying: as the Tosefta (T. Menaḥot 10.14; T. Temurah 3.9) makes clear, offerings made by several partners are still considered individual, and in such cases all the partners lay their hands on the offering.

60. M. Pesaḥim 5.6.

Perhaps the most powerful testimony to the extent to which the Passover was collectivized in rabbinic legislation is a ruling pertaining to a different offering altogether—the feast offering (*ḥagigah*). Following the common biblical paradigm in which a feast in the presence of God consists of both burnt offerings (*ʿolot*) and well-being offerings (*zevaḥim/shelamim*),[61] the Mishnah prescribes that each person pursuing a pilgrimage to the temple during festivals bring both a burnt offering and a well-being offering known as *ḥagigah*, roughly translated as "festive joy."[62] On the face of it, the feast offering is an individual offering par excellence: it comes as a result of private initiative, it is privately funded, it is not restricted in terms of the animals that may be used, and it does not override the Sabbath or impurity. Nevertheless, this offering is curiously categorized in the Tosefta as a congregational offering.[63] This classification, as Henshke has observed, reflects an implicit rabbinic analogy between the Passover and the feast offering: since both of them are offerings made at festival times and celebrated en masse (that is, with multiple people all sacrificing and eating at the same time in the courtyards of the temple), some rabbis consider both as congregational offerings that the community is required to provide as a community.[64] The identification of the feast offering as a congregational offering thus closely depends upon the sustained rabbinic collectivization of the Passover: through their collectivizing interpretation of the Passover, the rabbis created a model in which an offering made in line with an obligation that pertains to the people as a whole can be calibrated as a congregational offering. This expanded model of congregational offerings allows both for further minimization of the agency of the owner (as we see in the debates on hand laying on feast offerings, which I discussed in chapter 1) and for further promotion of the idealized view of "Israel" as one cohesive corporate entity.

Finally, it is worth noting that a collectivistic ethos governs not only facets of rabbinic legislation regarding the Passover, but also the literary description of the manner in which the Passover sacrifice was performed. The fifth chapter of tractate Pesaḥim of the Mishnah contains a short ritual narrative,[65] which poetically relates how priests and laypeople worked together in seamlessly orchestrated coordination to carry out the massive sacrificial operation of the Passover night. What

61. See Watts, *Ritual and Rhetoric*, 64–70.

62. The feast offering (*ḥagigah*) is referred to in various Tannaitic texts also as "joy offering" (*simḥah*). On the relation between the two names, see Henshke, *Festival Joy*, 24–86. Both these names are parallel with and perhaps reflect a direct translation of the Greek term *euphrosyne*, literally "merriment," a common way of describing a sacrificial banquet. On the term *euphrosyne*, see Dennis E. Smith, *From Symposium to Eucharist: The Banquet in the Early Christian World* (Minneapolis: Augsburg Press, 2003), 78–86.

63. See T. Temurah 1.17; cf. BT Yoma 50a–51a.

64. Henshke, *Festival Joy*, 140–44.

65. On the mishnaic genre of ritual narratives, see chapter 5.

one could have imagined to be a rather unstructured procedure in which different people come at different times of the afternoon with their lambs, slaughter them with the assistance of whichever priest is available, and proceed to roast and eat them, is depicted in the Mishnah as a process in which the people as a whole perform the sacrifice *together*—to the extent that this is possible:

> The Passover is slaughtered in three divisions (*kitot*), for it was said: "And all the assembled congregation of Israel (*qehal 'adat benei yisr'ael*) will slaughter it at twilight" (Exodus 12:6)—[hence three divisions:] assembly, and congregation, and Israel. The first division came in, and once the court was full, they locked the gates of the court. . . .[66]
>
> The priests stood in rows, and in their hands were beakers of gold and beakers of silver. . . .[67]
>
> An Israel[ite] [that is, layperson] slaughtered and a priest received [the blood], and gave it to his fellow and his fellow to his fellow, [such that each priest] receives a full [vessel] and gives back an empty one. A priest who is close to the altar tosses [the blood] once against the base.[68]
>
> Once the first division got out, the second division went in. Once the second one got out, the third one went in.[69]

The Mishnah presents here a creative compromise between the realistic space limitations of the temple's court and an idealized picture in which the people as a whole all perform the sacrifice together. It reads the three components of the collective appellation "the assembled congregation of Israel" as entailing a threefold division of this collective, thus making it possible to pragmatically split the congregation into three groups while still claiming that this manner of division itself bespeaks the congregation's unity.[70] The priests, on their end, are described as efficiently operating in a conveyor-belt manner, constantly and ceaselessly transmitting vessels with and without blood to and from the altar, thus making it possible for multiple sacrifices to take place simultaneously. Through this highly coordinated choreography, multiple persons offering multiple lambs can be seen to be operating as one entity.

The ritual narrative concludes with the comment that when the sacrificial procedure was completed for all three divisions (that is, after the lambs have been slaughtered, their blood tossed, and their suet burned), all three divisions remained at the Temple Mount. Only when it got dark did all three divisions leave and go to roast the lambs and have the Passover meal.[71] As several commentators noted, this comment

---

66. M. Pesaḥim 5.5.
67. M. Pesaḥim 5.5.
68. M. Pesaḥim 5.6.
69. M. Pesaḥim 5.7.
70. Cf. Mekhilta deRabbi Ishmael Bo 5 (ed. Horovitz-Rabin 17).
71. M. Pesaḥim 5.10.

probably pertains to a situation in which the Passover takes place on the Sabbath, which does not allow the people to carry the lambs away and roast them immediately after the slaughter, but forces them to wait until the sun is down and the Sabbath is over. The Mishnah, however, does not explicitly state that these stipulations pertain to the Sabbath alone. Rather, it puts forth the description of the three divisions all waiting at the Temple Mount together as a standard part of the Passover sacrifice ritual. This description "freezes" the dynamic ritual picture that the Mishnah portrays at a point in which all the people are assembled together in one place. Between the rapid movement of the sacrificial procedure itself (entry, slaughter, blood manipulation, burning, exit, and repeat with the next division) and the movement away from the Temple Mount toward the places in which small groups roast and eat the lambs, there is a hiatus in which the congregation as a whole stands still in manifestation of its oneness. This hiatus, I propose, expresses the rabbinic idealized vision of the Passover as a single sacrifice, despite its multiple instantiations.

Many vs. one, meat vs. blood

While rabbinic legislation reveals, as I have argued, a strong tendency toward presenting the Passover sacrifice as a collective enterprise, the rabbis nonetheless presumed that the Passover entails certain obligations vis-à-vis each individual. That is to say, even if the people of Israel offer the Passover as a congregation, a certain mode of personal participation in the sacrificial enterprise is still required of each member of the congregation. The language of Numbers 9:13 makes it very clear that the Passover commandment pertains to each and every person on an individual level: "Anyone who is clean and is not on a distant road, and yet refrains from doing the Passover, shall be cut off from the people for not presenting the Lord's offering at its appointed time; such person shall bear the consequences for the sin." What this verse does not make clear, however, is what "doing" (la'asot) the Passover actually means. Does it mean being physically present at the sanctuary when the Passover lambs are offered? Does it mean actively contributing money toward the procurement of a Passover lamb? Or does it mean feasting on the lamb's meat? The biblical sources do not provide answers to this question, thereby leaving all those interpretive options open.

In rabbinic legislation, "doing" the Passover takes on a rather formalistic meaning: one "does" the Passover by officially joining a group (ḥavurah) that agrees to partake in one Passover lamb or more together.[72] Those who comprise the group

---

72. A controversy appears in several rabbinic sources on whether a single person may perform the Passover for himself; the disagreement seems to pertain to the presumed inability of one person to consume an entire lamb by himself. See M. Pesaḥim 8.7; Mekhilta deRabbi Ishmael Bo 3 (ed. Horovitz-Rabin 11); Mekhilta deRabbi Shimon 12:4 (ed. Epstein-Melamed 10); Sifre Deuteronomy 132 (ed. Finkelstein 189–90).

are referred to as "enlisted" (*menuyim*), and one can choose to enlist in a specific group right up until the moment in which the lamb(s) in which the group partakes is(are) slaughtered. Once one joins such a group, he or she is not required to be physically present at the temple during the sacrificial process itself: a single representative of the group suffices for this purpose.[73] There is also no indication that one must actively participate in the procurement of the lambs to be part of a group, since women and slaves who have no funds of their own certainly constitute parts of such groups.[74] Rather, one's formal inclusion in a group establishes a legal association of this person with the Passover offering brought by this group. The essence of this legal association, according to various rabbinic texts, is that the Passover lamb at hand is officially slaughtered "for the sake" of each person enlisted in the group.[75] The recurring phrase "to slaughter for [someone's] sake" (literally "to slaughter on someone," *shaḥat 'al*) suggests that each member of the group is the implied reference point of the act of slaughter of a particular lamb. But what does it mean to slaughter an animal for someone's sake? What bearing does this official inclusion in the act of slaughter have on each enlisted individual?

At first glance, the answer to this question is simple: formal inclusion in the sacrificial act applied to the Passover lamb enables one to eat of its roasted flesh later on. The rabbinic emphasis that a Passover lamb must be slaughtered not only for those officially enlisted (*li-menuyav*) but also specifically "for its eaters" (*le-'okhlav*) indicates that the ultimate purpose of being included in the act of slaughter is to participate in the meal.[76] In order to slaughter the lamb for or "on" a particular person, it is not enough for this person to enlist with a certain group ahead of time: this person must also be capable of eating at least a token amount of the Passover meat.[77] The notion that one can slaughter the Passover only for persons who can eat of it strongly suggests that the quintessential obligation of the individual vis-à-vis the Passover is to partake in its meat, and it is thus reasonable to infer that for the rabbis, an individual who did not consume some of the Passover lamb's meat did not fulfill the biblically mandated commandment to "do" the Passover. While this position is indeed traceable in multiple Tannaitic passages, alongside it we find a contesting position according to which one fulfills one's obligation vis-à-vis the Passover by merely having the blood of the animal tossed "for his sake." In other words, as I will show in detail in the next section, rabbinic treatments

73. As stated explicitly in Mekhilta deRabbi Ishmael Bo 5 (ed. Horovitz-Rabin 17).

74. See, for example, M. Pesaḥim 8.7; cf. 7.13, 8.1, 8.2, 8.5.

75. This phrase is repeatedly used in M. Pesaḥim 8.1–7; T. Pisḥa 7.3–13.

76. M. Pesaḥim 5.3, 6.6; cf. T. Pisḥa 4.2.

77. M. Pesaḥim 8.3, 6–7; T. Pisḥa 4.2; 6.3–4, 10; 7.6, 12; Mekhilta deRabbi Ishmael Bo 3 (ed. Horovitz-Rabin 12); Mekhilta deRabbi Shimon 12:4 (ed. Epstein-Melamed 10); Sifre Deuteronomy 132 (ed. Finkelstein 190).

of the Passover reflect two opposing views on the question of wherein lies the essence of the Passover: in the meat or in the blood.

The question of whether it is the meat or blood that defines the Passover and the obligations pertaining to it cannot be disentangled from the question of whether the Passover is an individual or congregational offering. The relation between these questions is fleshed out most clearly in the statement attributed to R. Eliezer that I mentioned above, according to which a single Passover offering suffices to fulfill the Passover obligation of the people as a whole. It goes without saying that if only a single lamb is slaughtered as a Passover offering, most members of the congregation *cannot* eat of its meat. If all the members can fulfill their obligation through a single lamb, then it is something other than the eating of meat that defines the satisfactory performance of the Passover. In the Palestinian Talmud's rendition of this statement (there attributed to R. Nathan), it is made explicit that it is the act of tossing blood on the altar that serves as the fulfillment of the Passover obligation, and it serves as such for each and every member of the congregation:

> R. Nathan said: One can fulfill one's obligation by tossing [the blood] without eating [the meat]. What is the reason? "And all the assembled congregation of Israel (*qehal 'adat benei yisr'ael*) will slaughter it (*'oto*) at twilight"—even if there is only a single offering there, they all fulfill their obligation by a single tossing [of the blood].[78]

Whereas meat, the edible component of offerings, is a limited resource insofar as each participant must receive a discernible portion of it, sacrificial blood is, in terms of its efficacy, an unlimited resource. As the congregational rites of purification and atonement indicate, the blood of a single animal can serve efficaciously for multitudes of people. Accordingly, the more one is inclined to identify the Passover as a congregational offering, the more emphasis one is likely to place on the component of blood, which can unfailingly operate on a collective level, rather than on the component of meat, which is by definition rationed for a limited number of individuals. One could have the blood tossed "for her sake" even if she is part of a group of many thousands; but one can only partake in the meat if she is part of a manageable group of a few dozen at most.

However, the question of whether the tossing of blood suffices to fulfill one's ritual obligation resonates well beyond the specific issue of the Passover. As I showed in detail in chapter 2, one of the most notable rabbinic innovations is the notion that the sacrificial work effectively ends when the manipulation of blood is complete. In fact, we may recall that the very same R. Eliezer who claims that a single Passover offering suffices for the entire congregation is also quoted as saying that as long as the blood of an offering remains available, one can proceed with the

78. PT Pesaḥim 7:5, 34b.

sacrificial process even if no meat is left of it.[79] There thus seems to be a connection between the position that blood is the be-all and end-all of the sacrificial process, and the position that the Passover—indeed the one sacrifice in which blood seemingly plays very little part and meat stands at the center—is a congregational rather than an individual offering. These two interpretive-legislative stances readily serve each other: in the same way that the emphasis on blood over meat undermines the individual's part in the offering, the collectivization of the Passover offers a heuristic tool for underplaying the role of meat in this sacrifice.

To be clear, I am not proposing that rabbinic debates on one topic are fully congruent with debates on the other topic: the question of whether the Passover is individual or congregational and the question of whether at its center stands meat or blood are two separate questions, and one cannot be subsumed under the other. What I am proposing, nonetheless, is that the Passover emerges as a site in which two notable rabbinic tendencies—collectivization of the cult and equation of the sacrificial process with the work of blood—converge with each other, and very possibly inform each other. In what follows, I turn to examine the relation between blood and meat in the rabbinic constructions of the Passover, and the role that this relation plays in the different rabbinic configurations of the meaning and function of the Passover sacrifice.

FROM FEAST WITHOUT SACRIFICE TO SACRIFICE WITHOUT FEAST: THE PASSOVER BETWEEN BLOOD AND MEAT

As I mentioned above, the foundational story of the Passover in Exodus 12 does not entail any explicit sacrificial features. Despite various points of resonance between the Passover and other sacrifices, the instructions given to the Israelites in Egypt are effectively instructions for the preparation of a meal and for the consumption of food: "They shall eat the lamb that same night; they shall eat it roasted over the fire with unleavened bread and bitter herbs. Do not eat any of it raw or boiled in water, but roasted over the fire, with its head, legs, and inner organs."[80] The Passover of Egypt is best described as a sacrificial feast without a sacrifice, as boldly stated in the Babylonian Talmud: when one amora, R. Zeira, presents the question of what was done with the suet (the parts reserved exclusively for the altar) of the Passover lambs in Egypt, Abaye responds that it was, in all likelihood, eaten along with everything else.[81]

79. T. Zevaḥim 4.1.
80. Exodus 12:8–9.
81. BT Pesaḥim 96a.

While the rabbis emphasize that future performances of the Passover—which they refer to as "the Passover of the generations" (*pesaḥ dorot*)—do entail the application of blood and suet to the altar,[82] the spirit of the foundational Passover story is maintained in a large number of Tannaitic sources, which are guided by the assumption that the ultimate purpose of the Passover is to be eaten, and that if one failed to eat of it one failed to fulfill one's religious obligation. This assumption is reflected in the repeated ruling that the Passover may be slaughtered only for the sake "of its eaters" and that if one is not able to eat at least the token amount of an olive-volume of the Passover meat, one does not qualify to have the Passover slaughtered for one's sake.[83] Nevertheless, a closer look at those sources reveals that the consideration of eating as vital for the completion of the Passover obligation is a matter of contention in Tannaitic law. Alongside the more dominant view, according to which one does not fulfill one's obligation until one physically eats of the offerings, there surfaces time and again a persistent competing position that points to the tossing of blood, rather than to the eating of meat, as the definitive component of the Passover. I shall begin by discussing several notable passages in which this competing position comes to the fore, and then venture to reconstruct the interpretive, legislative, and ideational views that could be informing this position.

Is blood enough?

The Mishnah relates two interrelated rulings concerning the Passover, both of which notably emphasize the Passover's consumption as its defining trait:

> Five things are offered in [a state of ritual] impurity but are not eaten in [a state of] impurity: the ʿomer, and the two loaves of bread, and the showbread, and the well-being offering of the congregation, and the goats of the beginnings of months. [However], a Passover that is offered in [a state of] impurity is eaten in [a state of] impurity, *for it is not offered to begin with except in order to be eaten.*

> If the meat [of the Passover] became impure and the suet is viable, [the priest] may not toss the blood. If the suet became impure and the meat is viable, he may toss the blood. This is not the case for [other] sanctified objects (*muqdashin*), in which even though the meat became impure, if the suet is viable he may toss the blood.[84]

These two mishnaic passages convey the notion that the Passover is different from all other offerings because it is by definition offered in order to be eaten: put differently,

---

82. M. Pesaḥim 5.5–9; T. Pisḥa 8.14; Sifre Numbers 118 (ed. Horovitz 139–40); Sifre Deuteronomy 129 (ed. Finkelstein 186).

83. M. Pesaḥim 8.3, 6–7; T. Pisḥa 4.2, 6.3–4, 7.6; T. Ḥagigah 1.2; Mekhilta deRabbi Ishmael Bo 3 (ed. Horovitz-Rabin 12); Mekhilta deRabbi Shimon 12:4 (ed. Epstein-Melamed 10); Sifre Deuteronomy 132 (ed. Finkelstein 190). See also R. Yohanan ben Beroqah's ruling in M. Pesaḥim 7.9, according to which a Passover offering for which there are "no eaters" (since the owners became impure) is to be incinerated immediately.

84. M. Pesaḥim 7.4–5.

here the sacrificial process serves the meal rather than the meal being a fringe benefit of the sacrifice. For this reason, if the majority of the congregation is in a state of impurity when the Passover is sacrificed, they may also eat of the Passover meat in a state of impurity, which is not the case for any other congregational offering that can be made in a state of impurity. Similarly, whereas in all other offerings (as discussed in chapter 2) meat and suet are interchangeable, in the case of the Passover the meat is crucial, and the sacrificial process cannot be carried out without it.

When we compare these passages to their parallels in the Tosefta, two significant differences surface. First, both the phrase "the Passover is not offered to begin with except in order to be eaten" and the ruling that there must be sufficient meat in order to complete the sacrificial process are attributed in the Tosefta to R. Yehoshua (as opposed to the Mishnah, in which these statements are anonymous).[85] Attributing these statements to R. Yehoshua directly aligns them with R. Yehoshua's position in a related controversy, which in Tosefta Zevaḥim immediately precedes R. Yehoshua's ruling about the Passover: this is the controversy between R. Eliezer and R. Yehoshua on blood without meat and meat without blood. As we may recall, whereas R. Yehoshua maintains that if either the meat or the blood of a particular offering is not viable then one may not carry on with the sacrifice, R. Eliezer holds that as long as the blood is viable the sacrificial process can continue even without meat.[86] In the Tosefta, then, R. Yehoshua's insistence on the viability of meat in the Passover sacrifice appears as an offshoot of his position on blood/meat relations in general, rather than as a reflection of a unanimous position on the matter. This leaves open the possibility that for R. Eliezer and others of his persuasion, the Passover sacrifice is valid even with no meat at all—a possibility that, as we will see, receives hints of confirmation in other Toseftan passages.

Second, the Tosefta passage that comments on the Mishnah's ruling that "the Passover that is offered in [a state of] impurity is eaten in [a state of] impurity" presents a critical qualification of this ruling:

> When [i.e., for which case] did they say that the Passover is eaten in [a state of] impurity? When it was initially offered in a [state of] impurity. But if it was slaughtered [in a state of] purity, and then the congregation became impure, the blood shall be tossed in [a state of] impurity,[87] but the meat shall not be eaten in [a state of] impurity. If it was slaughtered [in a state of] purity, and then the congregation and the

85. T. Pisḥa 6.4; cf. T. Zevaḥim 4.3.

86. T. Zevaḥim 4.1–2.

87. "Let the blood be tossed in a state of impurity" (be-tum'a) is the version in all the Tosefta manuscripts. However, in PT Pesaḥim 7:4, 34b the version is "let the blood be tossed in a state of purity," as it is in BT Pesaḥim 78b in a slightly different rendition of this passage. Lieberman (Tosefta ki-peshuta Mo'ed, vol. 4, 580) maintains that the Tosefta's version is an error and should be corrected in accordance with the PT; however, I do not think the correction is necessary.

blood became impure, the blood shall be tossed in [a state of] impurity, but the meat shall not be eaten in [a state of] impurity.[88]

This Tosefta passage presents a bifurcation of the Passover into two separate components—tossing of blood and eating of meat—and presents the latter part as dispensable and the former as indispensable. Regardless of the circumstances, the blood must be tossed—even if the blood itself became impure!—but the consumption of the meat subscribes to a different protocol, and in some cases is not carried out. This bifurcation suggests that the sacrificial process of the Passover stands in its own right and is not strictly a prelude to the meal that follows: indeed there exists a scenario of a Passover sacrifice without a Passover meal.[89]

While the conceptual separation of the Passover sacrifice from the Passover meal does not necessarily entail the notion that the former suffices to fulfill the Passover obligation of individuals without the latter, several Tannaitic texts explicitly make the point that this is indeed the case, and that as long as the blood of the Passover is tossed for the sake of a person, this person does not actively have to eat of the meat to be seen as one who has "done" the Passover. This idea is presented most vividly in midrashic accounts of the story of the establishment of the "second Passover" in Numbers 9:1–14. In the biblical story, the people who were ritually impure and therefore unable to perform the Passover at its time approach Moses, asking: "Why must we be kept from presenting the Lord's offering at its appointed time among the Israelites?" Moses responds by asking for direct oracular guidance from God on this matter.[90] Between the people's complaint and Moses's turning to divine help, the midrash Sifre on Numbers incorporates an entire halakhic exchange:

> And these people said to him: Why must we be kept from presenting the Lord's offering?
>
> He [Moses] said to them: Holies cannot be offered in [a state of] impurity.
>
> They said to him: If not, then let the blood be tossed for the sake of the impure ones and the meat be eaten by the pure ones! Logic requires this. If in the case of a purification offering, which is [classified as] "holy of holies," its blood is tossed for the sake of the impure ones and the meat is eaten by the pure ones [i.e., the priests], does not logic require that in the case of the Passover, which is [classified as] "light holies," its blood be tossed for the sake of the impure ones and the meat be eaten by the pure ones?[91]

---

88. T. Pisḥa 6.1.

89. Indeed, in both the Palestinian and the Babylonian Talmuds this passage is associated with R. Nathan, who maintains that the tossing of blood suffices to fulfill the Passover obligation.

90. On the pericope of Numbers 9:1–14, see Simeon Chavel, *Oracular Law and Priestly Historiography in the Torah* (Tübingen: Mohr Siebeck, 2014), 93–164.

91. Sifre Numbers 68 (ed. Horovitz 63).

It is only after the impure persons present a series of compelling and sophisticated halakhic arguments that Moses is inclined to admit, "I did not hear" (that is, I do not know), and asks for guidance from God. This account is followed by a comment of R. Ḥidqa, who relates a tradition in the name of R. Aqiva, according to which "Moses knew that impure persons may not eat of the Passover: they only disagreed on whether the blood should be tossed for their sake or not."[92] A similar but significantly shorter version of this midrash appears in Sifre zutta on Numbers, in which the impure people's complaint is phrased even more incisively: "Why should we be like outcasts among the people of Israel? It is not that we seek eating and drinking, but rather that the blood be tossed for our sake."[93]

This midrashic tradition constructs the Passover sacrifice as consisting of two separate components—tossing of blood and eating—and makes the point that the former is powerful, efficacious, and desirable even without the latter. In fact, the component of eating is implied to be an enjoyable side benefit rather than the heart of the commandment, especially in the Sifre zutta, in which it is paired with drinking, and thus presented in an almost frivolous light. Particularly striking is the comparison of the Passover to a purification offering as the model for an offering in which "the blood is tossed for the sake of the impure ones and the meat is eaten by the pure ones." Whereas in purification offerings the blood, in its capacity as "ritual detergent," is quintessentially the tool through which the purpose of the offering is accomplished, in the Passover the blood—so one would think—does not play a significant part at all: it must be tossed on the altar, since this is the appropriate way to dispose of blood of sanctified animals, but what defines and completes the sacrifice is, presumably, the consumption of food. Here, in contrast, the tossing of the Passover's blood is depicted as sufficing to satisfy the people's desire to partake in the sacrifice.

A series of Tosefta passages similarly presents a persistent—although contested—position according to which the blood of the Passover suffices to fulfill the individual obligation pertaining to the Passover. These passages, all of which concern regulations regarding the performance of "the second Passover," make it clear that the emphasis on blood in the Sifre reflects a sustained rabbinic position that defines the tossing of blood and not the eating of meat as the completion of the Passover ritual. Chapter 7 of Tosefta Pisha presents a series of different scenarios in which something goes wrong—with the Passover offering itself or with those who are supposed to eat it—between the time in which the sacrificial actions (slaughtering and tossing of blood) are carried out and the time in which the meat is eaten.

---

92. Cf. Sifre Numbers 114, 133 (ed. Horovitz 123, 177).
93. Sifre zutta Numbers 9:7 (ed. Horovitz 259).

The first case the Tosefta discusses is of a servant who could not remember whether his master told him to slaughter a lamb or a kid, and so he slaughtered both.[94] Since as a rule a sacrificial animal must be slaughtered at the will of the owner, one of those two animals is considered an offering without owners and must therefore be incinerated (unless the servant, after finding out what the master originally wanted, claims the other animal for himself). If the master himself does not remember whether he asked for a kid or a lamb, both animals are considered ownerless and must be incinerated. The Tosefta presents a disagreement on the result of such a turn of events:

> If his master had forgotten what he told [the servant], both [the kid and the lamb] must be incinerated, and [those who planned to eat of this Passover] must perform the second Passover. R. Nathan says: They need not perform the second Passover, *since the blood was already tossed for them.*[95]

According to the anonymous voice in the Tosefta, since no one was able to eat of this Passover because the animals had to be incinerated after their sacrifice, those who were planning to eat of it did not fulfill their obligation and must repeat the Passover. According to R. Nathan, however, the tossing of blood on the altar, which had already been done for the sake of those planning to eat by the time the mistake was discovered, suffices as fulfillment of the Passover obligation.

The same disagreement is replicated in the following passage, which discusses a case in which the number of people who agreed to partake in a single Passover animal was greater than the number that the animal could feed. The Tosefta distinguishes between two cases: in the first case, the number of potential eaters was initially (that is, when the group was first formed) too great for the animal to feed, and in this case all agree that the sacrifice is inherently invalid. In the second case, the number of potential eaters was still small enough for the animal to feed when the group was first formed, but later on more potential eaters joined the group, thereby making the animal insufficient. In such a case,

> the first ones [that is, the initial members of the group], who have [enough food], will eat [of the meat], and those who joined later will not eat, and they must perform the second Passover. R. Nathan says: They need not perform the second Passover, *since the blood was already tossed for them.*[96]

As in the previous case, R. Nathan maintains, in contrast to the anonymous Tosefta, that those who were unable to eat still fulfilled their obligation, since they were included in the sacrifice when the blood was tossed.

---

94. In conjunction with M. Pesaḥim 8.2.
95. T. Pisḥa 7.5.
96. T. Pisḥa 7.6.

At the core of these two controversies stands an assumption that both sides share, according to which the Passover must be fit for consumption for a specific group of people at the time in which the sacrificial actions pertaining to it are performed. But whereas the anonymous Tosefta requires that the Passover actually be eaten, and maintains that if it could not be eaten those for whom it was slaughtered did not fulfill their obligation, R. Nathan maintains that actual consumption does not matter as long as the offering was fit for consumption when the blood was tossed. In other words, for R. Nathan it is the *consumability of the Passover during the work of blood* that defines the fulfillment of the commandment, not its actual consumption. The same principle is later applied in the Tosefta to cases in which it is the person rather than the offering that became unfit for consumption, because of ritual impurity. Whereas the anonymous Tosefta declares that "all those who have become impure after the tossing of blood ... must perform the second Passover,"[97] R. Yose ben Yehudah presents a contesting position. The passage discusses a woman who was considered ritually pure while the blood was tossed for her, but between the tossing of blood and the actual eating discovered that she was menstruating.[98] R. Yose ben Yehudah rules that although such a woman may not eat of the Passover meat, "she is exempt from performing the second Passover, since she has already fulfilled her obligation through the tossing [of blood]."[99]

It is worth noting that two of the cases discussed in the Tosefta are also discussed in the Mishnah: first, the case of the master who told his servant to procure an animal and forgot whether he asked for a kid or a goat,[100] and second, the case of persons who were ritually capable of eating the Passover during the time of slaughter and tossing of blood, but became impure before actually eating.[101] In both cases, the anonymous Mishnah rules that the people in question need *not* perform the second Passover. That is to say, the position that is presented in the Tosefta as a controversial minority opinion is presented in the Mishnah as an authoritative and uncontested ruling on this question. The same ruling appears also in regard to a case in which members of a particular group were unable to eat of their Passover, since two different offerings were made for them, and it is uncertain on which they were actually "enlisted": here too, according to the Mishnah, those who were unable to eat need not perform the second Passover.[102] Interestingly, however, in none of these cases does the Mishnah mention the notion that the second Passover is not necessary because the tossing of blood qualifies as a fulfillment of the obligation. Perhaps

---

97. T. Pisḥa 7.11.

98. The case is specifically of a woman who was in a liminal state between purity and impurity (*shomeret yom ke-neged yom*) at the time of the slaughter.

99. T. Pisḥa 7.13.

100. M. Pesaḥim 8.2.

101. M. Pesaḥim 8.6.

102. M. Pesaḥim 9.9.

this omission can be explained by the Mishnah's tendency toward brevity and refrainment from stating the obvious; but it is also possible that the redactors of the Mishnah, despite accepting the "bottom line" of those who do not require actual consumption for fulfillment of the Passover obligation, were disinclined to state explicitly that it is the tossing of blood, and not the eating of meat, that constitutes the defining pinnacle of the Passover ritual.[103]

Finally, an echo of the controversy regarding the action that fulfills the Passover obligation—whether it is eating or tossing of blood—can be found in a rabbinic dispute regarding the meaning of the phrase "distant road" (*derekh rehoqah*) in Numbers 9:10: "Anyone of you or your descendants who is impure by a corpse or on a distant road, shall still keep the Passover to the Lord, in the second month on the fourteenth day, at twilight they shall keep it." In the Mishnah, R. Eliezer and R. Aqiva disagree on the point from which distance is measured to determine if one was on "a distant road": according to R. Aqiva, this point is Modi'im at the outskirts of Jerusalem, while according to R. Eliezer this point is the threshold of the temple's court.[104] As the parallel passage in the Tosefta (in which these opinions are attributed to different named rabbis) explains, the first opinion is guided by the view that it is distance from the place in which the Passover is *eaten* (that is, Jerusalem) that matters, whereas the second opinion is guided by the view that it is the distance from the place in which the Passover is *sacrificed* (that is, the temple's court) that matters.[105] Even this seemingly technical controversy reflects, I contend, the pervasiveness of rabbinic disagreement on the question of wherein lies the essence of the Passover: in its blood or in its meat.

The Passover as blood ritual

Since the biblical origin story of the Passover ostensibly presents a picture of a sacrificial feast without the preceding sacrificial actions, and of the Passover itself as an offering in which nothing is offered (since no part of the animal is given to God), it is easy to understand the rabbinic position that considers the actual consumption of the Passover meat as the ultimate goal of the sacrificial process. But wherefrom comes the opposing view, according to which the tossing of blood on the altar—a

103. The exemptions in M. Pesaḥim 8.2 and 9.9 can also be understood differently, in light of the ruling in T. Pisḥa 7.12 that all cases of doubt are exempt from the second Passover. However, such a reading is not applicable to M. Pesaḥim 8.6.

104. M. Pesaḥim 9.2.

105. T. Pisḥa 8.2–3. In the Tosefta it is R. Eliezer who is prioritizing the place of consumption ('*akhila*), whereas R. Yose ben Yehudah is the one prioritizing the place of "performing" the Passover ('*asiyah*), which is the temple's court. R. Aqiva's opinion in the Tosefta considers "distant road" as a general impediment to performance of the sacrifice rather than a particular point in space. The version in Sifre Numbers 69 (ed. Horovitz 64) is identical with the Tosefta. In Sifre zutta Numbers 9:13 (ed. Horovitz 260), however, the attribution of opinions corresponds with the Mishnah.

ritual component that is not even mentioned in Exodus 12, in which there is no altar to speak of—suffices to fulfill one's obligation vis-à-vis the Passover? Furthermore, what does the phrase "to toss the blood for someone's sake" (or literally "to toss the blood on someone") actually mean in the context of the Passover? What is the blood of the Passover supposed to accomplish for those for whom it is tossed? In what follows, I suggest four different directions for answering these questions, some or all of which directions are likely at play in the rabbinic position that champions the blood of the Passover over its meat. None of these directions, to be clear, can be pointed to as the ultimate explanatory paradigm, and none is mutually exclusive of the others.

The first and most immediate direction for explaining the position that prioritizes blood over meat is to see the Passover in the context of the larger rabbinic sacrificial system, and to observe that the rabbis who insist on the tossing of blood and not on the eating of meat as the completion of the sacrifice thereby align the Passover with all other sacrifices. As I showed in detail in chapter 2, there is an overarching tendency in rabbinic legislation to identify the fourfold work of blood as tantamount to the sacrificial process as a whole, and to marginalize burning and eating as a desirable but dispensable sacrificial aftermath. The Passover is presented in some of the texts we have seen as downright anomalous in this regard, since "it is not offered to begin with except in order to be eaten." The position that points to the tossing of blood and not to the consumption of meat as the fulfillment of the obligation can thus be understood as an attempt to diminish the anomaly of the Passover and to apply to it the same rules as are applied to any other offering. Particularly interesting in this regard is the way in which this position transforms the requirement for *consumption after* the work of blood to a requirement of *consumability during* the work of blood. This legislative move replicates in reverse the rabbinic innovative notion of "wrongful thoughts" as capable of disqualifying offerings: in the same way that inappropriate intentions during the four works of blood suffice to disqualify an offering, since these four actions ritually encapsulate the entire process, so these four works suffice to *fulfill* the obligation of the offerer, since they ritually encapsulate the entire process. If the Passover offering could in principle be eaten at the time in which its blood is manipulated, it is seen as though it had been eaten. The work of blood thus serves in both cases as a critical juncture into which the sacrificial process as a whole is condensed.

However, in insisting on the preeminence of blood in the Passover sacrifice, the rabbis do not operate without concrete biblical precedent. A second direction for understanding the role of blood in the Passover ritual is to return to the biblical foundational narrative of Exodus 12, and to note that blood in fact does play a critical role in this narrative, even if not in a sacrificial way per se. The Israelites are instructed to apply the blood of the slaughtered lambs to the door frames, so that God will see the blood and not let the destroyer come inside. Some rabbinic homilies attempted to underplay this component of the Passover of Egypt, insisting that the blood merely served as a marker of the Israelites' performance of the commandment;[106] but alongside these homilies we find other interpretations, which assign this blood a crucial ritual function. Furthermore, the different interpretations that do assign the Passover blood a ritual function are notably continuous with ideas found in earlier postbiblical literature, thus indicating that these readings are deeply rooted in Jewish exegetical traditions. In the book of Jubilees, the blood is straightforwardly interpreted as an apotropaic substance keeping away the powers of evil,[107] and as shown by Ahron Shemesh, this apotropaic understanding of the Passover informs certain rabbinic views as well.[108] It is perhaps notable that this apotropaic reading is closely associated with R. Eliezer, whom we have seen stressing the centrality of blood in the sacrificial process elsewhere.[109] In contrast, Philo interprets the application of blood to the door frames as a preenactment of the temple ritual in which the blood is tossed on the altar,[110] and we similarly find in rabbinic texts the notion that "our ancestors had three altars in Egypt: the lintel and the two door frames."[111] Josephus presents a third approach and sees the application of blood as means of purifying the Israelites' homes, a reading undoubtedly informed by the resonance of the combination of blood and hyssop in Exodus 12 with other biblical purification rites.[112] Such a reading is also traceable in the rabbinic exegesis of Exodus 12, in which the application of blood to the door frames is construed and depicted using the exact same terminology as in other purification rites.[113]

106. See mainly the homilies in Mekhilta deRabbi Ishamel Bo 6, 7, 11 (ed. Horovitz-Rabin 18, 24, 38–39), and Mekhilta deRabbi Shimon 17:11 (ed. Epstein-Melamed 121).

107. See Betsy Halpern-Amaru, "The Festivals of Pesah and Massot in the Book of Jubilees," in *Enoch and the Mosaic Torah: The Evidence of Jubilees,* ed. Gabriele Boccaccini and Giovanni Ibba (Grand Rapids, MI: W.B. Eerdmans, 2009), 309–22; Segal, *The Book of Jubilees,* 149–59.

108. Ahron Shemesh, "What Is This Passover About" [Heb.], *AJS Review* 21, no. 2 (1996): א–ז.

109. As shown by Shemesh, "What Is This Passover About," ה–ט.

110. *Questions and Answers on Exodus* 1.12, pp. 21–22.

111. Mekhilta deRabbi Ishamel Bo 6, 11 (ed. Horovitz-Rabin 18, 37); see also BT Pesaḥim 96a.

112. Josephus, *Antiquities of the Jews* 2.14.6 (ed. Whiston 74).

113. In the Mekhilta's elaborate commentary on the way in which the blood application was performed, the biblical instruction "And touch the lintel and the two doorposts with the blood in the basin" (Exodus 12:22) is read as stipulating that the bunch of hyssop be dipped in the blood three times, before being applied to each of the sides of the door, or in the Mekhilta's words, "for every touching (*haga'a*) a dipping" (Bo 11, ed. Horovitz-Rabin 37–38). This phrase is almost identical to the formulaic phrase "for every sprinkling (*haza'a*) a dipping," which is used in rabbinic texts to describe the procedure of sprinkling purifactory blood, in which the priest is required to dip his finger in blood anew before each "flicking" of blood (M. Parah 3.9; T. Kippurim 3.2; M. Nega'im 14.10; Sifra ḥovah 3.3.8, ed. Finkelstein 17b; Sifra metzora 3.3.8, ed. Weiss 72a). This correspondence with other biblical purificatory rites evidently resonated so deeply for the rabbis that in M. Pesaḥim 9.5 the verbal noun used to denote the application of blood to the door frames is "sprinkling" (*hazaya*), even though "sprinkling" is not at all the appropriate description for the marking of door frames with blood, which is more akin to smearing or brushing.

Regardless of the exact manner in which one chooses to interpret the application of blood to the door frames in Egypt, the variety of these interpretive traditions suffices to show that the championing of blood as a significant, efficacious, and transformative substance entailed in the Passover can be traced back to the Pentateuch and to prerabbinic exegesis. Whether the blood is seen as protecting, purifying, or constitutive of a sacrificial act, it is viewed as playing a vital role in the Israelites' liberation from Egypt and their rescue from the plague of the firstborn. Thus, the position that considers the tossing of blood to be the determining component of the Passover may reflect adherence to one of the interpretive stances that sees the blood as critical—indeed more critical than the meal—in the exodus story.

The third direction for explaining the primacy of blood over meat in various rabbinic rulings was discussed in the previous section, and pertains to the debated nature of the Passover as an individual offering or a congregational offering. As I suggested above, the more one is inclined to identify the Passover as a congregational offering and to downplay its individual aspects, the more likely one is to identify the tossing of blood—of which a token quantity can be efficacious for the congregation as a whole—as the pinnacle of the ritual. The eating of meat, even if it is performed by multiple people at the same time, is fundamentally an individual act, which mandates visible forms of individual participation. Of course, one could bifurcate the Passover obligation and claim that the obligation to sacrifice rests on the community as a whole and the obligation to eat rests on each individual separately, and in all likelihood many rabbis adhered to this position; but when the view of the Passover as a congregational offering is carried to its most extreme form—namely, to the position that one offering suffices for the entirety of the people—the component of eating cannot maintain its prominence. It is probably not incidental that the two named rabbis who are quoted as saying that one Passover offering suffices for all the people—R. Eliezer and R. Nathan—are also quoted, in other contexts, as insisting on the primacy of blood and dispensability of meat in the sacrificial process.

The connection between the collectivization of the Passover and the emphasis on blood in its sacrificial performance can be understood not only on the pragmatic level described above but also on a theological level. Blood appears time and again in the Hebrew Bible as the marker of the covenant between God and God's people, most famously manifested in the rite of circumcision but most vividly depicted in the covenant ritual of Exodus 24:3–8, in which half the blood of sacrificial animals is tossed on the people and half of it is tossed on the altar.[114] As Ronald Hendel has shown, there is profound correspondence between Exodus 12 and

114. On blood and covenant in the Hebrew Bible, see Howard Eilberg-Schwartz, *The Savage in Judaism: An Anthropology of Israelite Religion and Ancient Judaism* (Bloomington: Indiana University Press, 1990), 141–76; Biale, *Blood and Belief,* 9–43.

Exodus 24, which proposes that the application of blood to the door frames in Egypt is in itself to be understood as a covenantal ritual of sorts.[115] In addition, the fact that the Passover is so closely connected with the rite of circumcision in biblical texts (circumcision is mentioned in Exodus 12:43–49 as a condition for participation in the Passover meal, and collective circumcision precedes the Passover celebration in Joshua 5:2–10) assigns the Passover sacrifice a covenantal dimension analogous to that of circumcision.[116] Thus a Tannaitic midrash reads the imploration of Ezekiel 16:6, "Live in your bloods" (*be-damayikh ḥayyi*), as follows: "The time has come for the Holy One, Blessed be He, to fulfill his oath to Abraham that he will redeem his children, and they had no commandments with which to preoccupy themselves. . . . Therefore the Holy One, Blessed be He, gave them two commandments, the blood of Passover and the blood of circumcision, with which to preoccupy themselves, so that they will be redeemed."[117] We can see how the collective nature of the redemption associated with the Passover, which reflects a collective covenant with the people as a whole, propels a collectivistic interpretation of the Passover sacrifice that places emphasis on blood as the quintessential covenantal substance.

At this point, it is necessary to pause and acknowledge what for some readers may have been an elephant in the room from the beginning of this chapter: the undeniable resonance between the rabbinic emphasis on the blood of the Passover and the Christian interpretation of Jesus as the Passover lamb.[118] The identification of Jesus as "our Passover" (*to pascha hēmōn*) appears already in Paul's first letter to the Corinthians (5:7), but is most thoroughly and systematically developed in the Gospel of John. Whereas in the Synoptic Gospels Jesus's crucifixion is dated to the first day of Passover, in the Gospel of John it is dated to the previous day (the fourteenth of Nisan),[119] thus corresponding with the slaughter and preparation of the paschal lambs.[120] Moreover, the manner in which Jesus is killed is explicitly compared with the manner in which the Passover is slaughtered, with emphasis on the spurting of blood in the process:

> Then the soldiers came and broke the legs of the first and of the other who had been crucified with him. But when they came to Jesus and saw that he was already dead, they did not break his legs. Instead, one of the soldiers pierced his side with a spear,

115. Hendel, "Sacrifice as a Cultural System," 384–89.

116. See Biale, *Blood and Belief*, 60–81.

117. Mekhilta deRabbi Ishamel Bo 5 (ed. Horovitz-Rabin 14).

118. On Jesus as a Passover offering and the biblical models at work in this interpretation, see Jeffrey Siker, "Yom Kippuring Passover: Recombinant Sacrifice in Early Christianity," in *Ritual and Metaphor: Sacrifice in the Bible*, ed. Christian A. Eberhart (Atlanta: Society of Biblical Literature, 2011), 65–82.

119. On the complexity of dating the crucifixion, see Scot McKnight, *Jesus and His Death: Historiography, the Historical Jesus, and Atonement Theory* (Waco: Baylor University Press, 2005), 260–75.

120. John 18:28.

and at once blood and water came out. . . . These things occurred so that the scripture might be fulfilled, "None of his bones shall be broken" (Exodus 12:46).[121]

The direct reference to blood in John's portrayal of Jesus as the Passover lamb corresponds with the statement attributed to John the Baptist in John 1:29, "Behold the lamb of God (*amnos tou theou*) who takes away the sins of the world."[122] This statement casts Jesus as a "lamb" in the Levitical paradigm of a purification offering (*ḥattat*), whose atoning efficacy depends on the correct manipulation of its blood.

In the Synoptic Gospels, while Jesus's death is never overtly analogized to the Passover sacrifice, the authors make notable efforts to cast the Last Supper—the account of which seems to have originally been unrelated to Passover[123]—distinctly as a paschal feast. Mark and Matthew mention that the meal was the Passover feast three times;[124] Luke mentions this six times.[125] This repetition creates a parallel between Jesus's last supper and the Passover of Egypt, which is reenacted in the annual paschal meal. In this framework, Jesus's statement in the course of the meal "This is my blood of the [new] covenant, which is poured out for many"[126] immediately alludes to the Passover of Egypt as a time in which the first covenant was established, and to the rich blood imagery associated with that covenant. In all four Gospels, then, blood features prominently—albeit differently—in constructing a new interpretation of the Passover sacrifice and of the Passover meal. This blood-oriented interpretation fundamentally relies on a view of Jesus as a *single* sacrifice, whose blood was efficacious collectively.[127]

This blood-centered model of Jesus as a collective Passover offering is further developed in the works of Christian authors from the second century, and is specifically pitted against the Jewish sacrificial practice, which these authors deem obsolete.[128] Justin Martyr in his *Dialogue with Trypho* insists that the injunction to sacrifice actual animals on Passover was only temporary, since the Passover of

121. John 19:32–36.
122. The identification of Jesus as "the lamb of God" recurs in John 1:36; it is also highly prominent in the book of Revelation. See Heyman, *The Power of Sacrifice*, 135–45.
123. See the discussion in McKnight, *Jesus and His Death*, 260–75.
124. Mark 14:12, 14, 16; cf. Matthew 26:17, 18, 19.
125. Luke 22:7, 8, 11, 12, 13, 15.
126. Matthew 26:26–28; Mark 14:22–24; Luke 22:17–20.
127. Interestingly, Origen (who rejects the paradigm according to which Jesus is equated with the Passover lamb) points to the discrepancy between the practice of multiple sacrifices and the notion of one sacrifice: "If the sheep with the Jews is a type of the sacrifice of Christ, then one should have been offered and not a multitude" (*Commentary on John* X.13, in *Ante-Nicene Fathers*, 9:389). See also Ruth Anne Clements, "Peri Pascha: Passover and the Displacement of Jewish Interpretation within Origen's Exegesis" (PhD diss., Harvard University, 1997), 180–94.
128. See Clements, "Peri Pascha," 141–218.

Egypt was merely a prefiguration of Christ: "The mystery, then, of the lamb which God enjoined to be sacrificed as the passover, was a type of Christ; with whose blood, in proportion to their faith in Him, they anoint their houses, i.e., themselves, who believe in Him."[129] Similarly, Melito of Sardis in his sermon *Peri pascha* presents the blood of the lamb (to which he refers consistently in the singular form, *probaton*) not only as protective of the Israelites but also as filling a function of initiation and constitution of a community.[130] After the same function of initiation has been accomplished through Jesus's blood for his believers, the Passover of the Old Testament is no longer valuable.

The early Christian paschal model, in which one "offering," through blood and blood alone, suffices for the whole community (whether "the whole world" or the community of believers) is notably commensurate with the position attributed to R. Eliezer, according to which a single Passover offering suffices for the entire congregation. This position, as we recall, is explained in a later rendition as reflecting the view that each member of the community fulfills his or her Passover obligation once the blood of the Passover offering has been tossed for his or her sake. Several conjectures can be raised to account for this similarity. One could suggest that the rabbinic position was set as a polemic against the Christian view, incorporating the same model but insisting on a literal and practical understanding of the biblical sacrificial commandments nonetheless. Alternatively, the fact that the "single offering" model in rabbinic literature is associated specifically with R. Eliezer might ignite the imagination of scholars who recognize R. Eliezer as one who had at least a temporary penchant for Christianity:[131] such scholars may propose that R. Eliezer's statements actually reflect direct appropriation, if not endorsement, of Christian ideas. My own inclination, however, is to identify this resonance between rabbinic and Christian constructions of the Passover sacrifice as stemming from a shared interpretive tradition that associates the blood of the Passover with the covenant, rather than to assume direct acquaintance between rabbinic and early Christian interpretive views. The recalibration of the Passover sacrifice as a communally efficacious blood ritual rather than as a feast of multiple offerings reflects, I suggest, corresponding attempts to infuse this sacrificial institution with mean-

---

129. *Dialogue with Trypho* 40 (*Ante-Nicene Fathers*, 1:214).

130. See Judith Lieu, *Image and Reality: The Jews in the World of the Christians in the Second Century* (New York: T&T Clark, 1996), 199–240.

131. The association of R. Eliezer with Christianity is based on an anecdote in T. Ḥullin 2.24 (cf. BT 'Avodah Zarah 16b). See Daniel Boyarin, *Dying for God: Martyrdom and the Making of Judaism and Christianity* (Stanford: Stanford University Press, 1999), 27–41; Peter Schäfer, *Jesus in the Talmud* (Princeton: Princeton University Press, 2007), 43–49; for a more qualified position, see Adiel Schremer, *Brothers Estranged: Heresy, Christianity, and Jewish Identity in Late Antiquity* (New York: Oxford University Press, 2009), 91–93.

ing, attempts that were conducted more or less simultaneously by two different communities seeking to establish a strong ethos of collective identity.

So far I have pointed to three directions for understanding the rabbinic position that prioritizes blood over meat. We could loosely define the first direction as procedural (aligning the Passover with all other sacrifices in terms of the workings of the process), the second as exegetical (responding to the prominence of blood in the foundational biblical narrative), and the third as theological-political (promoting a collectivistic, possibly covenantal ethos). As I stressed, these directions are not mutually exclusive but rather complementary. By way of conclusion to this chapter I would like to suggest a fourth complementary direction, which I would title here "counteractive": this direction is guided by the assumption that the rabbis who center the Passover on the tossing of blood do so in order to underplay or marginalize another ritual component of the Passover—in this case, the feast. I propose that the emphasis of blood over meat can be seen as reflecting a certain rabbinic discomfort with the gluttonous and self-indulgent potential of the Passover meal, and an attempt to create a clearer divide between sacrifice and banquet.

A TASTE OF AMBIVALENCE

"What sacrifice is acceptable to the gods without those feasting together?"[132] asked the Greek author Dio Chrysostom around the turn of the second century C.E., succinctly expressing what seems to have been self-evident for denizens of the ancient Mediterranean world: that sacrifice is not only a mode of pious religious and civic behavior, and not only an obligation that one has toward the gods or a way of acquiring and maintaining their favor, but also an opportunity to eat, drink, and be merry. As Dennis Smith has shown in detail, the sacrificial feast, in which those present partook after the portions designated for the deity had been burned on the altar, was not a separate "profane" component of an otherwise sacred ritual, but was rather understood as encapsulating the sacred essence of the event: the banquet was a manifestation of the deity's hospitality and goodwill toward his or her worshippers, and an affirmation and ratification of the social bonds among the participants.[133] In the concise words of John Scheid, "A sacrificial act consists not only in killing or eating, but rather in the association of both activities."[134]

---

132. Dio Chrysostom, *Discourses 1–11*, trans. J. W. Cohoon, Loeb Classical Library (Cambridge, MA: Harvard University Press, 1932), 3.97.

133. Smith, *From Symposium to Eucharist*, 67–86; see also Vernant and Detienne, *The Cuisine of Sacrifice among the Greeks*.

134. Scheid, "Roman Animal Sacrifice," 87.

As much as a joyous feast was an intricate part of the sacrificial process, numerous ancient authors professed concerns over the fact that such sacred banquets
often deteriorated into raucous displays of gluttony and drunkenness.[135] Moreover,
as Wendell Willis has shown, the most efficient way to defame and ridicule the
sacrificial practices of other groups was to present those practices as geared exclusively toward eating and drinking, and to present the sacrificial meal of the author's
group as tame, pious, and devoid of such lewd behavior.[136] Indeed, both Philo and
Josephus go out of their way to emphasize that the Jews always consume sacrificial
meat daintily and moderately, and never get drunk during sacred meals like other
people do.[137] Specifically in regard to the Passover, Philo stresses that "those who
are to share in the feast come together not as they do to other entertainments, to
gratify their bellies with wine and meat, but to fulfill their hereditary custom with
prayer and songs of praise."[138] Yet despite Philo's idealizing picture, it is quite prob-
able that the Passover feast—like any other sacrificial banquet, and as is only
natural—could sometimes entail unseemly behavior and ravenous eating.

For the early rabbis, a concern with potentially gluttonous behavior during sacrificial meals was largely theoretical in nature, as no actual sacrificial meals were
held in their time, at least not officially.[139] I do suggest, however, that this theoretical concern nonetheless informed their approach to the Passover sacrifice and the
Passover feast. One homily in the Babylonian Talmud, attributed to the third-
century Palestinian amora R. Yoḥanan, addresses this concern explicitly:

> "For the ways of the Lord are right, and the upright walk in them, but transgressors
> stumble in them" (Hosea 14:9). This resembles the case of two people who have
> roasted their Passover [lambs], one for the sake of [observing the] commandment
> and one for the sake of coarse eating ('akhilah gasah). [To] the one who ate for the

135. For multiple examples of Greek and Roman authors expressing this concern, see Willis, *Idol
Meat in Corinth*, 51–54; Redfield, "Animal Sacrifice in Comedy"; Ullucci, *The Christian Rejection of
Animal Sacrifice*, 51–64. Interestingly, a similar disdain for gluttonous behavior in sacrificial settings is
expressed in Zoroastrian texts, as shown by Albert de Jong, "Animal Sacrifice in Ancient Zoroastrian-
ism: A Ritual and Its Interpretations," in *Sacrifice in Religious Experience*, ed. Albert I. Baumgarten
(Leiden: Brill, 2002), 147–48.

136. Willis mentions Juvenal (*Sat.* 15), Philo (*Flaccus* 17.136), and Tertullian (*Apology* 39) as mock-
ing the excessive feasting in Egyptian cults (particularly the cults of Serapis). See Willis, *Idol Meat in
Corinth*, 44. We should also mention Hebrews 9:10, which dismisses animal sacrifices by associating
them with "eating and drinking."

137. Philo, *On the Special Laws* 1.190–92 (ed. Yonge 552); Josephus, *Against Apion* 2.8, 2.26 (ed.
Whiston 800, 806).

138. Philo, *On the Special Laws* 2.148 (ed. Yonge 582).

139. There are, however, various rabbinic expressions of disdain for gluttony and coarse behavior
during meals in general in Talmudic texts. For a discussion of this theme in rabbinic literature, see
Ruhama Weiss, *Meal Tests: Meals in the World of the Sages* [Heb.] (Tel-Aviv: Ha-kibbutz ha-meu'had,
2010), 120–47.

sake of the commandment [refer the words] "the righteous walk in them," but [to] the one who ate for the sake of coarse eating [refer the words] "transgressors stumble in them."[140]

R. Yoḥanan says that the commandment to eat of the Passover meat, which for pious people serves as an opportunity to accrue merit, can serve as a stumbling block for gluttonous people who will eat of the meat ravenously: for such people, the consumption of the Passover meat can actually turn into a form of transgression. R. Yoḥanan's homily is followed by an objection of Resh Lakish, who protests that even those who eat of the Passover in an unseemly way still fulfill their obligation, although they cannot be seen as performing a "choice commandment" (mitz-vah min ha-muvḥar).

While it is only in this Amoraic tradition that voracious eating of the Passover offering is discussed explicitly and directly, I believe that we do find an echo for a concern with such behavior in one Tannaitic tradition as well. Moreover, I suggest that there is a possible connection between this concern and the positions that prioritize blood over meat that we have seen above. The tradition I am referring to concerns the feast offering (ḥagigah) that accompanies the Passover offering, often referred to as "the feast offering of the fourteenth."

The notion that the Passover offering is to be accompanied by another well-being offering, which is slaughtered after the Passover and served in the meal alongside it, is based on an exegetical attempt to reconcile two contradictory biblical teachings: whereas according to Exodus 12:5 the Passover offering can be taken only from the flock (that is, is limited to lambs and goats), according to Deuteronomy 16:2 the Passover offering can be taken from either the flock or the cattle. The solution to this contradiction, which in rabbinic sources is attributed to Hillel the Elder, is that the verse in Deuteronomy refers to an additional offering made alongside the Passover.[141] This exegetical solution is already implied in 2 Chronicles 35:7, in a chapter that presents a consistent interpretive effort to harmonize the Passover pericopes of Exodus and Deuteronomy.[142] There is no evidence from the Second Temple period that such an additional offering was ever made alongside the Passover, and as noted by Joseph Tabory, it should be understood primarily as a literary construction.[143] Rabbinic sources, however, treat the "feast offering of the fourteenth" as an established fact, and present multiple debates on the exact

140. BT Nazir 23a; BT Horayot 10b.

141. Mekhilta deRabbi Ishmael Bo 4 (ed. Horovitz-Rabin 13); Sifre Deuteronomy 129 (ed. Finkelstein 187); and see David Henshke, "On the Rabbis' Way in Reconciling Biblical Contradictions" [Heb.], Sidra 10 (1994): 39–55.

142. See Sara Japhet, I and II Chronicles: A Commentary, Old Testament Library (Louisville, KY: Westminster John Knox Press, 1993), 1050–53.

143. Joseph Tabory, "The Paschal Hagigah—Myth or Reality?" [Heb.], Tarbitz 64, no. 1 (1995): 39–49.

workings of this additional offering and on the extent to which it is or is not subject to the same ritual protocol as the Passover offering.[144]

There is a consensus among rabbinic sources that the feast offering that accompanies the Passover is primarily meant to complement the meal and to provide additional sustenance to the eaters—that is, to make the Passover meal a more substantial one.[145] However, the Mishnah and the Tosefta disagree on one notable point. Whereas the Mishnah maintains that the feast offering is presented alongside the Passover *only* when the quantity of the Passover meat is not sufficient—that is, when it will not suffice to satiate its eaters[146]—the Tosefta maintains that a feast offering is *always* made alongside the Passover, regardless of the quantity of meat of the latter.[147] More importantly for our purposes, the Tosefta stresses that the feast offering is to be eaten *before* the Passover offering, so that the Passover will be eaten in a state of satiation (*'al ha-sov'a*).[148] For the Tosefta, then, the feast offering is used as a "buffer" between the people and the Passover meat, which ensures that by the time they get to the Passover meat they will be full enough not to eat it ravenously.[149] Thereby the Tosefta, much like Philo and much like R. Yoḥanan in the homily quoted above, positions the consumption of the Passover meat primarily as fulfillment of a commandment and not as a form of indulgence.

I would like to raise the possibility that the rabbinic traditions that locate the fulfillment of the Passover commandment in the blood and not the meat can be read in light of the concern that the Tosefta seems to be addressing. If there was indeed some concern among the rabbis that the Passover meal might feature unbridled gluttony and perhaps show too much resemblance to sacrificial feasts of "other" (presumably non-Jewish) groups, then a possible solution would be to try to distance the core of the commandment from the meal altogether. In other words, whereas the Tosefta and the homily in the Babylonian Talmud attempt to distinguish between eating as a pristine fulfillment of a commandment and eating for the purpose of indulgence, the rabbis who point to the tossing of blood as the fulfillment of the commandment obviate the need for this distinction, at least to some extent. The Passover feast, when construed as the aftermath of the sacrificial process rather than as its pinnacle, deflects the problem of intermixing of indul-

---

144. M. Pesaḥim 6.3–4; T. Pisḥa 5.3, 8.7.

145. See also Mekhilta deRabbi Ishmael Bo 4 (ed. Horovitz-Rabin 20).

146. M. Pesaḥim 6.3; cf. Sifre zutta Numbers 9:2 (ed. Horovitz 257).

147. T. Pisḥa 8.7.

148. T. Pisḥa 5.3.

149. In the Palestinian Talmud (PT Pesaḥim 6.4, 33c) it is explained that this arrangement is meant to prevent the eaters from hurrying to eat the Passover lamb and accidentally breaking its bones. It is also possible that this passage reflects a concern that if the Passover meat is served first, there will not be enough of it left for all the participants: cf. T. Pisḥa 7.10.

gence and piety, because the meal is conceptually distinguished and separated from the Passover commandment itself.

A strong indication that the emphasis on the tossing of blood can serve as an antidote to the potential appearance of the Passover meal as a display of gluttony can be found in the Sifre zutta tradition quoted earlier: there, as we recall, those who were unable to perform the Passover at its appointed time tell Moses: "It is not that we seek eating and drinking, but rather that the blood be tossed for our sake."[150] The midrash directly contrasts the feasting aspects of the Passover with the tossing of blood, using a rhetoric that marks "eating and drinking" as forms of self-interested pleasure implicitly contrasted with the religious reverence manifested in one's desire to have the blood tossed for one's sake. I thus propose that the view of the blood rather than the meat of the Passover as its ritual essence could be informed, in addition to the factors discussed in the previous section, by an attempt to underplay banquet-like aspects of "eating and drinking" in the sacrificial setting of the Passover, and thereby possibly to chart clearer distinctions between Jewish and non-Jewish sacrifice.[151]

Finally, the rabbinic inclination to underplay the role of meat and to highlight the role of blood can be understood as responding not only to the possibility of inappropriate or impious behavior in the sacrificial meal itself, but also to a possibility that was much more concrete for the rabbis: that people would eat a Passover or Passover-like meal without the appropriate sacrificial process at all. Several rabbinic traditions describe a practice of roasting a lamb on Passover night such that it would look like the Passover offering (or perhaps, roasting a lamb on Passover night with the thought that it actually *constitutes* a Passover offering).[152] This practice is hotly debated in rabbinic texts, which indicate that the Passover meal posed a genuine problem for the rabbis in an era in which there was no temple and no centralized sacrificial cult. The more the "official" Passover ritual of the temple resembles a regular feast in which a roasted lamb is eaten, the easier it is to replicate this feast outside the temple, and the blurrier the boundaries between legitimate sacrifice and illegitimate sacrifice become. In contrast, the more one points to the tossing of blood on an altar by priests as the heart of the Passover ritual, rather than to the group of laypeople enjoying a meal together, the clearer and

---

150. Sifre zutta Numbers 9:7 (ed. Horovitz 259).

151. It should be noted that feasting is never problematized in relation to other consumable offerings, and it is perhaps the Passover's special status as national-redemptive sacrificial event that leads to this problematization in its case.

152. M. Pesaḥim 4.4; T. Yom Tov 2.15; see Haim Licht, "Thodos of Rome and Consumption of Roasted Lambs on the Passover Night" [Heb.], *Tura* 4 (1989): 89–106. On the possible persistence of sacrificial-like Passover feasts after the destruction of the temple, See Tabory, *The Passover Ritual*, 92–105.

stricter the boundaries one charts between sacrifice and meal, between what can be done only in the temple and what can be done outside of it. Blood thus functions in the rabbinic construction of the Passover as the quintessential marker of sacrifice *as such*, thereby preventing the Passover—at least on a discursive level—from collapsing into an ordinary home-based meal.

Ordinary Miracles

The fifth chapter of tractate 'Avot ("Fathers") of the Mishnah, a tractate that uniquely contains teachings regarding morals and virtues rather than elaborations of particular legal or ritual topics, commences with six passages whose recurring theme is the number ten.[1] These passages highlight the centrality of the number ten in the sacred history of the people of Israel, following the biblical order: the world was created by ten utterances; there were ten generations from Adam to Noah and ten generations from Noah to Abraham; Abraham endured ten trials; there were ten miracles and ten plagues in Egypt, ten miracles and ten plagues in the Sea of Reeds, and ten times in which the Israelites tested God in the wilderness; finally, ten miracles regularly took place in the temple. The unit closes by coming back to its starting point, the creation of the world, and enumerates "ten things that were created on the sixth day at dusk"—an intriguing list that includes various miraculous objects, most of which were created specifically in anticipation of key moments during the events or times mentioned above. Beginning and ending with the act of creation, this mishnaic unit indicates that Israel's sacred history is intertwined with—if not indeed tantamount to—the history of the cosmos itself.

In this unit, the Jerusalem temple and the sacrificial worship performed therein not only constitute a quintessential part of Israel's sacred history, but also appear as its pinnacle. The Mishnah does not give any indication of whether "the temple" at hand is the First or the Second Temple; rather, it seems purposefully to mesh both temples into one ongoing reality, beginning in biblical times and ending in a

---

1. On this list, see Amram Tropper, *Wisdom, Politics, and Historiography: Tractate Avot in the Context of the Graeco-Roman Near East* (Oxford: Oxford University Press, 2004), 148.

past that is not too distant from the rabbis themselves. Interestingly, the miracles listed in this passage are of a rather mundane nature: they are not ones of extravagant audiovisual effects but of a subtle suspension of natural laws. With the exception of one, these are all "negative" miracles, marked by the fact that unpleasant things that could be expected to happen never happened in the temple: the sacred meat never became putrid, a fly was never found in the slaughterhouse,[2] the fire on the altar was never put out by rain, a scorpion or serpent never hurt anyone in Jerusalem, and so forth.[3] The Mishnah, however, makes the point that these ordinary, quotidian miracles are equal in every respect to miracles on the magnitude of splitting the sea. The juxtaposition of the miracles in the temple to the miracles in Egypt and on the Sea of Reeds powerfully frames the temple as a mythical space that existed in what Mircea Eliade called *illo tempore*,[4] a wondrous time wholly different from the readers'/listeners' own time.[5]

The mishnaic list of "ten miracles that were performed in the temple,"[6] like several other Tannaitic passages recounting wondrous occurrences in the temple,[7] serves as a potent reminder that for the rabbis the temple and the sacrificial cult were not only objects of scrutiny, regulation, and textual dissection, but also objects of admiration and allure. On the one hand Tannaitic texts, in their focus on the minutest details pertaining to the substances and sequences of various sacrificial activities, present temple-related legislation as akin to the laws of vows, marriage, or retrieval of lost objects: they do not indicate that aspects of temple cult are in any way less pragmatic or this-worldly than other areas of Jewish law. On the

2. The notion that flies miraculously stay away from sacrificial meat appears also in Greek and Roman literature, as discussed in Gilhus, *Animals, Gods, and Humans*, 140.

3. M. 'Avot 5.5. The full list of miracles in the passage is as follows: "A woman never miscarried from the smell of the sacred meat, and the sacred meat never became putrid, and a fly was never seen in the slaughterhouse, and the high priest did not have a seminal emission on the Day of Atonement, and the rain did not put out the fire of the altar, and the wind did not overcome the pillar of smoke, and the 'omer and the two loaves were never defiled; they would stand crowded but have space to prostrate; and a serpent or scorpion never hurt [a person] in Jerusalem, and never did a person say to his fellow 'I do not have sufficient room to spend the night in Jerusalem.'"

4. Mircea Eliade, *The Myth of Eternal Return, or, Cosmos and History* (Princeton: Princeton University Press, 1954), 4.

5. The mythization of the temple times is even more pronounced in the printed editions of the Mishnah, in which the version is "Ten miracles were performed *for our forefathers* in the temple."

6. In MS Parma 138: "Ten miracles were performed *for* the temple."

7. In particular, a lengthy unit in T. Sotah 13–15 integrates several anecdotes about miraculous occurrences in the temple into a narrative sequence whose overarching theme is continuous deterioration. This unit emphatically distinguishes between the earlier days of the temple (marked by the persona of the high priest Simeon the Righteous), during which miracles took place constantly, and later times, in which both the temple and the priesthood were significantly compromised. However, this unit also distinguishes between the times of the temple as a whole and the time after its destruction, since which the world exists as a lacking and pale shadow of what it used to be.

other hand, the temple clearly functions in early rabbinic literature as an emblem of a more perfect past, a "golden age" of sorts,[8] which can be discursively used to lend authority and credence both to certain ideas and to the rabbis themselves. As was shown by Martin Jaffee[9] and later on by Naftali Cohn,[10] the many places in which the rabbis incorporate themselves (under the moniker "the Sages") into accounts regarding temple-related legal or ritual decisions strongly speak to the fact that the temple served for them as a critical source of political capital. Furthermore, Ishay Rosen-Zvi demonstrated that the temple is often used in Tannaitic literature as a site through which greater cultural, social, and religious questions are negotiated—specifically because of the privileged position of the temple as a marker of a glorious era.[11] The temple thus simultaneously functions in Tannaitic texts both as ongoing halakhic reality and as idealized memory.

It is important to observe, however, that the temple era is not merely assumed by the rabbis to be a golden age, but is actively produced by them as such. The main textual sites in which the temple is constructed in an idyllic way, and portrayed through an admiring and enchanted lens, are the Mishnah's various ritual narratives, that is, play-by-play depictions of different rituals that took place in the temple or in its vicinity.[12] This mishnaic literary genre operates as what the Greeks called *ekphrasis,* a rhetorical exercise meant to produce "a vivid visual passage describing the topic so clearly that anyone hearing the words would seem to see it."[13] As Patricia Cox Miller explained, since the purpose of *ekphrases* is "turning listeners into spectators," such descriptions are not only technically elaborate but also affective, geared to instigate a subjective, emotional response.[14] Correspondingly, the temple and the rituals related to it are portrayed in the Mishnah's ekphrastic depictions not only in striking detail, which generates a strong sense of verisimilitude and eyewitnessing,[15] but often also with particular emphasis on aesthetics and sensual affect. Through artful choices of wording, imagery, and narrative sequence the temple emerges in many of these descriptions as a place of music, light, abundance, beauty, and joy; but perhaps even more important, these

8. See Tropper, *Wisdom, Politics, and Historiography,* 171.

9. Martin Jaffee, "The Taqqanah in Tannaitic Literature: Jurisprudence and the Construction of Rabbinic Memory," *Journal of Jewish Studies* 41, no. 2 (1990): 204–23.

10. Cohn, *The Memory of the Temple,* 39–56.

11. Rosen-Zvi, "The Body and the Temple."

12. On the genre of ritual narratives in the Mishnah, see Rosen-Zvi, *The Mishnaic Sotah Ritual,* 225–54; Moshe Simon-Shoshan, *Stories of the Law: Narrative Discourse and the Construction of Authority in the Mishnah* (New York: Oxford University Press, 2012), 42–45.

13. Liz James and Ruth Webb, "To Understand Ultimate Things and Enter Secret Places: Ekphrasis and Art in Byzantium," *Art History* 14, no. 1 (1991): 5–6.

14. Patricia Cox Miller, *The Corporeal Imagination: Signifying the Holy in Late Ancient Christianity* (Philadelphia: University of Pennsylvania Press, 2009), 9.

15. See Cohn, *The Memory of the Temple,* 57–72.

descriptions place emphasis on the harmony and camaraderie among all those who come to the temple, and more broadly among the people as a collective.[16] We have had an opportunity to see the rabbinic production of the temple as a social utopia in chapter 3, in which I showed how the collection procedure of the annual tribute and the acquisition of congregational offerings are shaped by the rabbis as manifestations of perfect solidarity, equality, and unity among the people. A similar emphasis on unity and harmony, perfectly displayed in the flawlessly orchestrated and coordinated movement of the priests and the laypeople in the temple, can be traced in the Mishnah's short account on the slaughter of the Passover offerings in tractate Pesaḥim, which I discussed briefly in the previous chapter.

The remarkable detail and elaborateness of ritual narratives in the Mishnah, as well as their occasional (and probably deliberate) use of archaic language, led some of the founding scholars of rabbinic literature to identify those textual units as particularly early in their provenance and as firsthand memories of individuals who actually witnessed the temple with their very eyes.[17] More recent scholarship has shown, however, that these texts are as much a product of Tannaitic study circles as other parts of the early rabbinic literature, and that they creatively weave together an array of rabbinic materials—history and fantasy, memory and ideology, early traditions and interpretive innovations—rather than reliably document or preserve "original" information from the time of the temple.[18] These narratives are linguistically and grammatically designed, as Yohanan Breuer has shown, to blend together "what was" and "what should be," and thereby simultaneously to idealize the past as the paradigm for the present/future and to affirm the rabbis' halakhic vision as congruent and compatible with the past.[19] In the words of Rosen-Zvi, the purpose of ritual narratives is "to shape the 'original' form of halakhic reality, as it ought to have been and as it should be remembered."[20] The temple is thus glorified and idealized in Tannaitic literature not (or not only) out of a sense of nostalgia, but rather because it is distinctly through its production as a semimythical space existing in a semimythical time, that the rabbis' own legal,

16. For prominent examples, see M. Bikkurim chapter 3; M. Pesaḥim chapter 5; M. Sukkah chapter 5; M. Menaḥot chapter 10.

17. See, for example, Hoffmann, *Die erste Mischna;* Epstein, *Prolegomena to Tannaitic Literature,* 25–46; Louis Ginzberg, "Tamid: The Oldest Treatise of the Mishnah," *Journal of Jewish Lore and Philosophy* 1, no. 1 (1919): 33–44.

18. See Rosen-Zvi, *The Mishnaic Sotah Ritual,* 162–64, 241–45. On the unreliability of rabbinic accounts of the Second Temple as historical sources, see also Tropper, *Rewriting Ancient Jewish History,* 118–33; Schwartz, "Sacrifice without the Rabbis."

19. Yohanan Breuer, "Perfect and Participle in Descriptions of Ritual in the Mishnah" [Heb.], *Tarbitz* 56 (1987): 299–326.

20. Rosen-Zvi, *The Mishnaic Sotah Ritual,* 245.

social, and religious ideology—when mapped onto the temple—can be seen as preservative and restorative rather than as revolutionary.

In this regard, there is significant similarity between the rabbinic descriptions of the Second Temple and the priestly descriptions of the tabernacle of the wilderness: both the priestly authors and the rabbis use an idealized past in order to legitimize a far-reaching legal and religious vision, claiming that their legislation originated in a perfect "golden age" and reflects the desired and appropriate order of the cult and of the people. David Wright cogently called the literary medium used by the priestly authors "pseudoarcheography": "Written much later than the events described, [the priestly texts] constructed an embroidered history by hermeneutically transforming sources, creatively filling in gaps, and inventing events and details."[21] The very same definition can be readily applied to the rabbis' "embroidered history" of the temple as shaped through their ritual narratives. However, whereas the priestly authors grounded their ritual legislation in a mythical era par excellence—Israel's time in the wilderness right after the revelation in Sinai—the early rabbis had to construct the Second Temple as an idyllic site and as the model of "things as they should be": they had to turn its routine procedures into something magnificent, and infuse its everyday life with a touch of the miraculous.

The purpose of this chapter is to examine the role that sacrifices play in the rabbinic production of the temple as an idealized site: in other words, it seeks to explore how the rabbis turned sacrifices into something magnificent. This chapter thus moves from the rules and regulations governing sacrificial procedures, on which I focused in the previous chapters, to the ways in which sacrifice as a procedure is used to create an affective portrayal of the temple's "golden age." For this purpose, I turn to the mishnaic genre of ritual narrative, in which normative halakhic and social visions are laid out in the form of eyewitness accounts, thereby turning the textual temple into a chronotope in which "thus it was" and "thus it ought to be" are one and the same. Specifically, I focus on ritual narratives that describe the sacrificial *routine* of the temple—the ordinary and repetitive rituals that recur every day—through an idealizing lens. Through an examination of Tannaitic constructions of the regular cultic work at the temple, I venture to trace the ideologies that inform the rabbinic depictions of the sacrificial worship, and to reveal how the idyllic past that these texts produce serves as infrastructure for the rabbis' own legislative and interpretive enterprise.

While various ritual narratives in the Mishnah depict or mention the making or bringing forth of offerings of various sorts to the temple (such as the firstfruits, the 'omer, the grain offering of the suspected adulteress, and the water libation of the festival of Sukkot), in this chapter I chose to concentrate on two tractates that consist almost in their entirety of ritual narratives relating elaborate sacrificial

21. Wright, "Ritual Theory, Ritual Texts," 200–201.

procedures: tractate Tamid, which describes the activities surrounding the daily burnt offering of the morning, and tractate Yoma, which describes the high priest's sacrificial work on the Day of Atonement. The lion's share of the chapter is dedicated to tractate Tamid, whereas my engagement with tractate Yoma is more limited in its scope, and focuses mainly on this tractate's thematic and structural correspondences with tractate Tamid—that is, on the ways in which the treatise dedicated to the Day of Atonement as an exceptional day repeatedly relates to the "everyday" of the sacrificial cult.

My choice to dedicate most of this chapter to tractate Tamid derives, in part, from the fact that this intriguing tractate received relatively little scholarly attention, whereas tractate Yoma has been the subject of several extensive studies that have covered much of its ground.[22] More important, however, this choice is motivated by my conviction that tractate Tamid—because of its preoccupation with the recurring, the quotidian, and even the banal in the sacrificial work of the temple—offers a distinctive and invaluable perspective on sacrifice *as such*. Because it engages with a type of sacrifice that is not bound with specific circumstances, with a specific time of year, or with specific cultic or public needs, tractate Tamid can be seen as a commentary on the very idea of sacrificial worship in the temple. It thus proposes both a theory of sacrifice and an ethos of sacrifice of its own, which often resonate with the rabbinic "sacrificial vision" that I reconstructed in the previous chapters, and yet introduces several new and intriguing conceptual and ideological tropes.

THE PRIESTLY MACHINE OF TRACTATE TAMID

According to Numbers 28:3–4, the daily sacrificial worship in the temple is always to be bookended by two burnt offerings, one of which precedes all other sacrifices and the other of which (usually)[23] seals them: "This is the offering by fire that you shall offer to the Lord: two male lambs a year old without blemish, daily, as a regular offering. One lamb you shall offer in the morning, and the other lamb you shall offer at twilight." Ostensibly, tractate Tamid of the Mishnah concerns the first of these two daily burnt offerings, the one made in the morning. Even a cursory look suffices, however, to see that only one chapter of the tractate's six chapters (or seven chapters, depending on the textual tradition[24]) is dedicated exclusively to

22. For a few notable examples, see Stökl Ben Ezra, *The Impact of Yom Kippur;* Swartz, "Judaism and the Idea of Ancient Ritual Theory" (as well as various other articles by Swartz cited in this chapter); and see also the multiauthor volume *The Day of Atonement: Its Interpretation in Early Jewish and Christian Traditions,* ed. Thomas Hieke and Tobias Nicklas (Leiden: Brill, 2012).

23. The only exception to this rule is the Passover, which is slaughtered after the daily offering (M. Pesaḥim 5.1).

24. In the Mishnah's manuscripts the tractate contains six chapters only, whereas in the printed editions M. Tamid 6.4–6 are marked as a separate, seventh chapter.

the treatment of the sacrificial lamb: the rest of the tractate discusses, at great length, an array of other preparations and rituals that are part of the morning routine in the temple. I will argue that the creators of this tractate purposefully shaped the morning routine as consisting of multiple activities, and also emphasized the divisibility of each major activity into even smaller activities. Thereby, I propose, the makers of this tractate replaced the biblical model of one offering made by one priest with a model of a complex but efficient machine consisting of many parts, in which no individual can claim greater importance or indispensability than others.

The temple that never sleeps

Structurally and thematically, the first four chapters of tractate Tamid take their cue from one passage in Leviticus 6, which relates the "law of the burnt offering" (*torat ha-'olah*) and clearly discusses the burnt offering that commences the sacrificial activities of the day:

> The Lord spoke to Moses, saying: Command Aaron and his sons, saying: This is the law of the burnt offering. The burnt offering itself shall remain on the hearth upon the altar all night until the morning, while the fire on the altar shall be kept burning. The priest shall put on his linen vestments after putting on his linen undergarments next to his body; and he shall take up the ashes to which the fire has reduced the burnt offering on the altar, and place them beside the altar. Then he shall take off his vestments and put on other garments, and carry the ashes out to a clean place outside the camp. The fire on the altar shall be kept burning; it shall not go out. Every morning the priest shall add wood to it, lay out the burnt offering on it, and turn into smoke the fat pieces of the offerings of well-being. A perpetual fire shall be kept burning on the altar; it shall not go out.[25]

The key theme in this passage is evident: three times it repeats the notion that the fire on the altar is never put out—that is, that even during the night, when no other activity is taking place in the tabernacle, the altar remains "awake." This message is further enhanced by the author's emphasis on direct continuity between the night burnt offering and the morning burnt offering: the former burns "all night" and is then immediately replaced with the latter.[26] In an effort to stress the direct continuity between the two offerings, the passage points that the priest's very first chore of the day is to remove the ashes of the evening's offering from the altar before setting the wood for the morning offering on it: this transitional phase between the two offerings turns the night and the day at the sanctuary into a single, continuous unit.

---

25. Leviticus 6:2–6.

26. As noted by Philo of Alexandria: "The lawgiver designed by this command to connect the old with the new sacrifices, and to unite the two by the duration and presence of the same fire by which all such sacrifices are consecrated" (*On the Special Laws* 1.286, ed. Yonge 561).

Following Leviticus 6:2–6, the description of the morning daily offering in tractate Tamid begins with the preceding night. But whereas in Leviticus the description of the tabernacle's nightlife focuses on the altar and on the burnt offering, in
tractate Tamid our attention is turned right at the outset to the nightly activities of
the priests:

> In three places the priests guard in the temple: in the Chamber of 'Avtinas, and in the
> Chamber of the Spark, and in the Chamber of Fire. The chamber of 'Avtinas and
> the Chamber of the Spark were elevated, and the young [priests] would guard there.
> The Chamber of Fire had a dome, and it was a large house surrounded with rows of
> stone: and the elders of the [priestly] family [that was serving at a given time] would
> sleep there with the keys to the temple's court in their hands, and the neophytes of
> the priesthood [would sleep] with their mattresses on the ground. They would not
> sleep in their sacred garments, but rather remove them and fold them and place
> them under their heads, and cover themselves with their own clothes. If a seminal
> emission would occur to one of them, he would go out and walk in a twisty road
> underneath the building, with candles burning on both sides, until he would reach
> the Chamber of Immersion. There was a bonfire there, as well as a toilet of respect-
> fulness. This was its respectfulness: if he would find it locked, he would know that
> there is someone there; [if he would find it] open, he would know that there is no one
> there. [That priest] would go down, immerse, go up and dry himself, and warm him-
> self by the fire. He would then come and sit by his brethren the priests until the gates
> would open, and then go out and leave.[27]

This lengthy passage enumerates three different kinds of "guarding" that are taking
place at night in the temple. The first kind, related in the opening sentence, is the
simplest: some priests would actually be assigned to stay awake at night and keep
watch in three places. But there is also another form of guarding: even the priests
who are asleep, the Mishnah points out, are actively guarding their sacred garments while sleeping. In addition, the unfortunate priest who happens to have a
seminal emission at night, who immediately gets up and goes to immerse himself,
waiting in the dark until he would be able to leave the temple (as he must stay away
from the holy precinct until the evening), is guarding the temple from his own
impurity. As Avraham Walfish has observed, this description is set to show that
"even at night the priests of the serving family do not take their mind off of the
service in the temple. . . . They are instructed to guard the temple, and even their
sleep takes place inside it while carefully watching the sanctity of their clothes and
the purity of their bodies."[28]

---

27. M. Tamid 1.1.

28. Avraham Walfish, "Ideational Tendencies in the Description of the Temple and Its Work in
Tractates Tamid and Middot" [Heb.], *Mekhkarei Yehudah ve-Shomron* 7 (1998): 82–83 (my translation).

Moreover, Walfish astutely noted the difference between the opening passage of tractate Tamid and the opening passage of tractate Middot, a mishnaic tractate whose main concern is the architecture and structure of the temple and the courts. Tractate Middot identically begins with the list of the three places in which the priests guard in the temple, but adds to it a list of twenty-one places in which the Levities guard and does not mention any of the priestly nighttime practices. Thus, Walfish writes, "tractate Tamid stresses the activity of guarding whereas tractate Middot stresses the fact that the temple is a well-guarded place."[29] The centrality of *activity* in tractate Tamid, as opposed to persons, substances, or places, will become increasingly evident as we continue our examination.[30]

In the passage that immediately follows, the Mishnah relates that it is not only those who guard the temple and those who had emissions who are awake before dawn: rising especially early is also the practice of priests who are eager to partake in the very first task of the day—clearing the altar of the waste and ashes of yesterday's offerings. Since the tasks in the temple are allocated through a lottery process (a point to which I will return in the next subsection), priests who wished to be included in the first "draw," which concerns the removal of ashes, had to be prepared for work before the appointed priest (*memuneh*) who administers the lottery would arrive:

> Anyone who wants to remove [the ashes from] the altar rises early and immerses before the appointed [priest] comes. At what time does the appointed [priest] come? Not all times are identical. At times he comes at the crow of the rooster, or soon after it or before it. The appointed one would come and knock at their [door], and they would open for him. He would tell them: anyone who had immersed, let him come and participate in the lottery. They would then draw a lottery, and whoever won [the task of removing the ashes], won.[31]

Consider the picture painted in this passage: a group of priests so eager to take on the first task of the day that they rise early, immerse in water in the chill of the night, and sit to wait for a person whose time of arrival is not entirely certain—all this in order to get a mere chance at performing what is for all intents and purposes a cleanup job. A corresponding passage in tractate Yoma mentions that the priests' alacrity and passion in performing this particular task were so great that one priest once violently pushed another in order to get to remove the ashes from the altar first, and it was

---

29. Walfish, "Ideational Tendencies," 82 (emphasis added).

30. Intriguingly, M. Middot 1.2 also describes how priests who accidently fell asleep were met with violent punishments, whereas tractate Tamid mentions nothing of the sort: this omission in Tamid is understandable in light of the tractate's continuous effort to describe the priests as flawless.

31. M. Tamid 1.2.

following that incident that the lottery was instituted.[32] It may seem curious that the Mishnah portrays this rather tedious and humble assignment as one that the priests are especially avid to perform: indeed, the Babylonian Talmud in tractate Yoma suggests that there was initially no lottery for this task because it was not assumed that anyone would ever compete for it.[33] I would like to suggest, however, that it is exactly *because* this task is so menial that the Mishnah portrays it as so coveted. By describing the exceptional effort made by the priests to perform a task that would not even register for most readers as consequential, the makers of tractate Tamid create an idealized picture of the priests as devoted workers for whom the very ability to participate in the cultic labor—in any aspect of it—is its own reward.[34]

Furthermore, the Mishnah describes the process of the removal of ashes as an ominous task of utmost sanctity, performed with the greatest of awe: like any other sacrificial activity, it must be performed with caution and following an exact protocol.[35] Notably, the Mishnah uses two literary motifs to shape the removal of the ashes as analogous to the offering of incense, which is discussed later on, in the sixth chapter of the tractate:

REMOVAL OF ASHES	OFFERING OF INCENSE
Whoever won [the lottery of] removal [of ashes] from the altar, he removes the ashes from the altar. *And they [the other priests] tell him: Be careful!* Lest you touch the vessel before you sanctify your hands and feet at the laver. . . . *No man would enter with him,* and there is no candle in his hand, but rather he walks by the light of the fire [on the altar]. *They would not see him and would not hear him* until they would hear the sound of the wooden wheel that Ben Qatin made for the laver, and then they would say: It is time![36]	Whoever won [the lottery of offering] the incense would take the censer out of the spoon and give it to his loved one or relative. . . . *And they [the other priests] would teach him: Be careful!* Lest you begin [scattering the incense on the side] close to you, so you will not burn yourself [as you continue scattering farther away from you] . . . the offerer [of incense] would not begin until the appointed [priest] would tell him: Offer! . . . *The people would leave,* and he would offer the incense, prostrate, and get out.[37]

---

32. M. Yoma 2.2; cf. T. Kippurim 1.12, which describes a case in which one priest killed another as they were running up the ramp. This anecdote in the Tosefta, however, is not explicitly connected to the removal of ashes from the altar.

33. BT Yoma 22a.

34. In this regard, the picture painted in M. Tamid 2.1 is significantly more positive than the picture in M. Yoma 2.2, which could be read as critical of the priests' behavior.

35. M. Tamid 1.4–2.2.

36. M. Tamid 1.4.

37. M. Tamid 6.3.

The removal of ashes from the altar and the offering of incense are the only two priestly tasks that are said to be performed in solitude, with no other person present or capable of seeing the priest in action. They are also the only tasks in which the priest is instructed to "be careful" before commencing. The literary resonance between those passages—one of which describes the first chore of the morning, and the other the last chore of the morning—is not only a stylistic flourish, but also, I suggest, reflects a deliberate effort to claim that the seemingly mundane task of clearing the altar of waste is fully equivalent to the most prestigious task of offering incense. We know well from various texts of the Second Temple period as well as from rabbinic literature that the offering of incense was considered to be the pinnacle of service in the temple,[38] and sometimes awarded the priest offering it direct theophany.[39] The creators of the Mishnah portray the removal of ashes from the altar as an activity inscribed with excitement and attunement—note the other priests harking for the sound of the laver and crying out "It is time!" when they hear it—thereby strongly putting forth the notion that what matters in the temple is not the nature of the work performed but the very prerogative of participating in the work. It is not about what the priests do; it is about the "doing" in itself.

The alacrity and enthusiasm associated with the removal of ashes from the altar are further expressed in the Mishnah's construction of this chore as one that consists of multiple stages. The first stage, in which the coals are removed from the altar using a shovel and placed on the floor, is performed only by the priest to whom this task was allotted.[40] But immediately when this priest descends, the Mishnah describes the other priests climbing up to the altar to continue the cleaning process, raking away the suet and limbs that were not fully consumed by the fire, and placing the ashes in their designated place.[41] The moment in which the other priests join is described as follows:

> Once his brethren saw that [the priest who was allotted the removal of ashes] descended, they would run and come. They would hurry and sanctify their hands and feet at the laver, pick up the rakes and the forks, and climb up to the top of the altar.[42]

The Mishnah, emphatically using both the verb "to run" and the verb "to hurry," constructs here a picture of a group of priests who impatiently wait for the moment

---

38. See Himmelfarb, "Earthly Sacrifice and Heavenly Incense"; Israel Knohl and Shlomo Naeh, "Milu'im and Kippurim" [Heb.], *Tarbitz* 62 (1993): 18–44. Indeed, M. Tamid 5.2 mentions that the lottery for the offering of incense was held only among priests who have not yet offered incense in their lives, thus indicating that this task was a particularly prized one; see also BT Yoma 26a.

39. See, for example, Luke 1:8–24; BT Berakhot 7a.

40. M. Tamid 1.4.

41. M. Tamid 2.1–2.

42. M. Tamid. 2.1.

they will be able to start doing their share of the cleaning of the altar. The division of the task into multiple stages (first coals, then unconsumed suet and limbs, finally ashes) is of significance here: even though this task is ostensibly allotted to a single priest, the Mishnah makes the point that it is effectively a collective task, in which everyone—or at least, everyone who wants to—gets to participate. Thereby, the menial task of clearing the altar, which commences the day of work in the temple, is shaped in the Mishnah as one of the most significant and emblematic components of the priestly service as a whole: it is not only a highly coveted task but also one in which multiple priests, even those not allotted the task, rush to participate.

As Michael Schneider has demonstrated, the notions that competition (*agon*) is an integral part of temple worship, and that running and hurrying are not only accepted but also expected manners in which one shows one's devotion to the deity, were prominent in the Greek-speaking world. Indeed, Greek athletic competitions—most famously the Olympics—were rooted in the practice of racing with a burning torch to the altar of the deity to place the fire on it.[43] This theme of "sacred competition," Schneider notes, is also traceable in various early Jewish traditions, whether they discuss sacrificial cultic practices or other sacred activities such as Torah study or the pursuit of mystical visions. In these traditions, "*agon* is [not only] related to the cult but also constitutes the body of the cult."[44] The mishnaic description of the priests rushing to the altar to remove the ashes should be understood, I contend, in this agonistic context: it is meant as an expression of the priests' piety and alacrity in the temple service. Crucially, however, the creators of the Mishnah chose to situate this sacred competition in the setting of one of the least glamorous tasks that the temple has to offer. The heightened emphasis on this unglamorous task is set to dismiss the idea that certain cultic actions are more important, transformative, or prestigious than others: it is the priestly labor itself that is valued, not the physical substances it involves and not the supposed results of the procedure. We can already identify resonance between this depiction of the priestly work and the emphasis on correct procedure (rather than on distributed "goods") that was discussed in chapter 2, and this resonance will become more evident as we continue to the next stages of the morning ritual.

The mishnaic unit on the first task of the day concludes with the comment "Not ever was the priest too indolent to take the ashes outside."[45] This comment refers back to Leviticus 6:4: "Then he shall take off his vestments and put on other garments, and carry the ashes out to a clean place outside the camp." While the Mishnah describes all other aspects of the altar's clearing in great detail, it does not elaborate on the final stage of taking the waste outside the city of Jerusalem (the

43. Schneider, *The Appearance of the High Priest*, 188–200.
44. Schneider, *The Appearance of the High Priest*, 199 (my translation).
45. M. Tamid 2.2.

rabbinic interpretation of Leviticus's "outside the camp"), which is not surprising: since this task does not take place in the temple itself it is not really seen as part of the temple's sacred labor. Nevertheless, the Mishnah goes out of its way to say that even a strenuous chore that had no cultic value—a chore that is literally the temple's equivalent of taking out the trash—was never neglected. This short comment powerfully captures both the Mishnah's continuous attempt to idealize the priests' diligence in their work and the underlying idea guiding this attempt: that no task pertaining to the temple is too lowly, too minor, or too trivial.

Here it is important to stress that this idealized description of the priests' eagerness to perform the most mundane of tasks in the temple is not meant to put any actual priests, whether past or present, on a pedestal as a particular clan or class among the people. As was shown in multiple studies, there is little reason to think that the rabbis in general were interested in elevating the priesthood or singing its praises.[46] The priests in tractate Tamid do not serve as historical or pseudohistorical figures, but rather as literary embodiments of the rabbis' fantasy of perfect temple laborers. These are not the priests as they were but the priests as they should be: selfless, enthusiastic, industrious, skilled, and above all, undiscriminating in their approach toward what has to be done, valuing the perfect fulfilment of their obligations for its own sake. The creators of tractate Tamid, in short, construct the description of the priests as a prescription for observance and piety *anywhere and anytime*—a point to which I will return at the end of this chapter.

The multiplication and division of priestly labor

Following the order of Leviticus 6:2–6, the first two chapters of tractate Tamid are dedicated to the priestly activities that mark the transition from the previous day to the new day: clearing the altar of ashes and waste, which I discussed at length above, and the arrangement of new firewood on the altar. Interestingly, the Mishnah does not make any comments about the priests' robing and disrobing of different sets of garments during these presacrificial preparations, despite the fact that this aspect of the morning preparation ritual is repeatedly mentioned in the biblical passage. The Mishnah's omission of this component of the morning routine attests, I suggest, that the main interest of its creators is not the priests as actors but the sequence of activities in the temple. Addressing the priests' robing and disrobing would have created an interruption in the sequential narrative that

---

46. For a few of the many studies on this topic, see Matthew Grey, "Jewish Priests and the Social History of Post-70 Palestine" (PhD diss., University of North Carolina, 2011), 6–12, 84; Seth Schwartz, *Josephus and Judean Politics* (Leiden: Brill, 1990), 96–109; Cohen, *The Three Crowns*, 158–71; Catherine Hezser, *The Social Structure of the Rabbinic Movement* (Tübingen: Mohr Siebeck, 1997), 487; Schäfer, "Rabbis and Priests"; Daniel R. Schwartz, *Judeans and Jews: Four Faces of Dichotomy in Ancient Jewish History* (Toronto: University of Toronto Press, 2014), 21–47.

the Mishnah presents here, in which each stage of the priestly activity is immediately and swiftly followed by another. As I will mention later on, a different approach is taken in tractate Yoma, which repeatedly mentions the high priest's immersions and changes of garments.

It is only in the third chapter of the tractate that the Mishnah first addresses the centerpiece of the morning ritual, the lamb designated for the daily burnt offering. As the Mishnah reminds us,[47] the slaughter of the lamb cannot commence before sunrise: all the activities described heretofore are still considered, in certain respects, to be nighttime tasks, and it is only upon the slaughter of the lamb that the day in the temple officially begins. Therefore, in the Mishnah the activities pertaining to the preparation of the morning burnt offering are intertwined with additional activities that mark the beginning of the day. Since the temple's inner hall (hekhal) was to remain locked during the night, the unlocking of the gate serves as a visible sign that the new day has started, and correspondingly services that take place in the inner hall (namely, offering incense and lighting the temple's lamp[48]) are performed at the same time as the preparation of the lamb outside, in the temple's court. The third chapter thus begins with a description of the second lottery of the day, which divides among the priests both the tasks related to the burnt offering and the tasks related to the inner hall:

> The appointed [priest] would tell them: Come and participate in the [following] lottery: who slaughters, who tosses [the blood], who removes [the ashes from] the inner altar [that is, the altar of incense in the inner hall], who removes [ashes from] the lamp, who raises [the lamb's] parts to the ramp: the head and the [right] hind leg, and the two forelegs, the tail and the [left] hind leg, the chest and the neck and the two sides, the intestines, and the fine flour [offering], and the pan offerings [of the high priest], and the wine [for immolation]. They would draw the lottery, and whoever won, won.[49]

This passage describes a lottery procedure at the end of which thirteen priests are allotted their assignments for the morning ritual: two of the assignments pertain to the service of the inner hall (the removal of ashes from the inner altar and from the lamp); two pertain to the preparation of the sacrificial lamb (slaughter and tossing of blood); and nine of the assignments are essentially transport assignments, in which each priest is designated different parts of the lamb or of the accompanying grain and wine offerings, which he will carry to the ramp at the bottom of the altar.[50] Following this opening passage, the third and fourth chapters of the tractate describe in detail exactly how these assignments were carried out.

---

47. M. Tamid 3.2.
48. Following Exodus 30:7–8.
49. M. Tamid 3.1.
50. The exact manner in which the lottery was held is described in M. Yoma 2.1.

In the fifth chapter we will hear of two additional lotteries, one pertaining to the offering of incense and one pertaining to the elevation of the sacrificial parts from the ramp to the altar.

The Mishnah's assertion throughout the tractate that all the chores of which the morning ritual consists were allocated through a lottery procedure is noteworthy. Unfortunately, the dearth of evidence on the actual workings of the Second Temple does not allow us to know whether the Mishnah's description of the lottery procedure is in any way grounded in historical reality.[51] We cannot rule out that the Mishnah relies here on concrete knowledge regarding the practices in the temple, in the same way that we cannot rule out that its description is largely imaginary and based mainly on fantasy and ideology. I am personally inclined to question the historicity of the lottery procedure, since such egalitarian mode of division of labor does not seem commensurate with other accounts of the temple and the priesthood as highly stratified and hierarchical institutions.[52] While such incommensurability is by no means sufficient evidence to dismiss the historicity of the Mishnah's account, it does mean that there is room to consider the literary and rhetorical effect of this repeated emphasis on the lottery process within the Mishnah's construction of an idealized temple. Here, I propose, we can discern three ways in which the lottery as an organizing principle of the tractate's narrative sequence serves the authors' greater ideational agenda.

First, the lottery procedure serves to depict all the priests both as equal to each other in rank—no priest is allotted tasks according to seniority or according to his family's station or wealth, but rather all priests are considered on an equal basis—and as equal in skill. If each and every one of the priests is capable of perfectly carrying out each and every one of the temple's chores, then they all emerge as unfailingly trained and skilled professionals who are able to perform their job flawlessly. Furthermore, the very fact that a lottery process is even required suggests that the priests are so eager to preform service works in the temple that they actively compete for these works, such that the competition has to be regulated. The lottery motif thus helps the creators of the tractate to construct an idyllic portrait of the priests as fervent and avid servers of the temple.

Second and related, the lottery procedure helps depict not only all the priests but also all the tasks performed in the temple as equal and interchangeable. In the

---

51. While the *Letter of Aristeas* describes in some detail the priests' daily service in the temple, and mentions that each priest had designated assignments, it does not provide any information on the manner in which the assignments were allocated: "For they all work hard of their own accord, with much exertion, and each one looks after his appointed task. And their service is carried on without interruption; indeed some undertaking the carrying of wood, but others oil, but others wheaten flour, but others the sweet spices, others offering the parts of the flesh for holocausts—all of them exerting their strength in different ways" (*Letter of Aristeas* 92–93, ed. Charlesworth vol. 2, 19).

52. See Büchler, *Die Priester und der Cultus,* 47–89; Schwartz, *Josephus and Judean Politics,* 58–109.

same way that the lottery indicates that there is no hierarchy among the priests, it indicates that there is no hierarchy among the components of the temple's service, and that they are all valuable and coveted. The lottery motif thus further bolsters the authors' agenda to which I pointed above, of highlighting participation in the temple's service rather than the "content" or substances of the service.

Third, by structuring and presenting the morning ritual through a series of lotteries the authors multiply and subdivide the priestly labor. As we will see, what could be easily conceived as a single task for a single priest is divided up in the Mishnah into multiple tasks occupying multiple priests. As opposed to biblical descriptions of the tabernacle's rituals, in which "the priest" (or more commonly, "Aaron") is always mentioned in the singular, the Mishnah makes clear that each component of the ritual is performed by a different priest, and more often than not, a single component of the ritual is further divided such that it requires more than one priest. We have already seen how the removal of ashes and waste from the altar is presented as consisting of multiple stages carried out by multiple priests, despite the fact that it is formally the task of a single priest. This tendency toward multiplication of priestly labors will become even more evident in the Mishnah's description of the division of the lamb's organs: I shall therefore address this description first, and then return to discuss the multiplication of priestly labor in the tractate more generally.

While the third chapter of tractate Tamid elaborates the preparatory activities that lead up to the sacrifice of the lamb for burnt offering (collecting all the vessels necessary for the day's work, retrieving the designated lamb from the pen and leading it to the slaughterhouse, and removing the ashes from the inner altar and the lamp), the fourth chapter describes in great detail the procedures applied to the lamb itself. These procedures, described in consecutive order, are the following:

1. Binding the lamb prior to its slaughter
2. Slaughter
3. Receiving the blood in a vessel
4. Walking the blood to the altar
5. Tossing the blood on the altar
6. Dissection of the lamb's limbs and internal organs, while dividing the lamb's parts among the priests who will carry them
7. Carrying the lamb's parts to the ramp leading to the altar and placing them on the altar.

As I showed in chapter 2, rabbinic texts that address questions of validity and efficacy in the sacrificial process leave no room for doubt that it is the second through the fifth stages mentioned above—slaughter, reception in a vessel, walking the vessel to the altar, and tossing of blood—that constitute the heart of the sacrificial process. It is the "work of blood," which consists of these activities, that makes or breaks the sacrifice. One could expect, accordingly, that the greatest amount of text in tractate Tamid's descriptive sequence would be dedicated to these activities, on which the entire sacrificial process hinges. Surprisingly, however, out of the 430 words that comprise this mishnaic chapter, only 47 are dedicated to the crucial stages of the work of blood, which are described rather briefly and tersely:

> The slaughterer slaughtered, and the receiver [of blood in a vessel] received [the blood]. He would walk to the northeastern corner [of the altar] and toss the blood [in the direction of] east and north; [he would then walk] to the southwestern corner [of the altar] and toss the blood [in the direction of] west and south. He would toss the remainders of the blood on the southern [side] of the base [of the altar].[53]

Whereas little textual attention is given to the second through the fifth stages of the sacrificial process, despite their ritual centrality, the sixth stage—cutting up the lamb and dividing it between the priests—is described with more elaboration and detail than any other procedure related in tractate Tamid (for the sake of comparison, the description of this stage takes up 347 of the chapter's 430 words). This, again, may seem surprising: neither the biblical texts nor other rabbinic texts indicate that there is any importance to the way in which the sacrificial animal's parts are dissected and removed, and even less so to the way in which those are carried to the altar. As we have seen, other rabbinic texts tend to dismiss the "flesh" component of the sacrificial ritual as secondary to the blood, if not as dispensable altogether.

The disproportionate relation between the textual treatment given in tractate Tamid to the most crucial sacrificial work (blood manipulation) and the textual treatment given to an ostensibly inconsequential work (dissection and division of the animal's parts) can be easily explained in pragmatic terms: whereas the work of blood is rather straightforward, the dissection of the lamb is intricate and complex and thus requires more text. To use an analogy, most people would probably agree that buttoning up one's shirt is more important than ironing it, and yet we would expect instructions for ironing to be more elaborate and detailed than instructions for buttoning, simply because of the complexity of the task. This disproportion, however, helps illustrate the uniqueness of tractate Tamid in the mishnaic landscape, and to bring out the ways in which the perspective and agenda of its authors differ from what we have seen in other Tannaitic texts: tractate Tamid's interest lies not in what is legally and ritually important, but in what helps construct an idealized picture of the temple as a place of devoted and careful priestly labor. The dissection and division of the lamb may be insignificant as far as the validity of the offering is concerned, but they are of great discursive value for the creators of the tractate for two main reasons. First, the dissection procedure

53. M. Tamid 4.1.

demonstrates great skill and accuracy, and highlights the priests' scrupulousness and meticulousness; second, and more pertinent to my discussion here, the division of parts among multiple priests emphasizes the priests' function as a group, in a way that does not allow any particular priest to stand at the center of the sacrificial process. Put differently, the division of the lamb into multiple parts helps the authors to portray the priests themselves not as one but as many.

Before I proceed, a few words are in order on the nature of priestly skill and specialty as it emerges from the Mishnah's lengthy depiction of the dissection and division process. Great attention is given in the tractate to the caution with which the priest separates the lamb's organs from one another, making sure that certain clusters of organs remain intact, whereas others are cut apart. The exactitude and vigilance required to carry out this process are strongly conveyed through several comments on what the priest would *not* do while dissecting the animal, for example: "He would take the knife and separate the lung from the liver and the lobe of the liver from the liver, but he would *not* move [the lobe of the liver] from its place," "he would cut downward toward the spine, but he would *not* touch the spine until he would reach the two soft ribs [of the neck]."[54] Pointing out that the priest would attentively avoid dissecting the lamb in certain ways—that he would not do what is easiest or least labor-intensive but rather meticulously operate according to a distinct protocol—serves well to indicate that even what may seem like a coarse butchering job was in fact a manifestation of utmost precision and care.

Nevertheless, it is important to note that while the priests are depicted here as specialists in slaughter and dissection, they are emphatically not depicted as possessing unique ritual knowledge. One aspect of the sacrificial process is strikingly missing from this account: the examination of the lamb's entrails for signs of injury or disease, signs that—according to rabbinic law—turn the animal into a *terefah*, an animal unfit for consumption.[55] Various other Tannaitic texts indicate that all animals that were offered on the altar were examined for such signs, and would not be offered if such signs were found in them.[56] However, tractate Tamid—the one mishnaic text that describes in great detail how the animal's organs are actually cut, separated, and divided—makes no mention of this examination procedure.

The omission of examination of the animal's parts from tractate Tamid, I suggest, can be explained in two possible ways. One possible explanation has to do with the conspicuous similarity between examination for *terefot* and Greek and Roman practices of extispicy, in which a priest or another specialist, in the course

54. M. Tamid 4.2.

55. The concept of *terefah* is mentioned in Exodus 22:12 and Leviticus 17:15, there probably referring to a "torn" or "devoured" animal. In the rabbinic tradition, however, this name is applied to any animal that, because of a serious injury, is unlikely to survive (see M. Ḥullin 3.1; BT Ḥullin 42a).

56. See, for example, M. Pesaḥim 6.6; M. Zevaḥim 7.6; M. Menaḥot 7.3; M. Temurah 6.5.

of the sacrificial process, would examine the animal's entrails so as to assess whether the sacrifice is accepted and approved.[57] Although the examination for *terefot* is ostensibly meant to discern whether the animal in question was healthy enough to live had it not been slaughtered, it is interesting to note that according to the Mishnah, the certification of an animal as *terefah* depends exclusively on *visible* signs of injury or disease. An animal that would have died for various reasons such as poisoning, suffocation, snakebite, and so forth, but whose cause of death does not leave visible marks in its body, does not fall under the category of *terefah*.[58] There is, at least on the surface, a palpable similarity between the examination of entrails in the rabbinic sacrificial setting and in the Greek and Roman sacrificial setting, and it is perhaps exactly this similarity that the authors seek to blur by eliminating the examination component from the procedure altogether. An alternative explanation for this omission has to do with the fact that the skill of discerning and identifying *terefot* is not limited to the realm of the temple, since it is also pertinent to nonsacral meat: accordingly, the rabbis develop an intricate and specialized system of knowledge regarding *terefot* to which they lay a special claim. It is possible that the authors of the tractate were reluctant to depict the priests as specialists in what they perceived as a distinctly rabbinic area of expertise. If this is so, we may conclude that the creators of tractate Tamid made a point of depicting the priests as skilled, devoted, industrious, and scrupulous—but emphatically not as possessing bodies of knowledge that the rabbis associated with themselves.

As I mentioned above, in tractate Tamid the dissection of the lamb's parts is intertwined with the distribution of those parts among the priests who were allotted them. Each sentence describing how the priest removes and separates a specific part of the lamb's body is immediately followed by the sentence "And he gave [the part he removed] to whomever won it"—that is, each priest who was designated by lottery to carry a particular part to the altar is standing by the priest who dissects the lamb and waits to be given his part. The sentence "And he gave it to whomever won it" recurs in the fourth chapter of the tractate no less than eleven times, and the last section of the chapter paints a vivid picture in which all the priests who have "won" parts of the lamb or other sacrificial supplements are standing in a row, each one balancing the parts he is about to carry in his two hands and sometimes also between his fingers. The chapter concludes with a

---

57. On inspection of entrails to assess the acceptability of a sacrifice in Greek and Roman rituals, see Beard, North, and Price, *Religions of Rome*, 2:173–78; Susanne William Rasmussen, *Public Portents in Republican Rome* (Rome: L'Erma di Bretschneider, 2003), 117–48; Kim Beerden, *Worlds Full of Signs: Ancient Greek Divination in Context* (Leiden: Brill, 2013), 33–34. The practice of extispicy (reading the entrails to see if the sacrifice was accepted) is not to be confused with the practice of attempting to predict the future through the reading of entrails, which was also widely common.

58. M. Ḥullin 3.1, 5.

festive procession of priests on their way to the altar, carrying the burnt offering in its constitutive pieces to its final destination.[59] This procession is effectively the last thing we will hear of the burnt offering. Even though the offering's parts have yet to be arranged on the firewood and to turn to smoke for the sacrifice to be completed, this crucial aspect of the ritual is not explicitly described in the tractate's play-by-play sequence, a point to which I will return below.

The mishnaic emphasis on the division of the lamb into multiple pieces, and on the division of those pieces among multiple priests, powerfully constructs the priestly work in the temple as a group effort, in which no single priest plays a decisive part. In the same way that the biblical icon of the single "lamb" of the daily offering is transformed in the Mishnah into an array of multiple limbs and organs, so the biblical icon of the single "priest" is transformed in the Mishnah into multiple priests, none more distinguished than the other, working together in an orchestrated manner. While again there is a clear pragmatic logic to the division of the lamb's parts among several priests (it is indeed too much for a single person to carry), the rhetorical effect of the Mishnah's multiplication and division of priestly labor is nonetheless evident: we are guided to view the priests as cogs in a machine of many parts.

We can fully register the significance of the Mishnah's rhetorical multiplication and division of priestly labor when we consider it against depictions of the priests' worship in the temple in various works from the Second Temple period. As Schneider has shown, texts ranging from Ben Sira, Jubilees, and the Aramaic Testament of Levi to the works of Philo all focus on a single priestly figure—most commonly the high priest—in their accounts of sacrificial and other ritual activities in the temple. These texts all reflect, albeit in different ways, one fundamental notion: that the high priest, as he is performing rituals in the temple, not only brings forth the divine presence (hence the term *hierophantes*, "the one who causes the holy to appear," used in Greek texts to describe the high priest), but also *embodies* the divine presence.[60] The high priest is conceived in ancient Jewish traditions not

59. On the centrality of processions in sacrificial rituals in the ancient world, see Schneider, *The Appearance of the High Priest*, 101. The only other mishnaic reference to a procession-like component in a temple ritual can be found in the third chapter of tractate Bikkurim; on the resonance between this description and Greek and Roman accounts of sacrificial processions, see Lieberman, *Greek in Jewish Palestine*, 141–46, 169.

60. Even the *Letter of Aristeas*, while it specifically notes that some seven hundred priests work in the temple every day, points to the high priest as the heart of the cult and as a figure that captures the divine: "Now it was an occasion of great consternation to us when we saw Eleazar engaged in his duty, with both his vestments and his glory, which was revealed in the tunic in which he was vested and in the stones around him. . . . Now the appearance of these things instills one with fear and disorder, so that a man would think he had entered the outside world. And I emphatically assert that every human who comes near the spectacle of what I have described will experience indescribable consternation and marvel, his very mind transformed by the holy arrangement on every single detail" (*Letter of Aristeas* 96–100, ed. Charlesworth vol. 2, 19).

only as a servant of God, but also as the living image of God, as the human form that God takes in the earthly sanctuary.[61] Other texts speak of the high priest's transformation into an angel as he enters the holy realm, an idea that has some resonance, as Schneider has shown, even in certain rabbinic texts.[62] In tractate Tamid, however, a conception of any specific priest, high or other, as an embodiment of the divine is immediately diffused by stressing time and again that whatever the priests do, they do as a group, and no one priest is unique or can be identified as the center of ritual. Thereby, the authors of the tractate systematically shift the readers' attention *from actors to activities*: the priests are not depicted as individual agents of the sacred, but rather as multiple organs in one large body whose sole task is to keep the temple going.

It is notable that even the priestly task most quintessentially identified as a lone activity, the offering of incense, regarding which it was said that "no person shall be in the Tent of Meeting until [the offering priest] comes out,"[63] is divided in the Mishnah into two constitutive tasks. We are told that the third lottery of the morning, which pertained to the offering of incense, consisted of two sublotteries: one priest was allotted the pan on which burning coals were placed, and another priest was allotted the censer in which the incense itself was held, and both walked to the altar of incense together.[64] Furthermore, we later on find out that when the priest holding the censer of incense is about to place incense on the altar, he is not alone: a friend or relative of his is standing next to him and holds the censer while the priest takes a handful of incense from it. All the while other priests are standing there and warning him to "be careful" as he is scattering the incense on the coals, and the appointed supervising priest, too, is standing next to him, ready to instruct him to commence the offering. It is only once the order has been given that everyone else departs.[65] Thus, even the most solitary sacrificial act in the temple, the one identified most widely as a moment of intimacy between the priest and the deity, is constructed in tractate Tamid as an operation involving multiple priests with multiple tasks.

One passing comment in the passage describing the offering of incense is particularly instructive for the purposes of this discussion:

> The offerer [of incense] would not begin until the appointed [priest] would tell him: Offer! *If it would be the high priest, the appointed one would tell him: My master the high priest, offer!* The people would leave, and he would offer the incense, prostrate, and get out.[66]

61. Schneider, *The Appearance of the High Priest*, 9–117.
62. Schneider, *The Appearance of the High Priest*, 201–48.
63. See Leviticus 16:17; see also Sifra Aḥare mot 3.4.6 (ed. Weiss 81d).
64. M. Tamid 5.4–6.
65. M. Tamid 6.3.
66. M. Tamid 6.3.

This is the first (albeit not the last) time in which the high priest is mentioned in the tractate, and he is mentioned specifically in a setting that stresses just how inconsequential he is. By pointing out the difference between the high priest and any other priest—the fact that the former is addressed in a more respectful and reverent way—the Mishnah here makes the point that in any other respect there is no difference whatsoever. In what concerns the daily ritual in the temple, the high priest is interchangeable with any other priest: while he has certain privileges (for example, he is not subject to the lottery and can perform any task he wants, and he also walks and enters ahead of the other priests), these privileges are ceremonial only.[67] The high priest of tractate Tamid does not play an indispensable role in the morning ritual of the temple such that it is incomplete without him, and thus the tractate does not allow its audience to identify the worship in the temple with any particular persona: rather, it maintains a picture in which it is the correctness and precision of the procedures that assure the success of the ritual, rather than the special qualities of the temple's personnel. The tractate's tendency to move the spotlight away from the high priest to the priests as a group will become evident again as we consider the last part of the tractate, which describes the concluding portions of the morning ritual.

The sacrifice that doesn't end

The fourth chapter of tractate Tamid, which concludes with the description of the procession of priests and animal parts to the altar, ends with a "cliff-hanger" of sorts: "They would go and place [the lamb's parts] at the midpoint of the ramp [leading up to the altar] and downwards on its west side, and salt them. They would then go down and come to the Chamber of Hewn Stone (lishkat ha-gazit), to recite the shema."[68] Immediately before the ritual of the burnt offering is completed with the definitive act of burning—that is, before the priests set the lamb's parts on the fire so that they are entirely consumed—the Mishnah prescribes a liturgical hiatus. The priests say an introductory blessing,[69] recite the Ten Commandments, recite the components of the shema creed and the blessing that follows it, and conclude with the blessing of "worship" ('avodah) and the priestly blessing of the people.[70] Without getting into the intricacies of this liturgical

---

67. Compare this to Josephus's account, according to which the high priest was required to officiate on Sabbaths, new moons, and festivals. Josephus, *The Wars of the Jews* 5.5.7 (ed. Whiston 708).

68. M. Tamid 4.3.

69. Elaborated in BT Berakhot 11b.

70. M. Tamid 5.1. On the components and structure of this liturgy, see Reuven Hammer, "What Did They Bless? A Study of Mishnah Tamid 5.1," *Jewish Quarterly Review* 81, nos. 3–4 (1991): 305–24; David Henshke, "The Prayer of the Priests and Their Blessing in the Temple: The Early Mishnah and the Teachings of the Late Tanna'im" [Heb.], in *Ke-Tabor be-harim: Studies in Rabbinic Literature in Honor of Joseph Tabory*, ed. Arnon Atzmon and Tzur Shafir (Alon Shevut: Tevunot, 2013), 51–87.

sequence, in terms of the logic of the sacrificial process this liturgical hiatus makes perfect sense: since the consumption of the offering by fire marks its acceptance by God, it is fitting that recitations of the creed, of the Ten Commandments (a text marking the covenant between God and the people), and particularly of the "worship" blessing in which God is explicitly asked to accept Israel's offerings[71] take place right before the burning commences.[72] Nevertheless, when the liturgical hiatus ends, the burning of the lamb's parts on the altar curiously does not follow.

In the next passage, the Mishnah reports two additional lotteries that were held after the liturgical portion: one for the offering of incense and one for raising the parts from the ramp to the altar so that they may be placed on the fire.[73] The Mishnah then proceeds to elaborate, as it has done so far, how the first assignment of the two was carried out once it was allotted: numerous passages (5.3–6.3) are dedicated to the offering of incense, which is described with great detail and flourish. What we would expect after the offering of incense, in accordance with the order of the lottery, is a description of the placement of the offering on the fire—that is, a description of the sacrificial burning that was ostensibly the purpose of all the preparations made so far. But what we find instead after the description of the offering of incense is a description of another liturgical portion, which includes prostration by the priests and another priestly blessing of the people:

> At a time in which the high priest enters to prostrate, three [men] support him: one on his right, and one on his left, and one [holds] the gems [of the high priest's breastplate]. Once the appointed [priest] would hear the footsteps of the high priest going out, he would raise the curtain for him, and he would prostrate and leave.[74] Then his brethren the priests would go in, and prostrate, and leave.
>
> They would come and stand on the steps of the hall . . .[75] and they would bless the people with one blessing; but in the region [that is, anywhere outside the temple]

71. On the blessing of "worship," see Yitzhak Landes, "Studies in the Development of Birkat ha-Avodah" [Heb.] (master's thesis, Hebrew University, 2015).

72. As Eyal Regev explained, there are good reasons to assume that in the Second Temple period prayer in general was inextricably connected to sacrificial worship in the temple: prayers were not seen to be efficacious without sacrifices, and at the same time prayers accompanied sacrifice as modes of verbalized communication with the deity. See Eyal Regev, "Temple Prayer as the Origin of Fixed Prayer: On the Evolution of Prayer during the Period of the Second Temple" [Heb.], *Zion* 70, no. 1 (2005): 5–29. However, according to Israel Knohl, the integration of prayer into the sacrificial ritual is a late development, which deviates from the priestly tradition of complete silence in the temple—and therefore takes places away from the altar, in the Chamber of Hewn Stone. See Knohl, "Between Voice and Silence."

73. M. Tamid 5.2. Thus the anonymous Mishnah describes the procedure. However, according to R. Eliezer ben Ya'aqov, there was no separate lottery for placing the parts on the altar, and whoever placed them on the ramp also raised them to the altar.

74. In the printed editions: "He would go in and prostrate and leave."

75. I skipped over a clause that describes the vessels held by the priests as they stand on the steps.

they would say [the priests' blessing for the people] as three blessings [that is, in three parts], and in the temple they would say it as one blessing. In the temple they would say the Name [of God] as it is written, and in the region as it is pronounced. In the region the priests would lift their hands [while blessing] up to [the height of] their shoulders, and in the temple above their heads, with the exception of the high priest, who does not raise his hands above the frontlet [on his forehead]. R. Yehudah says: Even the high priest raises his hands above the frontlet, for it was said (Leviticus 9:22): "Aaron lifted his hands toward the people and blessed them."[76]

The liturgical ceremony described above is clearly meant as the conclusion of the entire morning ritual. The biblical verse quoted in this mishnaic unit is instructive in this regard: its context is the sacrificial ritual of the inauguration of the tabernacle in the wilderness, which is related in Leviticus 9. Aaron's blessing of the people in this account emphatically takes place *after* the sacrificial parts were placed on the altar, just before he is about to step down from the altar and right before divine fire consumes the parts on the altar in indication of God's approval. This Levitical model, of a priestly blessing at the conclusion of the ritual, is upheld also in the book of Ben Sira, which poetically describes the high priest's blessing of the people as he concludes the sacrificial ritual.[77] The Mishnah clearly and explicitly models the liturgical portion that follows the offering of incense on the Levitical paradigm of the high priest's blessing as the concluding mark of the sacrifice, and indicates to its readers/listeners that with this blessing, the morning worship is complete. However, the Mishnah notably diverges from the biblical paradigm in two central respects. First, the blessing at hand is a communal priestly blessing rather than a blessing of the high priest; second, in the narrative sequence of the Mishnah the blessing does not follow the placement of limbs and organs on the altar but rather the offering of incense. Both these divergences, as I will argue, are very much in keeping with the general tendencies we have identified in tractate Tamid so far.

As in the case of the offering of incense, so also in the case of the concluding prostration and blessing, the Mishnah mentions the protocol pertaining to the high priest as but a possible variation on the standard ritual. It relates that *if* the high priest is present at the time of prostration, his prostration is conducted in a particular way; but under no circumstances is his prostration a vital component of the ritual. The concluding priestly blessing is described in the Mishnah as a collective blessing of the priests as a group: the high priest is distinguished from the

76. M. Tamid 7.1–3 (6.4–5 in the Mishnah's manuscripts).

77. Ben Sira 50:1–21. While some scholars have read this description as pertaining to the Day of Atonement, Fearghail has convincingly argued that it should be read as referring to the ritual of the daily offering. See Fearghas O. Fearghail, "Sir 50, 5–21: Yom Kippur or the Daily Whole Offering?" *Biblica* 69 (1978): 301–16; and the discussion in Patrick W. Skehan and Alexander A. Di Lella, *The Wisdom of Ben Sira* (New Haven: Yale University Press, 1995), 551–54.

group only insofar as he does not raise his hands as high as the rest of the priests (and according to one opinion, even in this regard he is not distinguished).

David Henshke, who has examined the liturgical descriptions of tractate Tamid closely, notes the odd redundancy of collective priestly blessings in this tractate: the priests are said to bless the people twice, both after the recitation of the *shema,* right before the offering of incense, and at the very end of the morning ritual. This redundancy, Henshke has convincingly argued, is the result of a deliberate replacement of the high priest's blessing at the closing of the ritual with a collective priestly blessing.[78] Whereas the priestly blessing after the recitation of *shema* is modeled after the priestly blessing of Numbers 6:22–27, a blessing that has nothing to do with sacrifices, the priestly blessing after the offering of incense is modeled after the high priest's blessing of Leviticus 9:22, which is explicitly connected with the sacrificial process. In the mishnaic setting, however, the high priest could not be afforded the same kind of centrality and import he is afforded in the priestly texts and in literature of the Second Temple period; therefore, the concluding blessing of the ritual is transformed into yet another collective priestly blessing. In Henshke's words, "The blessing can no longer rely on the special personality and standing of the high priest, and from now on it relies on the temple work (*'avodah*) performed by the priests that empowers them also to bless."[79]

Henshke explains this transformation as indicative of the erosion of the high priest's status toward the end of the Second Temple period: the position of high priesthood, he contends, has lost most of its cachet, and the prestige it once had was awarded to the priests a whole.[80] Perceptively, Henshke notes that the priests' collective prestige relies specifically on the tasks that they perform in the temple: it is not the priests' ancestry or inherent sanctity but rather their *activities* that make them worthy of blessing the people. While I entirely agree with this analysis, I suggest that the replacement of a blessing of the high priest with a collective priestly blessing should not be read as an indication of developments in the historical Second Temple period, but rather as a manifestation of the greater ideological agenda of tractate Tamid's creators. The makers of the tractate make a systematic effort to place emphasis on the priests' collective function as cogs in a machine and to prevent any emphasis from being placed on one specific priest at any given time. By constructing the priestly worship in the temple as a collective effort in which many different "hands" are working simultaneously, the Mishnah puts activities rather than actors at the heart of its account of the temple. The Mishnah's idealized temple thus becomes a model of *religious doing as such.*

78. Henshke, "The Prayer of the Priests."

79. Henshke, "The Prayer of the Priests," 85 (my translation).

80. Henshke is following the thesis of Shmuel Safrai, *At the Time of the Temple and at the Time of the Mishnah* [Heb.] (Jerusalem: Magnes Press, 1994), 40–41.

But here we must observe that even when the Mishnah focuses on activities, there is one activity that it chooses to obscure, and this obscured activity is the one to which almost all the activities that comprise the morning ritual presumably lead: the actual burning of the lamb's parts on the altar. Put differently, the one activity that quintessentially defines the ritual is exactly the one effectively missing from its mishnaic description. I use the word "effectively" here, since the burning component of the morning ritual is not entirely missing from the tractate. If one reads further in the chapter, beyond the seemingly conclusive description of the prostration and blessing, one finds that in the following passage (7.3) there appears a description of the manner in which the lamb's parts are to be arranged and burned on the altar. This description commences with the words "at a time in which the high priest wishes to burn [the organs on the altar] he climbs up the ramp with the deputy at his right," and proceeds to relate how the high priest receives the lamb's parts, lays his hands on them, places them on the altar, and performs the immolation.

The creators of the tractate thus made two curious editorial choices regarding the description of the burning procedure: first, they flipped the sequential order of the narrative, placing the burning *after* the concluding prostration and blessing rather than ahead of it (thereby blatantly diverging from the biblical pattern); second, they formulated the description of the burning process as a *variation* on the ordinary procedure—"This is how it is done in the unusual case that the high priest is officiating"—without first accounting for the ordinary procedure at all.[81] Thereby, the description of the burning component of the daily offering functions in the Mishnah as an appendix of sorts, rather than as an integral part of the ritual narrative: it is both out of place and formulated as a comment or afterthought. These editorial choices reflect, I suggest, a sustained effort on the side of the Mishnah's creators to marginalize the burning component and to prevent it from appearing as the pinnacle of the morning ritual.

In chapter 2, I showed that the rabbis marginalize the burning component of the sacrificial process as part of their overall rejection of an interactive model of sacrifice: I believe this greater tendency to underemphasize the burning component is also at play in tractate Tamid. However, I wish to highlight the rhetorical effect of this omission within the narrative structure of the tractate as a whole. By omitting from the ritual narrative of the daily offering the activity that quintessentially concludes the ritual, the creators of the tractate prevent the account of the morning ritual from having one decisive, definitive focal point. Since the last activity mentioned in the narrative sequence is the offering of incense and not the burning of limbs and organs, the reader/listener is left with a diffused impression

81. As noted by Albeck, *The Six Orders of the Mishnah: Qodashim,* 430; Henshke, "The Prayer of the Priests," 77.

of the worship in the temple as consisting of several unrelated tasks rather than as revolving around one particular offering.[82] In other words, the authors of tractate Tamid do not allow their description of the daily ritual to have an overarching telos, a discernible end point or purpose. Whereas in the account of Leviticus 6:2–6 the end goal of the priestly activities is to burn the morning offering on the altar, and all the other activities serve this goal, in the mishnaic account the successful completion of every activity is its own independent goal.

In this regard, tractate Tamid is guided by the same overarching ideology that governs the rabbinic reconfiguration of sacrifice as a blood ritual. In every aspect of its structure, its rhetoric, and its literary design tractate Tamid puts correct actions and ritual commitment at the center and underplays the individuals and the substances involved in those actions. The persons who perform the activities are of no special importance, and are in fact entirely interchangeable with one another; the substances that are handled in these activities are also not valued in and of themselves, and waste is treated with the same reverence as blood or incense; even the activities themselves are presented as bearing equal importance and as randomly designated. The ritual narrative of tractate Tamid thus powerfully and vividly demonstrates what I have identified as the rabbinic theory of sacrifice more broadly, according to which sacrifice is efficacious not because of *what* it does but because of *how* it is done: accurate and committed ritual performance, rather than blood or fat or smoke, rather than this or other participant, is what serves to maintain the temple and the people in peaceful prosperity. The description of the daily worship in the temple thereby serves, when seen as part of the greater rabbinic sacrificial vision, as an idealized model of halakhic performance as such—at any place, at any time, and by any person.

BETWEEN "THE DAY" AND EVERY DAY

On the face of it, tractate Yoma of the Mishnah, which describes in detail the temple rituals of the Day of Atonement, is diametrically opposed to tractate Tamid in several respects. First, whereas Tamid repeatedly refers to the priests as a collective and refrains from placing emphasis on one particular priestly persona, Yoma is almost exclusively focused on the high priest, who—in accordance with the ordinances of Leviticus 16—performs all the rituals of the day by himself. Not only the

---

82. It could also be argued that these editorial choices are specifically meant to highlight the offering of incense and to turn it into the centerpiece of the ritual. Considering the critical role that incense plays in Second Temple literature, a tendency to champion incense as the most "spiritual" of offerings could certainly account in part for the literary design of tractate Tamid. Interestingly, Jaś Elsner has shown that at the beginning of the third century incense became the most dominant motif in the visual depictions of sacrifices across the Roman provinces. Elsner, "Sacrifice in Late Roman Art."

high priest's sacrificial activities are of concern in the tractate, but also the priest's own body and its vicissitudes: the tractate elaborates how the priest was to be prevented from sleeping so that he would not have a seminal emission, and includes in its ritual narrative every instance in which the high priest washes, immerses, and changes his garments.[83] Second, whereas Tamid strives to describe all the temple's activities—even the most menial ones—as equally valuable and equally desirable to the priests, Yoma makes it abundantly clear which of the many activities that constitute the day's ritual are critical and central and which are more peripheral: the sprinkling of blood on the altar and the offering of incense in the inner sanctum receive greater textual attention than any other ritual component of the day, in complete congruence with the biblical account's emphasis on these particular activities.[84] Finally, the ritual narrative in Yoma is unquestionably complete, systematic, and sequential, as opposed to the narrative in Tamid, which conspicuously skips over the burning of sacrificial parts on the altar.

These differences can be accounted for by the fact that tractate Yoma closely follows the biblical account of Leviticus 16, which is in itself a rather complete, systematic, and coherent ritual narrative. While the Mishnah in tractate Yoma certainly adds various details to the biblical core, it remains highly committed to the structure and logic of the Levitical text, whereas tractate Tamid is more of a patchwork of several different biblical passages and additional traditions. Much could be said about Yoma's use of the Levitical sources in its interpretation of the biblical ritual, as well as on the overall nature and function of the tractate as a whole, which has been the topic of abundant scholarly analysis and speculation.[85] For the purposes of this discussion, however, I would like to focus not on the unique components of the Day of Atonement's ritual as described in the Mishnah, but rather on the correspondences between the mishnaic account of this special ritual and the mishnaic account of the daily routine of the temple. As I will show, the compilers of tractate Yoma carefully wove the unique activities of the Day of Atonement, which must be carried out by the high priest alone, into a greater framework of recurring and ordinary priestly activities. This framework, which closely intersects with the narrative sequence of tractate Tamid, highlights the special features of the Day of Atonement but at the same time neutralizes and trivializes them. Thereby, tractate Yoma as a whole valorizes the ordinary over the exceptional, the many over the one, and the correct performance of actions over the attribution of power to persons or substances.

83. M. Yoma 1.7, 3:4–7, 7.3–5.

84. On blood, see Michael Swartz, "The Choreography of Blood in Mishnah Yoma," in *Jewish Blood: Reality and Metaphor in History, Religion, and Culture*, ed. Mitchell B. Hart (London: Routledge, 2009), 70–82; on incense, see Knohl and Naeh, "Milu'im and Kippurim."

85. For a helpful summary of the different positions on this topic, see Stökl Ben Ezra, *The Impact of Yom Kippur*, 19–27; Swartz, "Judaism and the Idea of Ancient Ritual Theory."

Training up a priest

In my discussion of tractate Tamid I mentioned time and again the fact that the Mishnah discusses the priests as a collective, as a body of multiple organs, and does not allow the reader to identify the worship in the temple with any particular priestly individual. Insofar as the high priest is mentioned in tractate Tamid, he is mentioned in side notes, as differing from the other priests merely in ceremonial trivialities. At first glance, tractate Yoma, in which the high priest is the clear focal point and the one on whom the entire ritual of the day hinges, presents a radically different picture. Nevertheless, a closer look at the tractate reveals that the creators of the Mishnah made a notable effort to integrate other persons aside from the high priest into the ritual narrative of the Day of Atonement, and thereby managed to undermine, however subtly, the exclusivity and centrality of the high priest in this narrative.

Michael Swartz, who has compared the Mishnah's ritual narrative of the Day of Atonement to the poetic descriptions of the day's rituals in synagogue liturgy, has cogently observed that the rabbinic construction of the Day of Atonement is unique—both compared to the Bible and compared to Second Temple traditions—in positioning the high priest within a broader network of ritual practitioners: "Whereas Leviticus 16 presents the story of a man, his bull, and his goats, Yoma presents a full tableau depicting a complex institution peopled with sages, priests, guilds, and throngs of anxious worshippers."[86] In the Mishnah, while the high priest is the one who actually performs the required ritual actions, these actions are described as enabled by and dependent upon a well-orchestrated choreography of other priests who bring forth the animals, carry the instruments, complete the procedures,[87] and even give the high priest instructions. A brief comparison between renditions of priestly actions in Leviticus 16 and the rendition of the same actions in tractate Yoma suffices to illustrate this:

LEVITICUS	MISHNAH YOMA
He shall put on the holy linen tunic, and shall have the linen undergarments next to his body, fasten the linen sash, and wear the linen turban; these are the holy vestments. He shall bathe his body in water, and then put them on.[88]	*They would bring him* to the Chamber of Parva, which was in a holy place. *They would spread a sheet of fine linen* between him and the people. He would sanctify his hands and feet, and remove his garments.... *They would bring him white linen garments.*[89]

86. Swartz, "Ritual Is with People," 211.

87. I am referring specifically to M. Yoma 3.5, in which it is mentioned that the high priest performed the initial slaughter of the lamb for the daily offering, but another priest would finish the procedure.

88. Leviticus 16:6.

89. M. Yoma 3.6.

Aaron shall cast lots on the two goats, one lot for the Lord and the other lot for Azazel.[90]

[The high priest] would shake the urn and bring up two lots; on one was written "for the Name," and on the other was written "for Azazel." *The deputy is on his right, and the head of the priestly household [currently serving] on his left. If the [lot] for the Name came up on his right, the deputy tells him: My master the high priest, raise your right hand! And if the [lot] for the Name came up on his left, the head of the household tells him: My master the high priest, raise your left hand!*[91]

Aaron shall present the bull as a purification offering for himself, and shall make atonement for himself and for his house.[92]

[The high priest] would slaughter [the bull] and receive its blood in a bowl, and would *hand it over to whoever would stir the blood . . .* so that it would not congeal.[93]

He shall take a pan full of coals of fire from the altar before the Lord, and two handfuls of crushed sweet incense, and he shall bring it inside the curtain.[94]

They would take out for him a spoon and a pan, and he would take two handfuls [of incense] and place them in the spoon.[95]

He shall take some of the blood of the bull, and sprinkle it with his finger on the front of the mercy seat, and before the mercy seat, he shall sprinkle the blood with his finger seven times.[96]

He would take the blood *from whoever* was stirring it.[97]

As these and other passages make evident,[98] in the Mishnah the high priest is far from being a sole performer. While the Mishnah leaves no room for doubt that the high priest stands at the center of the Day of Atonement ritual and is indispensable to it, it also makes the point that the day's ritual is a collective production: the successful completion of the ritual is a function of the temple as an institution—indeed, as a machine of many cogs—and not of the high priest alone.

While this may seem obvious, it is also worth noting that the high priest is of interest to the Mishnah strictly insofar as he is the carrier of specific ritual actions,

90. Leviticus 16:8.
91. M. Yoma 4.1.
92. Leviticus 16:11.
93. M. Yoma 4.3.
94. Leviticus 16:12.
95. M. Yoma 5.1.
96. Leviticus 16:14.
97. M. Yoma 5.3.
98. For additional references to other people participating in the ritual procedures of the day, see M. Yoma 3.4–5; 6.3, 8; 7.1, 3–4.

and not as an instantiation of the divine. Unlike the book of Ben Sira or liturgical poems, the Mishnah does not dedicate any attention to the appearance of the high priest, to the radiance of his face, or to the beauty of his garments: it focuses exclusively on what the high priest does, not on what the high priest is. This focus on the technical aspects of the priest's activities rather than on the dazzling effect of his presence is, of course, in keeping with the overall genre and style of the Mishnah as a composition. Yet the Mishnah's insistence on the incorporation of other figures on whom the high priest is dependent shows that the makers of the tractate were actively working to shape the high priest as a *function* rather than as an *icon*. That is to say, the high priest of tractate Yoma is presented as a placeholder for certain designated activities, operating within a greater network of temple workers, rather than as a unique persona endowed with unique qualities.

While the depiction of the high priest throughout the tractate as dependent upon the help of other priests presents him in functional terms, as part of a greater mechanism, the depiction of the high priest as dependent upon the instruction and leadership of others blatantly undermines his individual agency altogether. Tractate Yoma commences with a description of a seven-day instructional procedure that precedes the Day of Atonement, during which the high priest "rehearses" various sacrificial procedures, and is taught "the order of the day" by the elders of the court.[99] During this instructional process, the high priest is treated in a rather condescending manner, not to say a demeaning one:

> [The elders of the court] read before him the order of the day, and they tell him: My master the high priest, you read this with your own mouth, lest you have forgotten or have not learned. On the day before the Day of Atonement at dawn they place him at the eastern gate and pass before him bulls and rams and sheep, so that he would know and be familiar with the [priestly] work.[100]

Not only is the high priest suspected of having forgotten or having not studied what he must do on the Day of Atonement; he is also treated as one who is not familiar with the basic features of domestic animals at all. Must the high priest really be shown bulls, rams, and sheep so as to be able to perform his tasks? This curious description of the high priest as entirely clueless in what concerns his ritual obligations makes it seem as though a new high priest would be appointed every year, such that no high priest would perform the ritual of the Day of Atonement more than once. While several rabbinic sources do suggest that during the Second Temple period one high priest would be replaced with another rather frequently,[101] a thorough study by Israel Knohl

---

99. The term "the order of the day" (*seder ha-yom*) probably refers to the biblical account in Leviticus 16, although Epstein (*Prolegomena to Tannaitic Literature,* 36) assumed that the "order of the day" was an early version of Mishnah Yoma itself.

100. M. Yoma 1.3.

101. T. Kippurim 1.7; BT Yoma 8b; PT Yoma 1:1, 38c; see Gedalyahu Alon, "Par'irtin: The History of the High Priesthood at the End of the Second Temple Period" [Heb.], *Tarbitz* 13 (1952): 1–24.

and Shlomo Naeh has proposed a different perspective, arguing that the Mishnah deliberately shaped the Day of Atonement in the pattern of the inauguration day of the tabernacle.[102] According to Knohl and Naeh, the seven days of instruction and preparation that precede the Day of Atonement in the Mishnah are meant to echo the eight-day inauguration ritual of the tabernacle described in Leviticus 8–10, and thereby to indicate that the Day of Atonement fulfills both the function of atonement and the function of resanctification of the sanctuary and its personnel. The Mishnah's description of the high priest's education thus serves to portray the high priest as newly dedicated to his sacred position, and thereby to depict the temple in its entirety as renewed and rededicated through the rituals of the day.

Knohl and Naeh's reading is persuasive, yet we cannot ignore the fact that the high priest is depicted in the Mishnah not merely as a novice who is in need of learning, but also as completely passive and inert, as one who is constantly acted upon by others rather than acting on his own. The Mishnah repeatedly uses the impersonal third-person plural to describe what is done to the priest—"They remove him from his home"; "They place him at the eastern gate"; "They do not let him eat much"—indicating that the high priest, despite his elevated status, is in fact subjugated to the authority of others. One mishnaic passage, which describes how "the elders of the court would hand him over to the elders of the priesthood," makes it especially clear that the high priest is entirely devoid of agency or authority in this instructional setting: not only is he "handed" from one group of elders to another like an object, but the elders of the court also make him take an oath that he will not deviate in any way from what they have told him—that is, they explicitly deny him any ability to make independent decisions or to follow alternative traditions.[103]

This description of the high priest as entirely subordinate to the authority of the court (which is governed, ostensibly, by rabbinic-like figures) can certainly be read as part of the rabbis' overarching effort to claim the Second Temple for themselves and to assert their authority over the priesthood, as several scholars have argued.[104] I propose, however, that this description serves not only to elevate the rabbis over the priests, but also to convey a specific message about the high priest and his function in the temple. The Mishnah's account of the training process of the high priest strongly makes the point that the high priest is manufactured rather than born: he is depicted as a blank slate, lacking any inherent qualities or skills, who is qualified to carry on the sacred tasks of the day strictly because he is taught how to perform them correctly. In other words, the high priest is portrayed in the Mishnah as a role rather than as a person. This portrayal, I suggest, serves the greater

---

102. Knohl and Naeh, "Milu'im and Kippurim."

103. M. Yoma 1.5. According to T. Kippurim 1.8, this oath had to do specifically with the manner in which incense is to be offered; see the discussion in Knohl and Naeh, "Milu'im and Kippurim."

104. See, for example, Cohn, *The Memory of the Temple*, 41–47; Swartz, "Ritual Is with People."

sacrificial vision of the creators of the Mishnah, which configures the temple and the worship therein in procedural terms and denies that there is any immanent value in either the persons or the substances involved.

But here we should note one curious feature of the Mishnah's account of the high priest's training: while the high priest is specifically taught "the order of the day"—that is, the Day of Atonement—his practical training during the seven days pertains to the *daily* burnt offerings, and to the recurring activities that take place in the temple every morning and every afternoon:

> During all those seven days he tosses the blood and offers the incense and sets the candles, and offers the head and the [right] hind leg, whereas on all other days if he wants to offer, he may offer, for the high priest offers his part first and receives his [meat] portion first.[105]

Knohl and Naeh have convincingly argued that the description of the high priest's training as pertaining to the everyday practices of the temple, that is, to the most basic sacrificial procedures, is set to construct the priest's preparation as a form of first-time initiation, in the pattern of the inauguration process of Leviticus 8–10.[106] The Mishnah also provides practical justification for the priest's rehearsal of the daily rituals by insisting that on the Day of Atonement it is incumbent upon the high priest to per-form all the sacrificial activities of the day, including the routine morning and after-noon burnt offerings. While the incorporation of the daily procedures into the priest's training program may very well derive from the Mishnah's effort to depict this pro-gram as basic education, I propose that the incorporation of these procedures into the narrative sequence of the Day of Atonement itself reframes and thereby reinterprets the meaning and structure of this day as a whole. The notion that the high priest must perform all the activities of the day—including the routine ones—rather than only the activities described in Leviticus 16 that have to do with the purification of the people and the sanctuary, reconstructs the day's rituals as one complete sequence defined by *time* (dawn to dusk) rather than by *purpose*. In other words, instead of presenting the high priest's task as "approaching the holy" in order to purify it and atone for Israel's sins, as is the case in Leviticus 16, the Mishnah presents the high priest's task as per-forming the full series of chores that must be performed on one specific day: some of these chores are ordinary and recurring, and some are unique, but they are all equally required as part of the protocol of the day as such.

In what follows, I will show that the tendency to frame the unique procedures of the Day of Atonement within the greater setting of the temple's daily routine can be identified as an overarching feature of tractate Yoma as a whole: its creators not only used the daily routine of the temple to give structure and context to the

105. M. Yoma 1.2.
106. Knohl and Naeh, "Milu'im and Kippurim," 20.

special procedures of the day, but in some ways even shaped the text of the tractate as a variation on tractate Tamid.

How is this day different from all other days?

Like all other ritual narratives of the Mishnah, tractate Yoma is generally structured in the form of a chronological sequence. Its first chapter describes the seven days that precede the Day of Atonement, up to the night before it (1.1–1.7), and the following chapters describe the work performed on the day itself, beginning with the burnt offering of the morning (3.4) and concluding with the burnt offering of the evening (7.4). However, this chronological sequence is interrupted several times to relate information about various other aspects of the worship in the temple. Most prominently, a very large portion of the first four chapters of the tractate (2.1–3.3) recounts different facts about the rituals pertaining to the burnt offering of the morning, in close correspondence with the account in tractate Tamid.

A closer look reveals that the first four chapters of tractate Yoma consist of four textual strands, which were all intertwined in the tractate as it stands before us: (A) the chronological sequence of the procedures preceding the day and of the day itself, which functions as the core of the tractate and extends from chapter 1 to chapter 7; (B) a series of comparisons contrasting the ordinary practices of the temple with the practices unique to the Day of Atonement, all structured in an identical pattern ("every day X . . . but on the Day of Atonement Y"[107]); (C) a lengthy unit on the daily ritual of the morning, which corresponds with tractate Tamid; (D) anecdotes about various persons and their contributions—monetary or functional—to the temple. To better understand the structure of these four chapters and the interplay of the different textual strands within them, I provide the following scheme:

A. Chronological sequence of the ritual (preceding seven days): 1.1–7
   B. "Every day . . . but on the Day of Atonement" I: 1.8
      C. The standard procedures of the morning ritual (corresponding with Tamid): 2.1–3.3
A. Chronological sequence of the ritual (from the first immersion of the day to the choosing of goats): 3.4–9
      D. Anecdotes about persons and objects in the temple (3.10–11)
A. Chronological sequence of the ritual (from the lottery of goats to the setting of coals for incense): 4.1–3
   B. "Every day . . . but on the Day of Atonement" II, III, IV: 4.4–6
A. Chronological sequence of the ritual (from the preparation of incense to the end): 5.1–7.4

---

107. Or, in some of the passages "every day X . . . but today Y."

It is not difficult to explain how textual strands B, C, and D were integrated into the narrative sequence A, which constitutes the core of the tractate. Since the activity that marks the transition from night to day in the temple is the removal of ashes from the altar, the redactors found it appropriate to shift from the depiction of the night before the Day of Atonement (1.7) to the immersion and change of garments that commences the high priest's activities of the day itself (3.4) by referring to this transitional activity. For this purpose they put forth a passage (1.8) that specifically contrasts the Day of Atonement with other days in what pertains to the clearing of the altar: "Every day they remove [the ashes from] the altar at the call of the crow or close to it, whether before it or after it; but on the Day of Atonement they start clearing it as of midnight." In turn, the Mishnah's reference to the daily procedure of the removal of ashes "drags" with it an entire unit (C), which comments on the morning procedures that regularly take place in the temple in preparation for the daily burnt offering: the removal of ashes and the various lotteries for priestly activities (2.1–4), the number of priests required to carry the sacrificial substances on different days and for different types of animals (2.5–6), and the preparation for slaughter, which must be done only upon sunrise (3.1–3).

Unit C follows the order of tractate Tamid so closely, and utilizes the same idioms and phrases as Tamid so noticeably, that the connection between the two tractates cannot be denied. Abraham Goldberg has argued, persuasively in my view, that this unit in tractate Yoma should be understood as a kind of "Tosefta" to tractate Tamid: it functions as an early commentary and expansion on the first chapters of tractate Tamid, in the same manner that a tractate in the Tosefta functions as an early commentary on a corresponding tractate in the Mishnah.[108] Whether or not one accepts Goldberg's thesis, it is evident that the compilers of tractate Yoma chose, for some reason, to include in a tractate dedicated to the Day of Atonement a large portion of text dedicated to the seemingly different topic of the daily morning ritual, only few parts of which are applicable or relevant to the specific ritual sequence of the Day of Atonement itself (for example, it is interesting that Yoma recounts in detail how the lottery process was carried out, considering that no lottery is held on the Day of Atonement).

After the chronological ritual sequence of the tractate resumes (3.4), it is interrupted twice more. First, since the golden lots that are to be cast for the two goats are mentioned in 3.9, and it is stated that "Ben Gamla made them and he was mentioned in praise," the Mishnah proceeds to recount various individuals who were mentioned favorably or unfavorably, depending on their contribution to the temple (D). Second, after the Mishnah describes how the priest takes coals from the

---

108. Abraham Goldberg, "Tosefta to Tractate Tamid: A Study of the Problem of the Relation between the Mishnah and the Tosefta" [Heb.], in *The Binyamin De-Fries Memorial Volume*, ed. Ezra Zion Melamed (Tel Aviv: Tel Aviv University Press, 1969), 18–42.

altar to be used in the offering of incense (4.3), we find a systematic comparison between the procedures pertaining to incense taken up every day and the procedures taken up on the Day of Atonement: the type of pan that is used, the quantity of incense, and how finely the incense is ground. The comparison of incense-related aspects is followed by additional comparisons between "everyday" practices and practices of "the Day": how the priest climbs up the ramp, what he uses to wash his hands, and how many arrangements of firewood are required. This series of comparisons (B) ties back to the comparison that commenced the initial digression from the chronological order in 1.8 ("Every day they remove [the ashes from] the altar at the call of the crow . . .; but on the Day of Atonement . . . as of midnight"), thereby bracketing passages 1.8–4.6 as one discernible subsection of the chapter, and allowing it to stand as a cohesive unit despite the multiple strands of which it consists.

Insofar as the first chapters of the tractate function as one cohesive unit, the most identifiable trait of this unit is a back-and-forth movement between "the Day"—that is, the Day of Atonement—and the everyday. The rhetorical effect of the Mishnah's recurring references to what is usually done at the temple, to the ordinary procedural protocol that applies on days that are *not* the Day of Atonement, is an overall reframing of "the Day" as a variation on "every day." In providing abundant information on the ordinary, whether with or without explicit comparison to the extraordinary, the redacted tractate guides its readers/listeners to consider the Day of Atonement in the greater context of the temple's routine work: it is constructed as essentially one day out of many in which the temple's machine operates skillfully and effectively. Setting the Day of Atonement in relation to the temple's everyday routine highlights, of course, all the ways in which the day is different and indeed of greater importance than any other day: it requires a special priest, special instruments, special garments, and so on. At the same time, however, this comparison draws attention to the fact that all these special things are merely more festive versions of the priests, instruments, and garments used every other day.

This is not to say, of course, that the creators of the tractate downplay or dismiss the ominous nature of the activities that are unique to the Day of Atonement alone—especially the high priest's entrance into the inner sanctum, which is assumed to harbor a very real risk of death.[109] The Mishnah leaves no room for doubt that the Day of Atonement is exceptional in what it requires of the high priest and in the incomparable importance of precision and caution on his end.[110]

---

109. As indicated by the people's anxious anticipation of the priest's exit from the inner sanctum (M. Yoma 5.1) and the high priest's celebration at the end of the day in gratitude for getting out in peace (M. Yoma 7.4).

110. See especially M. Yoma 5.7.

What I argue is that tractate Yoma in its redacted form firmly grounds the story of this exceptional day in a greater story of the temple as a seamlessly operating institution, and thereby brings this seamless operation to the center of attention to be appreciated and admired. Indeed, the "happy ending" of the ominous day is the return of the temple to its normal routine.

I propose that tractate Yoma's heightened emphasis on the everyday routine of the temple is indicative of the rabbis' greater agenda of presenting and interpreting sacrifices as manifestations of perfect procedure. As we have seen, the rabbis valorize accurately and scrupulously performed actions administered in devout fulfillment of a commandment, and maintain that sacrifice is efficacious in its capacity as a perfectly performed procedure, rather than as a channel of interaction between the human and the divine. Within the framework of this rabbinic theory of sacrifice, the more quotidian and recurring the sacrificial procedure, the more it lends itself to such practice-oriented and action-oriented interpretation. Thus, despite the fact that tractate Yoma is ostensibly concerned with the least mundane and most dramatic aspects of worship in the temple, its makers chose to frame those dramatic aspects in the nondramatic and repetitive setting of daily worship, giving special attention to the cleaning chores, the lottery process, and the division of multiple labors among the priests—the very same tropes that were used in tractate Tamid to put forth the message that what matters in the temple is not what is done, but rather how it is done. Not the blood or fat or incense, but how they are handled and used; not who the actors are, but their enthusiastic commitment to the task.

THE IDEALIZED TEMPLE AND RITUAL COMMITMENT

I opened this chapter with the question of what role sacrifices play in the rabbinic construction of the temple as an idyllic and semimythical site. In light of the analysis of tractates Tamid and Yoma that I have presented above, I suggest the following answer to this question: the rabbis' practice-oriented approach to sacrifices, which sees sacrifices first and foremost as ideal types of correct performance, underlies their admiring and glorifying view of the temple as they construct it as *the ultimate site of perfect performance.*

As I mentioned in passing in chapter 2, I find the concept of "ritual commitment" coined by anthropologists Caroline Humphrey and James Laidlaw to be particularly useful for conceptualizing the rabbis' approach to sacrifice in general, and to the temple as an idealized site in particular. Humphrey and Laidlaw argued that the main difference between ordinary actions and ritualized actions is the actor's stance vis-à-vis what she is doing: whereas ordinary actions are guided or motivated by the actor's intentions to attain something or to express something, ritual actions are guided by the intention to get the actions themselves right, with full awareness that the actor is not the author of those actions but rather follows preordained stipulations. "For the actor, the ritualized act is seen as ready for him or her to do. He or she 'enacts' it, that is, does not simply do something as in everyday life . . . but as it were mimics an idea of what should be done."[111] But what makes a ritual actor different from a soldier following orders or a narrator reading a script is that the ritual actor knowingly and willfully chooses to defer her own authorship of her actions because she is committed to the notion that there is value in following the stipulated actions *as such*—that is, not because of their content but because they are stipulated. Ritual commitment is thus the readiness to suspend one's own usual intention-based mode of action in favor of externally predetermined actions, and the desire to perform those predetermined actions flawlessly.[112] A critical aspect of the ritual commitment is that it is nondiscriminating: all ritual actions and subactions in a given sequence are assessed as "elemental," that is, as equally required and equally essential.[113]

The rabbinic vision of sacrifice is guided by a notion of ritual commitment very similar to the one laid out by Humphrey and Laidlaw. In the Mishnah's ritual narratives that focus distinctly on sacrificial procedures, these procedures are elaborated and presented in a manner that denies any inherent value to the sacrificial substances themselves or to the particular persons who handle them. The handling of sacrificial substances is presented as one among many things done at the temple, all of equal importance and all performed with the same alacrity. Sacrifices thus serve in the Mishnah's ritual narratives not as unique channels of communication or as means to an end, but as multiple routinized manifestations of ritual commitment. The temple is depicted in these narratives as an idealized space not because of what is done in it but because the manner of doing itself—steadfast, accurate, and devoted—is championed as a model of religious performance in general.

This, to be clear, does not mean in any way that the rabbis thought that sacrifices were unimportant or dispensable or meaningless. On the contrary: the ritual narratives we have seen make it abundantly clear that the rabbis considered the sacrificial cult a revered site that should be longed for and admired. What should be noted, however, is that the sacrificial cult is valorized in these narratives not in and of itself but as part of the greater workings of the perfectly orchestrated temple as an institution, and that those who keep this institution running are not celebrated for their beauty, their pedigree, or their ability to invoke the divine, but for their commitment and ability to *perform procedures correctly*. The sacrificial cult is a critical and integral part of the rabbis' vision of a full and complete life led in

111. Humphrey and Laidlaw, *The Archetypal Actions of Ritual*, 102.
112. Humphrey and Laidlaw, *The Archetypal Actions of Ritual*, 99.
113. Humphrey and Laidlaw, *The Archetypal Actions of Ritual*, 151.

accordance with the Torah, but its importance and value lie exactly in the notion that sacrificial activities are *comparable* to other commandments of the Torah, rather than in the notion that these activities are qualitatively different. In other words, what makes the temple cult so magnificent for the rabbis is exactly the fact that it is seen as a glorified expression of the most ordinary dimension of Jewish life as they envision it: a life guided by incessant, committed, and meticulous observance of *halakhah*.

Conclusion

The End of Sacrifice, Revisited

"Our slaughter of tame animals for sacrifices is common to us and to all other men," wrote the Jewish historian Flavius Josephus in his polemic work *Against Apion,* setting out to reject allegations according to which Jews engage in savage and barbarous forms of worship.[1] Josephus made this statement toward the end of the first century C.E., over two decades after the destruction of the Jerusalem temple, but there is no trace in his account that no centralized Jewish sacrifices were actually performed at the time. Rather, Josephus refers to Jewish sacrificial worship as an ongoing and uninterrupted reality, emphasizing especially the daily offerings made—at the public's expense, he stresses—for the well-being of the empire and emperor.[2] Josephus's apologetic defense of Jewish sacrificial practices, which insists on their commensurability with the sacrificial practices of all other civilized people (that is, the Greeks and Romans), serves as a potent reminder of the fact that Jewish sacrifice was seen and understood in the ancient world as a particular manifestation of a universal phenomenon. Moreover, Josephus reminds us that sacrifice was a tool through which communal relations were formed and political alliances were expressed, and that Jews—both as recipients of sacrificial gifts and as givers of sacrificial gifts[3]—regularly partook in sacrificial exchanges that were constitutive of the social fabric of the ancient Mediterranean.

1. Josephus, *Against Apion* 2.14. (ed. Whiston 968).
2. Josephus, *Against Apion* 2.6 (ed. Whiston 964).
3. On the sacrificial relations of the Jews with the Roman Empire, see also Philo, *The Embassy to Gaius* 157 and 356 (ed. Yonge 771 and 789); Josephus, *The Wars of the Jews* 2.17.3–4 (ed. Whiston 759).

Distinctly because sacrifice, which was a practice shared by the overwhelming majority of religious and ethnic communities in antiquity, consisted primarily of actions rather than of words, it was the most translatable mode of expression across linguistic and cultural boundaries: in many ways, it was the ultimate lingua franca of the ancient world.[4] The Jews of the Roman Empire, like its other peoples, were entangled in what we may call a "sacrificial network" that encompassed various different communities and played a definitive role in configuring the relations within these communities, between these communities, and between these communities and the empire. Jewish sacrificial practices were unique in the ancient Mediterranean landscape insofar as Jews sacrificed to one god only, and (generally speaking) sacrificed only in one place;[5] but in most other respects those practices were fully comparable to traditional Greek and Roman practices.

Josephus, writing at the end of the first century C.E., naturally could not envision a world in which animal sacrifice was not the ultimate mode of religious worship, the quintessential way in which individuals and communities expressed and managed both their relationships with the gods and their relationships with each other. But the story of the five hundred years that follow—of the period that came to be known as "late antiquity"—is to a great extent the story of the dissolving and undoing of that very sacrificial network to which he alludes. Within a span of half a millennium, the Mediterranean region saw age-old sacrificial practices turn from the most dominant form of religious activity to a neglected, if not despised, vestige of the past. Traditionally, the story of this seismic shift presented only one active protagonist group, namely, Christians, whereas both Jews and "pagans" were the passive subjects of processes or events that took place against their will. As the story goes, Christians, from the very inception of their movement, rejected animal sacrifice and instituted other (and ostensibly, better) forms of devotion, which eventually prevailed.[6] Jews did not necessarily *want* to stop sacrificing, but the destruction of their temple in 70 C.E. forced the cessation of sacrifice upon them such that they, too, had to adopt alternative forms of religious practices. "Pagans" strove to maintain sacrificial practices for as long as they could, but even-

---

4. See Rives, "Animal Sacrifice and Political Identity."

5. The only sustained evidence that we have on sacrifices outside of Jerusalem pertains to the temple of Onias in Leontopolis; see John J. Collins, *Between Athens and Jerusalem: Jewish Identity in the Hellenistic Diaspora* (Grand Rapids, MI: Wm. B. Eerdmans, 2000), 69–77. This, of course, does not preclude the possibility that there were other sacrificial settings outside Jerusalem during or after the Second Temple Period, but extant sources do not reflect that.

6. See, most notably, Robert Daly, *Christian Sacrifice: The Judeo-Christian Background before Origen* (Washington, DC: Catholic University of America Press, 1978) and various other works by the same author. This approach is strongly replicated in Petropoulou, *Animal Sacrifice*, 211–78.

tually, after the Christianization of the empire, had to succumb to the new regulations and decrees that forbade all animal sacrifice.[7]

More recent scholarship on the topic has challenged this traditional view by persuasively arguing that the early followers of Jesus did not reject animal sacrifice at all. Both the four Gospels and the letters of Paul introduce sacrifice as a completely integral part of religious life, and while they do stress that moral rectitude and compassion are more important than sacrifices (a well-established idea dating back to the prophetic books of the Hebrew Bible), they never indicate that sacrifices are dispensable.[8] Even the Letter to the Hebrews, the text most famously proclaiming that animal sacrifices have been superseded by the sacrifice of Christ, still completely subscribes to the notion that blood sacrifices are the quintessential and most effective channel through which human beings can approach the deity.[9] Christianity developed as a religion without animal sacrifice, the argument continues, not because it was initially disposed against this practice but because after the first century Christians simply did not have an appropriate sacrificial setting. They could not perform sacrifices in the Jerusalem temple because it no longer existed after 70 C.E., and they could not perform sacrifices in other local shrines because they were strictly prohibited from offering to idols. Eventually, as they set out to distinguish themselves both from Jews and from "idol worshippers," many Christian authors pronouncedly disentangled themselves from the sacrificial network and developed various doctrines and theologies that strongly rejected animal sacrifice: but those, as Daniel Ullucci has shown, were discursive moves set to justify a reality that was already established by a rather prosaic set of historical circumstances.[10]

This scholarly transition, which shifts the picture from "Christians were always averse to sacrifice" to "Christians did not sacrifice after the destruction of the Jerusalem temple and then followed up by turning it into a doctrine," in turn leads to a much more significant shift in the greater metanarrative of late antiquity: it effectively sets the destruction of the Jerusalem temple as one of the most cataclysmic events in world history. When taken as the crisis that caused Jews to stop sacrificing, and as a result ultimately caused Christians to reject sacrifice, and eventually caused all sacrificial practices in the Roman Empire to be banned, the destruction

---

7. For a refinement of this picture, see Saltzman, "The End of Public Sacrifice"; Edward J. Watts, *The Final Pagan Generation* (Oakland: University of California Press, 2015).

8. See, for example, Klawans, *Purity, Sacrifice, and the Temple*, 213–45; Heyman, *The Power of Sacrifice*, 95–160; Paula Fredriksen, "Judaizing the Nations: The Ritual Demands of Paul's Gospel," *New Testament Studies* 56 (2010): 232–52; Ullucci, *The Christian Rejection of Animal Sacrifice*, 69–90.

9. See Dunnill, *Covenant and Sacrifice*; Heyman, *The Power of Sacrifice*, 98–110 and the scholarship referenced there.

10. Ullucci, *The Christian Rejection of Animal Sacrifice*, 119–36.

of the Jerusalem temple emerges as more than the outcome of a tedious battle of Roman legions with local militias in a rather small and insignificant region of the empire. Rather, the demolished temple claims its place as the bedrock of completely new modes of religiosity. Embracing this view, Elias Bickerman proclaimed: "It was the Roman Emperor Titus who, in 70 C.E., put an end to the bloody sacrifices of the Jews and the Christians and thus eventually to paganism itself. He was certainly the greatest religious reformer in history."[11]

Guy Stroumsa, in his book *The End of Sacrifice*, expressed the same outlook: "More than any other singular action, it was the destruction of the Temple of Jerusalem by Titus in 70 CE, as a result of the Jewish revolt, that activated the slow—overly slow—transformation of religion to which we owe, among other things, European culture."[12] However, for Stroumsa the "great religious reformer" is not Titus but rather the Jews themselves, and more specifically the rabbis, as their presumed spiritual leaders. The Jews, he claims, were the very first to have invented—as a result of the destruction of the temple—religious practices and approaches that are based on "interiorization and privatization of worship" and therefore qualify as "modern" (insofar, of course, as one identifies modern religion with Protestant Christianity). "Since before the end of the first century CE," Stroumsa writes, "the Jews (much against their will) had offered the example of a society that had succeeded in conserving its ethnic and religious identity, even after the destruction of the only temple where daily sacrifices could be offered."[13]

For Stroumsa, then, the Jews were the pioneers of the religious revolution that set late antiquity in motion, a revolution whose governing principles were the replacement of public with private, the replacement of ritual actions with words, and the replacement of hierarchical and hereditary priesthood with democratized spiritual and scholastic pursuits.[14] In developing this argument, Stroumsa takes on the important and overdue task of integrating late ancient Jewish texts and traditions into the greater landscape of their times and places, and of showing that Judaism of the first half of the first millennium was not only a pertinent piece of the cultural fabric of its environment but in fact a definitive piece of it. He thus adopts a narrative about the development of post-temple Judaism that is well established among scholars of Jewish Studies—that is, the narrative about how the rabbis championed prayer, charity, fast, and Torah study as substitutes for sacrifices—and

11. Elias J. Bickerman, *Jews in the Greek Age* (Cambridge, MA: Harvard University Press, 1988), 139.

12. Stroumsa, *The End of Sacrifice*, 63.

13. Stroumsa, *The End of Sacrifice*, 62.

14. On this common view and its problematics, see also Daniel R. Schwartz, "Introduction: Was 70 C.E. a Watershed in Jewish History? Three Stages of Modern Scholarship, and a Renewed Effort," in *Was 70 CE a Watershed in Jewish History? On Jews and Judaism before and after the Destruction of the Second Temple*, ed. Daniel R. Schwartz, Zeev Weiss, and Ruth A. Clements (Leiden: Brill, 2012), 1–19.

weaves this narrative skillfully into a broader social and intellectual context in which corresponding transitions in religious discourse are apparent.

I fully agree with Stroumsa that the decline and ultimately the demise of animal and vegetable sacrifices in the Mediterranean world is of crucial historical significance, and is in many ways one of the most defining features of late antiquity as an epoch. I also wholeheartedly agree that the late ancient Jewish discourse on sacrifice, and most notably the rabbinic discourse (as the rabbinic corpus does constitute the overwhelming majority of Jewish material from this period), are critically important components in any attempt to understand and assess this transformation. I do, however, wish to point to the very limited nature of the rabbinic materials on which Stroumsa, like other scholars who have worked on this topic, chooses to rely. As I mentioned in the introduction, almost all the work that has been done on the topic of sacrifice in rabbinic literature has focused on a handful of statements in which the rabbis equate nonsacrificial practices with sacrificial practices in terms of their efficacy or religious value, and has virtually ignored the enormous legal-ritual corpus in which sacrificial practices are laid out, scrutinized, and explained. This skewed choice of materials has led to the view that the rabbinic project was essentially to create a sustained and durable nonsacrificial version of Judaism, and accordingly to the view that sacrifices were, for the rabbis, empty religious slots that they filled with new content. According to this view, the rabbis turned sacrifice into a language and a symbol that became the placeholder for practices and ideas that had nothing to do with sacrifice, and in this sense Judaism and Christianity can be seen as proceeding on parallel, if not intersecting, routes.

But what if instead of focusing on this handful of statements, almost all of which appear in later rabbinic (Amoraic) compilations, we took into account the vast corpus of legislative materials on sacrifices, which comprises almost a quarter of Tannaitic literature? What would the picture of "the end of sacrifice" as a key dimension of late antiquity look like if we attempted to reconstruct the rabbinic piece of this picture through what the rabbis say about sacrificing, rather than through what they say about *not* sacrificing? Would we still be able to point to correspondences, similarities, and resonances between rabbinic discourse and other contemporaneous discourses (Hellenistic, Roman, and Christian)? Would we be able to uphold the conviction that Jewish texts are part and parcel of the environment in which they were created? And most important, will the incorporation of those legal texts into the greater late antique conversation potentially change the terms of this greater conversation itself? In this conclusion, I wish to explore these questions in light of my discussions in the previous chapters. I venture to propose a more nuanced and complex account of the ideational transformation of sacrifice within the rabbinic tradition, and thereby to contribute to a richer and more accurate understanding of "the end of sacrifice" as a process of religious change.

SACRIFICE AFTER SACRIFICE:
A NONMETAPHORICAL PERSISTENCE

Before turning to particular facets of the rabbinic sacrificial system and to their resonances with contemporaneous discourses on sacrifice, it is important to reflect briefly on the very *existence* of a rabbinic sacrificial system—that is, to register the fact that the early rabbis dedicated enormous amounts of text and energy to discussing a set of practices that supposedly was of no practical consequence in their time. As I discussed in the introduction, this is by no means the only subset of legal-ritual material addressed in early rabbinic literature that was no longer applicable at the time of the rabbis (or may never have been applicable). The appearance of "obsolete" halakhic themes in rabbinic texts is not surprising if we realize, first, the rabbis' commitment to the biblical legal codes in their entirety, and second, the cultural function of legal rhetoric as an ideological platform. Here, however, I wish to highlight that the extensive rabbinic engagement with the topic of sacrifice cannot be understood strictly as a scholastic endeavor, but must also be seen as a mode of asserting that to be part of "Israel" is to partake in sacrificial procedures. The dedication of significant portions of rabbinic texts to the topic of temple worship and sacrifice is a way of conveying an idealized world-picture of which sacrifice is a key component. In other words, the rabbis, like Josephus (albeit possibly for different reasons), wanted their audience to perceive Jews as *people who sacrifice*.

The rabbis were not alone in actively maintaining the image of the Jews as people who sacrifice. The prominence of sacrificial scenes and themes in synagogue art of late antiquity, from Dura Europos to Shepphoris,[15] attests to the continuous centrality of sacrifice in Jewish religious imaginaries, as do the extensive references to sacrifices in Jewish liturgy.[16] To be clear, in these visual and poetic representations of sacrifice this theme is not invoked metaphorically: sacrifice is not a symbolic container for more abstract religious ideals such as devotion or giving oneself up, but rather a concrete physical practice involving rams and sheep, blood and incense, just as it is in halakhic rabbinic literature. Michael Swartz is certainly right in questioning the paradigm of "spiritualization" of sacrifice in late ancient

15. For discussions of representations of sacrifice in synagogue art, see Steven Fine, *Art and Judaism in the Greco-Roman World: Toward a New Jewish Archeology* (New York: Cambridge University Press, 2005), 172–83; Kära L. Schenk, "Temple, Community, and Sacred Narrative in the Dura-Europos Synagogue," *AJS Review* 34, no. 2 (2010): 195–229; Joan R. Branham, "Mapping Sacrifice on Bodies and Spaces in Late-Antique Judaism and Early Christianity," in *Architecture of the Sacred: Space, Ritual, and Experience from Classical Greece to Byzantium,* ed. Bonna D. Wescoat and Robert G. Ousterhout (New York: Cambridge University Press, 2012), 201–30.

16. See, for example, Swartz, "Liturgy, Poetry, and the Persistence of Sacrifice"; Ophir Münz-Manor, "Narrating Salvation: Verbal Sacrifice in Late Antique Liturgical Poetry," in *Jews, Christians, and the Roman Empire: The Poetics of Power in Late Antiquity,* ed. Annette Yoshiko Reed and Natalie Dohrmann (Philadelphia: University of Pennsylvania Press 2013), 154–66.

Judaism, and in arguing that even as late as the fifth and sixth centuries C.E. "sacrifice was not solely a utopian notion but rather a foundational concept that deeply informed the way [Jews] saw worship and the human connection with the divine."[17] Perhaps no less important, the image of Jews as people who sacrifice persisted not only in the works of Jewish cultural producers, but also in the ways in which non-Jewish authors represented the Jews.[18] It is telling, for example, that two authors of the fourth century C.E., living more than two centuries after the destruction of the Jerusalem temple, dedicate much effort to comparing Jewish sacrificial practices to Hellenistic sacrificial practices and to discussing both as essential to both groups. One of these two authors, the emperor Julian, draws this comparison approvingly, whereas his contemporary John Chrysostom does so with great vitriol and disdain; but both display a fundamental characterization of Jews as people who sacrifice, and utilize this characterization in their polemical writings.[19]

Thus, while Jews may have (as far as we know) stopped sacrificing in the last quarter of the first century C.E., on a *discursive* level they continued to sacrifice well into the middle of the first millennium of the Common Era, and continued, albeit in a changed way, to form a part of the sacrificial network that encompassed the ancient Mediterranean. They were, in their own eyes and in the eyes of others, *people who sacrifice* even when they did not actively sacrifice. Considering the fact that most Jews of the ancient world participated in sacrifice on a sporadic basis at most even when the temple still stood (since the journey to Jerusalem was costly and dangerous), the persistence of sacrifice as a discursive marker of Jewish identity is rather unsurprising: for many Jews it was more a discourse than a lived practice even before the temple was destroyed.[20] The rabbinic legal-ritual corpus concerning sacrificial procedures should be understood, I contend, as part of this discursive continuation of sacrifice rather than as an attempt to mummify the memory of "how things were" guided by the concession that things are now completely different. Rabbinic sacrificial manuals are not preservative but generative, and they engage with the topic of sacrifice because sacrifice is a fundamental religious reality even when it is not a practical reality.

17. Swartz, "Liturgy, Poetry, and the Persistence of Sacrifice," 412.

18. See the helpful survey in Laura Nasrallah, "The Embarrassment of Blood: Early Christians and Others on Sacrifice, War, and Rational Worship," in *Ancient Mediterranean Sacrifice*, ed. Jennifer Wright Knust and Zsuzsanna Várhelyi (New York: Oxford University Press, 2011), 146–47.

19. See Isabella Sandwell, *Religious Identity in Late Antiquity: Greeks, Jews, and Christians in Antioch* (New York: Cambridge University Press, 2007), 61–90.

20. As forcefully argued by Goodblatt, "The Jews of the Land of Israel," 162. See also Michael Tuval, "Doing without the Temple: Paradigms in Judaic Literature of the Diaspora," in Schwartz, Weiss, and Clements, *Was 70 CE a Watershed in Jewish History?* 181–239.

The very existence of the rabbinic sacrificial corpus, then, should lead us to question the most prominent pattern used in describing the transition from animal sacrifice to other modes of practice in late ancient religions, which I will call here "the pattern of analogical substitution." This pattern rests on the notion that when sacrifice is not physically practiced its only mode of survival is through calibrating other activities as analogous to sacrifice, and that the process of analogization depends on extracting an essence or higher meaning that ostensibly underlies both animal sacrifice and the comparable activity. This pattern explains how animal sacrifice can be transformed into almsgiving if sacrifice is identified as a manner of giving something up, can be manifested in a shared meal if it is framed as communion, can be replaced by prayer if it is seen primarily as a way of approaching the deity, and can be read into any situation in which violence is inflicted on the innocent (or even on the noninnocent) if it is perceived as an act of expiatory killing. Indeed, these analogizations are a common rhetorical trope in both Jewish and Christian writings of late antiquity; but the vast sacrificial corpus of the rabbis shows that sacrifice can and does survive as a central discursive category *without* turning into something else. The rabbis of the Mishnah are concerned with sacrifice exactly as the set of concrete practices that it is, not as a symbol and not as a placeholder for a more abstract religious value. The Tannaitic corpus thus urges us to reconsider the commonly held view that when sacrifice (or any other practice, for that matter) is not actually performed, it necessarily turns into a metaphor.

The persistence of sacrifice as a nonmetaphorical practice in rabbinic literature, that is, the rabbis' presentation of sacrifice as an organizing principle of time, of public life, and of economy, calls into question the assumption that change in religious practice is also necessarily a change in religious consciousness. Put differently, it casts doubt on the view that all elite cultural producers who did not engage in animal sacrifice saw themselves as creating alternative forms of worship, and suggests instead that perhaps they did not think in terms of alternatives at all.[21] By this I do not mean that the early rabbis thought that without sacrifices the world and humanity were doomed, but only that they did not attempt to envision a version of "Judaism without sacrifice" because for them this was a contradiction in terms. As Jonathan Klawans has rightly pointed out, the practices commonly identified as the rabbis' "substitutes" for sacrifice (such as prayer, charity, self-denial, etc.) are in fact not "substitutes" at all, but rather long-standing practices that prevailed among Jews back when the temple stood, and in fact often accompanied or

---

21. A possible reason for this is that the early rabbis may have not seen the absence of the temple as a permanent situation: as Ruth Clements has argued, it seems that it was long after 70 C.E. that the possibility of an imminent rebuilding of the temple became improbable. See Ruth Clements, "70 CE after 135 CE—The Making of a Watershed?," in Schwartz, Weiss, and Clements, *Was 70 CE a Watershed in Jewish History?* 517–36.

complemented sacrificial practices.[22] In the same way that the giving of charity does not obviate the practice of prayer and one is expected to engage in both, so neither charity nor prayer obviates the performance of sacrifices. In the rabbinic model one is expected, if one is able, to engage in all of those forms of piety.

Furthermore, the rabbis' continuous engagement with sacrifices can be understood not only as an interpretive and scholastic enterprise of a religious elite guided by a lasting commitment to a textual tradition, but also as one dimension of a broader picture in which a much larger Jewish population continues to think and very possibly act in sacrificial modes. We have no conclusive evidence on whether and to what extent Jews sacrificed outside the Jerusalem temple or after its destruction, but there are good reasons to assume that for Jews in the first centuries, as for their non-Jewish contemporaries, the consumption of meat was inextricably associated with sacrifice. Despite the fact that the distinction between "slaughter of sacred things" (shehitat qodashim) and "slaughter of nonsacred things" (shehitat hullin) was well established in early Judaism, rabbinic legislation reveals significant overlap between the two practices. Both sacral slaughter and nonsacral slaughter are performed in the same manner, and can be performed by the same people;[23] both sacral and nonsacral slaughter require one to dispose of the blood and the suet (although the disposal is not performed in the same way);[24] and in both sacral and nonsacral slaughter the priests are to receive a portion of the animal before the owners may consume it (although the nature of the portion is different).[25]

More generally, for most people in the ancient Mediterranean world, meat was a substance acquired and consumed so infrequently that it was almost always designated for occasions of a sacred nature, such as festivals, weddings, and so forth, even if it was not handled and eaten specifically in the precincts of a temple.[26] It is evident from rabbinic and nonrabbinic texts alike that the practice of cooking and consuming meat outside the temple was seen as imitation or continuation of the sacrificial practices of the temple, such that the former was effectively a reflection of the latter.[27] It is exactly this fundamental view of all meat eating as an offshoot of sacrifice that stands behind the famous rabbinic tradition regarding Jews who

---

22. Klawans, *Purity, Sacrifice, and the Temple*, 203–9.

23. See M. Ḥullin 1.1 and Zevaḥim 3.1. For an elaborate discussion of the parity between sacred slaughter and profane slaughter in the Mishnah, see Jacob Neusner, "Law and Theology in the Mishnah: The Case of Mishnah-Tractate Ḥullin," *Studia Orientalia Electronica* 99 (2004): 191–97.

24. M. Ḥullin 6.1–6, 8.6.

25. M. Ḥullin 10.1–3; consider also M. Bekhorot 2.1–5.6.

26. See M. Hullin 5.3; T. Ḥullin 5.9.

27. On the dependence of nonsacral slaughter on sacral slaughter, see Werman, "The Rules of Consuming and Covering the Blood"; Yoram Erder, "Qumranic Vestiges in Two Halakhot of the Karaite Benjamin Nahawandi on the Issue of Nonsacral Meat," *Zion* 63, no. 1 (1998): 5–38.

refused to eat meat and drink wine after the destruction of the temple, since meat and wine were no longer offered on the altar.[28]

In this close association of meat and sacrifice Jews were commensurate with their non-Jewish contemporaries. Scholars have long maintained that in the Greek and Roman world all meat was procured through sacrificial slaughter, and while this view has recently been contested as inaccurate, it is quite evident that there was a least a prominent attempt to *present* all or most meat sold in the market as deriving from sacrifices.[29] From a different angle, Andrew McGowan has argued that the eucharistic meal was deliberately shaped as excluding meat (and in some communities, also wine) in order to differentiate it from meals associated with sacrifice to idols.[30] It thus stands to reason that for many Jews after the destruction of the temple, sacrifice persisted as a meaningful category, and in a residual way as a lived practice, through the very regulated and unique set of rituals surrounding the eating of meat. This association of meat eating with sacrifice, which was so elemental in the ancient world, helps explain a much-discussed passage in Julian's *Against the Galileans,* in which he claims that Jews in his own time (that is, the mid-fourth century c.e.) still sacrifice regularly:

> No doubt some sharp-seeing person will say: "But the Jews also do not sacrifice." But ... they sacrifice (*thuousi*) in private places. Even now all things the Jews eat are holy and they pray before sacrificing and they give the right shoulder to the priests as first fruits. Having been deprived of the temple, or as is their custom to call it, the sanctuary, they are prevented from offering the sacred things to God.[31]

Scholars have debated whether we can surmise from Julian's description that Jews in Antioch in his time indeed sacrificed, or rather that we should assume that Julian wrongfully misunderstood (or intentionally misconstrued) some other kind of Jewish food-related practice.[32] However, I propose that for Julian, as a devout

---

28. T. Sotah 15.5; BT Baba Batra 60b.

29. The notion that all consumable meat in the Greek world came from animal sacrifice guides the work of Marcel Detienne and Jean-Pierre Vernant; see Detienne and Vernant, *The Cuisine of Sacrifice among the Greeks,* 8; for a careful examination and qualification of this view, see Fred S. Naiden, "Blessed Are the Parasites," in *Greek and Roman Animal Sacrifice: Ancient Victims, Modern Observers,* ed. Christopher A. Faraone and Fred S. Naiden (New York: Cambridge University Press, 2012), 55–83. For the observation that all meat was presented as associated with sacrifice, see Willis, *Idol Meat in Corinth,* 7–64.

30. Andrew McGowan, *Ascetic Eucharists: Food and Drink in Early Christian Ritual Meals* (New York: Oxford University Press, 1999), 33–88.

31. Translation quoted from Aryay Bennet Finkelstein, "Julian among Jews, Christians and 'Hellenes' in Antioch: Jewish Practice as a Guide to 'Hellenes' and a Goad to Christians" (PhD diss., Harvard University, 2011), 40.

32. See the elaborate discussion and survey of scholarship in Finkelstein, "Julian among Jews," 38–52.

Hellenist, any ritualized form of eating, especially of meat, *was* a form of sacrifice, most notably when it included distribution of portions among the priests. I dare to raise the conjecture that the Jews of Antioch, and maybe many others like them, saw it in the same way.

Rabbinic texts testify, with varying levels of approval or disapproval, to practices of meat eating after the destruction of the temple that either set out to imitate sacrificial meals or were actually understood, intentionally or accidentally, to be sacrificial meals for all intents and purposes. This pertains especially to the Passover meal, which, as I discussed in chapter 4, could be most easily calibrated as a meal without a sacrifice.[33] However, the Mishnah also mentions potential cases of individuals slaughtering animals outside the temple and designating them as different types of offerings.[34] The rabbis leave no room for doubt that such manner of slaughter is *not* sacrifice, and in some cases it even disqualifies the meat from being eaten, but nonetheless they envision a possibility of a blurring of boundaries between sacrifice and nonsacral slaughter, and seek to fortify those boundaries. We can thus understand the legislative enterprise of the rabbis in regard to sacrifices not only as a specialized parabiblical commentary, but also as their own intervention in a set of conversations and practices that were still sacrificial in nature, or were at least understood by some as sacrificial. The rabbinic sacrificial corpus charts out what sacrifices are and are not, how they are and are not to be performed, and what are the ritual considerations that underlie them, and it does so in a world in which people still think with sacrifices when they eat, when they celebrate festivals, when they perform magic,[35] and when they interact with their Greek and Roman surroundings, which are still saturated with sacrifice. In short, the rabbis—certainly the early rabbis—were still deeply entangled in a sacrificial network.

All of this is to say that even without a temple and without a centralized sacrificial cult, sacrifice continued for centuries after the temple's destruction to be thought of as a very concrete flesh-and-blood practice and not only as a rhetorical trope or placeholder for other religious activities. Thus, I contend, the early rabbis should not be understood primarily as creating substitutes for sacrifice, but rather primarily as *creating a discursive reform in understanding and approaching sacrifice.* This was not an attempt to envision a world without sacrifice, but rather an attempt to construct a ritual setting in which sacrifices qualified as certain things and not others, and fulfilled certain functions and not others. This discursive reform could

33. See my discussion at the end of chapter 4, and the evidence considered by Baruch Bokser, *The Origins of the Seder* (Berkeley and Los Angeles: University of California Press 1984), 101–6; Tabory, *The Passover Ritual*, 92–105.

34. M. Ḥullin 2.10; M. Menaḥot 13.10.

35. See Michael Swartz, "Sacrificial Themes in Jewish Magic," in *Magic and Ritual in the Ancient World*, ed. Paul Mirecki and Marvin Meyer (Leiden: Brill, 2002), 303–15.

very well have taken place when the temple was still fully operational, and perhaps some of its roots can actually be traced to that period. But the crystallization and solidification of this reform in texts redacted around the third century C.E., at a time in which the centralized sacrificial cult had already been gone for some decades, do set this reform at a historical crossroads that allows us to understand later developments in a new light. In what follows, I will reiterate how I understand this reform, and venture to place this reform in the broader intellectual and religious context of the transformations of sacrifice in late antiquity.

THE INTERACTIVE MODEL AND
THE METAPHYSICS OF SACRIFICE

In chapters 1 and 2, I argued that the rabbis transformed the biblical model of sacrifice, which can be described as a communicative or interactive model, into a noninteractive model. Whereas biblical depictions portray sacrifices—in different ways and to various degrees—as manners through which individuals or communities approach the deity, greet him, attempt to appease him, allay his anger, express gratitude toward him, and so forth, the rabbis present a series of innovations in their sacrificial legislation that significantly marginalize both the offerer and the deity, and place heightened emphasis on the procedure itself. I showed that the agency of the offerer is noticeably bracketed in rabbinic texts, both by emphasizing that it is the priest's intentions rather than the offerer's on which the validity of the sacrifice depends, and by dismissing the importance of hand laying, the one ritual component in which the offerer expresses his or her pertinence to the sacrificial process. In addition, I showed that the rabbis center the entire sacrificial procedure on the manipulation of blood, thereby relegating the burning component of the ritual— the part in which the deity visibly gets his share—to the position of an aftermath. The recalibration of the sacrificial process such that it is rendered efficacious even if nothing was received shifts the focus from the participants and the substances involved to the accuracy of the actions performed and their adherence to preordained protocols. My analysis of ritual narratives in chapter 5 further demonstrated how the rabbis reconceive of sacrifice, and indeed valorize it, as a manifestation of perfect ritual commitment and flawlessly carried out actions.

I contend that this revolutionary rabbinic vision of sacrifice, which goes much further than the already procedure-oriented Priestly Code in its elimination of interaction from the sacrificial scene, should be understood as a particular theory of sacrifice despite the fact that it is not presented as a theological or philosophical treatise but rather as a technical manual. At the heart of this theory stand two interrelated questions: a metaphysical question, namely, *what does sacrifice do,* and a normative question, namely, *whether and why ought one sacrifice.* These questions stem from a fundamental theological conundrum: how can the deity, whom the rabbis unquestionably took to be an entirely immaterial entity devoid of any human-like needs, want human beings to give him material things? How can the omnipotent, omnipresent creator of the world be satisfied by grain and meat and fat?

Several centuries before the rabbis, prophetic and poetic biblical texts proclaimed that it is sheer foolishness to think that God needs sacrifices, that he somehow takes pleasure in them, or that he can be bribed through them. "Has the Lord great delight in burnt offerings and sacrifices, as in obedience to the voice of the Lord? Surely, to obey is better than sacrifice, and to heed than the fat of rams," says Samuel,[36] whereas Isaiah wonders, "What to me is the multitude of your sacrifices? . . . I have had enough of burnt offerings of rams and the fat of fed beasts; I do not delight in the blood of bulls, or of lambs, or of goats."[37] Similar sentiments are expressed by Jeremiah,[38] Hosea,[39] and Amos.[40] The psalmist could not be clearer in rejecting the notion that God has any real use for offerings: "If I were hungry, I would not tell you, for the world and all that is in it is mine. Do I eat the flesh of bulls, or drink the blood of goats?"[41] Yet none of those authors, it must be emphasized, criticizes the practice of sacrifice as such: their critique is directed at those who misunderstand sacrifice, that is, at those who think that material offerings please God in and of themselves regardless of the offerers' moral rectitude. These biblical authors never call upon the Israelites to stop offering sacrifices (although they are often misperceived to be doing so, primarily because of centuries of Christian antisacrificial interpretation), but rather implore them to be decent human beings and not to assume that sacrifices suffice to maintain their relations with God.[42] To be sure, the psalmist's admonition against assuming that God needs sacrifices is immediately followed by the exhortation "Offer to God a sacrifice of thanksgiving, and pay your vows to the Most High."[43] It is not about refraining from sacrifice, but rather about sacrificing for the right reasons.

But what are the right reasons? If, on the one hand, human beings are expected to burn grains and animals on an altar as a form of worship, and, on the other hand, they are discouraged from believing that the deity has any use for those grains and animals, what is the value of sacrifice, and why sacrifice in the first place? According to Stanley Stowers, during the times in which sacrifice was the dominant form of worship in various Mediterranean cultures, "ordinary people" did not concern themselves with these questions at all. They sacrificed because

---

36. 1 Samuel 15:22.

37. Isaiah 1:11.

38. Jeremiah 7:21–24.

39. Hosea 6:6.

40. Amos 5:21–24.

41. Psalm 50:12–13.

42. As convincingly showed by Klawans, *Purity, Sacrifice, and the Temple*, 75–100.

43. Psalm 50:14.

that was what one did, and did so with a general sense that the mode of operation of sacrifice is reciprocal in nature, that is, that sacrifice is effectively an exchange with the deity in which each side gains something they need or want. In other words, Stowers argues, first, that most people in antiquity had absolutely no problem imagining the deity as benefiting from their offerings, and second, that most people did not even take too much time to think of why they were sacrificing: it was a habit, it was a form of piety, and it was a nice opportunity to have a good meal.[44] In contrast, those whom Stowers calls "experts"—that is, the narrow intellectual and religious elite that composed the texts and treatises through which we have gotten to learn of those ancient times—were very concerned with these questions. As quite a few texts composed by such elite authors reveal, the view that a deity cannot be bribed by human gifts, has no material needs, and takes no physical satisfaction in meat and smoke was by no means unique to Judeans or Jews. It was a pervasive assumption about divinity among Greek and Roman authors, from philosophers to poets and satirists, and in their writings these authors strove to condemn and deride exactly the reciprocal view of sacrifices that "ordinary people" at their time held.

I have some misgivings about Stowers's characterization of "ordinary people" as performing practices without troubling themselves with the meaning of their actions. In truth, we have no way of knowing the thoughts and perceptions of people who lived two thousand years ago and left no written documents, and we should be very wary of assuming, consciously or unconsciously, that only those educated enough to write and respected enough for their writings to be preserved actively reflected about issues like religious practices. I strongly agree with Bruce Chilton that even if lay offerers did not have a consistent and articulated theory regarding their act of sacrifice, they were highly aware of its economic, psychological, and sociological repercussions, and in all likelihood constructed certain meanings vis-à-vis those repercussions.[45] Nevertheless, I think Stowers is correct in his two fundamental observations: first, that the practice of bringing substances to a place of worship and placing them on an altar readily lends itself to a reciprocal interpretation or to a logic of exchange, and this interpretation was probably intuitive for many people; and second, that authors who held particular persuasions about the nature of divine entities as profoundly different from human beings could not accept this interpretation. Since most authors (with very few exceptions, such as the Pythagoreans) did not contest the legitimacy and indeed the religious value of sacrificial practices and did not advocate the cessation of sacrifice, they had to create new intellectual frameworks through which to explain and justify sacrifice.

44. Stowers, "The Religion of Plant and Animal Offerings."
45. Chilton, *The Temple of Jesus*, 37.

As Ullucci has shown in detail, the arguments used to reject the reciprocal metaphysics of sacrifice (that is, the notion that what makes sacrifices efficacious is their ability to please the gods) constitute a widely shared discourse across regions, genres, and religious and ethnic groups throughout antiquity and late antiquity. Those arguments resonate in texts from the fifth century B.C.E. to the fifth century C.E., appearing in different configurations among Platonists, Epicureans, Stoics, and Cynics, Jewish Hellenistic authors and Graeco-Roman comedians, Christian apologists and Neoplatonic revivalists.[46] Some of these authors set out only to dispel or ridicule the reciprocal model without necessarily proposing an alternative metaphysics, or merely point out that sacrifice should be performed primarily out of respect for local customs and traditions.[47] A few authors, most famously early Christian authors like Justin and Tertullian, use these arguments to reject the practice of sacrifice altogether.[48] Other authors, however, do attempt to provide alternative answers to the metaphysical question "What does sacrifice do?" as well as to the intertwined normative question "Why sacrifice?" One such answer is that sacrifices serve contemplative purposes: for example, Philo of Alexandria presents an allegorical interpretation of sacrificial rituals as evoking correct understandings of the nature of God and of the soul.[49] This interpretation is shared also by Clement of Alexandria some two hundred years later, but unlike Philo, Clement maintains that no actual performance of sacrifice is necessary.[50] A completely different answer, presented by Porphyry of Tyre and his devout disciple Iamblichus in the late third/early fourth century, is that sacrifices are directed not to gods but to *daimones,* who are the lowest forms of divinity to whom it is appropriate to offer material things (but whereas Porphyry had significant reservations about sacrifice, Iamblichus enthusiastically endorsed it).[51] Yet another approach is presented

46. Ullucci, *The Christian Rejection of Animal Sacrifice*, 31–118.

47. For example, Plato, *Euthyphro* 14b–15e and *Laws* 10.906–10. See Plato, *Complete Works,* ed. John M. Cooper (Indianapolis: Hackett, 1997), 14–15 and 1562–67; Philodemus, *On Piety,* ed. Dirk Obbink (Oxford: Clarendon Press, 1997), 873–95; Epictetus, *Enchiridion* 31, trans. George Long (Mineola, NY: Dover Books, 2004), 14.

48. Justin Martyr, *Dialogue with Trypho* 22 (*Ante-Nicene Fathers,* 1:205–6); Tertullian, *Apology* 27–30 and *Against the Jews* 25 (*Ante-Nicene Fathers,* 3:40–42 and 156).

49. See especially Philo, *On the Special Laws* 1.56–298 (ed. Yonge 539–63); on Philo's approach to sacrifice, see William K. Gilders, "Jewish Sacrifice: Its Nature and Function (According to Philo)," in Knust and Várhelyi, *Ancient Mediterranean Sacrifice,* 94–105.

50. Clement of Alexandria, *Stromata* 7.6 (*Ante-Nicene Fathers,* 2:537–38); see Ullucci, *The Christian Rejection of Animal Sacrifice,* 107–10.

51. Porphyry, *On Abstinence from Killing Animals,* trans. Gillian Clark (London: Bloomsbury, 2000), mainly book 2; Iamblichus, *On the Mysteries,* trans. Emma C. Clark, John M. Dillon, and Jackson P. Hershbell (Atlanta: Society of Biblical Literature, 2003), book 5. See also James B. Rives, "The Theology of Animal Sacrifice in the Ancient Greek World: Origins and Developments," in Knust and Várhelyi, *Ancient Mediterranean Sacrifice,* 187–202.

around the same period by Sallustius, who sees the gift of animals to the deity as the symbolic giving of life itself.[52] The attempt to create a compelling metaphysics of sacrifice was not only the domain of those whose communities regularly engaged in sacrifice: whereas some Christian writers dismissed blood sacrifice as altogether "barbaric" and as a concession that God made to the idolatrous Israelites,[53] authors like Irenaeus and Cyprian made concerted efforts to create a compelling sacrificial metaphysics to explain the workings of the Christian community[54] and of the eucharistic meal,[55] respectively.

The theological and philosophical conversation on sacrifices—what they are, how they work, how they benefit humans or gods, and what value there is in their performance—was thus an enduring conversation in the ancient and late ancient world. Rabbinic literature, however, was brought to bear on this conversation almost exclusively in one manner: insofar as it was assumed that the only thing that the rabbis had to say about sacrifices was that other practices could replace them. Since the common assumption among scholars was that the rabbis (and by extension, the Jews) ceased to be interested in sacrifices once they were no longer practiced, except as lifeless textual fossils, the fact that various rabbinic texts do present their own rich and fascinating attempts to explain the workings of sacrifice and to speak of their value has been practically overlooked.[56] In a recent article on the reframing of sacrifice in the fifth-/sixth-century Palestinian Midrash Leviticus Rabbah, I showed that rabbinic homilists not only used the imagery of sacrifice to endorse activities that they considered meritorious, but also used themes of self-denial, giving of life, and contrast between animal and divine to justify and elevate

52. Sallustius, *Concerning the Gods and the Universe*, trans. Arthur Darby Nock (Cambridge: Cambridge University Press, 1926), 15–16. Consider also the discussion of Neoplatonic approaches to sacrifice in Stroumsa, *The End of Sacrifice*, 58–62.

53. See Marcel Poorthuis, "Sacrifice as Concession in Christian and Jewish Sources: The *Didascalia Apostolorum* and Rabbinic Literature," in *The Actuality of Sacrifice: Past and Present*, ed. Alberdina Houtman, Marcel Poorthuis, Joshua Schwartz, and Joseph Turner (Leiden: Brill, 2014), 170–91.

54. Irenaeus, *Against the Heresies* 4.17–19 (*Ante-Nicene Fathers*, 1:482–86); see Townsend, "Another Race?," 244–49.

55. Cyprian, *Epistles* 62/63 and *On the Lapsed* 14–18 (*Ante-Nicene Fathers*, 5:358–63 and 440–42). See Andrew B. McGowan, "Rehashing the Leftovers of Idols: Cyprian and Early Christians Constructions of Sacrifice," in *Religious Competition in the Third Century CE: Jews, Christians, and the Greco-Roman World*, ed. Jordan D. Rosenblum, Lily Vuong, and Nathaniel DesRosiers (Göttingen: Vandehoeck and Ruprecht, 2014), 69–78.

56. While Aaron Glaim has correctly observed that "tannaitic texts are remarkable in that they do not treat the offering of sacrifices as the preeminent means of participating in reciprocal relations with God" (Glaim, "Reciprocity, Sacrifice, and Salvation," 25), his cogent conclusion rests only on the *absence* of reciprocal language from Tannaitic materials, rather than on the ways in which rabbinic sacrificial procedures are actively shaped.

sacrificial practices as such.[57] Here, in light of my analysis in the previous chapters, I want to argue that early rabbinic legal-ritual materials should also be integrated into this long-standing and cross-cultural conversation on the metaphysics of sacrifice, and should be viewed as providing their own answers to the two questions "What does sacrifice do?" and "Why sacrifice?"

Like other elite participants in the pervasive conversation on sacrifices, the early rabbis rejected the reciprocal model and the notion that God gains something from human gifts: indeed, in several homilies different rabbis stress that it is human beings who need sacrifices, rather than God.[58] Rabbinic legislation, however, takes this idea even further by effectively eliminating both the giver and the receiver from the sacrificial equation. The rabbis construct sacrifice as a procedure that cannot be described in terms of "giving" at all, since the "given" substances are immaterial to the ritual validity of the sacrifice. Sacrifice is also not a mode through which one can connect with the deity, because the individual who seeks to "connect" may as well not be present. In other words, the rabbis' sacrificial model is not only nonreciprocal but also noninteractive. But what metaphysics of sacrifice do the rabbis propose instead? If they do not see sacrifice as a mode of approaching the deity, then how do they explain its workings?

I would phrase the rabbis' answer to the interrelated questions "What does sacrifice do?" and "Why sacrifice?" as follows: sacrifice is the mechanism through which one is released from sacrificial obligations, and release from sacrificial obligations is tantamount to the attainment of atonement. By performing one's sacrificial obligation, whether as an individual or a group, one rehabilitates oneself as a member of the community and as a religious subject. While this answer may sound tautological, as though I am saying "sacrifice is the means through which one performs sacrifice," I contend that behind it stands a sustained and well-developed religious worldview.

The Priestly Code presents a host of various situations in which an individual or a community is obligated to bring offerings for the purpose of sacrifice: after committing different forms of transgression, in order to complete certain purification processes, as part of specific rites of transformation (like the rite of the suspected adulteress or the Nazarite rite), and so on. In addition, both priestly and nonpriestly texts mention occasions on which individuals or communities may bring offerings as an expression of joy and gratitude, as a form of celebration, as a means of making a petition to God, and so on. In the rabbinic construction, however, all sacrifices derive from obligations: as I showed in chapter 1, the rabbis present even voluntary sacrifices as preceded by a vow that instantly generates an

---

57. Mira Balberg, "The Animalistic Gullet and the Godlike Soul: Reframing Sacrifice in Midrash Leviticus Rabbah," *AJS Review* 38, no. 2 (2014): 221–47.

58. See the examples I cited in chapter 2.

obligation, such that only when the offering is brought to the temple is the offerer released from the obligation. Similarly, sacrifices pertaining to festivals or pilgrimages are presented as obligations that one must fulfill in order to have performed the festival or pilgrimage properly. These sacrificial obligations operate on two levels. First, they impact the persons or groups to whom the obligation applies, such that they are now in a state of debt (in some cases an actual financial debt; in other cases the debt is the lingering obligation itself).[59] Second, if particular substances have been designated for sacrificial purposes, then once the obligation is enacted upon these substances they become prohibited for use. The sacrificial process in the form of the fourfold work of blood pays the debt of those who owe a sacrifice, and turns the prohibited substance into a permitted substance that—with certain restrictions—can be used again. It is important to emphasize, however, that the debt is not paid through the actual transfer of goods from the offerer to the deity: it is paid once the procedure set to enable the transfer has been carried out appropriately by the officiating priests.

On the face of it, one could argue that the rabbis' depiction of sacrifice in these self-contained terms—as an obligation and a release from obligation—should not be understood as a commentary on the metaphysics of sacrifice but simply as a matter of genre. After all, any normative compendium that provides ritual instructions will tend to describe the ritual in terms of obligations that need to be fulfilled and without recourse to any reality outside the ritual.[60] But here I insist again that the rabbis do not merely redescribe the biblical sacrificial procedure but in fact modify it: they maintain that the ritual actions prescribed by biblical texts that signify the giver's part (laying of hands) and the receiver's part (burning on the altar) are not an integral part of the sacrificial process and are not required for the fulfillment of obligations. They subsume all forms of sacrifice under the heading of "atonement" and put forth that atonement is attained exclusively through blood, not because God desires blood or because blood is of any sanctity, but because blood functions as "permitter"—as the mechanism of release from injunction. I understand this innovative move as a way of proclaiming that the value of sacrifice lies not in the material gain that it involves, but in the careful and scrupulous performance of a ritual obligation.

On one level, this proclamation serves a "negative" purpose: it confirms what sacrifices are not (a way of communicating with the deity), and in this respect this proclamation strongly resonates with other ancient and late ancient texts from the Mediterranean region. But on another level, this proclamation is also part of a greater rabbinic cultural project—perhaps *the* rabbinic cultural project—of identi-

---

59. On the ubiquity of "debt" as an overarching way of understanding one's relation to the sacred realm around the turn of the Common Era, see Anderson, *Sin*, 27–110.

60. As powerfully shown by Staal, "The Meaninglessness of Ritual."

fying the fulfillment of commandments as the locus of holiness and of religious life regardless of the content of the commandment.[61] This facet of rabbinic theology was concisely captured by Ephraim E. Urbach in a brief comment on the rabbinic blessing that precedes the performance of any and every commandment, "Blessed are you, the Lord our God, who sanctified us with his commandments and commanded us to . . ."[62] As Urbach put it, "The sanctity is, as it were, withdrawn from the precept itself and transferred to the act of the precept and to him that performs it. The commandment is thus voided not only of any mythical-magical quality, but also of its very ritual-cultic basis."[63] There is no better way for the rabbis to make the point that fulfillment of commandments is the ultimate mode of religiosity regardless of their "ritual-cultic basis" than to take the ultimate ritual-cultic commandments—namely, sacrifice and temple worship—and to make the point that these commandments, like all others, are defined strictly in terms of their correct performance and not in terms of their sensual, emotional, or material effect. Sacrifices are not unique and indispensable ways of approaching the deity: they are commandments like all others, with no special ontological status.[64]

The question that immediately follows is whether this transformation in the metaphysics of sacrifice is necessarily a result of the destruction of the temple and the cessation of the sacrificial cult. It is tempting to propose that this is the coping

---

61. As Christine Hayes has demonstrated in detail, one of the key features of the rabbis' understanding of divine law is that God's laws do not necessarily correspond with discernible benefits or rational values, and can be seen to cultivate obedience for obedience's sake. See Christine Hayes, *What's Divine about Divine Law? Early Perspectives* (Princeton: Princeton University Press, 2015), 246–86.

62. The earliest discussion of this blessing in rabbinic sources is in T. Berakhot chapter 6.

63. Ephraim E. Urbach, *The Sages: Their Concepts and Beliefs,* trans. Israel Abrahams (Cambridge, MA: Harvard University Press, 1987), 368.

64. The distinction I am drawing here between viewing sacrifices as uniquely efficacious ways of connecting with the deity, on the one hand, and viewing sacrifices as "commandments among other commandments," on the other hand, may resonate for some with the realism/nominalism distinction that has prevailed in the study of ancient Judaism for the last two decades. In an influential piece, Daniel R. Schwartz described the rabbis' approach to biblical law as "nominalistic" in contrast to the priestly "realistic" approach: whereas the latter identifies the law as revealing something about the intrinsic nature of objects, phenomena, and actions, the former maintains that the status of things in the world is only determined by human acts of naming and identification. See Daniel Schwartz, "Law and Truth: On Qumran-Sadducean and Rabbinic Views of Law," in *The Dead Sea Scrolls: Forty Years of Research,* ed. Devorah Dimant and Uriel Rappaport (Jerusalem: Magnes Press and Yad Yitzhak Ben-Zvi, 1992), 229–40. Schwartz's approach was upheld but somewhat challenged by Jeffrey Rubenstein, "Nominalism and Realism in Qumranic and Rabbinic Law: A Reassessment," *Dead Sea Discoveries* 6.2 (1999): 157–83; and Vered Noam, "Is It True That 'a Corpse Does Not Defile?' On Ritual Contamination in Tannaitic Literature" [Heb.], *Tarbitz* 78, no. 2 (2009): 157–87. In her recent work, Christine Hayes has convincingly argued for the limited utility of this dichotomy in regard to rabbinic literature; see Christine Hayes, "Legal Realism and the Fashioning of Sectarians in Jewish Antiquity," in *Sects and Sectarianism in Jewish History,* ed. Sacha Stern (Leiden: Brill, 2010), 119–46; Hayes, *What's Divine about Divine Law?* 195–99.

mechanism that the rabbis devised for explaining how "life can go on" in the absence of a temple: they reconfigured the sacrificial cult as a nonunique part of a greater set of commandments. Thereby they equated the inability to perform sacrifice with the inability to perform any other commandment (for example, to observe agricultural commandments outside the land of Israel), rather than with a theological and existential catastrophe. While this hypothesis is compelling and certainly could account for the motivations of the rabbis in creating this corpus in the way they did, I submit that this mode of explanation is not truly necessary. The rabbis' attempt to explain sacrifice in a noninteractive manner could easily rest on ideas and themes that were developed back when the temple stood: as I mentioned above, such ideas were prominent in antiquity among other learned elites who lived in communities that actively engaged in sacrifice on a regular basis. There is no inherent contradiction between maintaining that the deity does not gain anything from sacrifices and actively and even enthusiastically engaging in sacrificial practices, and presenting sacrifice strictly in terms of obligation should not be mistaken as a way of undermining its importance.

Some scholars may be inclined to understand the rabbinic approach to sacrifices as a distinct product of the second or third century by situating it vis-à-vis the rise of Christianity. A long-standing position in the study of rabbinic literature has been that the early rabbis' emphasis on concrete observance of the commandments is a polemical reaction to what is understood as Paul's dismissal of the law in favor of "faith."[65] Following a similar path of reading rabbinic texts in polemical terms, one could argue that by emphasizing that sacrifices serve only to fulfill commandments and that therein lies their value, the rabbis assert two doctrines in response to contesting Christian arguments. First, they assert that Jewish sacrifices are indeed biblically required and therefore cannot be dismissed or superseded, and second, they assert that counter to Christian claims, Jewish sacrifices are not comparable to "pagan" offerings because they do not rest on misguided anthropomorphic assumptions. It is certainly possible that the rabbis consciously ventured to make those assertions, although it is very difficult to determine how much familiarity they even had with what we have come to call "Christian doctrines" and to what extent they perceived those as a threat in the first centuries of the Common Era.[66] Once again, however, I contend that it is not necessary to assume an anti-Christian polemical

65. For notable examples, see Arthur Marmorstein, "Judaism and Christianity in the Middle of the Third Century," in *Studies in Jewish Theology by A. Marmorstein,* ed. Joseph Rabbinowitz and Mayer S. Lew (New York: Oxford University Press, 1950), 77–92; Urbach, *The Sages,* 30–37; Devorah Steinmetz, "Justification by Deed: The Conclusion of Sanhedrin-Makkot and Paul's Rejection of Law," *Hebrew Union College Annual* 76 (2005): 133–87. On this scholarly assumption, see the helpful discussion in Schremer, *Brothers Estranged,* 107–17.

66. Indeed, Neusner ("Map without Territory," 117) raises the possibility that the sacrificial orders of the Mishnah constitute an anti-Christian polemic, but notes that there is no evidence whatsoever for the early rabbis' familiarity with Christian ideas.

context in order to account for the rabbinic understanding and presentation of sacrifice: those could have evolved organically as a result of engagement with theological and philosophical questions pertaining to the practice of sacrifice, in the same way that various different answers to the same questions evolved among other circles. To acknowledge the rabbis' acumen as intellectuals and as religious thinkers means not to perceive their innovations automatically as a "response" to some ominous reality that was imposed upon them, but instead to consider rabbinic concepts and ideas alongside other ancient and late ancient works that engage questions on humanity, divinity, belief, and practice.

While I do not think that the early rabbis generated the notion that sacrifices are not fundamentally different from other ritual and legal obligations specifically in order to diminish their centrality in Jewish life, I do believe that this notion facilitated and enabled such diminishment in the long run. This is of course not to say that if it were not for the rabbis' interpretive revolution (which would have been consequential and comprehensible only to a very small learned elite anyway) sacrifice would have remained the highest priority for late ancient Jews. Clearly many different factors, both conceptual and pragmatic, eventually pushed sacrifice to the periphery of what people perceived as a complete Jewish life. But I submit that we cannot settle for the paradigm of "substitutes" if we wish to account for the early rabbis' part in this process of marginalization. Tannaitic sacrificial legislation itself should be seen as creating (or at least, presenting) a paradigm shift in the way sacrifices were understood and approached, and without this paradigm shift later rabbinic statements to the effect of "practice X is just as good as sacrifice" cannot be properly understood.

SACRIFICES AND PUBLIC/PRIVATE RELIGION

So far my discussion of the rabbinic theory of sacrifice, as it emerges from the early rabbis' legal-ritual creation, has treated sacrifice primarily as a *problem*: like other elite authors of the ancient Mediterranean, I have argued, the rabbis were uncomfortable with the anthropomorphic implications of sacrificial practices and sought to dispel those implications without dismissing the importance of the practice itself. But throughout this book I have attempted to show that on a discursive level, sacrifice also provided the rabbis with an *opportunity*. Sacrifices and cultic practices, because of their traditional standing as pillars of Israelite-Judean worship, functioned for the rabbis as sites through which idealized modes of religiosity could be constructed and promulgated. In chapter 5 I argued that the mishnaic depiction of daily sacrificial worship in the temple, as performed by the priests with great alacrity and without discriminating between different aspects of the work, serves to paint an idyllic picture of ritual commitment, competence, and cooperation. In what follows, I would like to focus on the rabbis' discussions of congregational sacrifices as discursive opportunities to put forth a particular social and religious vision. Here too, I suggest, we will gain a better understanding of the rabbinic sacrificial project by putting it in a dialogue with other contemporaneous approaches to sacrifice, and will subsequently be able to establish a more complex picture of "the end of sacrifice" as a defining feature of late antiquity.

As I showed in chapters 3 and 4, the rabbis put much effort into constructing congregational sacrifices as settings in which solidarity, egalitarianism, and harmony among the people of Israel are manifested. In particular, their insistence that congregational offerings can be provided only through public funds and not through individual contributions establishes congregational offerings as emblems of the oneness of the people. The half-shekel tribute to the temple means that each and every member of the community actively participates in congregational sacrifices, and in the rabbis' literary imagination these sacrifices are also witnessed and observed by "the people." Moreover, the rabbinic elevation of congregational sacrifices above individual sacrifices, and the palpable tendency to "collectivize" offerings that could otherwise be construed as individual, put forth congregational sacrifices as constitutive of Jewishness (or "Israel-ness") itself. In other words, congregational sacrifices serve for the rabbis as a unifying mechanism through which different individuals, families, and local communities emerge as one polity.

I briefly suggested that the rabbis' championing of congregational offerings as instruments of unification and solidification of group identity resonates with the heightened importance of sacrifices in the formation of kinship and community throughout the Graeco-Roman world. Here I wish to be more specific, and to propose that the religious vision that the rabbis construct through their treatment of congregational sacrifices can be understood specifically against a Roman imperial background—and perhaps even distinctly against the Roman imperial background of the turn of the third century C.E.

As Clifford Ando has shown, imperial authorities in Rome made concerted efforts, from an early stage, to promulgate and spread various traditional cults throughout the empire in an attempt to create a sense of religious unity across the ethnically and culturally diverse regions of the empire. However, for as long as these attempts were made primarily in the form of transportation of cultic objects, they were not very successful. The one cult that became remarkably successful in spreading throughout the empire and effectively created something akin to "a religion of the empire" was the cult of the empire itself, namely, the celebration of the imperial *gens,* expressed primarily in the habit of sacrificing for the emperor's well-being.[67] It was the imperial cult that became most prevalent in the provinces,

---

67. Clifford Ando, *The Matter of the Gods: Religion and the Roman Empire* (Berkeley and Los Angeles: University of California Press, 2008), 95–119.

notably through the presence of the Roman army,[68] and that had the most lasting influence on the way local communities understood their relation to the empire at large.[69] James Rives has observed that the custom of sacrificing for the emperor's well-being was a mechanism through which the entire empire could be seen as operating as one political entity, especially because—as I mentioned at the beginning of this conclusion—sacrifice was a mode of practice that most communities in the empire were engaged in anyway.[70]

The first half of the third century C.E., a time of political unrest and financial crisis throughout the empire, was a turning point in the attempt to generate a unified Roman Empire, and to create a sense of imperial identity that would supersede local and regional identities. The *Constitutio Antoniana* of 212 C.E., an edict of the emperor Caracalla granting citizenship to all free-born denizens of the Roman Empire, may have been driven by an urgent need to increase tax revenue, but it nonetheless served also to foster a sense of imperial loyalty.[71] Thirty-seven years later, in 249 C.E., the newly coronated emperor Trajan Decius issued an edict requiring every citizen in the empire to perform a sacrifice in the presence of an imperial official, and to sign a certificate attesting that he had always been in the habit of making sacrifices and planned to continue doing so. Decius's edict does not seem to have pertained to any specific god or gods, nor does it seem to be associated with any particular date or event.[72] Rather, citizens were instructed to show that they were partaking in sacrifice qua sacrifice, as a form of worship. As Rives has convincingly explained, Decius's intention was to use sacrifice as a unifying mechanism in creating, as it were, a shared imperial religion.[73] His edict used sacrifices as manifestations of imperial citizenship and imperial loyalty in two ways: first, in the "content" of the sacrifices, which were offered explicitly for the sake of the well-being of the empire and emperor, and second, and perhaps more interestingly, in the sacrificial form itself: his edict reflects the view that to engage in sacrifice is to practice religion in the imperial way.

---

68. See Herz, "Sacrifice and Sacrificial Ceremonies."

69. See Simon R. F. Price, *Ritual and Power: The Roman Imperial Cult in Asia Minor* (New York: Cambridge University Press, 1984); Heyman, *The Power of Sacrifice*, 45–93; Monika Bernett, "Roman Imperial Cult in the Galilee: Structures, Functions, and Dynamics," in *Religion, Ethnicity, and Identity in Ancient Galilee*, ed. Jürgen Zangenberg, Harold W. Attridge, and Dale B. Martin (Tübingen: Mohr Siebeck, 2007), 337–56; Jeffrey Brodd and Jonathan L. Reed, eds., *Rome and Religion: A Cross-Disciplinary Dialogue on the Imperial Cult* (Atlanta: Society of Biblical Literature, 2011).

70. Rives, "Animal Sacrifice and Political Identity," 108–9.

71. See Hayim Lapin, *Rabbis as Romans: The Rabbinic Movement in Palestine, 100–400 C.E.* (New York: Oxford University Press, 2012), 25–37.

72. See David Potter, *The Roman Empire at Bay, AD 180–385* (New York: Routledge, 2004), 237–42.

73. Rives, "The Decree of Decius."

Although the Mishnah, the main Tannaitic text that develops the theme of congregational offerings keenly and systematically, presumably predates Decius's edict by a few decades, I have no doubt that the conceptual frameworks that identify the power of shared sacrificial practice as a unifying political mechanism were already prevalent when the Mishnah was formed. Accordingly, I suggest that the sacrificial vision that the Mishnah constructs is in essence an *imperial* sacrificial vision. As I have shown, the rabbis imagine the temple as its own "state," as a centralized locus of power that through a well-oiled bureaucratic machine governs not only itself, and not only the city of Jerusalem, but in a sense the Jewish world as a whole.[74] What sustains the temple in this idealized picture is an elaborate system of taxation for the purpose of sacrifice that extends to every corner of the world. Like the Roman Empire of the day, the sacrificial empire of the rabbis has a civic center (Jerusalem), a periphery (the outskirts of Jerusalem), and faraway provinces (such as Egypt, Asia Minor, Babylonia, etc.).[75] This empire relies for its survival not on military force but for the most part on the goodwill of the citizens, but there are also mechanisms of coercion and retribution for those who fail to demonstrate the appropriate goodwill. Within this rabbinic imperial vision, as in imperial Rome, participation in the sacrificial cult is a marker of citizenship, a marker of loyalty, and a marker of identity. In short, I propose that the rabbis absorbed the Roman notion of public sacrifice as a manifestation of civil allegiance and applied an idealized version of it to a Jewish setting. As they did in various other junctures in Tannaitic literature, the rabbis utilized a Roman model specifically in order to establish a vision that *rejects* (or forcefully denies) Roman rule: in the cogent words of Natalie Dohrmann, "Rabbinic theology draws on Roman imperial logics of self, justice, power, communication, and order—the raw materials from which it constructs a resistant counter nomos."[76]

The rabbinic emphasis on the civilizing power of congregational sacrifices, and on their importance both as manifestations and as facilitators of political and social unity, serves as another indication that the practical irrelevance of the temple cult to the everyday lives of the rabbis did not in any way make this cult marginal to their discourse. The centrality of sacrifice in Tannaitic works is not only the result of an antiquated commitment to the themes addressed in the Pentateuch: it also reflects, at least in part, the fact that the early rabbis lived in a world in which sacrifices played critical social, political, and religious roles. The building blocks of which the rabbinic sacrificial system is made are fundamentally biblical,

74. The elaborate bureaucracy of the temple is described especially colorfully in M. Sheqalim, chapters 1–5.

75. See M. Sheqalim 3.4.

76. Natalie Dohrmann, "Can 'Law' Be Private? The Mixed Message of Rabbinic Oral Law," in *Public and Private in Ancient Mediterranean Law and Religion,* ed. Clifford Ando and Jörg Rüpke (Berlin: de Gruyter, 2015), 207.

and as Naphtali Meshel has shown, the rabbis remain faithful to the priestly nomenclature and grammar of sacrifices,[77] but the conceptual and ideological edifices that give these building blocks theological and political meaning are unmistakably rabbinic. We are thus better positioned to understand these ideological edifices when setting them against the early rabbis' own time and place, namely, Roman Palestine of the first centuries of the Common Era.

Furthermore, I suggest that understanding the rabbinic sacrificial vision as an attempt to create an imperial-like religion through means of imagination and interpretation perhaps helps shed light on the Tannaitic legislative project more broadly. Here I follow in the footsteps of Karl Noethlichs, who identified the Roman efforts to form a religion of the empire, which reached a transformative turning point with Decius's edict, as an effective elision of the distinction between *sacra publica* and *sacra privata*.[78] This distinction, which was so elemental to Roman religious life,[79] traditionally pertained to the relative independence of local or familial forms of worship from cults performed at the state or city level: but the Roman requirement that all denizens throughout the empire sacrifice to *their own gods* for the sake of the emperor dismantled this dichotomy. The imperial cult infiltrated local (and with Decius, also familial and personal) forms of worship with a "universalizing element," thus making the public private and the private public. This elision of the public/private distinction in the course of creating a unifying imperial religion set in motion the process that would eventually reach a new turning point with Constantine and the subsequent adoption of Christianity as the religion of the empire in the fourth century. In Christian imperial legislation, as Noethlichs notes, the scope of possibility for individual and local variations in the practice of religion became exceedingly narrow.[80]

The rabbinic sacrificial vision presents an interesting counterpart to the picture portrayed by Noethlichs. On the one hand, the distinction public/private (or congregational/individual, in rabbinic terms) is a pervasive one in the rabbis' taxonomy, and plays a key role in categorizing and ordering the sacrificial system—as is the case in Roman discussions of religion and cult. But on the other hand, when one begins to examine up close how the categories congregational/individual actually play out in rabbinic texts, it becomes evident that at multiple points the distinction simply collapses. Sacrifices that could be construed as private are transformed into collective ones (whether formally or through legislative features), and

---

77. Meshel, *The "Grammar" of Sacrifice.*

78. Karl Leo Noethlichs, "The Legal Framework of Religious Identity in the Roman Empire," in *Group Identity and Religious Individuality in Late Antiquity,* ed. Éric Rebillard and Jörg Rüpke (Washington, DC: Catholic University of America Press, 2015), 13–27.

79. See Ando, *The Matter of the Gods,* 59–61.

80. Noethlichs, "The Legal Framework," 25.

we also identify a strong rhetoric that presents congregational offerings as filling the role of individual offerings such that the former effectively subsume the latter. The result is a picture in which the private is often public and the public is private: for example, a family that eats a feast offering in Jerusalem fulfills an obligation of the entire people, and congregational reparation offerings can atone for the misdeeds of a specific individual.

I therefore wish to offer a corrective to Stroumsa's claim that the postdestruction legislative project of the rabbis should be understood in terms of individuation, interiorization, and privatization of religion.[81] There is certainly truth to Stroumsa's claim that the rabbis dedicate much time and effort to developing modes of piety available to individuals as such, and that can be practiced in any place and in solitude. Yet if we take the rabbinic sacrificial corpus into account—and as I have stressed, this corpus does constitute about a quarter of Tannaitic literature—we could argue exactly the opposite, and identify a process of collectivization, exteriorization, and publification of religion. While different parts of the rabbinic corpus can of course be ideologically at odds with each other (and they often are), and it is certainly possible for the rabbis to apply different frameworks to the temple cult than they do to the home or the marketplace, in this case I think the incongruity is only surface deep: in truth what the rabbis do throughout their legislation is eradicate the distinction between private and public altogether. Rabbinic praying or eating or retrieving a lost object or hiring a worker or immersing in water to rid oneself of impurity—all are constructed in rabbinic literature as ways in which one performs one's pertinence to the collective. The idealized subject of rabbinic literature operates, even in the bedroom or in the toilet, as an instantiation of the corporate entity "Israel,"[82] and this subject is always placed under the implied gaze of this corporate entity, which assesses his or her actions. No place is hidden, and no action is silent or secret: the fundamental premise of rabbinic *halakhah* is that the private is public and the public is private, the internal external and the external internal.

One dimension of the dismantling of the public/private distinction in rabbinic *halakhah* is indeed the rabbis' claim on the domestic sphere, and more importantly on one's own body, which frames even the most mundane of daily activities as performances of collective identity. As Charlotte Fonrobert has shown, even an intimate experience like menstruation becomes a site through which a woman actively identifies herself as "a daughter of Israel."[83] But another dimension of this

---

81. Stroumsa, *The End of Sacrifice*, 67, 69.

82. On notions of corporate identity in rabbinic Judaism, see Sacha Stern, *Jewish Identity in Early Rabbinic Writings* (Leiden: Brill, 1994), mainly 10–13; see also Fonrobert, "Humanity Was Created as an Individual."

83. Charlotte Elisheva Fonrobert, "When Women Walk in the Way of Their Fathers: On Gendering the Rabbinic Claim for Authority," *Journal of the History of Sexuality* 10, nos. 3–4 (2001): 398–415.

dismantling is the claim that the rabbis make on the public sphere: the street, the city, the land, and in an implied way even on an "empire" of sorts. Those spaces, too, are imagined as sites inscribed with Jewish (rabbinic) law, in which Jewish (rabbinic) identity is performed. Here I again refer to Dohrmann's insightful observations on the ways in which rabbinic oral law mimics Roman written law. According to Dohrmann, because rabbinic legislation claims to cover every aspect of everyday life, this legislation appropriates the public sphere, that is, Roman urban space, and overwrites it with its own nomic script. "The rabbis inhabit and regulate a parallel city, their private public," writes Dohrmann,[84] reminding us of what we often tend to forget: that Tannaitic texts rarely make any substantial distinction between real and imaginary, past and present, practical and theoretical. The Tannaitic project is one of creating a world fully defined and controlled by rabbinic law, "a parallel city," and in this city, the public and private are of the same fabric, and there exists full continuity between them.

The notable resonance between rabbinic notions of the political and social power of sacrifice, on the one hand, and similar ideas in the Roman imperial landscape as well as in early Christian discourse, on the other hand, can thus productively lead us to look at the greater arc of the religious transformations of late antiquity from a different angle. Instead of approaching this transformation through a lens of "privatization," we could develop a paradigm for speaking of the erasure of the distinction between private and public, which is traceable across different religious communities throughout the Mediterranean region. Moreover, instead of identifying sacrifice as the "other" against which the transformations are defined, as the placeholder of the increasingly obsolete past that is rapidly being replaced with alternatives, we could acknowledge the critically important role that sacrifice plays, whether practically or discursively, in generating those very transformations, and more broadly in the making of late antiquity as a discrete era. As I hope to have shown, a conversation on religion in late antiquity cannot be complete without accounting for rabbinic legal and ritual texts, and often those texts hold an exciting potential for redirecting this conversation.

At the end of the day, the strong tendency to view the early rabbis as establishing a nonsacrificial version of Judaism derives from a teleological view of history: if we see today that self-proclaimed rabbinic Jews go through life without engaging in sacrifices and do not seem to feel that anything is missing, then it seems natural to surmise that it is the rabbis of the first centuries who recalibrated Judaism to fit a world without sacrifices. The rabbis who immediately postdated the temple, it is commonly assumed, sought to fill an enormous void, and did such a good job at it

84. Dohrmann, "Can 'Law' be Private?" 208.

that the void is no longer even recognized. What I have ventured to show through-out this book is that the early rabbis did not actually treat the sacrificial cult as a void at all, nor did they seek to fill a void by "replacing" sacrifices: they presented the sacrificial cult as an integral part of a greater system of Torah-guided life, which was neither qualitatively different from nor superseded by other forms of practice. The rhetoric of "filling the void" relies primarily on a handful of later rab-binic passages, and on historians' own projections on the rabbis' motivations and concerns: but it fails to describe how the Mishnah, Tosefta, and Tannaitic mid-rashim approach this topic.

The Tannaitic sacrificial corpus is not an aberration within the greater corpus of Tannaitic literature. It is not an archive into which the rabbis filed old docu-ments for posterity's sake while dedicating their creative efforts to other, more relevant aspects of Jewish life. It is also not a closed room into which the rabbis step every now and then to stretch some unused intellectual muscles, toying with scriptural concepts and hermeneutical principles for the sake of scholastic chal-lenge. Rather, Tannaitic sacrificial texts are part and parcel of an all-encompassing enterprise of rabbinic world-making, and they promulgate—through their own distinct ritual language and sets of concepts—ideas and ideals that are pertinent to the rabbis' visions of self, society, practice, and belief. Sacrifices, I have argued, play an important role in rabbinic modes of religiosity, and their role is by no means restricted to that of not-existing, or of being that against which everything else is defined. Reclaiming the integrity of Tannaitic texts as self-standing, sophisticated, and intellectually rich compilations rather than as mere precursors or substrates of what we view today as halakhic Judaism bears the reward of allowing us to rethink some deep-seated notions of the history of Judaism in particular, and of the evolu-tion of religious ideas and practices in general.

Abusch, Tzvi. "Sacrifice in Mesopotamia." In *Sacrifice in Religious Experience,* edited by Albert I. Baumgarten, 39–48. Leiden: Brill, 2002.

Albeck, Hanoch. "The Book of Jubilees and the Halakhah." *Jewish Studies* 45 (2008): 3–48.

———. *The Six Orders of the Mishnah.* [In Hebrew.] Jerusalem: Bialik Institute, 1952.

Alexander, Elizabeth Shanks. *Transmitting Mishnah: The Shaping Influence of Oral Tradition.* New York: Cambridge University Press, 2006.

Alon, Gedalyahu. "Par'irtin: The History of the High Priesthood at the End of the Second Temple Period." [In Hebrew.] *Tarbitz* 13 (1952): 1–24.

Altman, Peter. *Festive Meals in Ancient Israel: Deuteronomy's Identity Politics in Their Ancient Near Eastern Context.* Berlin: Walter de Gruyter, 2011.

Anderson, Gary A. *Sacrifices and Offerings in Ancient Israel: Studies in Their Social and Political Importance.* Atlanta: Scholars Press, 1988.

———. *Sin: A History.* New Haven: Yale University Press, 2009.

Ando, Clifford. *The Matter of the Gods: Religion and the Roman Empire.* Berkeley and Los Angeles: University of California Press, 2008.

Andrade, Nathanael J. *Syrian Identity in the Graeco-Roman World.* Cambridge: Cambridge University Press, 2013.

Attridge, Harold W. *Hebrews: A Commentary on the Epistle to the Hebrews (Hermeneia: A Critical and Historical Commentary on the Bible).* Minneapolis: Augsburg Press, 1989.

Balberg, Mira. "The Animalistic Gullet and the Godlike Soul: Reframing Sacrifice in Midrash Leviticus Rabbah." *AJS Review* 38, no. 2 (2014): 221–47.

———. *Purity, Body, and Self in Early Rabbinic Literature.* Berkeley and Los Angeles: University of California Press, 2014.

———. "Rabbinic Authority, Medical Rhetoric, and Body Hermeneutics in Mishnah Nega'im." *AJS Review* 35, no. 2 (2011): 323–46.

Bar-Ilan, Meir. "Are Tamid and Middot Polemical Tractates?" [In Hebrew.] *Sidra* 5 (1989): 27–40.

Bataille, Georges. *Theory of Religion.* Translated by Robert Hurley. New York: Zone Books, 1992.

Beard, Mary, John North, and Simon R. F. Price. *Religions of Rome.* 2 vols. Cambridge: Cambridge University Press, 1998.

Be'er, Haim. *The Time of Trimming.* [In Hebrew.] Tel-Aviv: Am Oved, 1987.

Beerden, Kim. *Worlds Full of Signs: Ancient Greek Divination in Context.* Leiden, Brill, 2013.

Berger, Michael. *Rabbinic Authority.* New York: Oxford University Press, 1998.

Berkowitz, Beth A. *Execution and Invention: Death Penalty Discourse in Early Rabbinic and Christian Cultures.* New York: Oxford University Press, 2006.

Bernett, Monika. "Roman Imperial Cult in the Galilee: Structures, Functions, and Dynamics." In *Religion, Ethnicity, and Identity in Ancient Galilee,* edited by Jürgen Zangenberg, Harold W. Attridge, and Dale B. Martin, 337–56. Tübingen: Mohr Siebeck, 2007.

Biale, David. *Blood and Belief: The Circulation of a Symbol between Jews and Christians.* Berkeley and Los Angeles: University of California Press, 2007.

Bickerman, Elias J. *Jews in the Greek Age.* Cambridge, MA: Harvard University Press, 1988.

Bokser, Baruch. *The Origins of the Seder.* Berkeley and Los Angeles: University of California Press, 1984.

———. "Rabbinic Responses to Catastrophe." *Proceedings of the American Academy for Jewish Research* 50 (1983): 37–61.

Boustan, Ra'anan S., and Annette Yoshiko Reed. "Blood and Atonement in the Pseudo-Clementines and *The Story of the Ten Martyrs:* The Problem of Selection in the Study of Ancient Judaism and Christianity." *Henoch* 30, no. 2 (2008): 333–64.

———. "Introduction: Blood and the Boundaries of Jewish and Christian Identities in Late Antiquity." *Henoch* 30, no. 2 (2008): 7–20.

Boyarin, Daniel. *Border Lines: The Partition of Judaeo-Christianity.* Philadelphia: University of Pennsylvania Press, 2004.

———. *Dying for God: Martyrdom and the Making of Judaism and Christianity.* Stanford: Stanford University Press, 1999.

Bradbury, Scott. "Julian's Pagan Revival and the Decline of Blood Sacrifice." *Phoenix* 49, no. 4 (1995): 331–56.

Branham, Joan R. "Mapping Sacrifice on Bodies and Spaces in Late-Antique Judaism and Early Christianity." In *Architecture of the Sacred: Space, Ritual, and Experience from Classical Greece to Byzantium,* edited by Bonna D. Wescoat and Robert G. Ousterhout, 201–30. New York: Cambridge University Press, 2012.

Bremmer, Jan N. *Greek Religion.* Cambridge: Cambridge University Press, 1999.

Breuer, Yohanan. "Perfect and Participle in Descriptions of Ritual in the Mishnah." [In Hebrew.] *Tarbitz* 56 (1987): 299–326.

Brodd, Jeffrey, and Jonathan L. Reed, eds. *Rome and Religion: A Cross-Disciplinary Dialogue on the Imperial Cult.* Atlanta: Society of Biblical Literature, 2011.

Brown, James R. *Temple and Sacrifice in Rabbinic Judaism.* Evanston, IL: Seabury Theological Seminary, 1963.

Buc, Philippe. *The Dangers of Ritual: Between Early Medieval Texts and Social Scientific Theory.* Princeton: Princeton University Press, 2001.

Büchler, Adolf. *Die Priester und der Cultus im letzten Jahrzehnt des Tempelbestandes.* Vienna: Israel-Theol. Lehranstalt, 1895.

Burkert, Walter. *Homo Necans: The Anthropology of Ancient Greek Sacrificial Ritual and Myth.* Translated by Peter Bing. Berkeley and Los Angeles: University of California Press, 1983.

Bynum, Caroline Walker. *Wonderful Blood: Theology and Practice in Late Medieval Northern Germany and Beyond.* Philadelphia: University of Pennsylvania Press, 2007.

Cartledge, Tony W. *Vows in the Hebrew Bible and the Ancient Near East.* Sheffield: JSOT Press, 1992.

Charlesworth, James H., ed. *The Old Testament Pseudepigrapha.* 2 vols. Peabody, MA: Hendrickson, 1983.

Chavel, Simeon. "A Kingdom of Priests and Its Earthen Altars in Exodus 19–24." *Vetus Testamentum* 65 (2015): 160–222.

———. *Oracular Law and Priestly Historiography in the Torah.* Tübingen: Mohr Siebeck, 2014.

Childs, Brevard S. *The Book of Exodus.* Old Testament Library. Louisville, KY: Westminster John Knox Press, [1974] 2004.

Chilton, Bruce. *The Temple of Jesus: His Sacrificial Program within a Cultural History of Sacrifice.* University Park: Pennsylvania State University Press, 1992.

Clements, Ronald E. *God and Temple.* Philadelphia: Fortress Press, 1965.

Clements, Ruth Anne. "70 CE after 135 CE—The Making of a Watershed?" In *Was 70 CE a Watershed in Jewish History? On Jews and Judaism before and after the Destruction of the Second Temple,* edited by Daniel R. Schwartz, Zeev Weiss, and Ruth A. Clements, 517–36. Leiden: Brill, 2012.

———. "Peri Pascha: Passover and the Displacement of Jewish Interpretation within Origen's Exegesis." PhD diss., Harvard University, 1997.

Cohen, Shaye J. D. "The Temple and the Synagogue." In *The Temple in Antiquity: Ancient Records and Modern Perspectives,* edited by Truman G. Madsen, 151–74. Provo, UT: Religious Studies Center, Brigham Young University, 1984.

Cohen, Stuart A. *The Three Crowns: Structures of Communal Politics in Early Rabbinic Jewry.* Cambridge: Cambridge University Press, 1990.

Cohn, Naftali S. *The Memory of the Temple and the Making of the Rabbis.* Philadelphia: University of Pennsylvania Press, 2012.

———. "The Ritual Narrative Genre in the Mishnah: The Invention of the Rabbinic Past in the Representation of Temple Ritual." PhD diss., University of Pennsylvania, 2008.

Collins, John J. *Between Athens and Jerusalem: Jewish Identity in the Hellenistic Diaspora.* Grand Rapids: Wm. B. Eerdmans, 2000.

Daly, Robert. *Christian Sacrifice: The Judeo-Christian Background before Origen.* Washington, DC: Catholic University of America Press, 1978.

Daube, David. "Rabbinic Methods of Interpretation and Hellenistic Rhetoric." *Hebrew Union College Annual* 22 (1949): 239–64.

De Jong, Albert. "Animal Sacrifice in Ancient Zoroastrianism: A Ritual and Its Interpretations." In *Sacrifice in Religious Experience,* edited by Albert I. Baumgarten, 127–48. Leiden: Brill, 2002.

Detienne, Marcel, and Jean-Pierre. Vernant, eds. *The Cuisine of Sacrifice among the Greeks.* Translated by Paula Wissing. Chicago: University of Chicago Press, 1989.

De Vaux, Roland. *Studies in Old Testament Sacrifice.* Cardiff: University of Wales Press, 1964.

Dio Cassius. *Roman History.* Translated by Earnest Cary. Loeb Classical Library. Cambridge, MA: Harvard University Press, 1925.

Dio Chrysostom. *Discourses 1–11.* Translated by James W. Cohoon. Loeb Classical Library. Cambridge, MA: Harvard University Press, 1932.

Dohrmann, Natalie. "Can 'Law' Be Private? The Mixed Message of Rabbinic Oral Law." In *Public and Private in Ancient Mediterranean Law and Religion,* edited by Clifford Ando and Jörg Rüpke, 187–216. Berlin: Walter de Gruyter, 2015.

Douglas, Mary. *Leviticus as Literature.* Oxford: Oxford University Press, 1999.

Drawnel, Henryk. *An Aramaic Wisdom Text from Qumran: A New Interpretation of the Levi Document.* Leiden: Brill, 2004.

Dunnill, John. *Covenant and Sacrifice in the Letter to the Hebrews.* New York: Cambridge University Press, 1992.

Eberhart, Christian A. "A Neglected Feature of Sacrifice in the Hebrew Bible: Remarks on the Burning Rite on the Altar." *Harvard Theological Review* 97, no. 4 (2004): 485–93.

———. "Sacrifice? Holy Smokes! Reflections on Cult Terminology for Understanding Sacrifice in the Hebrew Bible." In *Ritual and Metaphor: Sacrifice in the Bible,* edited by Christian A. Eberhart, 17–32. Atlanta: Society of Biblical Literature Press, 2011.

Eilberg-Schwartz, Howard. *The Human Will in Judaism: The Mishnah's Philosophy of Intention.* Atlanta: Scholars Press, 1986.

———. *The Savage in Judaism: An Anthropology of Israelite Religion and Ancient Judaism.* Bloomington: Indiana University Press, 1990.

Eliade, Mircea. *The Myth of Eternal Return, or, Cosmos and History.* Princeton: Princeton University Press, 1971.

Elior, Rachel. *Memory and Oblivion: The Secret of the Dead Sea Scrolls.* [In Hebrew.] Jerusalem: Van Leer Institute and ha-kibbutz ha-me'uhad, 2009.

Elsner, Jaś. "Sacrifice in Late Roman Art." In *Greek and Roman Animal Sacrifice: Ancient Victims, Modern Observers,* edited by Christopher A. Faraone and Fred S. Naiden, 120–63. New York: Cambridge University Press, 2012.

Epictetus. *Enchiridion.* Translated by George Long. Mineola, NY: Dover Books, 2004.

Epstein, Ya'akov N. *Introduction to the Text of the Mishnah.* [In Hebrew.] Jerusalem: Magnes Press, 2000.

———. *Prolegomena to Tannaitic Literature: Mishnah, Tosefta, and Halakhic Midrashim.* [In Hebrew.] Jerusalem: Magnes Press, 1959.

Epstein, Ya'akov N., and Ezra Z. Melamed, eds. *Mekhilta de-Rabbi Shimon ben Yohai.* Jerusalem: Sha'are Rahamim, 1955.

Erder, Yoram. "Qumranic Vestiges in Two Halakhot of the Karaite Benjamin Nahawandi on the Issue of Nonsacral Meat." [In Hebrew.] *Zion* 63, no. 1 (1998): 5–38.

———. "Second Temple Period Sectarian Polemic Concerning the Half-Shekel Commandment in Light of Early Karaite Halakhah." [In Hebrew.] *Meghillot* 8–9 (2010): 3–28.

Faraone, Christopher A., and Fred S. Naiden. "Introduction." In *Greek and Roman Animal Sacrifice: Ancient Victims, Modern Observers,* edited by Christopher A. Faraone and Fred S. Naiden, 1–10. New York: Cambridge University Press, 2012.

Fearghail, Fearghas O. "Sir 50, 5–21: Yom Kippur or the Daily Whole Offering?" *Biblica* 69 (1978): 301–16.

Festus, Sextus Pompeius. *De verborum significatu quae supersunt cum Pauli epitome.* Edited by Wallace M. Lindsay. Stuttgart: B. G. Teubner, 1997.

Fine, Steven. *Art and Judaism in the Greco-Roman World: Toward a New Jewish Archeology.* New York: Cambridge University Press, 2005.

Finkelstein, Aryay Bennet. "Julian among Jews, Christians, and 'Hellenes' in Antioch: Jewish Practice as a Guide to 'Hellenes' and a Goad to Christians." PhD diss., Harvard University, 2011.

Finkelstein, Louis, ed. *Sifra on Leviticus.* New York: Jewish Theological Seminary, 1990.

———. *Sifre on Deuteronomy.* New York: Jewish Theological Seminary, 1969.

Fishbane, Michael. *The Exegetical Imagination: On Jewish Thought and Theology.* Cambridge, MA: Harvard University Press, 1998.

Flavius, Josephus. *The Works of Josephus.* Translated by William Whiston. Peabody, MA: Hendrickson Publishers, 1980.

Flusser, David. "The Half-Shekel in the Gospel and among the Judean Desert Sect." [In Hebrew.] *Tarbitz* 31, no. 2 (1962): 150–56.

Fonrobert, Charlotte Elisheva. "'Humanity Was Created as an Individual': Synechdocal Individuality in the Mishnah as a Jewish Response to Romanization." In *The Individual in the Religions of the Ancient Mediterranean,* edited by Jörg Rüpke, 489–521. New York: Oxford University Press, 2013.

———. "When Women Walk in the Way of Their Fathers: On Gendering the Rabbinic Claim for Authority." *Journal of the History of Sexuality* 10.3–4 (2001): 398–415.

Frankfurter, David. "Egyptian Religion and the Problem of the Category 'Sacrifice.'" In *Ancient Mediterranean Sacrifice,* edited by Jennifer Wright Knust and Zsuzsanna Várhelyi, 75–93. New York: Oxford University Press, 2011.

Fredriksen, Paula. "Judaizing the Nations: The Ritual Demands of Paul's Gospel." *New Testament Studies* 56 (2010): 232–52.

Friedman, Shamma. "Anthropomorphism and Its Eradication." In *Iconoclasm and Iconoclash: Struggle for Religious Identity,* edited by Willem J. van Asselt, Paul van Geest, Daniela Müller, and Theo Salemink, 157–78. Leiden: Brill, 2007.

———. "Mishna-Tosefta Parallels." [In Hebrew.] *Proceedings of the 11th World Congress of Jewish Studies* C.1 (1994): 15–22.

———. "The Primacy of Tosefta to Mishnah in Synoptic Parallels." In *Introducing Tosefta: Textual, Intratextual, and Intertextual Studies,* edited by Harry Fox, Tirzah Meacham, and Diane Kriger, 99–121. Hoboken, NJ: Ktav, 1999.

Gane, Roy. *Cult and Character: Purification Offerings, Day of Atonement, and Theodicy.* Winona Lake, IN: Eisenbrauns, 2005.

Gardner, Gregg. "Giving to the Poor in Early Rabbinic Judaism." PhD diss., Princeton University, 2009.

Gesundheit, Shimon. *Three Times a Year: Studies on Festival Legislation in the Pentateuch.* Tübingen: Mohr Siebeck, 2012.

Gilat, Yitzhak. *Studies in the Development of Halakha.* [In Hebrew.] Ramat Gan: Bar Ilan University Press, 2001.

Gilders, William K. "Blood and Covenant: Interpretive Elaboration on Genesis 9.4–6 in the Book of Jubilees." *Journal for the Study of the Pseudepigrapha* 15 (2006): 83–118.

———. *Blood Ritual in the Hebrew Bible: Meaning and Power.* Baltimore: Johns Hopkins University Press, 2004.

———. "Jewish Sacrifice: Its Nature and Function (According to Philo)." In *Ancient Mediterranean Sacrifice,* edited by Jennifer Wright Knust and Zsuzsanna Várhelyi, 94–105. New York: Oxford University Press, 2011.

Gilhus, Ingvild Saelid. *Animals, Gods, and Humans: Changing Attitudes to Animals in Greek, Roman, and Early Christian Ideas.* New York: Routledge, 2006.

Ginzberg, Louis. "Tamid: The Oldest Treatise of the Mishnah." *Journal of Jewish Lore and Philosophy* 1, no. 1 (1919): 33–44.

Girard, René. *Violence and the Sacred.* Translated by Patrick Gregory. Baltimore: Johns Hopkins University Press, 1979.

Glaim, Aaron. "Reciprocity, Sacrifice, and Salvation in Judean Religion at the Turn of the Era." PhD diss., Brown University, 2014.

Goldberg, Abraham. "The Tosefta—Companion to the Mishna." In *The Literature of the Sages,* vol.1, edited by Shmuel Safrai, 283–302. Assen: Van Gorcum, 1987.

———. "Tosefta to Tractate Tamid: A Study of the Problem of the Relation between the Mishnah and the Tosefta." [In Hebrew.] In *The Binyamin De-Fries Memorial Book,* edited by Ezra Zion Melamed, 18–42. Tel Aviv: Tel Aviv University Press, 1969.

Goldenberg, Robert. "The Broken Axis: Rabbinic Judaism and the Fall of Jerusalem." *Journal of the American Academy of Religion* 45 (1977): 869–82.

Goldstein, Naftali. "Worship at the Temple in Jerusalem: Rabbinic Interpretation and Influence." [In Hebrew.] PhD diss., Hebrew University, 1977.

Goodblatt, David. "The Jews of the Land of Israel in the Years 70–135." [In Hebrew.] In *Judea and Rome: The Rebellions of the Jews,* edited by Uriel Rappaport, 155–84. Jerusalem: Am Oved, 1983.

Goodman, Martin. "Nerva, the Fiscus Judaicus, and Jewish Identity." *Journal of Roman Studies* 79 (1989): 40–44.

Graf, Fritz. "One Generation after Burkert and Girard: Where Are the Great Theories?" In *Greek and Roman Animal Sacrifice: Ancient Victims, Modern Observers,* edited by Christopher A. Faraone and Fred S. Naiden, 32–53. New York: Cambridge University Press, 2012.

Grey, Matthew. "Jewish Priests and the Social History of Post-70 Palestine." PhD diss., University of North Carolina, 2011.

Guttmann, Alexander. "The End of the Jewish Sacrificial Cult." *Hebrew Union College Annual* 38 (1967): 137–48.

Halbertal, Moshe. *On Sacrifice.* Princeton: Princeton University Press, 2012.

Halivni, David. *Mekorot u-mesorot Mo'ed.* [In Hebrew.] New York: Jewish Theological Seminary, 1982.

Hallewy, Elimelech E. "The First Controversy." [In Hebrew.] *Trabitz* 28, no. 2 (1959): 154–57.

Halpern-Amaru, Betsy. "The Festivals of Pesah and Massot in the Book of Jubilees." In *Enoch and the Mosaic Torah: The Evidence of Jubilees,* edited by Gabriele Boccaccini and Giovanni Ibba, 309–22. Grand Rapids, MI: W.B. Eerdmans, 2009.

Hammer, Reuven. "What Did They Bless? A Study of Mishnah Tamid 5.1." *Jewish Quarterly Review* 81, nos. 3–4 (1991): 305–24.

Harel, Yehoshafat. "Palestinian Sugyot for Seder Qodashim." [In Hebrew.] PhD diss., Hebrew University, 2004.

Hauptman, Judith. *Rereading the Mishnah: A New Approach to Ancient Jewish Texts.* Tübingen: Mohr Siebeck, 2005.

Hayes, Christine. "Legal Realism and the Fashioning of Sectarians in Jewish Antiquity." In *Sects and Sectarianism in Jewish History,* edited by Sacha Stern, 119–46. Leiden: Brill, 2010.

———. *What's Divine about Divine Law? Early Perspectives.* Princeton: Princeton University Press, 2015.

Heemstra, Marius. *The Fiscus Judaicus and the Parting of the Ways.* Tübingen: Mohr Siebeck, 2010.

Heger, Paul. *The Three Biblical Altar Laws: Developments in the Sacrificial Cult in Practice and Theology.* Berlin: Walter de Gruyter, 1999.

Hendel, Ronald. "Sacrifice as a Cultural System: The Ritual Symbolism of Exodus 24, 3–8." *Zeitschrift für die alttestamentliche Wissenschaft* 101, no. 3 (1989): 366–90.

Henrichs, Albert. "Animal Sacrifice in Greek Tragedy: Ritual, Metaphor, Problematizations." In *Greek and Roman Animal Sacrifice: Ancient Victims, Modern Observers,* edited by Christopher A. Faraone and Fred S. Naiden, 180–94. New York: Cambridge University Press, 2012.

Henshke, David. *Festival Joy in Tannaitic Discourse.* [In Hebrew.] Jerusalem: Magnes Press, 2007.

———. "On the Rabbis' Way in Reconciling Biblical Contradictions." [In Hebrew.] *Sidra* 10 (1994): 39–55.

———. "The Prayer of the Priests and Their Blessing in the Temple: The Early Mishnah and the Teachings of the Late Tanna'im." [In Hebrew.] In *Ke-Tabor be-harim: Studies in Rabbinic Literature in Honor of Joseph Tabory,* edited by Arnon Atzmon and Tzur Shafir, 51–87. Alon Shevut: Tevunot, 2013.

Herz, Peter. "Sacrifice and Sacrificial Ceremonies in the Roman Imperial Army." In *Sacrifice in Religious Experience,* edited by Albert I. Baumgarten, 81–100. Leiden: Brill, 2002.

Heyman, George. *The Power of Sacrifice: Roman and Christian Discourses in Conflict.* Washington, DC: Catholic University of America Press, 2007.

Hezser, Catherine. *The Social Structure of the Rabbinic Movement.* Tübingen: Mohr Siebeck, 1997.

Hieke, Thomas, and Tobias Nicklas, eds. *The Day of Atonement: Its Interpretation in Early Jewish and Christian Traditions.* Leiden: Brill, 2012.

Himmelfarb, Martha. *Between Temple and Torah: Essays on Priests, Scribes, and Visionaries in the Second Temple Period and Beyond.* Tübingen: Mohr Siebeck, 2013.

———. "Earthly Sacrifice and Heavenly Incense: The Law of the Priesthood in *Aramaic Levi* and *Jubilees.*" In *Heavenly Realms and Earthly Realities in Late Antique Religions,* edited by Ra'anan S. Boustan and Annette Yoshiko Reed, 103–22. New York: Cambridge University Press, 2004.

———. "'Found Written in the Book of Moses: Priests in the Era of Torah." In *Was 70 CE a Watershed in Jewish History? On Jews and Judaism before and after the Destruction of the Second Temple,* edited by Daniel R. Schwartz, Zeev Weiss, and Ruth A. Clements, 21–41. Leiden: Brill, 2012.

————. *A Kingdom of Priests: Ancestry and Merit in Ancient Judaism*. Philadelphia: University of Pennsylvania Press, 2006.

Hirschman, Marc. *A Rivalry of Genius: Jewish and Christian Biblical Interpretation in Late Antiquity*. Translated by Batya Stein. Albany: State University of New York Press, 1996.

Hoffmann, David Zwi. *Die erste Mischna und die Controversen der Tannaim*. Berlin, 1882.

Horovitz, Hayim Saul, ed. *Sifre on the Book of Numbers and Sifre Zutta*. 1st ed., Leipzig, 1917. Jerusalem: Shalem Books, 1992.

Horovitz, Hayim Saul, and Israel A. Rabin, eds. *Mekhilta deRabbi Ishmael*. 1st ed., Breslau, 1930. Jerusalem: Shalem Books, 1998.

Hubert, Henri, and Marcel Mauss, *Sacrifice: Its Nature and Functions*. Translated by Wilfred D. Halls. Chicago: University of Chicago Press, 1981.

Humphrey, Caroline, and James Laidlaw. *The Archetypal Actions of Ritual: A Theory of Ritual Illustrated by the Jain Rite of Worship*. New York: Oxford University Press, 1994.

Hurvitz, Avi. *Between Language and Language: The History of Biblical Language in the Second Temple Period*. [In Hebrew.] Jerusalem: Bialik Institute, 1972.

Iamblichus. *On the Mysteries*. Translated by Emma C. Clark, John M. Dillon, and Jackson P. Hershbell. Atlanta: Society of Biblical Literature, 2003.

Jaffee, Martin. "The Taqqanah in Tannaitic Literature: Jurisprudence and the Construction of Rabbinic Memory." *Journal of Jewish Studies* 41, no. 2 (1990): 204–23.

————. *Torah in the Mouth: Writing and Oral Tradition in Palestinian Judaism, 200 BCE–400 CE*. New York: Oxford University Press, 2001.

James, Liz, and Ruth Webb. "To Understand Ultimate Things and Enter Secret Places: Ekphrasis and Art in Byzantium." *Art History* 14, no. 1 (1991): 1–17.

Janes, Dominic. *God and Gold in Late Antiquity*. Cambridge: Cambridge University Press, 1998.

Janzen, David. *The Social Meanings of Sacrifice in the Hebrew Bible: A Study of Four Writings*. Berlin: Walter de Gruyter, 2004.

Japhet, Sara. *I and II Chronicles: A Commentary*. Old Testament Library. Louisville, KY: Westminster John Knox Press, 1993.

Jim, Theodora Suk Fong. *Sharing with the Gods: Aparchai and Dekatai in Ancient Greece*. New York: Oxford University Press, 2014.

Kahana, Menahem. "The Halakhic Midrashim." In *The Literature of the Sages*, vol. 2, edited by Shmuel Safrai, Peter Tomson, and Zeev Safrai, 3–106. Assen: Uitgeverij Van Gorcum, 2006.

Katz, Menachem. "The Stories of Hillel's Appointment as Nasi in the Talmudic Literature: A Foundation Legend of the Jewish Scholars' World." [In Hebrew.] *Sidra* 26 (2011): 81–116.

Klawans, Jonathan. *Purity, Sacrifice, and the Temple: Symbolism and Supersessionism in the Study of Ancient Judaism*. New York: Oxford University Press, 2006.

Knohl, Israel. "Acceptance of Offerings from Gentiles." [in Hebrew.] *Tarbitz* 48, nos. 3–4 (1979): 341–45.

————. "Between Voice and Silence: The Relations between Prayer and Temple Cult." *Journal of Biblical Literature* 115, no. 1 (1996): 17–30.

————. "A Parashah Concerned with Accepting the Kingdom of Heaven." [In Hebrew.] *Tarbitz* 53, no. 1 (1984): 11–31.

————. "Participation of the People in Temple Worship: Second Temple Sectarian Conflict and the Biblical Tradition." [In Hebrew.] *Tarbitz* 60, no. 2 (1991): 139–46.

————. *The Sanctuary of Silence: A Study of the Priestly Strata in the Pentateuch.* [In Hebrew.] Jerusalem: Magnes Press, 1993.

Knohl, Israel, and Shlomo Naeh. "Milu'im and Kippurim." [In Hebrew.] *Tarbitz* 62 (1993): 18–44.

Lake, Kirsopp. *The Apostolic Fathers.* Vol. 1. London: Heinemann, 1912.

Landes, Yitzhak. "Studies in the Development of Birkat ha-Avodah." [In Hebrew.] Master's thesis, Hebrew University, 2015.

Lapin, Hayim. *Rabbis as Romans: The Rabbinic Movement in Palestine, 100–400 C.E.* New York: Oxford University Press, 2012.

Leonhardt, Jutta. *Jewish Worship in Philo of Alexandria.* Tübingen: Mohr Siebeck, 2001.

Levenson, Jon D. *The Death and Resurrection of the Beloved Son: The Transformation of Child Sacrifice in Judaism and Christianity.* New Haven: Yale University Press, 1993.

Levine, Baruch. *In the Presence of the Lord: A Study of Cult and Some Cultic Terms in Ancient Israel.* Leiden: Brill, 1974.

Levinson, Bernard M. *Deuteronomy and the Hermeneutics of Legal Innovation.* New York: Oxford University Press, 1997.

Licht, Haim. "Thodos of Rome and Consumption of Roasted Lambs on the Passover Night." [In Hebrew.] *Tura* 4 (1989): 89–106.

Lieberman, Saul. *Greek in Jewish Palestine/Hellenism in Jewish Palestine.* New York: Jewish Theological Seminary, 1994.

————. *Tosefta ki-peshuta.* 12 vols. New York: Jewish Theological Seminary, 1962.

Lieu, Judith. *Image and Reality: The Jews in the World of the Christians in the Second Century.* New York: T&T Clark, 1996.

Lim, Richard. "Christianization, Secularization, and the Transformation of Public Life." In *Companion to Late Antiquity,* edited by Philip Rousseau, 497–511. Oxford: Wiley-Blackwell, 2012.

Liver, Jacob. "The Edict of the Half-Shekel." [In Hebrew.] In *The Yehezkel Kaufman Jubilee Volume,* edited by Menahem Haran, 54–67. Jerusalem: Magnes Press, 1961.

————. "The Half-Shekel in Scrolls of the Judean Desert Sect." [In Hebrew.] *Tarbitz* 31, no. 1 (1962): 18–22.

Lorberbaum, Yair. "Anthropomorphisms in Early Rabbinic Literature: Maimonides and Modern Scholarship." In *Traditions of Maimonideanism,* edited by Carlos Fraenkel, 313–53. Leiden: Brill, 2009.

————. *Disempowered King: Monarchy in Classical Jewish Literature.* New York: Continuum Books, 2011.

Lott, J. Bert. *The Neighborhoods of Augustan Rome.* New York: Cambridge University Press, 2004.

Maclean, Jennifer K. Berenson. "Barabbas, the Scapegoat Ritual, and the Development of the Passion Narrative." *Harvard Theological Review* 100, no. 3 (2007): 309–34.

Mandell, Sara. "Who Paid the Temple Tax When the Jews Were under Roman Rule?" *Harvard Theological Review* 77, no. 2 (1984): 223–32.

Marmorstein, Arthur. "Judaism and Christianity in the Middle of the Third Century." In *Studies in Jewish Theology* by A. Marmorstein, edited by Joseph Rabbinowitz and Mayer S. Lew, 77–92. New York: Oxford University Press, 1950.

McClymond, Kathryn. *Beyond Sacred Violence: A Comparative Study of Sacrifice.* Baltimore: Johns Hopkins University Press, 2008.

———. "Don't Cry over Spilled Blood." In *Ancient Mediterranean Sacrifice*, edited by Jennifer Wright Knust and Zsuzsanna Várhelyi, 235–50. New York: Oxford University Press, 2011.

McGowan, Andrew B. *Ascetic Eucharists: Food and Drink in Early Christian Ritual Meals.* New York: Oxford University Press, 1999.

———. "Rehashing the Leftovers of Idols: Cyprian and Early Christian Constructions of Sacrifice." In *Religious Competition in the Third Century CE: Jews, Christians, and the Greco-Roman World*, edited by Jordan D. Rosenblum, Lily Vuong, and Nathaniel DesRosiers, 69–78. Göttingen: Vandehoeck and Ruprecht, 2014.

McKnight, Scot. *Jesus and His Death: Historiography, the Historical Jesus, and Atonement Theory.* Waco: Baylor University Press, 2005.

McLean, Bradley H. "The Absence of Atoning Sacrifice in Paul's Soteriology." *New Testament Studies* 38, no. 4 (1992): 531–53.

Meshel, Naphtali S. "The Form and Function of Biblical Blood Ritual." *Vetus Testamentum* 63 (2013): 1–14.

———. *The "Grammar" of Sacrifice: A Generativistic Study of the Israelite Sacrificial System in the Priestly Writings.* New York: Oxford University Press, 2014.

Milgrom, Jacob. "Israel's Sanctuary: The Priestly 'Picture of Dorian Gray.'" *Revue Biblique* 83 (1976): 390–99.

———. *Leviticus 1–16: A New Translation with Introduction and Commentary.* Anchor Bible 3. New York: Doubleday, 1991.

Miller, Patricia Cox. *The Corporeal Imagination: Signifying the Holy in Late Ancient Christianity.* Philadelphia: University of Pennsylvania Press, 2009.

Mor, Sagit, and Ronen Ahituv. "Sacrifice through Sin: The Place of Values in Respect to Sacrifices in Talmudic Literature." [In Hebrew.] *Molad* 16 (2006): 40–60.

Münz-Manor, Ophir. "Narrating Salvation: Verbal Sacrifice in Late Antique Liturgical Poetry." In *Jews, Christians, and the Roman Empire: The Poetics of Power in Late Antiquity*, edited by Annette Yoshiko Reed and Natalie Dohrmann, 154–66. Philadelphia: University of Pennsylvania Press, 2013.

Naiden, Fred S. "Blessed Are the Parasites." In *Greek and Roman Animal Sacrifice: Ancient Victims, Modern Observers*, edited by Christopher A. Faraone and Fred S. Naiden, 55–83. New York: Cambridge University Press, 2012.

———. *Smoke Signals for the Gods: Ancient Greek Sacrifice from the Archaic to the Roman Periods.* New York: Oxford University Press, 2013.

Nasrallah, Laura. "The Embarrassment of Blood: Early Christians and Others on Sacrifice, War, and Rational Worship." In *Ancient Mediterranean Sacrifice*, edited by Jennifer Wright Knust and Zsuzsanna Várhelyi, 142–66. New York: Oxford University Press, 2011.

Neusner, Jacob. *Judaism: The Evidence of the Mishnah.* Atlanta: Scholars Press, 1988.

———. "Law and Theology in the Mishnah: The Case of Mishnah-Tractate Hullin." *Studia Orientalia Electronica* 99 (2004): 191–97.

———. "Map without Territory: Mishnah's System of Sacrifice and Sanctuary." *History of Religions* 19, no. 2 (1979): 103–27.

Neuwirth, Oriel. "Between Intention and Action: An Ethical and Theological Analysis of the Conception of Mitzvah in Rabbinic Literature." [In Hebrew.] PhD diss., Bar-Ilan University, 2012.

Noam, Vered. *From Qumran to the Rabbinic Revolution: Conceptions of Impurity.* [In Hebrew.] Jerusalem: Yad Ben Zvi, 2010.

———. "Is It True That 'a Corpse Does Not Defile?' On Ritual Contamination in Tannaitic Literature." [In Hebrew.] *Tarbitz* 78, no. 2 (2009): 157–87.

———. *Megillat Ta'anit: Versions, Interpretation, History.* [In Hebrew.] Jerusalem: Yad Ben Zvi Press, 2003.

Noethlichs, Karl Leo. "The Legal Framework of Religious Identity in the Roman Empire." In *Group Identity and Religious Individuality in Late Antiquity,* edited by Éric Rebillard and Jörg Rüpke, 13–27. Washington, DC: Catholic University of America Press, 2015.

Novick, Tzvi. *What Is Good and What God Demands: Normative Structures in Tannaitic Literature.* Leiden: Brill, 2010.

Olyan, Saul. *Rites and Rank: Hierarchy in Biblical Representations of Cult.* Princeton: Princeton University Press, 2000.

Orlin, Eric M. *Temples, Religion, and Politics in the Roman Republic.* Leiden: Brill, 1997.

Orr, David G. "Roman Domestic Religion: The Evidence of Household Shrines." In *Aufstieg und Niedergang der römischen Welt* II.16.2: *Religion (Heidentum: Römische Religion, Allgemeines),* edited by Wolfgang Haase, 1557–91. Berlin and New York: Walter de Gruyter, 1978.

Petropoulou, Maria-Zoe. *Animal Sacrifice in Ancient Greek Religion, Judaism, and Christianity, 100 BC to AD 200.* Oxford: Oxford University Press, 2008.

Philo. *Questions and Answers on Exodus.* Translated by Ralph Marcus. Cambridge, MA: Harvard University Press, 1953.

———. *The Works of Philo.* Translated by Charles D. Yonge. Peabody, MA: Hendrickson Publishers, 2006.

Philodemus. *On Piety.* Edited by Dirk Obbink. Oxford: Clarendon Press, 1997.

Plato. *Complete Works.* Edited by John M. Cooper. Indianapolis: Hackett, 1997.

Poorthuis, Marcel. "Sacrifice as Concession in Christian and Jewish Sources: The *Didascalia Apostolorum* and Rabbinic Literature." In *The Actuality of Sacrifice: Past and Present,* edited by Alberdina Houtman, Marcel Poorthuis, Joshua Schwartz, and Joseph Turner, 170–91. Leiden: Brill, 2014.

Porphyry. *On Abstinence from Killing Animals.* Translated by Gillian Clark. London: Bloomsbury, 2000.

Potter, David. *The Roman Empire at Bay, AD 180–385.* New York: Routledge, 2004.

Price, Simon R. F. "Between Man and God: Sacrifice in the Roman Imperial Cult." *Journal of Roman Studies* 70 (1980): 28–43.

———. *Ritual and Power: The Roman Imperial Cult in Asia Minor.* New York: Cambridge University Press, 1984.

Propp, William H. C. *Exodus 1–18 with a New Translation and Commentary.* Anchor Bible 2. New York: Doubleday, 1999.

Pummer, Reinhard. "Samaritan Rituals and Customs." In *The Samaritans,* edited by Alan D. Crown, 650–90. Tübingen: J.C.B. Mohr, 1989.

Pyyhtinen, Olli. *The Gift and Its Paradoxes: Beyond Mauss.* Farnham, Surrey: Ashgate, 2014.

Rasmussen, Susanne William. *Public Portents in Republican Rome.* Rome: L'Erma di Bret-schneider, 2003.

Redfield, James. "Animal Sacrifice in Comedy: An Alternative Point of View." In *Greek and Roman Animal Sacrifice: Ancient Victims, Modern Observers,* edited by Christopher A. Faraone and Fred S. Naiden, 167–79. New York: Cambridge University Press, 2012.

Reed, Annette Yoshiko. "From Sacrifice to the Slaughterhouse: Ancient and Modern Per-spectives on Meat, Ritual, and Civilization." *Method and Theory in the Study of Religion* 26, no. 2 (2014): 111–58.

———. "When Did Rabbis Become Pharisees? Reflections on Christian Evidence for Post-70 Judaism." In *Envisioning Judaism: Essays in Honor of Peter Schäfer on the Occasion of His Seventieth Birthday,* edited by Ra'anan S. Boustan, Klaus Herrmann, Reimund Leicht, Annette Y. Reed, and Giuseppe Veltri, 2: 859–96. Tübingen: Mohr Siebeck, 2013.

Regev, Eyal. "Offerings of Righteousness: Visiting the Temple and Bringing Sacrifices as a Religious Experience in the Psalms." [In Hebrew.] *Tarbitz* 73, no. 3 (2004): 365–86.

———. *The Sadducees and Their Law: Religion and Society in the Second Temple Period.* [In Hebrew.] Jerusalem: Yad Ben Zvi Press, 2005.

———. "Temple Prayer as the Origin of Fixed Prayer: On the Evolution of Prayer during the Period of the Second Temple." [In Hebrew.] *Zion* 70, no. 1 (2005): 5–29.

Rives, James B. "Animal Sacrifice and Political Identity in Rome and Judea." In *Jews and Christians in the First and Second Centuries: How to Write Their History,* edited by Peter J. Tomson and Joshua Schwartz, 105–25. Leiden: Brill, 2014.

———. "The Decree of Decius and the Religion of the Empire." *Journal of Roman Studies* 89 (1999): 135–54.

———. "The Theology of Animal Sacrifice in the Ancient Greek World: Origins and Devel-opments." In *Ancient Mediterranean Sacrifice,* edited by Jennifer Wright Knust and Zsu-zsanna Várhelyi, 187–202. New York: Oxford University Press, 2011.

Roberts, Alexander, James Donaldson, and Arthur Cleveland Coxe, eds. *Ante-Nicene Fathers.* Vols. 1–9. New York: Scribner Books, 1903–6.

Rosenfeld, Ben-Zion. "Sage and Temple in Rabbinic Thought after the Destruction of the Second Temple." *Journal for the Study of Judaism in the Persian, Hellenistic and Roman Period* 28, no. 4 (1997): 437–64.

Rosen-Zvi, Ishay. "The Body and the Temple: The List of Priestly Blemishes in the Mishnah and the Place of the Temple in the Tannaitic Study House." [In Hebrew.] *Jewish Studies* 43 (2006): 49–87.

———. *Demonic Desires: "Yetzer Hara" and the Problem of Evil in Late Antiquity.* Philadel-phia: University of Pennsylvania Press, 2011.

———. "The Mishnaic Mental Revolution: A Reassessment." *Journal of Jewish Studies* 66, no. 1 (2015): 36–58.

———. *The Mishnaic Sotah Ritual: Temple, Gender, and Midrash.* Translated by Orr Scharf. Leiden: Brill, 2013.

Rosen-Zvi, Ishay, and Adi Ophir. "*Goy:* Towards a Genealogy." *Dine Israel* 28 (2011): 69–122.

Rubenstein, Jeffrey. "Nominalism and Realism in Qumranic and Rabbinic Law: A Reassess-ment." *Dead Sea Discoveries* 6, no. 2 (1999): 157–83.

Safrai, Shmuel. *At the Time of the Temple and at the Time of the Mishnah.* [In Hebrew.] Jeru-salem: Magnes Press, 1994.

————. "The Pilgrimage Commandment and Its Observance during the Second Temple Period." [In Hebrew.] *Zion* 25, no. 2 (1960): 67–84.

————. "The Recovery of the Jewish Population in the Yavneh Generation." [In Hebrew.] In *Eretz Israel from the Destruction of the Second Temple to the Muslim Conquest,* edited by Zvi Baras, Shmuel Safrai, Menahem Stern, and Yoram Tsafrir, 18–37. Jerusalem: Yad Ben Zvi, 1982.

Sagiv, Yonatan. "Studies in Early Rabbinic Hermeneutics as Reflected in Selected Chapters in the Sifra." [In Hebrew.] PhD diss., Hebrew University, 2009.

Sallustius. *Concerning the Gods and the Universe.* Translated by Arthur Darby Nock. Cambridge: Cambridge University Press, 1926.

Saltzman, Michele Renee. "The End of Public Sacrifice: Changing Definitions of Sacrifice in Post-Constantinian Rome and Italy." In *Ancient Mediterranean Sacrifice,* edited by Jennifer Wright Knust and Zsuzsanna Várhelyi, 167–83. New York: Oxford University Press, 2011.

Sandwell, Isabella. *Religious Identity in Late Antiquity: Greeks, Jews, and Christians in Antioch.* New York: Cambridge University Press, 2007.

Schäfer, Peter. *Jesus in the Talmud.* Princeton: Princeton University Press, 2007.

————. *The Jewish Jesus: How Judaism and Christianity Shaped Each Other.* Princeton: Princeton University Press, 2012.

————. "Rabbis and Priests, or: How to Do Away with the Glorious Past of the Sons of Aaron." In *Antiquity in Antiquity: Jewish and Christian Pasts in the Greco-Roman World,* edited by Gregg Gardner and Kevin Osterloh, 155–72. Tübingen: Mohr Siebeck, 2008.

Schechner, Richard. *Performance Studies: An Introduction.* New York: Routledge, 2013.

Scheid, John. *An Introduction to Roman Religion.* Translated by Janet Lloyd. Bloomington: Indiana University Press, 2003.

————. "Roman Animal Sacrifice and the System of Being." In *Greek and Roman Animal Sacrifice: Ancient Victims, Modern Observers,* edited by Christopher A. Faraone and Fred S. Naiden, 84–98. New York: Cambridge University Press, 2012.

Schenk, Kära L. "Temple, Community, and Sacred Narrative in the Dura-Europos Synagogue." *AJS Review* 34, no. 2 (2010): 195–229.

Schiffman, Lawrence. *The Courtyards of the House of the Lord: Studies on the Temple Scroll.* Leiden: Brill, 2008.

————. "Sacrifice in the Dead Sea Scrolls." In *The Actuality of Sacrifice: Past and Present,* edited by Alberdina Houtman, Marcel Poorthuis, Joshua Schwartz, and Joseph Turner, 89–106. Leiden: Brill, 2014.

Schilderman, Hans. "Religion as Concept and Measure." *Journal of Empirical Theology* 27, no. 1 (2014): 1–16.

Schmidt, Francis. *How the Temple Thinks: Identity and Social Cohesion in Ancient Judaism.* Translated by J. Edward Crowley. Sheffield: Sheffield Academic Press, 2001.

Schneider, Michael. *The Appearance of the High Priest: Theophany, Apotheosis, and Binitarian Theology from the Priestly Tradition of the Second Temple Period through Ancient Jewish Mysticism.* [In Hebrew.] Los Angeles: Cherub Press, 2012.

Schott, Jeremy M. *Christianity, Empire, and the Making of Religion in Late Antiquity.* Philadelphia: University of Pennsylvania Press, 2008.

Schremer, Adiel. *Brothers Estranged: Heresy, Christianity, and Jewish Identity in Late Antiquity.* New York: Oxford University Press, 2009.

Schwartz, Baruch J. "The Bearing of Sin in Priestly Literature." In *Pomegranates and Golden Bells: Studies in Biblical, Jewish, and Near Eastern Ritual, Law, and Literature in Honor of Jacob Milgrom*, edited by David P. Wright, David N. Freedman, and Avi Hurvitz, 3–21. Winona Lake, IN: Eisenbrauns, 1995.

Schwartz, Daniel R. "Introduction: Was 70 CE a Watershed in Jewish History? Three Stages of Modern Scholarship, and a Renewed Effort." In *Was 70 CE a Watershed in Jewish History? On Jews and Judaism before and after the Destruction of the Second Temple*, edited by Daniel R. Schwartz, Zeev Weiss, and Ruth A. Clements, 1–19. Leiden: Brill, 2012.

———. "The Jews of Egypt between the Temple of Onias, the Temple of Jerusalem, and Heaven." [In Hebrew.] *Zion* 62, no. 1 (1997): 5–22.

———. *Judeans and Jews: Four Faces of Dichotomy in Ancient Jewish History.* Toronto: University of Toronto Press, 2014.

———. "Law and Truth: On Qumran-Sadducean and Rabbinic Views of Law." In *The Dead Sea Scrolls: Forty Years of Research*, edited by Devorah Dimant and Uriel Rappaport, 229–40. Jerusalem: Magnes Press and Yad Yitzhak Ben-Zvi, 1992.

———. *Studies in the Jewish Background of Christianity.* Tübingen: J.C.B. Mohr, 1992.

Schwartz, Joshua. "Sacrifice without the Rabbis: Ritual and Sacrifice in the Second Temple Period according to Contemporary Sources." In *The Actuality of Sacrifice: Past and Present*, edited by Alberdina Houtman, Marcel Poorthuis, Joshua Schwartz, and Joseph Turner, 123–48. Leiden: Brill, 2014.

Schwartz, Seth. *Josephus and Judean Politics.* Leiden: Brill, 1990.

———. *Were the Jews a Mediterranean Society?* Princeton: Princeton University Press, 2009.

Scott, James C. *The Art of Not Being Governed: An Anarchist History of Upland Southeast Asia.* New Haven: Yale University Press, 2010.

Segal, Michael. *The Book of Jubilees: Rewritten Bible, Redaction, Ideology, and Theology.* [In Hebrew.] Jerusalem: Magnes Press, 2008.

Shemesh, Ahron. *Halakhah in the Making: The Development of Jewish Law from Qumran to the Rabbis.* Berkeley and Los Angeles: University of California Press, 2009.

———. "What Is This Passover About?" [In Hebrew.] *AJS Review* 21, no. 2 (1996): א–יז.

Siker, Jeffrey. "Yom Kippuring Passover: Recombinant Sacrifice in Early Christianity." In *Ritual and Metaphor: Sacrifice in the Bible*, edited by Christian A. Eberhart, 65–82. Atlanta: Society of Biblical Literature, 2011.

Simon-Shoshan, Moshe. *Stories of the Law: Narrative Discourse and the Construction of Authority in the Mishnah.* New York: Oxford University Press, 2012.

Skehan, Patrick W., and Alexander A. Di Lella. *The Wisdom of Ben Sira.* New Haven: Yale University Press, 1995.

Smith, Dennis E. *From Symposium to Eucharist: The Banquet in the Early Christian World.* Minneapolis: Augsburg Press, 2003.

Smith, Jonathan Z. *Relating Religion: Essays in the Study of Religion.* Chicago: University of Chicago Press, 2004.

Smith, William Robertson. *Lectures on the Religion of the Semites.* New York: Macmillan, 1927.

Staal, Frits. "The Meaninglessness of Ritual." *Numen* 26, no. 1 (1979): 2–22.

Steinfeld, Tzvi Arye. "On the Definition of Individual and Congregational Offerings." [In Hebrew.] In *Shoshanat Yaakov: Jewish and Iranian Studies in Honor of Yaakov Elman*, edited by Shai Secunda and Steven Fine, 1–28. Leiden: Brill, 2012.

Steinmetz, Devorah. "Justification by Deed: The Conclusion of Sanhedrin-Makkot and Paul's Rejection of Law." *Hebrew Union College Annual* 76 (2005): 133–87.

Stern, Sacha. *Jewish Identity in Early Rabbinic Writings.* Leiden: Brill, 1994.

Stevenson, Kalinda Rose. *The Vision of Transformation: The Territorial Rhetoric of Ezekiel 40–48.* Atlanta: Scholars Press, 1996.

Stökl Ben Ezra, Daniel. *The Impact of Yom Kippur on Early Christianity.* Tübingen: Mohr Siebeck, 2003.

Stowers, Stanley K. "Greeks Who Sacrifice and Those Who Do Not." In *The Social World of the First Christians: Essays in Honor of Wayne A. Meeks,* edited by L. Michael White and O. Larry Yarbrough, 293–333. Philadelphia: Fortress Press, 1995.

———. "On the Comparison of Blood in Greek and Israelite Ritual." In *Hesed ve-emet: Studies in Honor of Ernest S. Frerichs,* edited by Jodi Magness and Seymour Gitin, 179–96. Atlanta: Scholars Press, 1998.

———. "The Religion of Plant and Animal Offerings versus the Religion of Meanings, Essences, and Textual Mysteries." In *Ancient Mediterranean Sacrifice,* edited by Jennifer Wright Knust and Zsuzsanna Várhelyi, 35–57. New York: Oxford University Press, 2011.

Stroumsa, Guy. *The End of Sacrifice: Religious Transformations in Late Antiquity.* Translated by Susan Emanuel. Chicago: University of Chicago Press, 2009.

Sussman, Ya'akov. "The Study of the History of Halakhah and the Dead Sea Scrolls: First Talmudic Contemplations in Light of the *Miqsat Ma'ase ha-Torah* Scroll." [In Hebrew.] *Tarbitz* 59 (1990): 12–76.

Swartz, Michael D. "The Choreography of Blood in Mishnah Yoma." In *Jewish Blood: Reality and Metaphor in History, Religion, and Culture,* edited by Mitchell B. Hart, 70–82. London: Routledge, 2009.

———. "Judaism and the Idea of Ancient Ritual Theory." In *Jewish Studies at the Crossroads of Anthropology and History: Authority, Diaspora, Tradition,* edited by Ra'anan S. Boustan, Oren Kosansky, and Marina Rustow, 294–317. Philadelphia: University of Pennsylvania Press, 2011.

———. "Liturgy, Poetry, and the Persistence of Sacrifice." In *Was 70 CE a Watershed in Jewish History? On Jews and Judaism before and after the Destruction of the Second Temple,* edited by Daniel R. Schwartz, Zeev Weiss, and Ruth A. Clements, 393–412. Leiden: Brill, 2012.

———. "Ritual Is with People: Sacrifice and Society in Palestinian Yoma Traditions." In *The Actuality of Sacrifice: Past and Present,* edited by Alberdina Houtman, Marcel Poorthuis, Joshua Schwartz, and Joseph Turner, 206–27. Leiden: Brill, 2014.

———. "Sacrificial Themes in Jewish Magic." In *Magic and Ritual in the Ancient World,* edited by Paul Mirecki and Marvin Meyer, 303–15. Leiden: Brill, 2002.

Tabory, Joseph. "The Paschal Hagigah—Myth or Reality?" [In Hebrew.] *Tarbitz* 64, no. 1 (1995): 39–49.

———. *The Passover Ritual throughout the Generations.* [In Hebrew.] Tel Aviv: Ha-kibbutz ha-me'uhad, 1996.

Townsend, Philippa L. "Another Race? Ethnicity, Universalism, and the Emergence of Christianity." PhD diss., Princeton University, 2009.

Tropper, Amram. *Rewriting Ancient Jewish History: The History of the Jews in Roman Times and the New Historical Method.* New York: Routledge, 2016.

———. *Wisdom, Politics, and Historiography: Tractate Avot in the Context of the Graeco-Roman Near East.* Oxford: Oxford University Press, 2004.

Tsukermandel, Moshe Samuel, ed. *Tosefta nach den Erfurter und Wiener Handschriften.* Trier: Fr. Lintzschen Buchhandlung, 1892.

Turner, Victor. *The Forest of Symbols: Aspects of Ndembu Ritual.* Ithaca: Cornell University Press, 1967.

Tuval, Michael. "Doing without the Temple: Paradigms in Judaic Literature of the Diaspora." In *Was 70 CE a Watershed in Jewish History? On Jews and Judaism before and after the Destruction of the Second Temple,* edited by Daniel R. Schwartz, Zeev Weiss, and Ruth A. Clements, 181–239. Leiden: Brill, 2012.

Ullucci, Daniel C. *The Christian Rejection of Animal Sacrifice.* New York: Oxford University Press, 2012.

Urbach, Ephraim E. *The Sages: Their Concepts and Beliefs.* Translated by Israel Abrahams. Cambridge, MA: Harvard University Press, 1987.

Van Straten, Folkert T. "Gifts for the Gods." In *Faith, Hope, and Worship: Aspects of Religious Mentality in the Ancient World,* edited by Henk S. Versnel, 65–150. Leiden: Brill, 1981.

Walfish, Avraham. "Ideational Tendencies in the Description of the Temple and Its Work in Tractates Tamid and Middot." [In Hebrew.] *Mekhkarei Yehudah ve-Shomron* 7 (1998): 79–92.

Watts, Edward J. *The Final Pagan Generation.* Oakland: University of California Press, 2015.

Watts, James W. "The Rhetoric of Sacrifice." In *Ritual and Metaphor: Sacrifice in the Hebrew Bible,* edited by Christian A. Eberhart, 3–16. Atlanta: Society of Biblical Literature, 2011.

———. *Ritual and Rhetoric in Leviticus: From Sacrifice to Scripture.* New York: Cambridge University Press, 2007.

Weisman, Zeev. "The Nazariteship in the Hebrew Bible: Its Types and Its Origins." [In Hebrew.] *Tarbitz* 36 (1967): 207–20.

Weiss, Isaac, ed. *Sifra de-bei rav.* 1st ed., Vienna, 1862. New York: Om Publishing, 1946.

Weiss, Ruhama. *Meal Tests: Meals in the World of the Sages.* [In Hebrew.] Tel-Aviv: Ha-kibbutz ha-meu'had, 2010.

Weitzman, Steven. *Surviving Sacrilege: Cultural Persistence in Jewish Antiquity.* Cambridge, MA: Harvard University Press, 2005.

Wellhausen, Julius. *Prolegomena to the History of Israel.* Translated by J. Sutherland Black and Allan Menzies. Edinburgh: Adam & Charles Black, 1885.

Werman, Cana. "The Rules of Consuming and Covering the Blood in the Priestly Halakha and the Halakha of the Sages." [In Hebrew.] *Tarbitz* 63 (1994): 173–83.

Werman, Cana, and Ahron Shemesh. *Revealing the Hidden: Interpretation and Halakha in the Dead Sea Scrolls.* [In Hebrew.] Jerusalem: Bialik Institute, 2011.

Wheeler Robinson, Henry. *Corporate Personality in Ancient Israel.* Philadelphia: Fortress Press, 1973.

Willis, Wendell L. *Idol Meat in Corinth: The Pauline Argument in 1 Corinthians 8 and 10.* Atlanta: Scholars Press, 1985.

Wright, David P. "Ritual Theory, Ritual Texts, and the Priestly-Holiness Writings of the Pentateuch." In *Social Theory and the Study of Israelite Religion,* edited by Saul M. Olyan, 195–216. Atlanta: Society of Biblical Literature, 2012.

Yadin-Israel, Azzan. *Scripture and Tradition: Rabbi Akiva and the Triumph of Midrash*. Philadelphia: University of Pennsylvania Press, 2014.

Zohar, Noam. "Purification Offering in Tannaitic Literature." [In Hebrew.] Master's thesis, Hebrew University, 1988.

———. "Repentance and Purification: The Significance and Semantics of חטאת in the Pentateuch." *Journal of Biblical Literature* 107, no. 4 (1988): 609–18.

SOURCE INDEX